# Economic Policy Towards the Environment

# Economic Policy Towards the Environment

Edited by

Dieter Helm

BLACKWELL
Oxford UK & Cambridge USA

First published 1991

Blackwell Publishers
108 Cowley Road
Oxford OX4 1JF
UK

Three Cambridge Center
Cambridge, Massachusetts 02142
USA



A CIP catalogue record for this book is available from the British Library.

**Library of Congress Cataloging in Publication Data**

Economic policy towards the environment / edited by Dieter Helm.
p. cm.
Includes bibliographical references and index.
ISBN 0-631-18201-2 ISBN 0-631-18202-0 (pbk.)
1. Environmental policy. 2. Natural resources—Government policy.
I. Helm, Dieter.
HC79.E5E273 1991
333.7—dc20 91-15713
CIP

Typeset in Times Roman 10 point by OXERA Publishing Ltd., Blue Boar Court, Oxford.
Printed in Great Britain by T. J. Press Ltd, Padstow, Cornwall.

This book is printed on acid-free paper.

# Contents

# List of Contributors


| | |
|---|---|
| Scott Barrett | London Business School |
| Wilfred Beckerman | Balliol College, Oxford |
| Vanessa Brechling | Institute for Fiscal Studies |
| Dallas Burtraw | Resources for the Future, Washington, D.C. |
| Partha Dasgupta | Stanford University; University of Cambridge; World Institute for Development Economics Research |
| Dieter Helm | New College, Oxford |
| Per-Olov Johansson | Stockholm School of Economics |
| Karl-Göran Mäler | Stockholm School of Economics |
| David Pearce | University College London |
| Paul Portney | Resources for the Future, Washington, D.C. |
| Stephen Smith | Institute for Fiscal Studies and University College London |
| Timothy Swanson | University College London |
| Tom Tietenberg | Colby College, Maine |

# Preface

This volume has developed from an issue of the *Oxford Review of Economic Policy* and a subsequent conference. A number of the chapters are revised versions of papers which appeared in that issue. Other chapters have been written in response to the debate opened by these earlier papers, and in the desire to present a much more comprehensive coverage of our theme.

In developing the project and in presenting an integrated volume, we have found the book falling naturally into a number of parts. These deal with the conceptual analysis; the international nature of the new environmental problems of the 1990s; and applications to particular problems—from rain forests and the law of the sea to more microeconomic issues such as energy conservation.

The editor is grateful for the patient co-operation of the authors. In addition, the considerable support and encouragement provided by Mark Allin at Blackwells has been appreciated. Finally, the volume has been improved immeasurably by the careful and professional guidance of Alison Gomm.

# Introduction

*Dieter Helm*

The environment has assumed a status as *the* economic problem of the 1990s, as did oil in the 1970s and inflation in the 1980s. It is increasingly obvious that the ways in which we use cars, burn coal for electricity, drop our waste into landfill sites, and our sewerage into rivers and the sea cannot continue indefinitely. In the 1990s the environment has become a regional and global problem. Acid rain, global warming, the destruction of tropical forests, and the exploitation of the oceans, are now the subjects of international concern and diplomacy.

To assess the extent of the problem and to devise technical solutions will require a major scientific effort. However, it is apparent that, whatever the proximate cause of environmental damage, the underlying cause is human behaviour. Growing population and the development of modern industrial economies have resulted in a process of environmental degradation. Human behaviour must change if the damage is to be contained.

Part of that change will require new moral attitudes. The values which motivate our approach to the environment are hardly benign. But changes in values are longer term, and highly uncertain. The destruction of the oil fields of Kuwait demonstrates how fragile the appeal to values can be.

For this reason, environmental policy must largely take values as given, and focus instead on the context within which humans act. Within this framework, the economic process plays a leading role. By changing the constraints that individuals face—by including the environment within economic calculations—the market can become less at odds with the environment. The problem then has an efficiency dimension: the same level of output must be produced at less cost to the environment. It is its exclusion from economic policy which accounts for much of the damage now witnessed.

The inclusion of the environment within economic calculations requires that we assign value to it, and therefore treat it as if it is a commodity. To many, such a categorization involves a debasing of the environment. The placing of monetary values fails to recognize its special moral status. However, it remains true that, *ex post*, values are in fact assigned, in the sense that environmental assets are harmed or destroyed in the name of economic development. Without monetarization, we have no basis for comparison, and therefore no criteria to aid decision-making. Whilst the environment may be 'priceless' (as may human life) we do in fact spend a given amount of money on preserving it and this is not infinite. Preventing environmental damage (as with preventing death) involves the allocation of scarce resources. Scarce resources are rationed: in a market, by price; in a planned economy, by outputs. The environmental problem is therefore an economic one—as well as a scientific and ethical one. The tools of economic analysis provide a useful aid to the design of policy. The aim of this volume is to illustrate their role.

The environmental problem has many components, and the first task of economic analysis is to provide a categorization of the causes of damage. Why precisely does the market over-exploit the environment? The traditional approach, surveyed in the first article by Dieter Helm and David Pearce, focuses on the identification of 'market failures'—ways in which the market fails correctly to take account of the complex set of environmental costs and benefits of economic activity. These are typically characterized under the general heading of externalities. Helm and Pearce analyse the concept, and distinguish between two traditions in the literature—the Meade–Pigou tax/subsidy approach, which focuses on marginal adjustments to damage and benefit functions, and the Chicago approach associated with Coase, which focuses on property rights.

The former approach is essentially aimed at corrections of the consequences of market operations. The latter considers how market institutions can be reformed to internalize externalities. In most cases, the environment is not owned, but rather treated as free. Consequently no proper rate is paid for its exploitation, permitting the polluter to escape the full costs of damage. The task for the Coase school, then, is to create appropriate property rights, and then leave individuals to bargain through the market (or the courts) to arrive at optimal solutions; for Meade–Pigou it is to adjust the prices and costs of market participants, so that account is taken of the damage resulting from their actions.

Helm and Pearce show that, whatever the underlying theoretical differences, in practice the two approaches have much in common. The principal differences are ones of emphasis—on courts and legal adjudication for Coase; or on civil servants and the tax system for Meade–Pigou. In part, this difference reflects institutional differences—between the US (and to a certain extent European) reliance on legal systems as regulatory agencies, as against the administrative approach to regulation typical in the UK.

Externalities rarely arise in isolation. Other market failures typically exacerbate environmental problems. Environmental benefits are frequently undercaptured because they display public good aspects. A natural scenery may be enjoyed by many people who cannot be charged. Many environmental benefits accrue to future generations, yet their preferences are only implicitly taken into account by current generations. Finally, economic decisions now about future developments may not properly incorporate the risks associated with our incomplete knowledge of how the environment functions. This is especially worrying when decisions are irreversible—such as the extinction of a species. Where there are multiple market failures, the design of policy is much more complex. Monopoly, for example, tends to lower output—including the pollutant. Competition policy may therefore in some circumstances worsen pollution. Similarly, public goods are typically underprovided by markets, and therefore if their production creates pollution, public intervention will again exacerbate pollution. Conversely, if market failures inhibit investment in the reduction of pollution (for example, in insulation and energy conservation) policies aimed at correcting these other market failures may be environmentally benign.

The answer then to our question—why does the market over-exploit the environment?—is couched in terms of the particular market failures identified in each case. The approach is therefore inevitably pragmatic. The task of economic policy is to design methods for intervention which temper the market, so that the environment is properly taken into account on a case-by-case basis. However, as Helm and Pearce also point out, such interventions must pass another test: they must not make matters worse. Economics is at best a very imprecise science. The complexity of human behaviour is only crudely captured by economic models. Thus, account must be taken of the unintended consequences of interventions. Furthermore, governments—which must introduce and administer policies—have their own agendas. Government failure is conspicuous in the environment. It is not accidental that many of the worst examples of pollution have arisen in public sector industries—in water and sewerage, in road-building, and in the electricity industry. Producer-oriented governments in Eastern Europe provide a graphic illustration of the failure of state planning in the absence of democratic control. Thus we have first to identify and evaluate market failures, and second take adequate account of government failures. Again the approach is pragmatic: *a priori* general rules are inferior to case-by-case analysis.

The market failure approach treats the environment as a commodity. It has an implicit price, and can therefore be evaluated. This commodity approach is addressed in the article by Partha Dasgupta. His starting point is that 'all commodities are . . . traceable to natural resources', including labour. The optimal allocation of these resources rests on the presence of markets whose institutions are, for him, much more general than the price mechanism alone. To Dasgupta, markets are 'institutions which make available to affected parties the opportunity to negotiate courses of actions'. Thus the wider framework governing human behaviour—including social norms and customs and common ownership rights—falls within the ambit of market failures. His approach is therefore much richer and more encompassing than that offered by focusing either on property rights or the adjustments of costs and benefits in the two traditional approaches. Externalities, and especially reciprocal externalities, depend upon the social framework of exchange, and it is the design of this social fabric which is critical to our utilization of natural resources, not just the price mechanism. The relative merits of government and markets lie in their ability to facilitate exchange, and that in turn depends upon the incentives of the parties and the quality and costs of information.

The relevant economic analysis is then the application of economic cost–benefit analysis to environmental problems. This is starkly illustrated in Wilfred Beckerman's paper. Environmentalists have been quick to conclude from the preliminary scientific research on global warming that emissions of greenhouse gases should be dramatically reduced over a relatively short period of time. Indeed some appear to conclude that the optimum amount of pollution is close to zero. In 1990 the Intergovernmental Panel on Climatic Change (IPCC) suggested that emissions should be reduced by 60% to stabilize the level of carbon dioxide in the atmosphere. Beckerman provides a reasoned sceptic's case. He points out that, on existing economic evidence, the costs may well exceed the benefits. In doing so, he places the current environmental issues in a wider perspective, pointing out that the current environment is not necessarily the optimal one.

The note of caution introduced by Beckerman has a particular consequence: that the order of policy intervention is important. Given uncertainty and given the magnitude of the costs of intervention, Beckerman argues that we should start with 'no regret' policies—policies which would be desirable whether or not global warming occurs. For example, improving the distortions caused by other market failures (like information and monopoly) may well improve the efficient use of energy and thereby have an incidental environmental pay-off. This theme is picked up later in the volume by Brechling, Helm, and Smith.

Beckerman's evaluation is, of course, controversial. It is predicated upon assumptions, particularly the growth and discount rates, which are open to challenge. Nevertheless, it illustrates strikingly the issues upon which policy should turn. In order to substantiate the claim that rapid reductions of emissions of greenhouse gases are required, the precise parameters related to costs and benefits need to be estimated. Beckerman indicates which are crucial to the case.

The example of global warming provides a good illustration of the problems of cost–benefit calculations. Since the environment is typically unpriced or at best underpriced, the level of damage is usually excessive. The valuation of damage therefore forms a crucial part of policy design. Per-Olov Johansson provides a survey of the latest techniques employed by economists in estimating environmental impacts. Although he is mainly concerned with demand-side valuations—what people are willing to pay to avoid harming the environment and willing to accept as compensation—there is a broader distinction between these demand-side techniques and supply or cost-based techniques. Johansson notes the quite wide variations in estimates which the willingness-to-pay and willingness-to-accept compensation yield. More generally, demand and supply-side approaches will only be equivalent in perfect competition. In all other circumstances (i.e. always), they will diverge. This observation (and Johansson's observation) has an important policy consequence. Cost–benefit studies should wherever possible incorporate a range of estimates, including both demand and supply-side estimates. Cost–benefit estimates are always uncertain, and the degree of uncertainty should form a significant element in the choice of optimal pollution targets.

The setting of targets for pollution reduction is however only the first stage in the design of environmental policy. The second step is the specification of instruments to achieve those targets. The traditional approach, very much reflected in UK pollution regulation, has been *command-and-control*. Regulatory bodies evaluate each case on its own merits and then specify the permitted maximum quantity of pollution. The alternative approach is to use market-based mechanisms. These attempt to utilize the informational advantages of the price mechanism and the institutional framework provided by markets to decentralize pollution control to individuals and firms. Pollution is priced, and market exchange then incorporates this valuation in its decisions. The advantage of this approach is its economy over information and the reduction in government failures.

Broadly, there are two types of market-based mechanism. These are the setting of taxes and subsidies—like carbon taxes for global warming and set-aside subsidies for agriculture—to alter the prices confronting market participants; and the creation of property rights through tradable or marketable permits. In the tax/subsidy case, the aim is directly to alter the costs to bring pollution back to the target level. Thus a tax on fossil fuels might be imposed to encourage a substitution effect amongst producers away from coal towards nuclear power, and to encourage consumers to reduce their demands in the face of higher prices. The tax or subsidy can then be raised or lowered according to the degree of success in reaching the target. The higher the required tax/subsidy, the more expensive is the necessary adjustment. Thus, carbon taxes to meet the IPCC targets would be very high indeed, as illustrated in Beckerman's article.

The second method, tradable permits, has a number of attractive features. The idea is very simple. The government sets the desired level of pollution in the form of a target reduction. Permits are then created equal to the amount of pollution. Then those who wish to pollute must buy a permit for the amount they wish to emit. Those producing products which are most valuable to consumers (i.e. demand-inelastic) and for whom the costs of pollution reduction through a supply-side substitution of technology are high, will pay the highest price for the permits. The right to pollute is more valuable to them than to producers of products which are demand-elastic, and for which it is relatively cheap to substitute more environmentally benign production technologies. A market then develops, allocating the permits efficiently between polluters. In effect, the market calculates the price of pollution and therefore, in theory, the price of the permits and the optimal pollution tax are identical. The advantage of the permit system is that the market works out the price (the tax) rather than the government. All the government has to do is to check that nobody pollutes without a permit.

The tradable permits approach, which draws directly on the Coase school discussed above and set out in the article by Helm and Pearce, is advocated forcefully in this volume by Tom Tietenberg. It is however open to a number of objections, and its implementation raises a series of practical difficulties. These relate to the issuing of the permits, the assignment of the initial rent, the degree of competition in the permits market, and the monitoring and enforcement procedures. Tietenberg addresses each of these issues.

Some types of pollution lend themselves more naturally to permit-based solutions—for example, sulphur-dioxide emissions from power stations. Other more diffuse sources of pollution—such as nitrate pollution of groundwater—are less amenable to this solution. Thus the design of instruments is likely to be pluralistic: in some cases permits, in others taxes, and for very complex or particularly dangerous substances, command-and-control.

One new area where permits might be considered appropriate is in global environmental protection. Targets could be set for each country, and these could be achieved by national governments through the issuing of permits. However, the setting of international targets is beset by a number of problems. In effect, in international negotiations, countries are attempting to reduce pollution through collusion: each wishes along with others to reach an optimal state. The theory of collusion, developed for oligopolistic market structures, illustrates how hard the achievement of a stable solution can be. Using the traditional prisoners' dilemma characterization of the problem, Scott Barrett illustrates the incentives to free ride by individual countries if cheating is hard to detect and the agreement is hard to enforce. Each nation would be better off if everyone else cut back emissions (and therefore bore the costs in lower growth) while it maintained production.

The implementation of an effective international approach to global environmental problems would require an international monitoring and enforcement agency. In the absence of such institutions—and the diplomatic and military force to back them up—the attractions of unilateral domestic targets are much reduced. Though the gains of co-operation are potentially large, the likelihood is that at least some players will be non-co-operative. Although the theory of non-co-operative games suggests that there may be fruitful opportunities to solve the collusion problem, these models point to the formidable obstacles to co-operation emerging without formal protocols, treaties, and supporting organizations. In such circumstances, some may conclude that adaptation to the consequences, rather than attention to the causes of pollution, may be the best policy.

The problem of international co-ordination and the setting up of optimal targets is also taken up by Karl-Göran Mäler. In evaluating different kinds of externalities, he provides a game-theoretic model of the acid rain problem. He considers the importance of the very different distribution of costs and benefits from acid rain reduction at the regional level, and illustrates by example the significance of setting targets differentially between co-operating countries to reflect these different costs and benefits. Thus, for example, the UK is predominantly a coal-burning generator of electricity, but much of its resulting emissions of sulphur dioxide fall on other countries. Czechoslovakia also has a coal-based electricity industry, though the domestic consequences are more severe than in the UK.

Other examples of global environmental problems include oceanic resources and rain forests. Timothy Swanson reviews the development of the law of the sea. His analysis focuses on international regulatory failures exemplified by the various attempts to deal with the over-exploitation of oceanic resources, including, most notably, fishing and whaling. The enforcement of international agreements—like those required for global warming and acid rain—is a complex legal task. At the European level, the use of Directives—such as that for sulphur-dioxide emissions for large combustion plants—can be enforced, precisely because the Treaty of Rome is backed by a court and the implicit and explicit sanctions are sufficiently strong to facilitate compliance. At the level of global resource management, the legal support is in its infancy. As Swanson illustrates, the lessons learnt from the history of attempts to manage oceanic pollution provide a sobering guide to how to proceed (and how not to proceed) with the new global pollution problems.

The tropical forest problem, examined here by David Pearce, has a number of distinctive features which illustrate the value of a pluralistic approach to pollution policy. The article shows how the application of cost–benefit analysis can translate a seemingly intractable problem into one for which there are practical ways forward. David Pearce systematically presents empirical estimates of the value of the outputs of the tropical forests, and the opportunity cost of reducing the destruction. Once the problem has been bounded by empirical estimates, methods for conservation can be designed. In the case of the tropical forests, Pearce shows that, for plausible values from a number of alternative approaches, the economic case for conservation is compelling.

Not all global problems require large-scale policy interventions. Often the solutions are typically much more local. The ultimate polluters are individuals, who demand the products whose production creates pollution. Countries and firms create pollution in response to individual demands. The design of environmental policy must therefore always be ultimately focused on the micro-level—on changing human behaviour. Policy must be designed not only to create supply-side substitutions, but also more directly to reduce demands for polluting products. The prime candidate is energy. The article by Vanessa Brechling, Dieter Helm, and Stephen Smith considers one aspect of energy conservation: how to reduce domestic consumption. In addition to providing an example of the local nature of policy design, the article also illustrates another general theme of environmental policy; namely that 'no regrets' policies should typically be pursued first. A 'no regrets' policy is one which makes economic sense even if the environmental benefits from the policy are negligible. For example, it may turn out that new scientific evidence demonstrates that climatic warming is a temporary phenomenon. We would then 'regret' having incurred the costs of engaging in policy which reduced emissions of greenhouse gases, unless they had offsetting net benefits. For example, the insulation of houses may be of benefit to domestic consumers even if global warming turns out to be an illusion. The policy of encouraging insulation could be justified because other barriers inhibited take-up, provided the net present value of the insulation, in the absence of any environmental benefit, was positive. Brechling *et al.* illustrate the kinds of market failure—in addition to environmental externalities—which pervade the market for energy.

The appropriate approach to policy also depends upon the wider institutional framework. The UK has, for example, placed considerable emphasis on command-and-control techniques, reflecting, as we noted in discussing the property rights approach above, its administrative institutional history. The US, by contrast, has traditionally placed much more emphasis on the legal process and the use of the courts. The final article provides a survey of the American tradition. Dallas Burrows and Paul Portney review the origins of recent pollution policy in the US, and focus in particular on the Environmental

Protection Agency, or EPA. They note the experience of more market-based mechanisms, though their analysis does provide some cause for caution amongst those who see EPA as a model for a new UK or indeed European Community regulatory body. The US experience with 'environmental federalism' provides some useful lessons for the parallel European issue of national jurisdiction and the application of subsidiarity.

The comparison of approaches between the US and UK provides the final theme of the volume. It complements the search for pragmatic and practical methods for setting targets and designing policy instruments. Though there is amongst many economists a general preference for market-based mechanisms over command-and-control, there can be no escape from the need to evaluate each problem on a case-by-case basis. The tools of economics provide in cost–benefit analysis the appropriate techniques for evaluating and estimating the costs of market and government failures. Economic analysis also indicates the importance of information, and the economy of information provided by markets.

The limitations of economic analysis are also apparent. It does not provide a simple panacea—a straightforward and simple answer to environmental pollution. Furthermore, economics cannot improve on scientific knowledge. Yet although global phenomena such as warming, tropical-forest destruction and oceanic pollution are scientific phenomena, their causes are largely the result of economic activity. Only by changing the decisions of individuals, preferably through markets, will the new global environmental problems be overcome. Going with the grain of the market will typically be more conducive than planned solutions. Eastern Europe provides a graphic example of the damage planners can do to the environment.

# 1
# Economic Policy towards the Environment: An Overview

*Dieter Helm*
*David Pearce*

## 1.1 Introduction

When Mrs Thatcher declared that the challenge of the 1990s will be to preserve the environment for the next generation she was highlighting a perceptual change in the nature of environmental problems. What had hitherto been viewed as a local and, at best, national issue, became in the 1980s an international and global one. The fate of natural environments was suddenly everyone's concern. The globalization of environmental degradation had been anticipated in the 1970s with warnings about ocean pollution, ozone layer damage, and climate change. But the popular focus was misdirected: resources were running out; the world was getting colder, not warmer; and the ozone layer was under threat from supersonic air transport. A mixture of poor and incomplete science combined with alarmism to produce *Limits to Growth* (Meadows *et al.*, 1972) and *Blueprint for Survival* (Goldsmith *et al.*, 1972).

Global concerns at the end of the 1980s remain subject to scientific uncertainty: rates of loss of biological diversity are not known, the greenhouse effect is not yet a scientific fact, and the precise functioning of global and regional ecosystems is ill-understood. But the scientific base is clearer and, above all, the manifestations of environmental neglect are now conspicuous.

Dieter Helm is Fellow in Economics at New College, Oxford. David Pearce is Professor of Economics at University College, London. The authors are grateful for detailed comments on early drafts from Christopher Allsopp, Patrick Lane, Derek Morris, and Mark Pearson. The usual disclaimers apply.

While scientific evidence is essential to identify the extent of the problem, the policy questions are largely ones for social science. The problem can only be addressed through changing human behaviour—altering the demand for environmental services and changing and controlling their supply. Indeed, a major feature of the modern environmental debate is the widespread acceptance of the role which economics must play in analysing the causal processes of environmental decay and in formulating policy. In the 1970s the economic voice was heard, often in critical response to alarmist environmentalism, in defence of economic growth, and in favour of the use of economic policy instruments.[1] But it seems fair to say that, with exceptions, economists then were transfixed by a presumption that environmental issues were localized examples of externalities, fairly minor deviations from the reasonably efficient workings of market and quasi-market economies. Transboundary pollution (acid rain, ocean pollution) and mutual destruction of the global commons (ozone layer holes over the Antarctic and Arctic, tropical deforestation, biodiversity loss) soon ended the misconception, backed by demonstrations of the theoretical foundations of the pervasiveness of the environment in economic life.[2]

In order to construct a viable environmental policy, it is necessary to start with a proper analysis of environmental problems. It is a task to which economic theory is well suited. To an extent, the relevant literature already exists. Environmental effects are externalities—effects of which the costs and benefits are not fully reflected in potential or actual market exchanges. They represent incomplete or missing markets. A huge literature exists on the nature of these market failures and on theoretical solutions.[3] In part, the objective of this chapter is to highlight the relevance of some of the major results to current policy problems.

However, much of the existing literature focuses on externalities as special cases in otherwise perfect markets. In practice, market failures rarely arise in neatly segmented boxes. Externalities arise in oligopolistic and monopoly markets, where there is risk and uncertainty, in conjunction with public goods, and in areas where the state is already involved. Indeed, a distinctive feature of global externalities is the requirement for international co-operative solutions. The conventional economic approach to externalities is therefore unlikely to prove sufficient to define the policy options. The institutional context and the associated market structure matter.

[1] See, for example, Beckerman (1974).

[2] See, notably, Ayres and Kneese (1969).

[3] See for recent surveys Cornes and Sandler (1986) and Baumol and Oates (1988). Other definitions, based on different conceptual approaches, are provided by Buchanan and Stubblebine (1962), Arrow (1970), and Heller and Starrett (1976).

Complexity also arises from the fact that most environmental assets are not marketed. There is no explicit market in clear air, in unpolluted bathing beaches, in forest views, and in the carbon-fixing properties of tropical rainforests. Though many regard these assets as priceless, such an approach is devoid of policy implications unless it is to leave the existing structure of environments untouched. Practical policy responses require trade-offs, and these in turn necessitate that values are placed on non-market goods in order to construct the appropriate policy interventions.

The task of environmental economics is therefore to adapt theoretical tools to provide an integrated framework of analysis and to develop existing tools to place valuations on environmental assets and consequences and, thereby, to develop appropriate policies. No doubt this task will take decades to perfect. However, since the lags are long and the effects may be irreversible, there is a substantial expected pay-off to early imperfect policy initiatives. The global nature of many environmental problems exacerbates the scale of the pay-offs. Investing in sea defences, inland water supplies, drainage, and flood-control schemes now yields potentially very large benefits in the future in the form of avoided risks of massive sea-water inundation in, say, Bangladesh or Guyana. Moreover, the first steps in a cost-effective ladder of investments to combat global warming would, in any event, yield other benefits. Energy conservation reduces acid rain and saves foreign exchange costs in resource-impoverished economies. Many of the policies will, no doubt, of necessity be crude, but they must be evaluated against the do-nothing option, not against an idealized solution. The purpose of this chapter is to provide an overview of progress to date in constructing an analytical framework, and to suggest a number of policy conclusions which follow.

The structure is as follows. Following the Introduction, section 1.2 provides a classification of environmental externalities differentiated by their institutional contexts. Section 1.3 considers the conventional economic theory approaches, based upon relatively strong informational assumptions. Section 1.4 then introduces the informational problems and indicates why co-operative solutions to global externalities may prove particularly hard to achieve. Section 1.5 concentrates on valuation of the future, and indicates a number of issues that arise with conventional discounting procedures. Section 1.6 looks at the potential role of the market in environment policy and in particular the consequences of privatization, taxes, and marketable permits. Finally section 1.7 sets out some tentative suggestions for the way forward.

## 1.2 The Context of Externalities

Recognizing environmental problems as externalities is essential in framing economic policy. It is, however, important to note that there are many different contexts within which they arise. These may be classified according to the number of parties respectively causing and suffering the consequences of pollution, the jurisdictions, and the economic systems within which the externalities arise.

### *The Number of Generators and Affected Parties*

The numbers involved in producing and receiving an externality have an important effect on the ability of different institutions to deal with the consequences. The classic textbook examples of externalities which arise between two identified parties are in fact special cases. Though these one-to-one cases are easiest to model and hence are the ones on which the literature concentrates most heavily, nearly all pollution problems are more general. Indeed the distinctive feature of the current environmental agenda is its global nature. Results which hold in the bilateral case do not necessarily carry over to the global one.

In these simple one-to-one cases, the parties are easily identified, and the costs of pollution can typically be evaluated. These cases can often be tackled either through taxes and subsidies or through negotiation and bargaining. For example, neighbours can often resolve problems of smoke, waste disposal, and noise through direct discussions and complaints, use of police, and through the legal process, whilst the Pollution Inspectorate can relatively straightforwardly regulate and if necessary prosecute individuals and firms.

Greater complexity is introduced when a large number of individuals and firms are affected. Many standard pollution problems fall into this one-to-many category: chemical spillages into water systems and oil tanker disasters, for example. In this case it remains relatively easy to identify the source of the pollution, but the affected parties are usually each too small to warrant the expense of solving the problem as in the one-to-one case above. The major new features introduced are the complexity of measuring environmental damage and the problems of establishing co-operative action amongst the affected parties where the costs to each are small relative to the costs of taking effective action against the polluter. The free-riding incentives for some affected parties on others are typically strong given the costs of enforcement. Class actions and the use of the political and regulatory process are typically required, introducing their own transactions costs and the burden of associated government failures.

The most persuasive externalities combine many generators with many recipients. These many-to-many cases include a number of new problems which have arisen in the 1980s, most noticeably the increasing concentration of greenhouse gases (carbon dioxide, methane, nitrous oxide), ozone depletion, and biodiversity losses. They can be called global mutual externalities. They also include the range of household and industrial wastes, including sewage, paper, and plastics. Measurement problems[4] are much more pressing with multiple pollution generators. Their identification can itself pose difficulties and detailed emissions data is typically costly to collect. Greater reliance on the polluters to provide information is necessitated, increasing the chances of regulatory bias and even capture. Distributional considerations can also arise in this category. Many of the associated products, especially energy and transport, are inelastic in demand, and have strong income effects.

### *Jurisdictions*

Since, as we shall see in section 1.3 below, property rights play an important role in the defining and solving of externalities, the legal system matters greatly in framing economic policies towards the environment. In cases where externalities are within nations, the legal base is co-extensive with the externality, and existing taxation and regulatory systems can typically be adapted for environmental policy. Environmental consequences do not, however, always respect national boundaries. Hence the domain of the externality and judicial boundaries do not always coincide. National law and national regulation provide weak methods of control, while general international law is usually too weak to provide adequate remedies. For example, the UN Convention on the International Law of the Sea in 1982 has yet to be signed by the US and the UK, and the UN International Whaling Convention has not yet been signed by the major whaling countries. In these circumstances, the benefits to the polluters from the polluting activity frequently exceed the costs of resisting international pressure from the affected parties, or indeed, in some cases, of breaking signed agreements.

### *Economic Systems*

All these problems are common to different types of economic regime, from free market through to planned. Nevertheless the type of economic system is likely to affect the extent of externalities and the efficiency of environmental policy. Planned economies reduce the likelihood of bargaining between the polluters and pollutees to internalize externalities, and the emphasis on production rather than consumption in many planned systems is likely to result

[4] See Johansson, chapter 5 of this book, for a survey of the evaluation problems.

in less weight being placed on the consequences of environmental degradation. Where planning is associated with single party dominance of the political process, the growth of regulation via the political process is also likely to be hindered. It is widely agreed that pollution problems in Eastern Europe and the USSR are more severe than in the Western European market-based economies.

The policy options are also constrained by the type of economic system. The creation of marketable pollution permits does assume a market system, as does the wider use of property rights. The impact of taxes rather than direct controls also presumes a price system.

The emergence in the last decade of regulatory activity and privatization in the developed and developing world has further highlighted the relationship between environmental concerns and free market activity. The shift of emphasis towards markets in Eastern Europe and in the Soviet Union can only increase this focus.

Whatever the economic system, the distribution and incidence of pollution, and the burden of environmental policy are unlikely to be even. The developing world faces particular concerns over environmental quality owing to its much greater direct reliance on natural resources—e.g. wood for fuel, direct abstraction of water, and the use of marginal lands for subsistence crops—and its extensive sensitivity to ecosystem shocks and stresses (droughts, wars, and floods). Hence the emergence of an environmental economics applied to the Third World.

## 1.3 Conventional Economic Approaches

Having established the salient institutional characteristics, the range of possible economic instruments can then be considered. The conventional economic approaches to externalities provide the framework of environmental policy. The models are simplistic, and deliberately so, to illustrate the fundamental theoretical characteristics which pervade both simple and complex practical examples. We examine first the early ideas for using taxes and subsidies to modify imperfect markets—to alter costs and incentives. These pragmatic tax/subsidy interventions are then contrasted with the more full-blooded free market approaches, associated with Coase and the Chicago school. Together they provide a number of quite general results and a framework for assessing the extent to which markets, regulation, and planning are appropriate policy regimes. More complex global problems require the addition of co-operative models, and therefore can be analysed through models of collusion and games.[5]

[5] Accessible texts surveying the literature include Mäler (1974), Tietenberg (1988), Baumol and Oates (1988), and Pearce and Turner (1990). See also Gruenspecht and Lave (1989).

### *Pragmatic Solutions to Market Failures: Pigouvian Taxes and Subsidies*

The standard economic approach to externalities is typically ascribed to Pigou (Pigou, 1920). While regarding externalities as a minor problem (compared, for example, to monopoly), Pigou devised a system of taxes and subsidies to correct for the social costs which were not incorporated in private decision-making. Crudely, a tax is placed on the polluter to bring his cost function into line with what it would have been had he faced the true social costs of production. The polluter pays, and therefore reduces his output to the socially optimal level. Conversely, a subsidy can be paid to the pollutee, to compensate for the damage done.[6]

The government provides the mechanism to force the polluter to pay the full costs of his activities. The tax may or may not be exactly offset by the subsidy, depending on whether the tax revenue is transferred to the victim or not, and on demand and supply elasticities. Clearly, if, for example, the revenue from an energy tax were spent on energy conservation, as opposed to reducing income tax, the impact on energy demand and supply would be much more marked.

This problem corresponds to the simple one-to-one case identified in the previous section. The model provides a number of insights into the policy problems besetting governments. Indeed it is this Pigouvian model which remains the basis of the taxation proposals currently being actively discussed. It provides a simple benchmark, and its shortcomings have provided much of the research agenda in the literature.

The following points are particularly important. First, there is no suggestion that any level of pollution is *per se* bad. It is, after all, the by-product of an activity which is economically valuable. Rather, its full cost needs to be reflected in decision-making. The problem of the market is not the creation of pollution, but rather the wrong amount of it. The optimal level of pollution is only zero in the extreme case that the externality costs require a tax so great that the firm stops production altogether.

Second, it is assumed that, after the tax, firms face the true marginal costs of production. There is therefore no distortion of competition between polluting firms. Thus it is assumed in this simple analysis that an externality arises in a context in which there are no other market failures. In particular, there is no oligopoly or monopoly, no uncertainty, no co-ordination problems, or other public goods. However, since externalities in practice always arise in markets riddled with other failures, models with joint-failures are of great importance. The design of more complex optimal Pigouvian taxes must therefore take these into account.

[6] The payment of subsidy does not, however, reduce the level of pollution in this case. It is purely compensatory.

Third, it is assumed that the costs of the polluting firm and the damage function of the polluted firm or consumer are known. In particular, there is no private information unavailable to the regulator, no strategic revelation of information by the affected parties, and there is no uncertainty about the pollution impacts. Thus, this approach is informationally very demanding.

Finally, there are no regulatory failures associated with the incentives of authorities. Regulators are concerned only with maximizing economic efficiency. Other social objectives—such as distribution and rights—are ignored. There is no regulatory capture.

These assumptions provide a menu of issues which the policy-maker needs to evaluate empirically in designing optimal interventions. The presence of monopoly or of substantial distributional consequences will modify the optimal form of intervention. Only if all the assumptions of the model are met will simple tax/subsidy solutions be the obvious first-best solution. Nevertheless, the Pigouvian model does carry a number of policy presumptions. The most important basic insight is that environmental damage has a cost, and that this should be reflected in economic decisions by facing the participants with a price. Furthermore, to the extent that taxes rather than subsidies are utilized, there is a presumption in favour of the *polluter-pays principle*. There is certainly no role for the *victim-pays principle*. Furthermore, since social costs are uniquely defined for each case of pollution, the Pigouvian model points inevitably towards pragmatism in the uses of taxes and subsidies to regulate markets, and provides the basis for the piecemeal case-by-case approach which is the hallmark of UK environmental policy.[7]

### *Laissez-Faire Approaches: Coase and Property Rights*

The pragmatic approach to externalities has been directly challenged by the more full-blooded market theorists. This challenge is associated most closely with Coase's seminal article (1960).

The free-market approach identifies the problem of externalities as the absence of markets and the associated property rights. An economy in which every asset is owned would internalize all externalities. On this view, overgrazing of pastures and pollution of the oceans and atmosphere result from the fact that common land, seas, and air are not owned. If they were, then the resolution of damage levels and payments would be organized through the valuation and enforcement of the relevant property rights. These are determined either through the market or through the legal system. Crudely, if a chemical

[7] See Vogel (1986) for a contrast between US and UK policy approaches. It should be noted that European Community regulation typically pursues a rule-based approach in contrast to that of the UK.

firm pollutes a river, the river owner, if he owns the right to clean water, will demand compensation, or sue. Alternatively, if he does not own the right to clean water, it will be in his interest to bribe the chemical firm to reduce pollution.

In Coase's original model, the externality problem is one-to-one.[8] The parties bargain with each other, with the result that the equilibrium is determined irrespective of the allocation of the property rights between polluter and polluted. Thus, whether the polluter pays compensation for the damage done, or the affected party bribes the polluter to reduce emissions, is irrelevant to the efficiency of the outcome, being only of distributional concern.

If correct, Coase's bargaining model would have quite radical implications for policy. First, emphasis on the polluter-pays principle would be invalid, or, at least, an equity judgement with no foundation in economic efficiency. It would be equally appropriate for the injured party or the government itself to bribe polluters with subsidies.[9] Second, the assignment of property rights to 'free' assets—such as air and water—would solve externalities. Finally, the fact that most environmental assets are not owned by identified individuals creates a very strong presumption against do-nothing policies.

The simple Coasean model inevitably suffers many deficiencies. First, Coase tends to assume that markets exist. In practice, the major global environmental problems arise in circumstances where property rights are impossible to define. The essential feature—excludability—is not present. Second, like the Pigouvian tax solution, it, too, assumes well-functioning markets. Yet, if there is monopolistic competition, the bargain becomes more complex, involving polluter, polluted, and consumer (Buchanan, 1969). Third, when there are many parties involved, there may be significant free-ride incentives and transactions costs reducing the efficiency of the bargaining process. Finally, in the intergenerational context, bargains take on a new meaning because it is not clear who is bargaining on behalf of the next generation. (We return to this aspect in section 1.5.)

Yet, despite the unreality of the examples frequently cited in support of the Coasean argument, the idea that the optimality of the outcome is unaffected by whether the polluter or pollutee pays is much exploited in international problems. The notion that the victim should pay the polluter is a stark reality in the context of international environmental policy. This is the import of Mäler's exposition, in this volume, of the underlying principles of international environmental negotiations. The reality of global or regional environmental

[8] See Farrell (1987) for an exposition and critique.

[9] There are other reasons why the polluter pays principle might be sub-optimal. Affected parties may have little incentive to minimize their exposure to pollution—there may be moral hazard. See on this Olson and Zeckhauser (1970).

problems is that they are a game in which those who gain by co-operation must devise incentives to make those who lose play the game. Game theory predicts that this requires side payments—inducements to participate to those who stand to gain little by co-operation, but whose co-operation is essential to the objective. Inducements are all the more essential when the polluter is poor and therefore lacks the economic resources to tackle control.

### *Comparing the Pigouvian and Coasean Approaches*

A fundamental difference between the two approaches lies in the mechanisms proposed for resolving externalities. The Pigouvian approach creates a presumption in favour of pragmatism with civil servants and government agencies evaluating each case on its individual merits. The official identifies the parties and then attempts to estimate the marginal costs and benefits to each. Information is gathered from the parties, and demand and cost functions are estimated. The 'optimal' tax is then imposed.

The Coasean approach, by contrast, relies on the market itself to facilitate bargaining between the affected parties. If they cannot agree, the dispute is viewed as one about the definition of their respective property rights. The appropriate forum is then the courts, with the legal process providing for the resolution of the differences between the parties. Lawyers and judges calculate the costs and benefits to the parties of the externality, and in practice conduct a similar enquiry to that of the Pigouvian civil servant. In deciding the rival claims, and in assigning compensation, the legal process requires the same information as government regulation. The differences therefore lie less in the specification of the problem than in the costs of each method of resolution—the relative transaction costs of legal and government failure. It is by no means obvious that the legal approach is the more cost-effective. We turn now to the common problem—information.

## 1.4 Imperfect Information, Strategic Behaviour, and Global Co-operation

Both the Pigouvian and Coasean approaches assume that markets function well. The associated assumptions, as we saw above, rule out precisely those aspects of environmental problems which are so endemic in practical examples. The analysis of cases where these assumptions have been relaxed has provided the subsequent research agenda. We shall concentrate on two related aspects—imperfect information and the problems of global co-operation.

### *Imperfect Information and the Assessment of Environmental Risks*

In contrast to the case of the simple full-information models, we typically lack precise information on the nature of externalities and the costs and benefits of alternative methods of dealing with them. Uncertainty is a pervasive characteristic of environmental problems.

The first question to be addressed is that of the appropriate method of scientifically modelling uncertainty. Second, there is the incentive problem of individuals, firms, and countries revealing private information, and negotiating co-operative agreements. Many of the major environmental externalities are uncertain in their effect. For example, it will be at least a decade before we can be certain whether global warming is really occurring, or whether it is merely a climatic cycle caused by non-greenhouse-gas phenomena. Although the increases in carbon can be measured and predicted relatively accurately, the process of climatic change is very poorly understood. Furthermore, the impact of carbon is complex. Its effects are not limited to simply increasing *pro rata* the total greenhouse ability to absorb and retain solar energy; carbon has effects on other gas impacts, on cloud cover, and water vapour content.[10]

Our degree of uncertainty can be reduced by further research. The question is: should we take action now on the basis of very imperfect information, given that if we do not and the problem turns out to be serious, it may be very much worse to start later? Alternatively, should we engage in research now in the hope of better-designed policies later and indeed better technologies for tackling the problem? The answer must be pragmatic: the expected costs and benefits must be evaluated and a balanced decision taken.

Cost–benefit analysis, however, requires a method for measuring uncertainty. Conventional economic approaches assume that we at least know the subjective expected utility loss to individuals of the environmental damage, their risk preference, and the marginal costs of pollution control to firms. These assumptions are always questionable. They are increasingly so where the environmental problems are global, requiring the aggregation of individuals' preferences, and where uncertainty about costs and consequences is great. In these circumstances, it is often appropriate to consider a series of scenarios: what would happen if the probabilities were some assumed set? Crudely, a worst- and best-case scenario maps the range of possible outcomes. This kind of approach has the added advantage of helping to specify the bounds within which particular problems are nested, and may be extremely useful in providing a framework for considering the gains from co-operative solutions, to which we now turn.

[10] See House of Commons Select Committee on Energy (1989) for a survey of the evidence.

*Global Co-operation*

The chapters by Dasgupta, Mäler, and Barrett in this volume elaborate on the idea that modern environmental problems are instances of the 'tragedy of the commons' (see Hardin, 1968). Essentially, the atmosphere, the oceans outside exclusive economic zones, and the stratosphere are open-access resources, *res nullius*—owned by no one. Biological models predict a steady-state equilibrium for open-access resources, but one that may be perilously close to the carrying capacity of the habitat (see Pearce and Turner, 1990). Put another way, the risk of extinction of the resource—the tragedy—is potentially high under open-access. Common property—*res communes*—on the other hand, relates to resources held in common by a reasonably well-defined group of owners who, typically, establish rules of use. The distinction helps to characterize modern international environmental agreements as attempts to modify property rights away from open-access towards common property rights.

But even common property agreements risk breakdown because of the essential internal contradiction between the maximization of individual gains and the maximization of the collective good. This is the essence of the 'Prisoners' Dilemma' characterization of the common property problem.[11] Each player in the game stands to gain by not co-operating with other players, but all players would be better off if they did co-operate. Non-co-operative equilibria are inefficient and co-operative solutions require binding agreements. Any agreement that is not wholly binding risks individual defection by free-riders.

Are environmental agreements in the global sphere subject to the Prisoners' Dilemma? Many would argue that they are and that binding agreements require incentive systems in the form of side payments, cash or technology or in-kind transfers, to potential defectors. As Mäler notes in chapter 7 below, such side payments can easily turn the morality of the polluter-pays principle upside down, so that victims pay polluters not to pollute—the victim-pays principle. Examples of the victim-pays principle are already evident, as with Sweden's technical assistance to reduce acid emissions from Poland, and the currently negotiated technology transfers to China and India with respect to chlorofluorocarbons (CFCs) emission reductions. The issue of 'side payments' will dominate the 1992 United Nations Environment Conference in Brazil.

Global environmental negotiation and agreement need not be as bleak a prospect as the Prisoners' Dilemma suggests. In game theory pay-offs tend to be characterized by single-dimensions—time spent in jail or monetary fines in the original Prisoners' Dilemma example, profits or utility in the generalized case. In the real world, however, multiple objectives characterize the game.

[11] On the Prisoners' Dilemma, see Taylor (1976) and Dasgupta, chapter 2 in this volume.

Countries may be prepared to act counter-preferentially for a greater good, out of obligation, fairness, or out of environmental stewardship motives. A second feature of real-world games, familiar in game theory as well, is that they are repeated. If one player defects in the first game, he may face a coalition to his disadvantage in a second game, and so on. *Sequential games* may not face the Prisoners' Dilemma syndrome, particularly if the time period over which games are played is a long one.[12]

The weapons at the disposal of co-operative coalitions are familiar, including international disapprobation, as Britain has learned from its unco-operative stance on European Community environmental legislation.

Game theory models suggest that the incentives to co-operate depend critically on the analysis of the counterfactual—what happens if the parties do not agree? In particular, if the two parties are differentially affected so that, for example, one country experiences large-scale destruction before others, or if the parties take different views of the probability of significant damage, they may have differential incentives to pay the pollution costs. Bankruptcy—in the sense of inability to pay—may also be highly significant. Many developing countries simply cannot meet the costs of environmental degradation.

In environmental problems, the end-game can at least be sketched in outline. If increasing concentrations of greenhouse gases lead to rising temperatures, and if these raise sea level, then those countries with low-lying, densely populated areas will face major population displacement and increased sea defence and drainage costs. Furthermore, agricultural areas sensitive to temperature change would experience depopulation. Large-scale population movements, adverse food production trends, and higher population levels are likely to create instability in international relations and ultimately these may become security issues.[13]

Although such an analysis is, of course, conjectural, it indicates which countries face the greatest costs if repeated games fail to produce a co-operative outcome and which countries are likely to gain little by co-operation. Bangladesh would face very high costs but lacks the resources to build appropriate sea defences. The UK, by contrast, might even benefit from an improved climate, and the costs of sea defences might be manageable.

A further important consideration in appraising the prospects for international co-operation is noted in Barrett's chapter in this volume. Global environmental agreements are not homogeneous in nature. An agreement on CFCs was feasible, first because of the small number of players in the game (the CFC producers of USA, Europe, and the Eastern bloc) and the small number

[12] See, for example, Axelrod (1984) for an exposition of tit-for-tat rules. For a formal treatment of sequential games, see Kreps and Wilson (1982).

[13] See Grubb (1989) for an extensive discussion of the role of international negotiations in framing agreements on greenhouse-gas emissions.

of potentially interested parties (industrializing developing countries). Second, the costs of substituting for CFCs in several major uses are small. No such conditions apply to greenhouse gases. All the world becomes the set of players and the costs of carbon cutbacks are formidable for some of the players. Offsetting this is the potential for some major emitters to co-operate in the initial stages and use demonstrated reductions in carbon dioxide as a bargaining instrument.

International environmental issues represent very fruitful ground for economic analysis in terms of game theory. The chapters by Mäler and Barrett in this volume reveal some of the potential and some of the insights.

## 1.5 Valuing the Future

Most of the major consequences of global externalities will fall on the next generation and beyond. Almost all environmental externalities have an intertemporal dimension. Nuclear waste generated now imposes a cost on future generations in terms of disposal costs and hazards; greenhouse-gas emissions now may commit the future to irreversible global warming; a species lost now imposes a user cost on future generations in terms of foregone benefits from that species.

Intertemporal resource allocations are incorporated into economic analysis by discounting the future. The value of £100 now is greater than £100 in a year's time because of the return between now and a year's time if the money is invested, or because consumption now is certain, whereas consumption in one year's time depends on being alive to consume it.[14] Discounting allows for the lower weight that individuals place on the future—their myopia —compared to the present. But discounting in the environmental context is contentious precisely because it justifies the forward shifting of environmental costs to future generations. Although it may be rational for individuals to value the future consumption at a discount to present consumption, it is by no means obvious that society should make the same trade-off.[15] Although technical progress may enhance the consumption possibilities of future generations over the present, environmental damage may have the opposite effect.

The first-best solution to this intertemporal bias is the downwards adjustment of discount rates, perhaps to zero to reflect indifference about the temporal incidence of costs and benefits.[16] Indeed, if society is risk-averse concerning

[14] Respectively, we consider the cost to society of waiting as the social opportunity cost, and the demand valuation as the social time preference rate. Only in competitive equilibrium will the two approaches yield the same answer.

[15] See Parfit (1984, Annex F).

[16] For a survey of environmental concerns about discount rates see Markandya and Pearce (1988).

the environment, and wishes to hand on to future generations environmental assets at least as good as it inherited, it may even be negative.

In practice, however, the optimal policy towards future generations is not so straightforward. Again, the treatment of one aspect of the environmental problem—valuing the future—cannot be considered in isolation from other market failures. There are, in consequence, a number of additional factors which should be borne in mind. First, by altering the normative balance between aggregate investment and consumption, lowering discount rates across the board could accelerate environmental degradation if investment is more materials/energy intensive.[17] This effect is of particular importance in considering the impact of privatization. As we argue below, privatization typically raises the discount rate and may consequently have the environmentally beneficial effect of providing a premium to small, less capital-intensive production techniques. Second, the impact of lowering the discount rate may be affected by the size of the errors in calculating the costs and benefits of projects. If, for example, the benefits of a project are overstated and the environmental consequences undervalued, a lower discount rate may exacerbate the total effect. It is therefore important to incorporate externality costs fully before applying a discount rate.

It is therefore not surprising that the discount-rate debate remains unresolved. One suggestion is that discounting is permissible only within an ecological constraint which sets limits on the degradation that would be permitted and which would protect future generations' capability to enjoy an undegraded environment.[18]

## 1.6 Market-orientated Solutions

It is currently fashionable to advocate the use of markets to solve environmental problems. This approach draws upon the basic Pigouvian insight, noted above in section 1.3, that individuals and firms should be explicitly faced with the costs of environmental damage resulting from their activities. It also fits neatly with the trend towards expanding the role of markets in traditional production areas and in the provision of welfare services. The collapse of state planning in Eastern Europe has given powerful impetus to this trend, while the continuing world debt crisis has encouraged developing countries to sell assets.

Environmentalists have, however, typically argued for greater state intervention. It has often been assumed that, since environmental problems result from market failures, state intervention is necessitated. This simplistic approach is

[17] Markandya and Pearce (1988).
[18] See, for example, Page (1977).

not, however, supported by evidence from the planned economies of Eastern Europe. It ignores the costs of intervention: market failure only justifies intervention if the costs of that failure are greater than the resultant costs of government failure consequent upon the intervention. The latter are often at least as important as the former.

Furthermore, there are typically a number of different responses to market failure: the options are, broadly, to replace the market; to make it work better by altering the incentives and costs; or to extend the market by the application of property rights.[19] These strategies are exemplified by a number of practical policy suggestions which are currently the focus of debate: introducing private ownership; utilizing the taxation system; and creating a market in pollution permits.

*Privatization*

Privatization in the narrow sense involves the transfer of assets from one set of owners (the government) to another (private shareholders). It does not introduce new property rights (*à la* Coase). Rather it changes the nature of existing property rights. Its impact thus depends upon the incentives and constraints faced by the two sets of owners. Despite almost a decade of privatization, the efficiency consequence of changing incentives and the replacement of government control by shareholders remains poorly understood. Nevertheless, since the sectors which have been privatized are frequently those which are most environmentally sensitive—water, energy, and transport—the consequences of this policy are important.

Government objectives in operating firms reflect wider considerations than profit maximization. Recent models have focused on the maximization of output (Rees, 1984, 1989) rather than profit, leading to over- rather than under-provision. In the public sector in the UK, electricity has witnessed substantial over-capacity, and coal output has been maintained beyond profit maximization. This trend towards output rather than profit has been reinforced by the lower cost of capital to government compared with private ownership. In this sense, if output and pollution are correlated, public ownership may result in higher pollution.

Privatization can, in these models, be assumed to reduce output and investment at the margin, given the profit objective and a higher cost of capital. A higher discount rate induces shorter-term investment horizons and therefore the assignment of lower valuations to the future. In the case of electricity investments, for example, Sizewell B nuclear power station passed the critical

[19] See Helm (1986) for an overview of these strategies and Helm (ed.) (1989) for applications to a range of economic activites.

5 per cent real rate of return requirement laid down in the 1978 White Paper. In the private sector, Hinkley B would face at least 11 per cent, and therefore not be viable (Dimson, 1989). Choice of technique for long-term utility industries will, therefore, on this argument, be profoundly affected by privatization. Paradoxically, this change in discount rates may actually be environmentally beneficial in the electricity case. It will raise the price of electricity, reducing consumption at the margin. It will also place a premium on small generating units, and especially favour combined heat-and-power plants.[20]

Some commentators have argued that the efficiency of the resources controlled in the private sector will be greater, thereby economizing on environmental damage. These effects fall into three categories: that more output will be produced from given inputs (thereby reducing the demands on natural resources); that the ratio of capital to labour will be closer to the optimum (correcting for labour bias in the public sector) and hence reduce costs of production of environmental improvements; and finally that prices and hence outputs will be more closely related to costs, thereby eliminating overproduction.[21]

Since the magnitude of these factors will vary on a case-by-case basis, the dynamic effects on investment will need to be compared with static efficiency gains. The more substantial the environmental impact of longer-term investments—as for example in the electricity and water industries—the greater the impact of privatization. When investment is environmentally benign—as in the water industry—privatization may only be beneficial if the static efficiency gains are large. When investment is environmentally damaging, the balance goes the other way.

Private firms do not, however, operate in a vacuum. In developed countries virtually all firms are subject to environmental regulation. The final and perhaps most important aspect of privatization is its impact on regulation. Is regulation likely to be tougher and easier to impose and monitor in the private or the public sector? The intuitive and conventional answer that greater control is engendered through ownership is highly misleading. It may be much better not to own the regulatee. The problem can be modelled through 'principal-agent' analysis.[22] The incentives of government regulators need first to be assessed. If they also own the polluter, they are likely to be susceptible to its financial performance. In the public sector, a politician is answerable for the performance of the firm, and will inevitably want to defend its record. In the UK water industry, government ministers frequently acted as *de facto* apologists for the low standards of water quality. Now that the industry is privatized,

[20] In the case of water, the effects may go the other way.
[21] See Bishop and Kay (1988) for some early efficiency estimates.
[22] See Rees (1985) for a survey of the principal–agent literature.

ministers are still answerable for water quality, but have no financial responsibility to the shareholders of the water companies. There is an incentive gain through privatization.

On the other hand, access to the relevant information to monitor performance is much reduced and there may be an offsetting cost created by the strategic behaviour of regulatees. This provides another opportunity for regulatory capture.[23] On balance, UK evidence suggests that privatization has significantly improved regulation. The establishment of the National Rivers Authority and the Office of Water Supply have provided an opportunity to create a programme of sustained environmental improvement.

*Taxes*

As we noted in section 1.3 above, the Pigouvian approach to externalities suggests that the tax system may provide a mechanism by which the incentives of polluters can be brought closer to a position reflecting the costs of environmental damage. Its attractions to government are considerable. Environmental taxes raise revenue, they elicit widespread acceptance and therefore compliance, and they leave the market to sort out the most efficient methods of pollution production and control. Once the desired level of pollution is set, the need for further complex regulatory oversight is minimal.

As we saw in section 1.3 above, the ideal tax from an efficiency point of view is one which exactly reflects the costs of pollution at the margin. However, it is often impractical to tax the pollution precisely, and therefore a number of proxy solutions are often adopted. The options can be illustrated by considering the example of carbon emissions from power stations.

The first option is to tax carbon-producing fuels, on the basis of their approximate carbon pollution potential. This alters the polluting input price and encourages substitution towards fuels with lower pollution potential (gas for coal, for example) and towards non-fossil fuels, like nuclear, water (barrages), and wind (windmills). The disadvantage of this method is that it treats all coal plants alike, and therefore penalizes coal plants with higher efficiency levels and hence fails to match actual pollution. A second option is to tax power station emissions, on a plant-by-plant basis. On this approach, each station is regarded as a unit converting inputs into two outputs, e.g. electricity and pollution. The tax exactly penalizes plants according to pollution emission.[24]

The third option is to tax the output of electricity: to tax final consumers. This could be achieved through the imposition of VAT. This would, however, be a

[23] See Helm and Yarrow (1988) for a summary of the major problems in regulating utilities.

[24] The optimal ranking of the electricity merit order is then, given the inputs, a function of the two efficiency parameters (electricity and pollution) considered jointly.

crude measure, creating no incentive to substitute cleaner technology at the margin because it taxes all inputs equally, with no account being taken of their different carbon contents. It is also unlikely to achieve the desired effect of significant reductions in emissions since the price elasticity of demand is very low.[25] Very substantial price increases would be required, illustrating the point that careful case-by-case empirical studies are required if policy is not to be misdirected.

Thus far, taxes have been considered in terms of their substitution effects. Income effects are also likely to be important. Income effects from taxes may at least partially offset the substitution effect. Many goods produced by polluting technologies are merit goods. Electricity, transport, and water are obvious examples and the resulting demand behaviour from taxes may conflict with distributional objectives. Indeed, in the case of a tax on electricity, the substitution effect is very small, while the income effect is very large.[26] On an international scale, environmental taxes would require a compensating redistribution to developing countries. Taxes may also be non-neutral at the national level, adversely affecting aggregate demand, and thus requiring compensatory expenditure or reductions in other taxes.

The latter point raises the question of the use to which additional revenues are put. For example, the low electricity price effect discussed above would not be so much of a problem if the resulting revenues were spent on energy conservation measures—i.e. if the tax funded a subsidy. This would create a double effect, and have the attractive feature of avoiding an extra call on the exchequer. Similarly, an environmental tax on rich countries (perhaps on energy consumption) may provide a politically more acceptable method of funding a transfer to developing countries to provide side-payments for reducing their pollution.

Taxes on a national scale may therefore provide an attractive policy option to reduce national pollution and to fund subsidies. In isolation, however, the impact may induce perverse substitution effects between countries. A unilateral tax on energy users in the UK would disadvantage the competitiveness of some UK traded goods. The competitors without the tax would gain market share, and hence increase total pollution. This is another example of the Prisoners' Dilemma, discussed above in section 1.4. The policy implication is clear: tax-based solutions of international externalities are best dealt with consistently at the international level. Unilateral action may have a considerable demonstration effect, but it may be counterproductive.[27]

[25] See Department of Energy (1989).

[26] See Baker *et al.* (1990) for micro disaggregated consumption patterns for electricity, and Pearson and Smith (1990) for estimates of the impact of electricity taxes on different consumer groups. See also Dilnot and Helm (1987) on energy as a merit good.

[27] In this context, it is interesting to note that UK discussion of the possibility of carbon taxes has stressed the international discussion. See Ridley (1989).

*Marketing Pollution Rights*

Pollution taxes seek to regulate waste, effluent, and ambient emissions through prices. But economists have long debated the merits of price incentives compared to quantity incentives. The idea of regulating the environment through emission quotas which are then traded was first espoused in the 1960s.[28] The environmental quality objective can be translated into an emissions target. Suppose the target is 100 units of pollution. Permits allowing the emission of 100 units can be issued to polluters. The initial allocation rule is important. Typically, the historical pattern of emissions will form the basis of the allocation: polluters will each receive permits according to their emissions at some agreed baseline date—'grandfathering'. Polluters are then free to trade the permits which then command a market price. For some polluters with low abatement costs, the market price ($P$) will exceed the abatement cost ($A$). As long as $P > A$, such polluters have an incentive to sell permits, thus surrendering the right to pollute, and to abate pollution. High-cost polluters will face a context in which $P < A$, giving them an incentive to acquire permits in the market. The attraction of tradable permits is that the concentration of abatement in low-cost polluters will minimize the compliance costs.

Tietenberg, in chapter 4 of this volume, shows how this result can be achieved in addition to environmental quality being improved. Any polluter able to emit pollutants below the initial allocation will secure certified emission-reduction credits. It is these credits that become the currency of the emissions trading programme. A new source of pollution can be allowed only if it acquires adequate credits, thus offsetting the initial gain in quality. By allowing trade only if credits exceed debits, the regulating authority can actually improve environmental quality. Some debate exists as to whether emissions trading under the US Clean Air Act has achieved improvements in air quality. Certainly it appears not to have deteriorated, so that trading has fared no worse than the alternative of command and control and has certainly achieved cost compliance benefits of several billion dollars (see Hahn and Hester, 1987, 1989).

The potential for using the tradable permit as an incentive system is enormous. It does, however, require imaginative administration. Most of the cost-savings under the US legislation have come from within-plant (internal) trading (see again Hahn and Hester, 1987, 1989). The greatest potential almost certainly lies with inter-firm trading. Moreover, trading offers a means of handling international environmental agreements. A carbon convention, for example, will have to function via emission targets allocated to individual countries. Grandfathering with some initial discount—e.g. carbon dioxide emissions in 1990 less, say, 20 per cent—is the most likely initial allocation.

[28] See Dales (1968).

Emissions trading options are then twofold. At the very least, within-country trading can occur, just as the US proposes for compliance with the Montreal Protocol on the protection of the ozone layer.

More imaginatively, permits could be traded between nations. A country that is able to secure carbon dioxide reductions of more than the initial discount can secure credits which can be traded with other countries. The obvious problem with this solution lies with the grandfathering clause, since developing countries will acquire a fairly low initial allocation if rights are allocated on the basis of base-year emissions, and will be unable to afford traded permits. One solution is to bias the initial allocation to developing countries according, say, to population. Trade will then be from developing countries to the richer world, with a consequent significant transfer of funds to the Third World.

Such a prospect opens up imaginative possibilities. Permit trading could be subject to its own form of conditionality. For example, sales might be contingent upon agreed proportions of permit revenues being used for energy-conservation expenditure in the Third World. Offsets would also be permitted in the form of carbon-fixing investments such as afforestation. New additions to carbon-dioxide-emitting capacity would be allowed if the potential permit holder agreed to fund tree-planting anywhere in the world. Tietenberg's enthusiasm for permits is therefore warranted at least in terms of the potential for tradable permit solutions to major environmental problems. Moreover, the quantity solution avoids a major pitfall of tax policy—the political difficulty of getting new taxes accepted. This difficulty might be significantly reduced by aligning green taxes with reductions in taxes on labour and capital. The advantage here is that the incentive effects of green taxes are preserved in a revenue-neutral budget, and the excess burden of the supply-side disincentive taxes is reduced. None the less, the psychology of tax burdens is likely to remain an obstacle to pricing solutions. Tradable permits thus have considerable attractions.

## 1.7 Conclusions

The prospect for the 1990s will be one of movements towards green economies. Both planned and free markets have failed lamentably to provide adequate environmental protection. Moreover, green market phenomena, in the form of green consumerism and, potentially more important, the green investor, cannot be relied upon to solve environmental problems. Major new policy initiatives will be required.

Environmental economics offers a number of important insights into the appropriate economic policies. The Pigouvian framework provides a strong presumption in favour of market-based approaches which utilize the price mechanism to confront individuals and firms with the real costs of environmental damage. The Coasean approach suggests that policy should be pragmatic between the polluter and the victim paying. Much, however, depends on the number of parties involved, and the institutional and legal framework.

The presumption in favour of market-based policies does not, however, imply the unfettered operation of market forces. Rather, the market should be harnessed to generate the most efficient method of achieving desired pollution reductions. The role of the state is to regulate through command-and-control procedures, in setting maximum pollution levels. The role of the market is to find the best method of achieving them. Although it may be possible in some cases to create property rights, the scope is limited. None of the current major environmental concerns falls into the pure Coase category.

The type of intervention will vary on a case-by-case basis. There is no general first-best solution. The pursuit of single instrument solutions is naïve and possibly even dangerous. The universal pursuit of taxes or command-and-control regulations is sub-optimal and sometimes perverse. There is no escape from pragmatism: the application of empirically based cost–benefit analysis to the evaluation of alternative policies. Market and government failures vary on a case-by-case basis, and so inevitably must the solutions.

The balance of the argument will, however, generally favour the exploitation of the market's mechanisms for revealing information, as compared with the excess costs and bureaucracy associated with total reliance on the command-and-control approach. Governments will be forced to search out cost-minimizing procedures to lower the projected costs of future environmental policy. The way forward lies with market-based incentives—taxes, charges, deposit-refund systems, tradable permits, and offset policies.

## Bibliography

Arrow, K. (1970), 'The Organisation of Economic Activity', in R. Haverman and J. Margolis (eds.), *Public Expenditures and Policy Analysis*, Chicago.

Axelrod, R. (1984), *The Evolution of Cooperation*, New York, Basic Books.

Ayres, R. V. and Kneese, A. (1969), 'Production, Consumption and Externality', *American Economic Review*.

Baker, P., Blundell, R., McKay, S., Symons, E., and Walker, I. (1990), 'A Simulation Programme of Consumer Expenditure', Institute for Fiscal Studies Working Paper.

Baumol, W. and Oates, W. (1988), *The Theory of Environmental Policy*, 2nd edn., Cambridge, Cambridge University Press.

Beckerman, W. (1974), *In Defence of Economic Growth*, London, Jonathan Cape.

Bishop, M. and Kay, J. A. (1988), *Does Privatisation Work? Lessons from the UK*, London Business School, Centre for Business Strategy.

Buchanan, J. M. (1969), 'External Diseconomies, Corrective Taxes and Market Structure', *American Economic Review*, March.
— and Stubblebine, W. C. (1962), 'Externality', *Economica*, 29, 371–84.
Coase, R. H. (1960), 'The Problem of Social Cost', *Journal of Law and Economics*, 3, 1–44.
Cornes, R. and Sandler, T. (1986), *The Theory of Externalities, Public Goods, and Club Goods*, Cambridge, Cambridge University Press.
Dales, J. H. (1968), *Pollution, Property and Prices*, Toronto, University of Toronto Press.
Department of Energy (1989), 'The Demand for Energy', in D. R. Helm, J. A. Kay, and D. Thompson (eds.), *The Market for Energy*, Oxford, Oxford University Press.
Dilnot, A. and Helm, D. R. (1987), 'Energy Policy, Merit Goods and Social Security', *Fiscal Studies* (reprinted in Helm *et al.*, (eds.) 1989).
Dimson, E. (1989), 'The Discount Rate for a Power Station', *Energy Economics*, 11.
Farrell, J. (1987), 'Information and the Coase Theorem', *Journal of Economic Perspectives*.
Goldsmith, E. *et al.* (1972), *Blueprint for Survival*, London, Penguin Books.
Grubb, M. (1989), *The Greenhouse Effect: Negotiating Targets*, London, Royal Institute of International Affairs.
Gruenspecht, H. K. and Lave, L. B. (1989), 'The Economics of Health, Safety and Environmental Regulation', in R. Schmalensee and R. D. Willig (eds.), *Handbook of Industrial Organisation*, Vol. 2, Amsterdam, North-Holland, 1507–50.
Hahn, R. and Hester, G. (1987), 'The Market for Bads', *Regulation*, 3–4.
— (1989) 'Where did all the Markets Go? An Analysis of EPA's Emissions Trading Program', *Yale Journal of Regulation*, 6(1), 109–53.
Hardin, G. (1968), 'The Tragedy of the Commons', *Science*, 162, 1243–8.
Heller, W. P. and Starrett, D. A. (1976), 'On the Nature of Externalities', in S. A. Lin (ed.), *Theory and Measurement of Economic Externalities*, New York, Academic Press.
Helm, D. R. (1986), 'The Economic Borders of the State', *Oxford Review of Economic Policy*, 2(2).
— (ed.) (1989), *The Economic Borders of the State*, Oxford, Oxford University Press.
— and Yarrow, G. (1988), 'The Regulation of Utilities', *Oxford Review of Economic Policy*, 4(2).
— Kay, J. A., and Thompson, D. (eds.) (1989), *The Market for Energy*, Oxford, Oxford University Press.
House of Commons Select Committee on Energy (1989), 6th Report, *Implications of the Greenhouse Effect*, HMSO.
Kreps, D. and Wilson, R. (1982), 'Reputation and Imperfect Information', *Journal of Economic Theory*, **27**, 253–79.
Mäler, K.-G. (1974), *Environmental Economics: A Theoretical Inquiry*, Baltimore, Johns Hopkins University Press.
Markandya, A. and Pearce, D. W. (1988), 'Environmental Considerations and the Choice of the Discount Rates in Developing Countries', Environment Department, World Bank Working Paper No. 3, Washington, D.C.

Meadows, D. H., Meadows, D. L., Randers, J., and Behrens, W. (1972), *Limits to Growth*, New York, Earth Island.

Olson, M. and Zeckhauser, R. (1970), 'The Efficient Production of External Economies', *American Economic Review*, 60, 512–17.

Page, T. (1977), *Conservation and Efficiency*, Baltimore, Johns Hopkins University Press.

Parfit, D. (1984), *Reasons and Persons*, Oxford, Oxford University Press.

Pearce, D. W. and Turner, R. K. (1990), *The Economics of Natural Resources and the Environment*, London, Harvester-Wheatsheaf.

Pearson, M. and Smith, S. (1990), 'Taxation and Environmental Policy: Some Initial Evidence', IFS Commentary No. 19, Institute for Fiscal Studies.

Pigou, A. (1920), *The Economics of Welfare*, London, Macmillan.

Rees, R. (1984), 'A Positive Theory of Public Enterprise', in M. Marchand, D. Pestieau, and H. Tulkens (eds.), *The Performance of Public Enterprises*, Amsterdam, North-Holland.

— (1985), 'The Theory of Principal and Agent, Parts 1 and 2', *Bulletin of Economic Research*.

— (1989), 'Modelling Public Enterprise Performance', in Helm *et al.* (eds.), 1989 .

Ridley, N. (1989), *Policies against Pollution*, London, Centre for Policy Studies.

Taylor, M. (1976), *Anarchy and Cooperation*, Chichester, John Wiley.

Tietenberg, T. (1988), *Environmental and Natural Resource Economics*, 2nd edn., Glenville, Illinois, Scott Foresman.

Vogel, D. (1986), *National Styles of Regulation: Environmental Policy in Great Britain and the United States*, Ithaca and London, Cornell University Press.

# 2
# The Environment as a Commodity

*Partha Dasgupta*

## 2.1 The Production of Commodities by Means of Resources

All economic activity is based ultimately on resources found in nature. Whether it is consumption or production, or whether it is exchange, the commodities which are involved are made of constituents provided by nature. Thus, the ingredients of any manufactured good are other produced goods, labour time and skills, and natural resources. Each of *these* constituent produced goods is in turn made up from the ingredients that went into *its* manufacture, namely labour time and skills, natural resources, and further produced goods. It follows that any manufactured commodity is ultimately a combination of labour and natural resources.

Labour too is a produced good. Even raw labour is an output, manufactured by those natural resources which sustain life, resources such as the multitude of nutrients we consume, the air we breathe, and the water we drink. *All* commodities are therefore traceable to natural resources.

The point in exposing the morphology of produced goods and services is not to construct a resource theory of a value. There are any number of natural resources, and this alone precludes such an attempted theory from being coherent. My purpose, rather, is to use it to express surprise at the fact that

Partha Dasgupta is Professor of Economics at Stanford University and the University of Cambridge. This paper was given as part of the Stevenson Lectureship series in the University of Glasgow, and appeared in *Information Strategy and Public Policy* edited by David Vines and Andrew Stevenson, published by Basil Blackwell in 1991.

despite the centrality of natural resources in economic activity, they find little room in economics discourses. Interest in resource economics, more particularly environmental economics, has only been intermittent, and if we are currently witnessing a resurgence (and this volume is an example of it), we have also just lived through a decade-long neglect, during which much valuable research could have been done.[1] We are way behind where we should have been, and could have been, to confront the many environmental problems we have again become conscious of.

In fact, there is another problem with periodic intellectual slumber. It is that with each reawakening, much of what had been developed earlier is not known or acknowledged: economists are notoriously ignorant of intellectual capital. (In many instances, however, the extent of ignorance is so astonishing that one can only assume it is feigned.) Much energy is then spent rediscovering ideas. Thus, there is no credible reason today why economists should have to write on the analytical foundations of environmental taxes, or the informational parsimony afforded by transferable pollution permits. Nor is there any reason why politicians, journalists, and international agencies have *now* to be told that estimates of net national product ought to take account of the degradation of environmental stocks; nor indeed, why we need now to try and fathom what 'sustainable development' might plausibly mean; or what ethical drive the concept of social discount rates may possess. These issues were the subject of a rather successful research programme among technical economists a decade and a half ago.[2] As subjects for analytical investigation, these topics are now very cold. As research problems they are dead.

There is even today a widespread misconception that 'economic' calculations and environmental concerns are in conflict. The view is so pervasive that thoughtful commentators on the environment often find it necessary first to state it and then to correct it by talking of the resurgence of 'green economics' (see, for example, *The Economist*, 2 September 1989). In fact, this greening began a long while ago, at least as far back as Pigou (1920) in his classic development of the concept of *externalities*, and his exposure of the difference between private and social costs (and benefits) in the phenomenon of externalities. Pigou, of course, did not complete the analysis. He could not, because there were analytical difficulties he was incapable of handling, most especially those connected with time, uncertainty, and the pervasiveness of asymmetric

[1] This neglect has been a persistent phenomenon in British universities. Courses on resource economics have been regularly on offer in major economics departments in Scandinavia, the United States, and Canada over the past fifteen years or so. But even there, interest has been muted in recent years.

[2] See below in the text for references and sources for further references.

information, and those involving a small number of economic agents.[3] During the decade of the 1960s, and even more the decade of the 1970s, what we today call environmental economics, and more generally resource economics, was developed and codified. (See, for example, Coase, 1960; Kneese, 1964; Brown and McGuire, 1967; Krutilla, 1967; Dales, 1968; Arrow, 1971; Starrett, 1972; Meade, 1973; Arrow and Fisher, 1974; Mäler, 1974; Baumol and Oates, 1975; Kneese and Schultze, 1975; Krutilla and Fisher, 1975; *Review of Economic Studies* (Symposium, 1974); Clark, 1976; Mäler and Wyzga, 1976; Dasgupta and Heal, 1979; Dasgupta, 1982; and Lind (ed.), 1982. Excellent elementary texts on the subject are Hartwick and Olewiler (1986) and Tietenberg (1988). Ulph (1989) is a useful readers' guide to existing textbooks and treatises on the subject.) Its incorporation into development economics, especially development planning, has been rather slower. (For an early attempt, see Dasgupta, 1982.) But the analytical elements are all available for use.

In this chapter, I will not produce a litany of environmental losses. This has been done to great and fruitful effect by others more knowledgeable on these matters. (See, for example, the documents published regularly by the Worldwatch Institute in Washington, D.C., and the several State of the Environment reports, e.g. CSE, 1982, 1986; IIED/WRI, 1987.) I shall approach matters instead from the analytical corner and borrow from the literature which I have cited to provide an outline of the main features of the economics of the environment.

By an environmental problem I do not of course mean only the classical one of the factory chimney polluting the atmosphere. I mean a great deal more and I shall try to present a unified viewpoint which will be wide enough to catch within its net a seemingly disparate class of resource problems. The advantage of a unified formulation is that it enables us to economize in our thinking. Given an embracing framework, we can borrow from our understanding of one class of issues when we consider some other class of issues. And it puts the onus on us to prove when we claim, as we rightly do in many cases, that a given environmental problem has its own special features, reflected not only by the specific nature of the resource under study, but also by its location, the time in question, and the socio-economic context in which it occurs.

As it happens, even here there are a number of routes along which one can enter a discussion. I shall, to begin with, adopt one which is hallowed by tradition, and is in other respects as good as any other route. Later in this chapter (section 2.6), I shall adopt a different route. We will see that the two will have

[3] Even Hotelling's great article (Hotelling, 1931) merely scratched the economics of exhaustible resources. The incorporation of substitutability among resources, of technological change, and, more generally, the placing of the subject in the context of intertemporal general equilibrium, could be completed only over four decades later.

the same implications for public policy. Our starting gate will therefore not matter. The two avenues will lead us to the same destination.

## 2.2 Missing Markets and the Breakdown of Social Norms

I want to begin by thinking of *market* failure and I begin with the observation that in many cases where markets malfunction, their malfunctioning can be ascribed to the fact that for certain commodities markets simply do not exist. Sometimes they happen not to exist for accidental or historical reasons, sometimes there are logical reasons why they cannot exist, sometimes the nature of the physical and political situation keeps them from existing, or makes them function desperately wrongly when they do exist. What are usually called environmental resources are, as it happens, particularly vulnerable to this problem.

By markets I do not necessarily mean price-guided institutions, I mean something a good deal more general. By markets I mean *institutions which make available to affected parties the opportunity to negotiate courses of actions*. And by malfunctioning markets I mean circumstances where such opportunities are not present, where they are at best present only partially, or where they are somewhat one-sided. (This last, the often one-sidedness of opportunities, means that I am thinking of distributional issues as well, not merely those bearing on efficiency.) The existence of competitive market prices presupposes only one set of institutional arrangements within which such negotiations can take place (as it happens they render unnecessary any negotiation!). Bilateral bargaining is another; and there are a whole host of intermediate institutions, those providing the scope for multilateral bargaining, the agreements arising from which are on occasion codified over the years through the emergence of *social norms*, and the associated social sanctions imposed upon those in violation of such norms; and upon those who fail to impose sanctions upon those in violation of such norms; and upon those who fail to impose sanctions upon those who fail to impose sanctions upon those in violation of such norms, and so on indefinitely.

This is important to recognize, that social norms can be seen as implicit social contracts. Put another way, social norms are strategies of behaviour. But they are strategies that are sustained by self-enforcement, and not by the law courts. Provided people are not unduly myopic (see Appendix), the contract could be enforced if each person were able credibly to threaten a withdrawal of his co-operation from any person who violated the contract. Since so much of resource management in traditional societies has been sustained by norms of behaviour, I shall try to make all this a bit more precise. It will also suggest why norms can break down during periods of change. And if they are not replaced by new, effective norms, the society begins to suffer from 'market failure'.[4]

At any date, call a person a *conformist* if he co-operates with a person if and only if that person has shown himself at the previous date to have been a conformist.[5] At the starting date, we define a conformist to be one who co-operates; that is, one who keeps his side of the bargain. From the definition of a conformist, this society can then recursively determine at any future date whether a given person *is* a conformist. It is then possible to show that if people are not unduly myopic, it is in the *self*-interest of each person to be a conformist if all others conform. But this means that universal conformism is self-enforcing.

Notice that the social norm in this example is conformism. A non-conformist is a deviant. And a conformist punishes him by withdrawing his co-operation. Thus, in particular, a conformist punishes a person who has failed to punish someone who has violated the social norm. This is because in failing to punish the violator, the person in question himself is a violator of the social norm! In the Appendix, I will present the simplest version of the formal argument. It will make clear the role individual discount rates play in sustaining social norms, and thus tacit co-operation. But even this informal account demonstrates that my starting gate, the phenomenon of market failure, has allowed me immediate access to the province of anthropologists who have so often illuminated our understanding of customs regarding the use of environmental resources in communities that are at first sight not easy to comprehend. As it happens, such social customs are often instrumental in supporting objectives that are not dissimilar to those of a 'modern' bent, and they are often under erosion—this is the market failure—through shifting demographic features, newly emerging economic opportunities, and changing social mores and lifestyles. Recent work on the theory of bargaining, particularly in the context of repeated games, has shown how fragile such social customs can be, how dependent they are on the ability of affected parties to monitor the actions of others—that is, compliance of implicit contracts—and on the ability of each party to assess the value that others attach to the resource in question. And so on. I shall come back to these issues in the following section.

[4] In the Appendix I give a formal account of this line of argument for a simple 2-person model of negotiation. I should add that norms can be *inefficient*. The Folk Theorem in game theory is an articulation of this fact. But in what follows I shall be thinking of norms which *are* efficient.

[5] This assumes that individual actions are publicly observable.

## 2.3 Reciprocal Externalities

Much of this has been studied under the general rubric of what is today called the Problem of the Commons, a problem which is associated with resources to which no property rights have been awarded. Such resources are therefore free to all who wish to avail themselves of them. Being free and finitely available they are used excessively. (One needs to add some qualifications to make this inference, but I will ignore theoretical niceties here.) We may conclude that the social value, or accounting price, of a 'common property' resource is positive, on occasion large and positive, even while it is free to individual users.

Such resources abound. The earth's atmosphere, which is in a continual state of diffusion, is a paradigm. It is a global commons, and such problems as are thought to arise from various greenhouse gases, including carbon dioxide which is not recycled by vegetation and plankton, are global problems and have to be attacked at an international level of discourse. Moreover, all nations will have to be involved in negotiation. It will not be enough if only a few nations agree on a joint co-ordinated policy; those not party to the agreement will follow policies that will vitiate the point of the agreement. So too with other global commons, such as international fisheries, deep-sea nodules, and the international waters as a repository of our garbage. The United Nations Law of the Sea Conferences have been an instance of this; not an inspiring instance, but it was better to have had them than not.

The global commons associated with greenhouse gases poses particularly interesting questions because it is twin-edged. Recall that the common property here is the earth's atmosphere, measured by a quality index, what one might call a generalized air-quality index. The burning of fossil fuels adds to the emission of greenhouse gases. If the greenhouse effect is indeed significant and if this in fact does lead to overall damage in crop production, fisheries, habitation, and so forth, we would say *ceteris paribus* the emission of greenhouse gases lowers this quality index. As we noted earlier, from the fact that we are all free to emit carbon dioxide, nitrous oxides, methane, etc. we may conclude that we emit too much of it. This is a problem of global commons with a vengeance. Unhappily, it is only one side of the matter. The other side is the fact that carbon dioxide is recycled by plants and vegetation, and if their stock is allowed to fall, the retention of carbon dioxide by the atmosphere will be increased. Brazil is one major repository of such vegetation. Notice that the private cost to Brazil of pursuing a depletion policy—insofar as the carbon dioxide issue is concerned—will be far less than the global cost. Brazil will not take account of the damages incurred by the rest of the world. So then, one will expect Brazil to deplete at a faster pace than is globally warranted, thus exacerbating the carbon dioxide problem. As it happens, Brazil is engaged in a murderous depletion policy. The gap between theory and application in environmental economics is a pleasantly narrow one.

So what is one to do? I cannot think it will do to look solemn and utter pious sentiments concerning our moral duty. Morality is a scarce resource, and one needs to economize its use when considering implementable public policy. Truly multilateral bargaining about reductions in carbon dioxide emission is one way. However, multilateral bargaining, leading to mutual reduction in pollution emission is a plausible way only when the problem is somewhat common, and is perceived to be common, with the stakes being roughly the same for all parties. This is so when the damages which are inflicted are reciprocal; that is, when each of the parties damages all the other parties through its actions to roughly the same extent. It is a less feasible way when the damage is somewhat unilateral, as with Brazilian deforestation. The idea of international compensation to the depleter for reducing the rate of depletion should no longer be regarded as far-fetched. Partial debt-relief for a lower rate of plunder of the Amazonian forest is something that will probably be on the agenda in the near future. This is Pigouvian subsidy. It is hard to imagine that there are many other options open to us.

I have begun with global commons because they are as good as any on which to fix ideas, and in any case they are the ones that receive the greatest attention in both the national and international press. But as we go about our daily lives, it is local commons which we encounter most often. Their effect is more immediate and is often shattering, most especially for those whose livelihood is based directly on them. Overgrazing, overfishing, the depletion of trees and shrubs from common land for use as fuel are familiar problems. They are traceable to the common property nature of such resources as grazing land, fisheries, and forest cover. So too with the drawing of water from aquifers which by the nature of things must usually be common property even when the land covering the aquifer is privately owned.[6]

One reason why the problem of the commons has been studied so intensively by economists is that the policy issues they give rise to possess the agreeable feature of our not having to choose between equity and efficiency. If the users of a common property resource are pretty much symmetrically replaced, a joint policy of restricting their use will be beneficial to all, and to roughly the same extent. It may even save the resource from ruin and this will benefit future users who are not currently a party to the social contract. Nothing could be nicer.

[6] I am ignoring the pressure of population growth on natural resource use in this chapter. This raises a somewhat wider set of issues, connected not only with common property resources and the absence of an adequate set of capital markets. It is also tied to the fact of the subjugation of women, a phenomenon that is particularly acute in poor countries.

## 2.4 Commons, Customs, and Norms

It may seem that geographically localized commons have a better chance of being protected from excessive use than global commons. It is not so much the smaller number of users that make local commons easier to manage, it is rather that the users' activities are easier to monitor. If private action cannot be monitored publicly, sanctions cannot be imposed on violators, and a social contract, even if it were to be reached, would amount to nothing. An unenforceable contract is no contract. Then of course, there is the question whether an agreement would in practice be reached. Agreement is presumably easier to reach if the parties have long known one another, expect to continue to know one another, and hope to avail themselves of the resource for a long while. It is not merely a question of social niceties, although this can be important. It is also that the parties are then likely to know how the resource is valued by each. (This is important, although it is often overlooked in discussions on these matters. You cannot effectively bargain with someone if you have no clue what his values are. Indeed, you may think that he thinks there is nothing to bargain over; that is, there is no mutually beneficial set of actions to agree upon.) And finally, yet another reason why these conditions are a prerequisite is that it is only under such circumstances that each party will have a long-term interest in the resource. It will then discount its future value at a low rate. This, as I shall argue in a rather different context, is in practice of great significance.

Social contracts, whether or not they are explicit, have to be simple to be effective. More specifically, contractual obligations need to be pretty much invariant across states of nature, or eventualities. This is partly because the mind has limited capacity for processing information, for evaluating information, and for acting *upon* information. And so it will not do for such a contract to have too many qualifications, to allow for too many exceptions to the rule. But it is partly also because a great many states of nature are only privately observable, and not publicly confirmable, and one should recall that obligations which are conditional only on privately observable states of nature are not enforceable, unless they are compatible with private incentives.[7] For these reasons, social contracts need to be simple if they are to promote individual or group well-being. As we noted earlier, social norms can be regarded as implicit contractual obligations.[8]

[7] As a half-serious illustration, the reader should ask if it is feasible to engage in bets on people's states of mind.

[8] In a highly original piece of work, Gauthier (1986) argues that even morality should be so regarded.

In stationary socio-economic environments they are enshrined in customs and rituals, with the result that the contractual behaviour is adopted effortlessly. If you are steeped in norms that are socially codified, you do not calculate every five minutes how you should behave. You simply follow the norm. This saves on computation costs all round, not only for you as an actor, but also for you as 'policeman' and 'judge'. This will be fine so long as the background environment remains pretty much the same. But it will not be fine if the environment changes suddenly. You might even be destroyed. It is this heightened vulnerability, often more real than perceived, which is the cause of some of the greatest social tragedies in contemporary society. This additional vulnerability is brought in their wake by shifting populations, ageing populations, predatory governments, and thieving aristocracies (see sections 2.5 and 2.6), and technological progress; but a part of the underlying causes is the absence of adequate property rights and the psychological and learning costs involved in altering one's behavioural norms. As noted earlier, a stationary society need not tamper with the commonality of a common property; it can arrive at an efficient use through an implicit contract. The tragedy I am alluding to is the breakdown of the contract unreplaced by a new and, for the historical users, beneficial contract. The locus of the problem does not usually lie in the place identified by Hardin (1968) in his famous essay. It lies where I have identified it.

## 2.5 Unidirectional Externalities

A defining characteristic of the problem of the commons is its reciprocal nature. If I bring an additional cow into the common pasture I harm you and all other cattle people: there will be just that much less grass for your cattle and for those of others. If you bring an additional cow into the pasture you harm me and all other cattle people.

The commons may, of course, involve many economic actors. In this situation, the damage each actor inflicts on one is often negligible. But the *sum* of the damages inflicted by the many on one can be substantial.[9] Now, all this makes for a certain simplicity of analysis and, as we have noted, for an ease in locating mutually beneficial policies. Matters are greatly more problematic, in need usually of public action, for damages which are unilaterally inflicted. A most significant instance of this is deforestation in the uplands inflicting damages on the lowlands. As always, it pays to concentrate first on the assignment of property rights before seeking remedies. The common law, if one

[9] Formal demonstration of this can be found in many writings. See, for example, Dasgupta and Heal (1979, ch. 3).

may be permitted to use this expression in a universal context, usually recognizes polluters' rights, not those of the pollutees. Translated into our present example this means that the timber merchant who has obtained a concession in the upland forests is under no obligation to compensate farmers in the lowlands. If the farmers want to reduce the risk of heightened floods, it is they who have to compensate the timber merchant for reducing the rate of deforestation. Stated this way, the matter does look morally bizarre, but it is how things are. Had property rights been the other way round, one of *pollutees'* rights, the boots would have been on the other set of feet, and it would be the timber merchant who would have had to pay compensation to farmers for the right to inflict the damages that go with deforestation. However, when the cause of the damage is located hundreds of miles away and when the victims are thousands of impoverished farmers, the issue of a bargained outcome does not really arise. It is difficult to see such farmers grouping effectively as a negotiating party. Judged even from the viewpoint of efficiency, the system of polluters' rights in such an example is disastrous. We would expect excessive deforestation. The timber merchant, it will be recalled, does not have to compensate the lowland farmers. Put another way, the merchant's private cost of logging falls short of its social cost. The problem is exacerbated if the timber concession is a short-lived one and if the concession is not allied to any serious form of public regulation. In such situations the merchant would discount the future value of the forest at a high rate, and thereby log at a fast rate, faster than the long view would warrant. The combined effect of high rates of discount and the infliction of damages to farmers can be shattering, and we now see evidence of this in many parts of the globe.

In each of the examples I have so far alluded to, whether it involves reciprocal damages (as in the problem of the commons) or unidirectional ones (as with upland deforestation) there is a wedge between the private and social costs associated with the use of some natural resource: in extreme cases private costs are nil. But the fact that social costs are higher, sometimes a great deal higher, means that, other things being the same, resource-based goods are underpriced in the market. Quite obviously, the less roundabout, or less distant, the production of the final good from its resource-base the greater is this underpricing, in percentage terms. Put another way, the lower is the value added to the resource, the larger is the extent of this underpricing of the final product. We can conclude therefore that *countries which export primary products do so by subsidizing them, possibly at a massive scale*. Moreover, the subsidy is paid not by the general public via taxation, but by some of the most disadvantaged members of society: the sharecropper, the small landholder or tenant farmer, and so on. The subsidy is hidden from public scrutiny; that is why nobody talks of it. But it is there. It is real. Such subsidies are both inefficient and inequitable.

We should be in a position to estimate them. As of now we have no such estimates.

## 2.6 Government Failure

All expositions on the economics of environmental resources with which I am familiar begin with market failure. There are pedagogical advantages in their doing so. This is why I began with it here. But once you start from there, you know what the next step is. It is to develop a conceptual basis for government intervention—in the design of environmental taxes, regulations, licences, and so forth.[10]

But in fact we could as well have begun from the opposite end: the failure of centralized modes of control in the allocation of resources. The record of East European governments on environmental matters is as good a starting point as any. Now, the reason why we would not expect systems of centralized control and command to work well are familiar. There is, first of all, the enormous potential for corruption to become engrained in a system where bureaucrats and the military have extensive powers to control resources. There is also a technical reason. It has to do with the massive quantities of information a centralized agency would be required to possess and process if it were to apply controls effectively. No single agency can ever *obtain* such amounts, let alone *use* it in a reliable manner. It is, of course, the single most telling characteristic of decentralized resource-allocation mechanisms that *information* is decentralized in them. In the field of environmental resources, where matters pertain to soil erosion, deforestation, air and water pollution, fisheries extraction, and so forth, the necessity of relying on mechanisms which make essential use of dispersed information is immediate.

It follows therefore that ideal resource-allocation mechanisms are mixed-'market' systems, where 'markets' are allied to judicious forms of government intervention in the allocation of a wide range of resources.[11] Current experiments in the United States with transferable permits in the field of pollution are an instance of this. (See Dales, 1968, for the original proposal, and Tietenberg, 1980, for an overview of the experience accumulated on the use of such permits.) A fixed number of marketable permits has two virtues at once. It first of all puts a ceiling on *total* emission in any given period. If this ceiling is chosen judiciously, there is little chance that serious damage will occur. Secondly, their marketability means that polluting firms' private information concerning their

[10] Kneese and Schultze (1975) is a good early discussion of these issues.

[11] I qualify the term 'market' because, as we have seen in sections 2.2 and 2.3, markets should be interpreted in a sense which is wider than the one in which they are commonly understood.

technologies is allowed to play an effective role in the allocation of these permits among them. The conceptual simplicity of tradeable permits has much to commend it. But at an analytical level, there are superior allocation mechanisms. They involve firm-specific, non-linear pollution taxes. (See Dasgupta *et al.*, 1980, and also Dasgupta, 1982, ch. 4.)

Let us recall that an environmental problem exists whenever there is a gap between the *accounting* price of a natural resource and its *actual*, or *market*, price.[12] In earlier sections we have seen that such a gap can arise because of missing markets. But, of course, it can arise also as a direct consequence of faulty government policy. When the state subsidizes the use of pesticides and fertilizers with an eye *solely* to agricultural production, it creates a wedge between their accounting and market prices. This is because it has not simultaneously kept an eye on the environmental damages that in future will be triggered by the chemicals. More generally, when public policy is determined under the supposition that natural resources are unlimited, a gap appears between accounting and actual prices. Nowhere has this been occasioned more dramatically than in the process of conversion of agricultural and forest land into ranches and unused, denuded land in Latin America. What has attracted most attention in recent years is the deforestation of the Amazon Basin accompanying this territorial expansion. In an early and neglected pair of articles, Feder (1977, 1979) described how massive private investment in the expansion of beef-cattle production in fragile ecological conditions has been supported by domestic governments in the form of tax concessions and provision of infrastructure, and by loans from international agencies.[13] As a case-study in policy mismanagement—more accurately, as an example of predatory behaviour on the part of the state—this one is difficult to improve upon. Government policy, prompted by the landed and industrial aristocracy, and the military, and aided by international agencies, was instrumental in degrading vast tracts of valuable environmental resources. And it simultaneously disenfranchised large numbers of small farmers and agricultural labour-

[12] Accounting prices are often called shadow prices. I should add that a commodity, or resource, should be specified not only by its physical characteristics, date, location, and state of nature, as in Debreu (1959); it should also be specified by the *agency* transacting in it. This is vital for environmental resources. It is important to think of them as *named* goods. (See Hahn, 1971. See also Arrow, 1971, and Starrett, 1972.) Another way of putting this is to say that these goods are *agent-relative*. Thus, to give an example, a polluting firm's smoke emission, as it is perceived by the neighbourhood laundry, is a different commodity from that same emission as perceived by the automobile tyre shop in the same neighbourhood.

[13] Ironically, the World Bank was much involved in loans to this agri-business. It has in recent years reversed its policies, and it is now more sensitive to environmental matters. As we noted in section 2.1, concern with the environment is an intermittent affair.

ers from the economy, and made at best destitutes of traditional forest-dwellers. There is absolutely nothing to commend it.[14]

As with market failure, government failure of the kind we have just studied results in an *excessive* use of environmental resources. We can conclude then that policy reversals designed to remove such self-inflicted distortion can be expected to yield at least two kinds of benefits: an increase in aggregate income and a discouragement of excessive environmental destruction. And to top it, such policy reversals could well improve the well-being of the poorest in society. Feder's analysis of Latin American agri-business suggests this last strongly.

## 2.7 The Environment as Renewable Natural Resources

Thus far we have been thinking of environmental resources as those naturally occurring commodities and services whose markets malfunction for a particular set of reasons: those arising from imperfectly monitorable rights of use and, in extreme cases, from an absence of specified rights. As we have noted, this allows us to draw fairly strong conclusions about appropriate public policy.

But it is only a partial view. It is a view from the *institutional* side of things. There is another, complementary perspective from which one may look at environmental resources. It is to study their *physical* characteristics. As it happens, there is a simple and useful way of describing them, one which I elaborated upon in Dasgupta (1982). I will sketch this now.

Environmental problems are almost always associated with resources that are naturally regenerative—we could call them *renewable natural resources*—but which are in danger of exhaustion from excessive use.[15] Notice first that this is very much consonant with common parlance. Resources such as minerals and fossil fuels do not fall into this category; they are non-renewable, except in geological time. One should also note that we usually do not regard the depletion of a non-renewable resource as an environmental issue, except insofar as the act of extraction and use in production have 'environmental effects'. Thus, to take two examples, the burning of fossil fuels increases the global mean temperature, and the smelting of ores is a common source of atmospheric pollution. The environmental issue here, as is usually understood, pertains not to the fact that the world's supply of fossil fuels and minerals is

[14] For further discussion, see Dasgupta (1982, ch. 2). Mahar (1988) and Binswanger (1989) have recently compiled a more complete list of macroeconomic policies in Brazil which have encouraged deforestation of the Amazon Basin. Repetto (1988) is a fine survey of the general issue, the effect of government macroeconomic policy on the environment.

[15] There are exceptions of course, such as the ozone layer. It is an exhaustible resource, pure and simple. But nothing is lost in my ignoring these exceptions here.

being reduced, but rather to the fact that such activities have a deleterious effect on the earth's atmosphere, which *is* a renewable natural resource. In these examples, the atmosphere is used as a sort of sink, a repository of certain forms of waste products. Stated only a bit differently, we are concerned here with natural resources which are capable of regenerating themselves so long as the 'environment' in which they are nurtured remains favourable.

The earth's atmosphere, as we noted earlier, is a paradigm of such resources. Under normal courses of events the atmosphere regenerates itself in terms of its composition. But the speed of regeneration depends upon the rate at which pollutants are deposited into it and it depends also on the nature of the pollutant. (Smoke discharge is clearly different from the release of radioactive material.[16]) Now, whenever we talk of a resource, we should think of its stock and of ways of measuring it. In the case at hand we ought to think of an atmospheric quality index. We ought also to think about its rate of regeneration. This last will depend upon the nature and extent of the pollutants discharged. It will, however, also depend upon the current index of quality; that is, the current level of stock. These are immensely complex, ill-understood matters. There is a great deal of synergism associated with the interaction of different types of pollutants in the atmosphere sink, but the analytical point I am making remains a valid one.

Animal, bird, plant, and fish populations are also typical examples of renewable resources. And there are today a number of studies connected with the reproductive behaviour of different species under a wide variety of 'environmental' conditions, including the presence of parasitic and symbiotic neighbours. (For the use of such ideas in economic models, see Barrett, 1989.) Land is also such a commodity, for the quality of arable and grazing land can be maintained by careful use. Overuse, however, impoverishes the soil and eventually produces a wasteland. (The symbiotic relation between soil quality and vegetation cover is, of course, at the heart of the current anxiety over sub-Saharan erosion.)

Underground basins of water often have a similar characteristic, the matter being even more problematic because we are concerned both about its quality and quantity. Under normal circumstances an aquifer undergoes a self-cleansing process as pollutants are deposited into it. But the effectiveness of the process depends, as always, on the nature of the pollutants and the rate at which they are discharged. Furthermore, many aquifers are recharged over the annual cycle. If, however, the rate of water extraction exceeds the recharge rate, the water table drops, thereby raising extraction costs. In fact aquifers display another characteristic. On occasion the issue is not one of depositing pollutants into them. If, as a consequence of excessive extraction, the water table is

[16] As noted in the previous footnote, the ozone layer is another example.

allowed to fall to too low a level, then in the case of coastal aquifers there can be salt-water intrusion, resulting in the destruction of the basin.

I conclude from these examples that one unifying characteristic of environmental resources is their regenerative capability, a capacity which can be destroyed if they are exploited unwittingly. In this sense, issues concerning what is usually labelled 'pollution' can be studied in the same general sort of way as those concerning animal, bird, plant, and fish populations, aquifers, forests, and soil quality.[17] And this brings us naturally back to a point already made, that markets for such resources can easily function badly. If we now add to this a further point we have noted, that their malfunctioning is *biased*, that for reasons we have identified, there is a strong tendency towards *excessive* use, rather than insufficient use, then we begin to obtain a consistent picture of what we are up against and what policy debates should be about.

It is worth reiterating the importance of viewing these commodities as renewable natural resources. They force us to look at the intertemporal structure of economic policies with all its attendant difficulties. Stated this way one may be led to think that we are up against yet another problem in what economists have labelled 'capital theory', of which we have a good understanding. It is certainly such a problem, but it is allied to a number of additional complexities, of which one central class was discussed at some length earlier, concerning imperfectly operating rights. But there is another class of problems associated with environmental resources, and I want to probe it a bit in what follows.

## 2.8 Net National Product

To begin with, the kinds of resources we are thinking of are, on occasion, of direct use in consumption (as with fisheries), in production (as with plankton, which serves as food for fish species), or both (as with drinking and irrigation water). Their stock is measured in different ways, depending on the resource: in mass units (e.g. biomass for fisheries), in quality indices (e.g. air and water quality), in volume units (e.g. acre-feet for aquifers), and so on. When we express concern about environmental matters we in effect point to a decline in their stock. Environmental resources are therefore a part of our capital assets. And yet, we have little quantitative feel for the extent of these stocks and their rates of change. There are countries which suffer from an almost total paucity of information on the extent of their forest cover, rates of soil erosion, water supply, and so forth. This gets reflected in the biased manner in which indices

[17] For further discussion of the analytical commonality among disparate environmental resource stocks, see Dasgupta (1982).

of economic performance are computed. In what follows, we will discuss the most common indicator of aggregate well-being: real net domestic product.[18]

Real net domestic product estimates are in bad odour today. It is often thought that such estimates are even in principle incapable of reflecting aggregate well-being. This is not correct. For it is possible to show that, subject to certain technical restrictions, for any conception of aggregate well-being there exists a set of (agent-relative) accounting prices which, if used in the estimation of net domestic product, will ensure that the measure reflects aggregate well-being. (See Dasgupta and Weale, 1989.)[19]

Now, this is a statement of principle. In practice, estimates of net domestic product are biased, in that the prices which are used for valuing certain categories of goods are systematically different from their accounting prices. This is especially so for natural resources, and for reasons we have already identified: their accounting prices are positive, but their values are set at zero in estimates of net domestic product.

Real net domestic product is by *definition* the sum of the social (or accounting) value of an economy's consumptions and the social value of the changes in its stocks of real capital assets.[20] Provided accounting prices have been estimated accurately, an optimizing economy will choose the flow of its consumptions and net investments so as to maximize real net domestic product at each date.[21] It was shown by Samuelson (1961) and Weitzman (1976) that real net domestic product at any date along an optimal economic path reflects its long-run consumption possibilities.[22] But they proved it in the context of economies that are capable of sustaining a steady economic state; that is, those that can maintain a balanced composition of all assets. Now, this precludes exhaustible resources. Dasgupta and Heal (1979) and Dasgupta (1982) showed how exhaustible and renewable natural resources should be incorporated into an ideal measure of real net domestic product. Thus, for example, when net domestic product of a country is estimated, the depreciation of fixed capital is deducted. An ideal index would deduct depreciation of the country's resource

[18] The analysis which follows was presented originally in Dasgupta and Heal (1979, ch. 8) and Dasgupta (1982, ch. 5).

[19] The technical restrictions amount to the requirement that both the set of feasible allocations and the social ordering reflecting aggregate well-being are convex.

[20] Thus, capital gains or losses are not included.

[21] Readers who are mathematically inclined will recognize that the Hamiltonian associated with in intertemporal well-being-optimization exercise is real net domestic product. This is what provides the motivation behind the definition of net national product; that it is a reduced form of aggregate well-being. This statement requires a mild modification if aggregate well-being at any given date is *strictly* concave in consumptions. But it is so mild that we may ignore it.

[22] This is a *theorem* concerning real net national product: it is not a *definition* of real net national product.

stocks as well—valued, of course, at accounting prices.[23] To the best of my knowledge, no country as yet deducts this latter magnitude, even while it simultaneously expresses concern about its declining resource base. This is schizophrenia with a vengeance. The reason for this dual attitude is not hard to find. It is connected with the characteristics of market failure we discussed earlier. But it is more pernicious in the present context because governments ought to know better than to fail to impute any value to an entire set of capital assets. Real net domestic product is therefore lower than it is currently estimated. This is almost certainly so for all countries. It is also almost certainly the case therefore that the rates of growth of net domestic product are lower than they are alleged to be.

The question arises whether these biases are in practice quantitatively significant. Suppose by way of illustration that environmental losses amount only to some 1–3 per cent of national income, not more. If this is the order of magnitude in economies we know, such corrections as those I have been advocating here would seem hardly worth the bother. In fact they are very much worth the bother. Recall that when correctly estimated, net national product is a measure of long-run consumption possibilities facing an economy. Therefore, when we ignore environmental depreciation we may well be way off the mark in our estimate of the economy's rate of growth of net national product. Our assessment of the economy's performance could be quite wrong.

To see this, let $Y(t)$ be net national product (as conventionally measured) in year $t$, and let $D(t)$ be environmental depreciation at $t$.[24] Consider two adjacent years, say 1 and 2. Suppose $D(1)/Y(1) = 0.01$. Being only 1 per cent of national product, environmental depreciation is negligible. Now suppose $[Y(2) - Y(1)]/Y(1) = 0.02$. This is a fairly healthy growth rate, and we would be tempted to commend the economy. However, this increase in national output may have come about at the expense of environmental stocks: soil erosion, groundwater depletion, deforestation, and so on. We would not know this if these losses were not to appear in national income accounts. Thus, suppose that $D(2)/Y(1) = 0.03$. As a ratio of national product, environmental losses are still negligible. But the real growth in net national product is not 2 per cent, but rather

$$\{[Y(2) - D(2)] - [Y(1) - D(1)]\} \,/\, [Y(1) - D(1)],$$

and this is *zero*. The economy has not actually grown at all. Our assessment of the economy should be quite different now.

[23] This leads to the seemingly paradoxical result that net domestic product in a country which lives solely off its exhaustible resources is nil, and it is nil no matter how high the current consumption is. See Dasgupta and Heal (1979).

[24] These are in *per capita* units.

Difficulties associated with the estimation of real net domestic product are compounded by the fact that unlike computers and tractors, environmental resources usually affect welfare directly as stocks, not merely as service flows. (An exception is noise pollution.) Fisheries and aquifers are useful not only for the harvest they provide (this is the flow); as a stock they are directly useful, because harvesting and extraction costs are low if stocks are large. Tropical forests are beneficial not only for the timber they may supply (this is the flow of service); as a stock they prevent soil erosion and, in the case of large tropical forests, help maintain a varied genetic pool and contribute substantially to the recycling of carbon dioxide. Likewise, air and water quality have direct well-being effects; (it is, let us remember, the concentration of pollutants which is relevant here). And finally, the direct effect of the *stock* of ozone in the ozone layer on the *flow* of well-being is obvious.

The direct well-being effects of environmental resource stocks are in some cases relatively easy to estimate, as with fisheries and groundwater, in others almost impossibly difficult. But the point remains that ignoring what one might refer to as environmental overhead durable consumption leads to a further bias in estimates of real net domestic product, in the direction of *over*estimation.

To make this precise, let us assume that aggregate well-being in an economy at any given date, $t$, depends not only on the flow of consumption, $C(t)$, but also directly on the stock of its assets, $S(t)$.[25] Let $U(C(t),S(t))$ denote the flow of aggregate well-being at $t$. Using the all-purpose commodity as our numeraire, it is easy to show that real net domestic product, $Y(t)$, in this economy should read as:

$$Y(t) = C(t) + dS(t)/dt + (U_S/U_C)S(t). \qquad (1)$$

In equation (1), $U_S$ and $U_C$ are, respectively, the marginal aggregate well-being of the resource stock and consumption flow. We have earlier commented on the second term on the right-hand side of (1)—the depreciation of environmental capital. It is the final term I am alluding to now. If the stock is directly beneficial (as with the current stock of the ozone layer), $U_S$ is positive. If it is damaging (as with atmospheric pollution), $U_S$ is negative.[26] In the latter case the final term

[25] For simplicity of exposition I shall think of an economy possessing a single, all-purpose good. The reader can easily generalize to the case where there are many kinds of real assets and many consumption goods.

[26] Notice that a commodity can have direct well-being effects which are deleterious even while being indirectly beneficial because of the consumption benefits it provides. Pollutants like pesticides have this property. The model in the text is merely illustrative. A proper model of pollution will lead us to the idea of *negative* accounting prices. See Dasgupta (1982, ch. 8).

in equation (1) is *negative*. Once again, neglecting environmental resources in national accounting would lead to an *overestimation* of aggregate well-being.[27]

I am of course using the measurement of real net domestic product merely as a prop on which to hang a number of issues concerning public policy. Appropriate criteria for public investment, and the public screening of private investment, are intrinsically related to the correct way of measuring real net domestic product. They hang together through a network of accounting prices. Optimal investment criteria are merely a way of ensuring that real net domestic product at each instant is maximized. And this in turn is a means of ensuring that the economic path which is followed indeed maximizes the present discounted value of the flow of aggregate well-being.[28] While we ignore resource accounting in our aggregate reporting of economies, we overlook as well to include them in the evaluation of investment projects. At an analytical level this amounts to regarding resource stocks as valueless. They are regarded free. In this chapter I have tried to trace a chain of implications this has on biases in resource use and resource accounting.

## 2.9 Inadequate Incentives for Obtaining Information

In fact there is another implication of this, equally grave, and which I hope will finally justify my choice of starting point in this article: the non-existence of generalized markets for environmental resources. It is the implied absence of private incentives for *obtaining* information about resource stocks and the technology of resource regeneration; or, in other words, the ecology of the matter. It is remarkable how little we know of things that are of such long-run interest, remarkable not because we cannot offer an explanation for why we do not know—I have just provided it—but because of the extent of our ignorance. Often enough, the data one sees, when scrutinized, are merely anecdotal, no more than pure guesses. As noted earlier, there are a number of countries which have no reasonable estimates of the extent of their forest cover, soil losses, water evaporation rates, and so on. Public knowledge of ecological processes is usually negligible. I am thinking here of the functional, or instrumental, value

[27] It is unfortunate that for the most part public debates on environmental matters have concentrated on those resources, such as the atmosphere and tropical-forest cover, whose direct well-being effects are unusually difficult to estimate. This usually has the effect of making one think that environmental issues cannot really be *analysed* in the way we analyse other economic issues. Witness the fact that the label 'conservation movement' sets off a chain of images in one's mind. As I have tried to elaborate in this essay, a great many environmental problems, of immense importance to human well-being, are ones concerning resources whose direct effects are not all that difficult to measure.

[28] Arrow and Kurz (1970) continues to be the most thorough treatment of this topic. But they do not include an account of natural resources.

of such knowledge. I am thinking of knowledge of ecological processes on a par with knowledge of technological transformation possibilities. There is a strong case for the *public* acquisition of such knowledge, because private incentives are particularly dull in this field. If the farmers in the lowlands can claim no compensation from the upland timber merchant, neither party has an incentive to discover the functional relationship between deforestation and soil erosion. These massive uncertainties are real, and a great deal in excess of what they should be.

At a more general level, the *direction* of technological change is biased on account of all this. When environmental resources are free, there is absolutely no incentive to economize in their use. Technological innovations which are profligate with them look profitable, certainly more so than they ought to look. Over time, an entire sequence of resource-intensive technologies is thus installed. And if we add to all this the fact that there are often strong learning-by-doing and learning-by-using effects, even at the stage of research and development, we arrive at a depressing conclusion: it may require a big push to move societies away from their current profligacy in the use of environmental resources. We may well have got locked into bad habits, not only as consumers and manufacturers, but also as scientists and technologists. In the mean time, a move towards a more appropriate set of price signals is clearly the right one.

## Appendix

In the text (sections 2.2 and 2.3), we presented an informal account of how co-operation may be sustained over time by means of norms of conduct. A social norm is a behaviour strategy. The critical point in the exercise is to show that there is no need for an outside agency to enforce the norms, and thus to assure co-operation. We have therefore to show that co-operation can be *self-enforcing* if appropriate norms are followed. (If the strategy needed outside enforcement, e.g. the law courts, it would not be a social norm, it would be something else.)

In this Appendix I shall provide a formal account of this by means of a very special example, that of a two-person, repeated game. Specifically, I shall study the two-person, repeated Prisoners' Dilemma game, and I shall develop *two* types of norm. (There are other norms that can sustain the same co-operative outcome.) I begin by describing their dilemma when the prisoners face each other only once.

There are two agents, 1 and 2. They are generically labelled $i$ and $j$. Thus, $i,j = 1,2$. Agent $i$ has two strategies to choose from, $A(i)$ and $B(i)$. The pay-off matrix is given below. Agent 1 chooses row and agent 2 chooses column. The first number in each box is the pay-off to player 1; the second, to player 2. I

| 1 \ 2 | A(2) | B(2) |
| --- | --- | --- |
| A(1) | (25,25) | (6,30) |
| B(1) | (30,6) | (10,10) |

**Figure 2.1** *Prisoners' Dilemma*

assume throughout that the game is common knowledge. (See, for example, Binmore and Dasgupta, 1986; Aumann, 1987, for expositions of this.) Plainly, the game has a unique non-co-operative (Nash) equilibrium outcome (10,10). In fact, $(B(1),B(2))$, which supports the equilibrium, is a pair of dominant strategies. But the equilibrium is sub-optimal: both parties would be better off were they to choose the pair $(A(1),A(2))$. We now assume that the parties do not have access to any co-operative infrastructure which would enable them to enforce the choice of the strategy pair $(A(1),A(2))$.[29] Thus, $(B(1),B(2))$ will prevail. All this is well known.

In what follows, we call the Prisoners' Dilemma just analysed the *stage game*, and we assume that this stage game will be repeated.

It is an easy matter to confirm that if the stage game is to be repeated only a *finite* number of periods, and if this number is common knowledge, the unique

[29] By a co-operative infrastructure I mean a machinery, such as that provided by the law courts, which can enforce agreements. When such an infrastructure is not present, agreements are not binding. Since $(B(1),B(2))$ is a pair of dominant strategies, it will unquestionably be chosen in the absence of any possibility of binding agreements. This *is* the dilemma. Notice that if the resource costs involved in establishing a co-operative infrastructure were small enough, it would be in the mutual interest of the parties to establish it. The 'infrastructure' could then impose a stiff penalty to any party which plays the $B$ strategy. By so imposing a penalty, the game is changed into one where $A(i)$ becomes the dominant strategy for person $i$. Notice that in this altered game the penalty is never actually paid! There is no occasion to, because $A(i)$ is now $i$'s dominant strategy. Herein lies the advantage of the co-operative infrastructure. In recent years it is these ideas from game theory which have been used in articulating social contract theories. See Rawls (1972), Gauthier (1986), Hampton (1986), and Hardin (1988). The more general idea behind the possibility that one can in many circumstances improve one's lot by tying one's hands was a central theme in Schelling (1960).

non-co-operative outcome will be the repeated play of $(B(1),B(2))$. The players are thus locked in a Prisoners' Dilemma even in this case.[30]

The interesting case is therefore one where the stage game is to be repeated *ad infinitum* and where this is common knowledge. The banal observation, that people are mortal, does not provide an argument against this hypothesis. The point in studying an infinitely repeated stage game is to avoid having the players use the final date of play as an anchor from which to work backwards. Discounting future pay-offs is a way of introducing uncertainty about the actual duration of the play: the higher the discount rate, the lower the weight players give to future pay-offs relative to present ones. Discounting is a way of capturing in an analytical model the fact that the actors know that play in all probability will not go on for ever, but that neither knows for sure when the game will terminate.[31] We suppose for simplicity of exposition that both players discount their future pay-offs at a constant, positive rate, $r$.

Individual strategies can be extremely complicated in the repeated Prisoners' Dilemma game. A strategy is now a plan of action at each possible contingency. To be precise, choice of an action by either party at date $T$ can be made to depend on how the game has been played until the previous period $T–1$. We are interested in checking whether an indefinite sequence of (25,25) can be realized as a non-co-operative equilibrium outcome by tacit co-operation; that is, where the policing is done by the players themselves and no co-operative infrastructure, such as government, is involved.

Consider the following strategy for player $i$ ($i$=1,2) which I shall call strategy Z:

Z: Play $A(i)$ in the first period, and continue to play $A(i)$ so long as the other player, $j$, plays $A(j)$. Switch to $B(i)$ the period following the first time $j$ plays $B(j)$, and play $B(i)$ thereafter.[32]

We want to locate conditions under which it is in each party's interest to choose Z, were the other to choose Z. In other words, we want to locate conditions under which (Z,Z) is a non-co-operative (Nash) equilibrium of the

[30] To confirm this, use the backward induction argument, and have the players reason back from the last period. See Luce and Raiffa (1957).

[31] A constant discount rate implies, of course, that no matter how long is the horizon, there is a positive (though vanishingly small) probability that the stage game will be repeated beyond the horizon.

[32] To the best of my knowledge, the efficacy of this strategy was formally studied first by Friedman (1971). It should be noted that Z is not tit-for-tat, a strategy made famous by Axelrod (1984). Z is not at all forgiving. A single deviation from the (implicitly) agreed play of $A(j)$ by $j$ is punished for ever by $i$ when $i$ plays Z. This means of course that after a possible deviation, renegotiation is not possible. If it is, strategy Z is not credible. Strategies supporting (25,25) indefinitely, which are invulnerable to renegotiation, have been much studied recently. See strategy $X$ below. See also Farrell and Maskin (1987), Bernheim and Ray (1987), and Abreu and Pearce (1989).

infinitely repeated Prisoners' Dilemma game. Notice that if both parties play Z, the outcome to each is the infinite pay-off sequence (25,25, . . . ).

Time is discrete. Play begins at $t = 0$. If both parties choose Z, the present discounted value of the flow of pay-offs to each is:

$$25 + 25/(1+r) + 25/(1+r)^2 + \ldots = 25(1+r)/r. \quad (A1)$$

We wish to locate conditions under which it does not pay either party to deviate from Z, given that the other is playing Z.

Towards this, consider an alternative strategy for, say player 1, which consists, among other things, of playing $A(1)$ until date $T\!-\!1$, and then switching to $B(1)$ at $T$.[33] We are *assuming* that 1 is playing against strategy Z. We can therefore conclude that it will be in his interest to switch permanently to $B(1)$ once he has played $B(1)$. Thus, if it is ever in 1's interest to switch to $B(1)$, it is in his interest to play $B(1)$ thereafter. Now notice that *if* 1 plans to switch to $B(1)$ at $T$, and *if* the plan is credible, it will be in 1's interest to switch to $B(1)$ at *T when T arrives*. But at $T$, $T$ *is* the present; it is no longer the future. It follows that, without loss of generality, we may as well assume that $T = 0$. In other words, we may as well assume that 1 plays the sequence ($B(1)$,$B(1)$, . . . ) against 2's choice of Z. We wish to see if it is in 1's interest to do so.

Now if 1 were to play an infinite sequence of $B(1)$s against 2's play of Z, his pay-off sequence will be (30,10,10,10, . . . ). And the present discounted value of this stream is:

$$30 + 10/(1+r) + 10/(1+r)^2 + \ldots = 30 + 10/r. \quad (A2)$$

We may conclude that it is in 1's interest to play Z against 2's choice of Z if expression ($A1$) is at least as large as expression ($A2$). It follows that for (Z,Z) to be an equilibrium pair of strategies in the infinitely repeated Prisoners' Dilemma game, we must have

$$25(1+r)/r \geq 30 + 10/r,$$

or

$$r \leq 3 = 300\%.$$

Stating matters more generally, tacit co-operation can be self-enforcing in an infinitely repeated Prisoner's Dilemma game if neither party discounts future pay-offs at too high a rate. In our specific example, if the parties discount at a rate in excess of 300 per cent, (Z,Z) is not self-enforcing. It is not a non-co-operative equilibrium pair of strategies.

[33] If $T=0$, this means that 1 starts by playing $B(1)$.

All this is congenial to intuition. There is a one-period gain to player $i$ in reneging and playing $B(i)$ for ever against Z. The gain is $30-25=5$. Set against this a loss of $25-10=15$ in each period starting the period after the first deviation. If $i$ is myopic he will renege. If he is not, he will not.

We should note how this analysis provides a reductionist explanation for such notions as 'custom', 'codes of conduct', 'social norm', 'social sanctions', and so forth. However, we should also note that there are many possible 'norms' for sustaining the mutually beneficial, co-operative outcome. The strategy we have studied in this Appendix is unforgiving, in that even one deviation (that is, one lapse) on the part of a person is met with eternal punishment. The norm lacks compassion. But it has analytical appeal. It allows us to say that, in the numerical example at hand, were the parties to discount future pay-offs at a rate in excess of 300 per cent, no social norm could take hold.

How do we know this? We know this because $Z$ inflicts the severest possible punishment for a single deviation. Any other norm would therefore inflict less severe punishment. It follows that the cost borne by a person for deviating once is less under any other norm. But the benefit remains at 5 for the period at which the norm-breaker breaks the norm. We can conclude then that if $r$ exceeds 300 per cent no norm can sustain an indefinite play of $(A(1),A(2))$.

An alternative social norm, which we called *conformism*, was outlined in section 2.2. We formalize it now, and call it strategy $X$.

$X$: At any date, choose $A(i)$ if and only if the other party had 'conformed' at the previous date, where 'conformism' at the first date is defined as the play of $A(\mathrm{i})$, $i=1,2$.

From this definition we can, by recursion, calculate what action is required under $X$ at any date. We now wish to find the critical discount rate for this norm.

If, say, 2 were to play $X$, then were 1 to deviate from $X$ at any date, his gain would be 5 at that date. Now, we have already noted that the maximum loss he needs to incur for this deviation is 15 at the next date. It follows that he will deviate if

$$5-15/(1+r)>0,$$

or

$$r>2=200\%. \qquad (A3)$$

We conclude that if $(A3)$ holds, then $X$ is not a viable social norm. We can also show that any set of deviations can be broken up into a sequence of such simple deviations, and thus conclude that if $r \leq 200\%$ per period, $(X,X)$ *is* a self-enforcing pair of strategies. $X$ is therefore a viable social norm if parties discount future pay-offs at a rate less than or equal to 200 per cent per period. Note, finally, that $X$ is tit-for-tat in disguise.

## Bibliography

Abreu, D. and Pearce, D. (1989), 'A Perspective on Renegotiation in Repeated Games', mimeo, Stanford, Hoover Institution.

Arrow, K. J. (1971), 'Political and Economic Estimation of Social Effects of Externalities', in M. Intriligator (ed.), *Frontiers of Quantitative Economics*, Vol. 1, Amsterdam, North-Holland.

— and Kurz, M. (1970), *Public Investment, the Rate of Return and Optimal Fiscal Policy*, Baltimore, Johns Hopkins University Press.

— and Fisher, A. (1974), 'Environmental Preservation, Uncertainty, and Irreversibility', *Quarterly Journal of Economics*, 88.

Aumann, R. (1987), 'Correlated Equilibrium as an Expression of Bayesian Rationality', *Econometrica*, 55.

Axelrod, R. (1984), *The Evolution of Cooperation*, New York, Basic Books.

Barrett, S. A. (1989), 'Economic Growth and Environmental Conservation', Ph.D. Dissertation, London School of Economics.

Baumol, W. and Oates, W. (1975), *The Theory of Environmental Policy*, Englewood Cliffs, Prentice-Hall.

Bernheim, B. D. and Ray, D. (1987), 'Collective Dynamic Consistency in Repeated Games', mimeo, Department of Economics, Stanford University.

Binmore, K. and Dasgupta, P. (1986), 'Introduction', in K. Binmore and P. Dasgupta (eds.), *Economic Organizations as Games*, Oxford, Basil Blackwell.

Binswanger, H. (1989), 'Brazilian Policies that Encourage Deforestation in the Amazon', World Bank Environment Department Paper No. 16.

Brown, G. and McGuire, C. B. (1967), 'A Socially Optimal Pricing Policy for a Public Water Agency', *Water Resources Research*, 3.

Clark, C. W. (1976), *Mathematical Bioeconomics: The Optimal Management of Renewable Resources*, New York, John Wiley.

Coase, R. (1960), 'The Problem of Social Cost', *Journal of Law and Economics*, 3.

CSE (1982, 1986), *The State of India's Environment*, New Delhi, Centre for Science and Environment.

Dales, J. H. (1968), *Pollution, Property and Prices*, Toronto, University of Toronto Press.

Dasgupta, P. (1982), *The Control of Resources*, Oxford, Basil Blackwell.

— Hammond, P., and Maskin, E. (1980), 'On Imperfect Information and Optimal Pollution Control', *Review of Economic Studies*, 47.

— and Heal, G. (1979), *Economic Theory and Exhaustible Resources*, Cambridge, Cambridge University Press.

— and Weale, M. (1989), 'On International Comparisons of Well-Being', mimeo. University of Cambridge.

Debreu, G. (1959), *Theory of Value*, New York, John Wiley.

Farrell, J. and Maskin, E. (1987), 'Renegotiation in Repeated Games', Department of Economics, University of California, Berkeley.

Feder, E. (1977), 'Agribusiness and the Elimination of Latin America's Rural Proletariat', *World Development*, 5.

— (1979), 'Agricultural Resources in Underdeveloped Countries: Competition between Man and Animal', *Economic and Political Weekly*, 14.

Friedman, J. (1971), 'A Non-cooperative Equilibrium for Supergames', *Review of Economic Studies*, 38.
Gauthier, D. (1986), *Morals by Agreement*, Oxford, Clarendon Press.
Hahn, F. (1971), 'Equilibrium with Transaction Costs', *Econometrica*, 39.
Hampton, J. (1986), *Hobbes and the Social Contract Tradition*, Cambridge, Cambridge University Press.
Hardin, G. (1968), 'The Tragedy of the Commons', *Science*, 162.
Hardin, R. (1988), *Reason and the Limits of Justice*, Chicago, University of Chicago Press.
Hartwick, J. and Olewiler, N. (1986), *The Economics of Natural Resource Use*, New York, Harper and Row.
Hotelling, H. (1931), 'The Economics of Exhaustible Resources', *Journal of Political Economy*, 39.
IIED/WRI (1987), *World Resources 1987*, New York, Basic Books.
Kneese, A. (1964), *The Economics of Regional Water Quality Management*, Baltimore, Johns Hopkins University Press.
— and Schultze, C. (1975), *Pollution, Prices and Public Policy*, Washington, D.C., Brookings Institution.
Krutilla, J. (1967), 'Conservation Reconsidered', *American Economic Review*, 57.
— and Fisher, A. (1975), *The Economics of Natural Environments: Studies in the Evaluation of Commodity and Amenity Resources*, Baltimore, Johns Hopkins University Press.
Lind, R. (ed.) (1982), *Discounting for Time and Risk in Energy Policy*, Baltimore, Johns Hopkins University Press.
Luce, R. D. and Raiffa, H. (1957), *Games and Decisions*, New York, John Wiley.
Mahar, D. (1988), 'Government Policies and Deforestation in Brazil's Amazon Region', World Bank Environment Department Working Paper No. 7.
Mäler, K.-G. (1974), *Environmental Economics: A Theoretical Enquiry*, Baltimore, Johns Hopkins University Press.
— and Wyzga, R. E. (1976), *Economic Measurement of Environmental Damage*, Paris, OECD.
Meade, J. E. (1973), *The Theory of Externalities*, Geneva, Institute Universitaire de Hautes Etudes Internationales.
Pigou, A. C. (1920), *The Economics of Welfare*, London, Macmillan.
Rawls, J. (1972), *A Theory of Justice*, Oxford, Oxford University Press.
Repetto, R. (1988), 'Economic Policy Reform for Natural Resource Conservation', World Bank Environment Department Working Paper No. 4.
Samuelson, P. A. (1961), 'The Evaluation of "Social Income": Capital Formation and Wealth', in F. Lutz and D. Hague (eds.), *The Theory of Capital*, London, Macmillan.
Schelling, T. (1960), *The Strategy of Conflict*, Cambridge, Mass., Harvard University Press.
Starrett, D. (1972), 'Fundamental Non-Convexities in the Theory of Externalities', *Journal of Economic Theory*, 4.
Tietenberg, T. (1980), 'Transferable Discharge Permits and the Control of Stationary Source Air Pollution: A Survey and Synthesis', *Land Economics*, 56.

Tietenberg, T. (1988), *Environmental and Natural Resource Economics*, Glenview, Ill., Scott, Foresman & Co., 2nd edition.

Ulph, A. (1989), 'A Review of Books on Resource and Environmental Economics', *Bulletin of Economic Research*, 42.

Weitzman, M. (1976), 'Welfare Significance of National Product in a Dynamic Economy', *Quarterly Journal of Economics*, 90.

# 3
# Global Warming: A Sceptical Economic Assessment

*Wilfred Beckerman*

## 3.1 Introduction

The majority of respondents in a recent Louis Harris poll in the USA rated a clean environment more important than a satisfactory sex life.[1] This may tell us something about American sex life. It may also tell us something about the impression made on many people in advanced societies by the widely proclaimed imminence of ecological disaster and the threat to human existence posed by a specific form of environmental damage, namely that associated with 'global warming'.

As is widely known there is a possibility that serious climate change, including a significant rise in average global temperatures, will result from excessive emissions of greenhouse gases (GHGs) in the course of innumerable human activities. Like most externalities, excessive emissions of GHGs, or other atmospheric pollutants (including some believed to reduce global warming through increasing the albedo effect of cloud cover) reflect the absence of well-defined or enforceable property rights, in this case rights to clean air. And in the case of GHGs the people who may be most harmed by the excessive emissions are future generations, to whom it is obviously not easy to give any rights that can be enforced today (though I am working on it).

There are several specific economic characteristics of global warming. One of them is that it represents a particular class of externality, often known as 'the tragedy of the commons'. This refers to situations in which nobody can be excluded from the use of an asset—such as common grazing land, or fishing

Wilfred Beckerman is a Fellow in Economics at Balliol College, Oxford. He wishes to express his indebtness to conversations with more people than he can enumerate here, including many who are not responsible for his errors.

[1] Reported in *The Atlantic Monthly*, October 1990, p. 46.

grounds, or the atmosphere—on account of either the technical characteristics of the asset (e.g. radio broadcasts, or light from lighthouses) or the legal arrangements, but where, nevertheless, one person's use of the asset reduces the amount available to other potential users (unlike radio broadcasts or the light from lighthouses). All nations have a right to pollute the atmosphere as much as they like but the atmosphere's absorptive capacity is no longer believed to be inexhaustible in certain important respects. In particular, it is feared that the concentration of 'greenhouse gases' (GHGs) in the atmosphere is being raised by anthropogenic activity to a level at which the effect on global climate will be significant and, in some peoples' opinion, highly damaging to life on this planet. At the same time it is neither rational nor effective for any one country to act alone to reduce GHG emissions, for reasons which are discussed more fully in the final section of this paper. Hence, there is an obvious call for internationally co-ordinated action, and failures of international conferences on the subject to agree to universal draconian measures to restrict GHGs invariably lead to wholesale condemnation in the media. However, a little economic analysis shows that the case for urgent action—international or unilateral—is by no means as clear as is widely assumed.

Many people believe that the problem of global warming is one on which scientists, not economists, have an exclusive right to pronounce and that the degree to which countries should try to reduce GHG emissions is a matter for scientists to decide. For example, a recent major report on global warming has twenty contributors, almost all of them scientists of one kind or another, and not one economist among them. This report deplored the fact that the Response Strategies Working Group (of the UN International Panel on Climate Change)

> did not even come down on the side of a freeze in greenhouse-gas emissions, much less the deep cuts the scientists clearly indicate will be necessary if any attempt is to be made to slow or arrest the greenhouse effect. The IPCC scientists calculate 'with confidence' that, to stabilize the carbon dioxide composition of the atmosphere at its present level, cuts in global emissions of that particular greenhouse gas would need to exceed 60 per cent. (Leggett, 1990)

But, to the economist, the question of how much one should cut GHG emissions now in order to reduce global warming in the future is a matter of the relative costs and benefits of alternative courses of action. And, as shown below, in the light of current information, such a cut could be much greater than can be justified by the costs of achieving it compared with the damage done by global warming.

Of course, scientists have to provide the information about the technical and physical characteristics of global warming. And their contribution to the construction of models to predict long-run changes in the climate constitutes an outstanding intellectual achievement of the first degree. But values have to be attached to the effects and to the costs of reducing GHGs which have then to be incorporated in the economist's paradigm of balancing costs and benefits at the margin.

For example, just to put the problem into perspective, if the growth rate of output per head in the world were to be, say, 1.5 per cent per annum over the next century, which is well below the rate achieved in the post-war period,[2] real incomes per head in 100 years' time would be 4.4 times as high as they are now. If the economic estimates of the reduction in total world output resulting from a doubling of $CO_2$ concentrations in the atmosphere are to be believed then, at the outside, real incomes would be reduced by about 1 or 2 per cent in 100 years' time. In that case, instead of being 4.4 times as rich as today the population in 100 years' time would be only about 4.3 times as rich. It is not up to scientists, any more than it is up to economists, to decide that present generations—which include vast numbers of very poor people—should accept heavy costs and economic burdens in order that the population in the year 2090 should be 4.4 times as rich as they are now rather than only 4.3 times as rich. How much resources society should devote today to curbing GHGs is not a matter that can be decided purely on scientific grounds.

Apart from its international aspect global warming has other important economic characteristics. These include the time dimension, with its associated problem of the appropriate discount rate to use, and the uncertainties involved, with the associated theory of decision-making under uncertainty. It would be impossible in a paper of this length to go into these matters in great detail and the most that can be done is to sketch in the main features of the problem in order to emphasize the fact that there is no need for urgent action and that we do have time to think. The next section of this paper, therefore, attempts to give some broad-brush idea of the overall costs and benefits of action to curtail GHG emissions.

## 3.2 Global Warming in Perspective

In the first place, it should be appreciated that GHGs are not produced only by human activities. Indeed, the anthropogenic contribution is relatively very

[2] Over the whole period 1950 to 1985 the average annual compound rate of world output has been 4.0 per cent and the rate of growth of output per head has been 2.1 per cent. (Estimates from UN Statistical Yearbooks, 1965, 1971, 1978, and 1985/86). Insofar as the rate of growth of world population is slowing down considerably whereas the rate of spread of education, which is the mainspring of technical progress, is increasing, the postulated increase of output per head of only 1.5 per cent p.a. over the next century is a very conservative figure.

small. Burning of fossil fuels emits about 5 billion tons of carbon per annum, which is small compared to the natural exchange between the atmosphere and the earth's surface (including the oceans) of about 200 billion tons per annum.[3] Much carbon is emitted by vegetation, such as rotting and decaying trees, but it would be difficult to impose a carbon tax on nature.[4]

After all, records from air bubbles trapped in ice cores revealed in the Vostock ice-core experiment show enormous variations over the last 150,000 years in $CO_2$ concentrations, long before humans were having any impact.[5] The concentration declined from about 320 parts per million (ppm) 130,000 years ago to around 200 ppm about 15,000 years ago, when the last ice age is believed to have come to an end, and has since been rising to reach its present level, which is nearly back to the level of 150,000 years ago. Human activity played no part in these changes in $CO_2$ levels. Indeed, although it is sometimes asserted that the apparent rough correlation between the $CO_2$ concentrations and the estimated temperatures over this period provides evidence for the effect of $CO_2$ concentrations on temperature, the direction of causality is generally believed to be the other way round. The decline in temperature over the period in question was largely the result of a small change in the earth's orbital characteristics and this contributed to a fall in the $CO_2$ concentration since cooler oceans have a higher rate of absorption of $CO_2$.

There are, of course, great uncertainties about this, as there are about the scientific characteristics of global warming and the greenhouse effect in general. At the same time there is enormous and legitimate public concern about the environment, and it is desirable that policy priorities genuinely reflect the relative importance of alternative environmental problems. For the current near-hysteria about global warming greatly exceeds the concern being expressed about twenty years ago—sometimes by the same scientists—over the

[3] Mason (1989). The author, Sir John Mason, was Treasurer and senior Vice-President of the Royal Society 1976–86, President of the Royal Meteorological Society 1969–70, President of the British Association for the Advancement of Science 1982–3, Permanent Representative of the UK at the World Meteorological Organization and a Member of its Executive Committee 1965–83, President of the Institute of Physics 1976–8. He was Professor of Cloud Physics at Imperial College of Science and Technology 1965–83, and Director-General of the Meteorological Office 1965–83.

[4] Of course, one could cut down all the trees, so that the net effect of their unfavourable impact on $CO_2$ concentrations from decay notably their catastrophic impact when growing would be zero, but leaving aside other objections to this policy (and their favourable effects on rainfall) one would still be left with the problem of how to dispose of them in a manner that did not equally add to carbon emissions.

[5] In fact, with the aid of the analysis of isotope Oxygen-18 obtained from drilling cores from the ocean floor it has been possible to reconstruct the climatic history of the earth for the last 100 million years. And this shows enormous fluctuations in temperature that cannot be satisfactorily explained. If anything, the available evidence suggests that the onset of the next glacial period is, if anything, overdue. In fact it may already have been under way for 6,000 years! (Ellsaesser, 1990; Berger, 1988)

impending ice age.[6] As a result, there are pressures on governments to allocate resources in a way that probably does not reflect what the relative preferences of a well-informed society would be as between the effects of climate change on very distant, and no doubt much richer, future generations, and other urgent environmental needs—such as dealing with current local water and air pollution that severely affects the lives of current generations in many parts of the world—or numerous other current concerns, such as housing, health and hospitals, education, research and training, industrial investment, transport, population control, crime, drugs, and so on, not to mention social problems such as peace, stability, tolerance, and racial harmony—the absence of which all over the world probably causes far more suffering than would the effects of the sort of climate change predicted over the course of the next century. It is important, therefore, to try to get a rough idea of the costs and benefits of global warming or of policies to attenuate it.

Even this is an immensely difficult task since what the economist wants is to sort out the costs and benefits of *different degrees* of abatement of GHG emissions. In general it is preferable to avoid all-or-nothing scenarios, since if there is one thing that we learn from economics it is that optimal policy consists of equating benefits from different courses of action at the margin. (It is rarely optimal to go out shopping with the determination to buy only fruit or only fish or only vegetables, according to which happens to be cheaper, rather than some combination of them.) Hence, ideally, one would like to draw up a schedule of costs of different levels of carbon dioxide emissions and the costs of different degrees of abatement in order to arrive at the optimum policy. Unfortunately, most of the estimates that have been made of the economic effects of global warming relate to specific degrees of warming or of abatement, at specific dates, although some attempts have been made, notably by Professor William Nordhaus of Yale University, to convert such estimates as are available of the costs and benefits of alternative $CO_2$-emission scenarios into schedules of the kind required (Nordhaus, 1990*a*).

As indicated above, the scientific side of global warming is a matter of considerable debate and uncertainty. But the general consensus amongst

[6] Stephen Schneider, the author of a well-known book, *Global Warming*, was the author of a book about the coming ice age, entitled *The Genesis Strategy*, at a time—the late 1960s and early 1970s—when global temperatures seemed to have been following a downward trend for about twenty years and ice-age predictions were fashionable amongst many 'concerned scientists'. See references to other assertions about the coming ice age in Bessemer (1990). William D. Nordhaus reminds us of a series of studies carried out about twenty years ago, under the auspices of the National Research Council, of the impact of global cooling. As he points out, many of the losses resulting from global cooling, which would be likely candidates for gains in the event of global warming, have not been considered at all in the recent major study of global warming consequences by the US Environmental Protection Agency, from which he invites us to draw the conclusion that 'environmental impact studies can find the cloud behind every silver lining' (Nordhaus, 1990*a*, draft).

scientists, such as it is, is that in the absence of special measures to restrict $CO_2$ emissions the concentration of $CO_2$ in the atmosphere will double some time towards the end of the next century and that this would lead to a rise in average world temperature of between 1.5°C and 4°C.[7] Of course, the average effect is not predicted to be uniform. One of the shared conclusions of the current models on which the dire predictions are based is that the rise in temperature will be least near the equator, and greatest near the poles. Since it is hottest in the former regions and coldest in the latter, one might be tempted, as Thomas Schelling points out (Schelling, 1990), to conclude that this would be a desirable outcome.

Furthermore, as Schelling has put it:

> it is fair to point out that most people will not undergo in the next 100 years changes in their local climates more drastic than the changes in climate that people have undergone during the past 100 years. No climate changes are forecast that compare with moving from Boston to Irvine, California, or even perhaps from Irvine to Los Angeles. The Goths and the Vandals, the Romans and the Vikings, the Tartars and the Huns migrated through more drastic changes than any currently anticipated; Europeans who migrated to North and South America similarly underwent drastic climate changes. In this country in 1860 barely 2 per cent of the population lived outside the humid continental or subtropical climates; in 1980 the percentages outside these zones had increased from 2 per cent to 22 per cent... Furthermore the microclimates of urbanized Tokyo, Mexico City, and Los Angeles have not deterred their population growth; the microclimates of London and Pittsburgh changed dramatically during the century before 1950 and have changed again almost as dramatically since then. (Schelling, 1990, p. 76)

Some of the US internal migration over the course of the last few decades to which Schelling refers relates of course to the millions of US citizens who have moved south in order to live in the warmer climates of California or Florida. Global warming could mean that future generations would not have to go to all the trouble!

However, some people are hard to please and everybody will have heard predictions of all sorts of alleged likely terrible consequences of a 3°C rise in temperature, to which I shall refer in more detail below. But meanwhile, let us

[7] IPCC (1990): 'the average rate of increase of global mean temperature during the next century is estimated to be about 0.3°C per decade ... This will result in a likely increase in global mean temperature of about ... 3°C above today's (about 4°C above pre-industrial) before the end of the next century' (p. 13).

consider another simple fact. As can be seen in the following table, at present the world's population is distributed over parts of the globe that differ enormously with respect to their average temperatures. Yet over a very wide range there is no obvious correlation between average temperature and the income level of the countries in question. In other words, without doing any complicated and highly conjectural calculations to predict how a 3°C rise in temperature would affect world output in 100 years' time it is perfectly clear that the human race can flourish in a great variety of average temperatures and climates. One does not get the impression that it is some fragile species that can only produce and survive in a museum with a controlled temperature the variation of which is confined within some 3°C band.

**Table 3.1** *Distribution of World Population by Temperature Zone*

| | *Winter* | | *Summer* | |
|---|---|---|---|---|
| *Temperature** | *Population* | | *Population* | |
| *°C* | *millions* | *%* | *millions* | *%* |
| < –6 | 317.3 | 6.3 | | |
| > –6 < –3 | 41.9 | 0.8 | | |
| > –3 < 0 | 152.2 | 3.0 | | |
| > 0 < 3 | 1,625.1 | 32.3 | | |
| > 3 < 6 | 132.2 | 2.6 | | |
| > 6 < 9 | 182.1 | 3.6 | 17.5 | 0.3 |
| > 9 < 12 | 46.9 | 0.9 | 35.0 | 0.7 |
| > 12 < 15 | 947.1 | 18.8 | 92.4 | 1.8 |
| > 15 < 18 | 187.4 | 3.7 | 206.5 | 4.1 |
| > 18 < 21 | 299.7 | 5.9 | 567.8 | 11.3 |
| > 21 < 24 | 344.6 | 6.8 | 813.9 | 16.1 |
| > 24 < 27 | 735.1 | 14.6 | 2,570.6 | 51.0 |
| > 27 < 30 | 34.0 | 0.7 | 469.9 | 9.3 |
| > 30 < 33 | | | 240.7 | 4.8 |
| > 33 | | | 31.3 | 0.6 |
| Total | 5,045.6 | 100.0 | 5,045.6 | 100.0 |

*Note*: * Average temperature of coldest or hottest month of period indicated.
*Sources*: *The World Weather Guide*, 1984, for temperatures, and *Readers Digest Atlas of the World*, 1988, for population. The total population of the world shown here excludes about 300 million people living in countries too small to be shown in one or other of these two sources.

## 3.3 The Scientific Consensus—Such As It Is

As indicated above, the general consensus amongst scientists in this field is that in the absence of special policies the concentration of $CO_2$ in the atmosphere will double some time towards the end of the next century and that this will lead to a rise in average world temperatures of about 3°C, but most reputable scientists seem to agree that there are still major gaps in their understanding of the global warming phenomenon in general and, in particular, the relationship between carbon dioxide and global warming, with corresponding very large differences in the predictions made by alternative climate models.[8] There appear to be three main reasons for these uncertainties:

1. Modelling the earth's climate is a task of heroic proportions and there are still enormous gaps in the models currently used. For example, everybody with the slightest interest in this issue knows by now that global warming is feared to arise on account of the fact that an increase in the atmospheric concentration of certain GHGs, of which carbon dioxide is the most important for practical purposes and which is produced by burning fossil fuels (as well as other means, some of them natural), tends to block some of the outgoing long-wave radiation which is one of the ways that the earth cools and sends back some of the incoming energy from the sun. The latter is mainly in the short-wavelength end of the spectrum, which is not absorbed so much, if at all, by the GHGs.

However, what is not so widely known amongst laymen is that the surface of the earth is not cooled primarily by the long-wave radiation that is trapped by the greenhouse gases. It is cooled primarily by evaporation, with the evaporated moisture being carried upwards by convection. In fact, in the absence of convection it is estimated that the globally averaged temperature would be about 72°C, by comparison with its current level of about 15°C.[9] And amongst the many uncertainties in the existing climate models there are major gaps on account of the absence of any proper treatment of the behaviour of water vapour and cloud cover and of the interaction between the atmosphere and the oceans and the way that the mix of water at different depths and of different temperatures affect the models. And it is generally agreed that better modelling of the increased evaporation and convection that would occur as a result of warming could have negative feedback effects and hence moderate the increase in warming that would otherwise take place (IPCC, 1990, p. 19). For example, improvements in the modelling of cloud cover recently introduced in the British

[8] For example, whilst all the main models predict that there will be increased precipitation as a result of global warming the estimated increases in precipitation range from +3% to +15%!

[9] See Lindzen (1989 and forthcoming). A comprehensive but simplified exposition can be found in various other texts, such as Moran *et al.* (1986), chapter 9.

Meteorological Office model reduced the estimates of the temperature increase associated with a doubling of the $CO_2$ concentrations from 5.2 degrees to 1.9 degrees.[10]

2. Contrary to widespread belief, the models that predict increases in world temperature as a result of increased $CO_2$ concentrations are not confirmed by temperature changes over the past century, for various reasons. First, the only reliable data on temperatures relate to the forty-eight contiguous states of the USA, and these data show no upward temperature trend at all.[11] Secondly, very recent satellite observations, which are far more reliable than the surface observations used so far, not merely show no global warming over the last ten years—by itself of no great significance one way or the other—but show that the ground-level observations used to support the view that there has been a long-run upward trend are unreliable. Thirdly, insofar as one does accept the estimated world average-temperature estimates purporting to indicate a trend increase of about 0.5°C over the last century, it is difficult to match these observations with the global warming models since (1) most of the trend rise occurred between 1900 and 1940, when $CO_2$ concentrations were increasing by only about 0.1 per cent per annum compared with 0.5 per cent per annum now; (2) there was a fall in temperature between 1940 and the early 1970s; (3) the models predict that more warming would take place at higher latitudes than near the equator, whereas the opposite has occurred. Hence, as Sir John Mason concludes, with reference to such upward trend in temperature as can be observed, 'The timing of the fluctuations in the temperature record, and the fact that any significant greenhouse warming is likely to be delayed for several decades because of the thermal inertia of the oceans, strongly suggest that these are natural climatic fluctuations.'[12]

[10] See Mason (1989), table 2, p. 428; Lindzen (1990), p. 9 and Section 3, p. 10; and Mitchell (1989), who says 'the major shortcoming is our poor understanding of the processes governing the formation and radiative properties of clouds' (p. 136). One of the many reasons for this is that their impact depends partly on the precise composition of clouds and that 'anthropogenerated pollutants can therefore serve to "brighten" clouds, reflecting away increasing amounts of solar radiation, and possibly compensating for greenhouse warming. A recent calculation demonstrates that the magnitude of this effect could indeed explain the fact that the Northern Hemisphere, where most sulphate emissions occur, shows no net warming during the last half century' (Michaels, 1990).

[11] There are various reasons why the data usually quoted are unreliable, such as the fact that the methods used to measure sea temperatures have changed over the decades in a manner that will have raised the recorded temperatures, or the fact that, since temperatures in cities are usually higher than in rural areas, growing urbanization will have biased estimated land temperatures in an upwards direction. See Lindzen (1990) p. 4, and White (1990). (Robert White was Chief of the US Weather Bureau and has held numerous top-level positions in the meteorological world, including being chairman of the first World Climate Conference of the World Meteorological Organization.)

[12] Mason (1989), p. 421, and Lindzen (1990). See also devastating statistical criticism of the proposition that data for the past century provide evidence of an upward trend in world temperature that can be associated with $CO_2$ concentrations in Solow and Broadus (1989 and forthcoming).

3. Furthermore, there are natural influences on the climate, not all of which are understood, and which include some relatively short-term natural variations such as changes in the angle at which the equatorial plane is inclined to its orbital plane (about 23°). Indeed, there is some reason to believe that there has been a slight long-run upward trend in global temperature since the end of the 'Little Ice Age' that began around the thirteenth century and ended towards the end of the eighteenth century, so that insofar as there is some upward trend in average temperature it could well be the continuation of a recovery from this Little Ice Age.[13] Hence, even if it had been true that the rise in global temperature over the last century fitted the rise that would be predicted by the current models on account of the increase in man-made emissions of $CO_2$, to conclude that this correspondence confirmed the model's prediction would amount to asserting that, by some fantastic coincidence, all the other variables affecting climate happened to have been completely inoperative during the period in question. To have lived in a period in which all these natural variables suspended operations simultaneously would have been a rare privilege indeed.

### 3.4 Some Economic Magnitudes

However, this is not a paper about the science, and the above points are made not only because they raise the question of how to make choices under conditions of uncertainty, but because of their much more practical relevance to the problem of achieving international agreement about the sharing out of costs and benefits of reductions in GHGs in a situation in which each country's scientists, as well as economists, will easily be able to challenge the assumptions and estimates made by those of other countries. This is particularly relevant insofar as the models used for prediction ('generalized climate models' or 'GCMs') are so far very bad at predicting relatively local effects, and from the point of view of individual countries what matters is not so much whether the world as a whole will get a little warmer or whether there is a slight increase in average rainfall in the world as a whole but whether their particular patch of it gets hotter or not, and by how much, and whether it gets more rain or less rain.

But meanwhile, let us concentrate on the average effect on the world as a whole and adopt, for the sake of argument, the current existing consensus amongst most scientists indicated above,[14] namely that in about 100 years' time

[13] Important evidence for this includes records of the freezing over of Lake Konstanz in Switzerland that go back to the year AD 875, which show the main frequency of freezing over to have taken place in the 15th and 16th centuries, with a declining frequency since then. See Solow (forthcoming, 1991). See also Ellsaesser (1990) and Crowley (1983).

[14] This is also the prediction reported at the recent Sundsvall meeting to produce the final report of the Intergovernmental Panel on Climate Change (IPCC) set up in 1988 under the auspices of the UN Environment Programme and the World Meteorological Organization.

average world temperature will rise by about 3°C—though there are many eminent scientists who dispute this consensus—and, too, that this will lead to an overall increase in rainfall, though, again, the opposite effect will occur in some large continental regions far removed from seas.

What can be said, in a rough and ready way, about the orders of magnitude of the economic effects that such climate changes would produce? Here, too, once one looks at some such estimates that have been made, and before trying to perform a 'Nordhaus' on them to estimate marginal cost and cumulative discounted marginal-benefit schedules for different degrees of reduction in greenhouse-gas emissions, one sees that the economic impacts hardly justify the alarm and the calls for dramatic action that are characteristic of much public discussion of this issue. In other words, whatever one does with the estimates they are unlikely to demonstrate that the present state of scientific knowledge justifies great trouble and expense to cut $CO_2$ emissions by a very large amount. The reasons for this become quickly apparent.

However, the estimates referred to below are confined to estimates of the effects of the $CO_2$ doubling, which are not expected to occur until the second half of the next century. It has been argued, notably by William Cline (to whose estimates for the doubling scenario considerable reference is made below), that one should extend one's time horizon much further. For a distinction needs to be made between the amount of warming that will have occurred by any particular date and the amount of eventual warming that is expected to result from the cumulative emissions and future emission levels by the time that the global climate system has reached equilibrium. Given the time-lags in the dynamics of climate change, notably those caused by the inertia introduced into the system as a result of the take-up of $CO_2$ by the oceans, it is quite possible that although global temperatures have risen by only 3°C by the end of the next century, there is a further unavoidable rise in the pipeline of a few more degrees.[15]

Of course, the further one projects into the future the more uncertainty has to be attached to the projections, and Cline's projections, which are, in effect, projections over another century of what are already projections of trends well beyond the predictive power of the models, are open to serious question on this account. Faced with the vast technological changes that have taken place in the last 100 years and the near certainty that these will be totally dwarfed by the

[15] This point is stressed in the IPCC reports (e.g. IPCC, 1990, pp. 13–16) in which a distinction is drawn between 'realized' and 'equilibrium' climate change. The relationship between the two is not proportional so that, for example, 'the realized temperature rise at any time is about 50 per cent of the committed temperature rise if the climate sensitivity (the response to a doubling of carbon dioxide) is 4.5°C and about 80 per cent if the climate sensitivity is 1.5°C . . . but it is not certain whether it would take decades or centuries for most of the remaining rise to equilibrium to occur' (loc. cit., box on p. 16).

changes that will take place over the next century, let alone the following century, during which an incomparably greater number of people will be engaged in technological and scientific research all over the world, nobody can suppose that the world of the late twenty-first century will bear much resemblance to the world that we know today and that energy will still be produced on a large scale by dirty and polluting substances such as coal. Furthermore, the need to discount the future implies that the benefits in two centuries' time from abating GHG emissions now, would have to be astronomic to justify significant current sacrifices. Hence, we shall confine ourselves here to such estimates as have been made of the effects of the $CO_2$ doubling/3°C rise scenario selected above.

### *Agriculture*

One of the most important effects of global warming, if any, will be on agriculture. The climate models predict that global warming will cause the interior of most continents to be drier, which will have an unfavourable effect on agriculture in many areas. But there will also be favourable effects in other areas, partly on account of longer growing periods in higher latitudes, partly on account of greater rainfall owing to generally increased evaporation over land and sea, and partly because of the fertilization effect on plants of higher $CO_2$ concentrations. Experiments at the US Water Conservation Laboratory have shown enormous increases in plant growth as a result of increased $CO_2$ concentrations. In other words, with higher $CO_2$ concentrations the same plant growth can be obtained with less water.[16] For the USA alone estimates by the Environmental Protection Agency show that the net effect on USA agriculture is uncertain in direction, with the possible range of effect lying between a net gain of $10 billion and a net loss of $10 billion.[17]

Now this may sound like big money to the layman, but, of course, by the standards of the American economy it is negligible—about the size of an

[16] See White (1990), p. 23. However, such experiments under somewhat artificial conditions are not a totally reliable guide to the effects of a genuine global rise in $CO_2$ concentrations, as has been pointed out in a survey of various experiments by Easterling *et al.* (1989), p. 98.

[17] The estimates of an approximately zero net effect on agricultural output made by the EPA in 1988 (pp. 21–2) have been confirmed in a more recent and very detailed study, breaking down the USA into a large number of regions and using alternative climate models (see Adams *et al.*, 1990). William Cline (Cline, 1990), however, refers to some estimates of much higher agricultural losses. But his own calculations, taking these estimates into account, still only suggest a loss of agricultural output of $150 billion as a result of eventual warming of 10°C. Since this is not predicted to occur (in Cline's extrapolations) until about the end of the 22nd century when, assuming the same 1.5% p.a. growth rate, the USA's GNP would amount to over $100 trillion, the loss of agricultural output would still be only 1.15 per cent of GNP. Of course, the whole of this sort of analysis is totally fatuous, since it is quite likely that US agriculture as we know it will have completely disappeared long before the end of the 22nd century.

average monthly trade deficit. Agricultural net output constitutes about 3 per cent of total US national product—i.e. about $150 billion out of a national product of about $5.2 trillion. Thus even if one takes the extreme worst-case estimate of a cut in net agricultural output of about $10 billion, this still constitutes only 0.2 per cent of total national product. Even if the estimates are wildly optimistic and the actual effect is to halve US agricultural output, this is still only 1.5 per cent of total national product—i.e. less than one year's growth. If US national product per head grows by about 1.5 per cent per annum, in real terms, over the next 100 years, by the year 2090 it would be over four times as large as it is now. In other words, even a cut of 50 per cent in net agricultural output as a result of global warming, which nobody would suggest is likely, would merely mean that the index of *real* national product in the USA in the year 2090, taking 1990 = 100, would be 436 instead of 443. To use a way of looking at it employed by Schelling, it means that the American population will have to wait another year, in 2090, to achieve the living standards that they could otherwise have expected to achieve in that year (see Schelling, 1983). I think the American population will find ways of adapting to this disappointment over the course of the years.

Of course, in other countries the effects will be different. In some, notably Canada, the USSR, and China, the net effects will be favourable as the production regions move northwards and growing periods are extended (see Cline, 1991). Nordhaus surveys estimates for other countries and reports that 'Detailed studies for the Netherlands and Australia found that the overall impact of a $CO_2$ equivalent doubling will be small and probably difficult to detect over a half-century or more. The Coolfont Workshop (in which teams of experts gathered on a very short-term basis) estimated the impact of climate change upon six large regions—the US, Europe, Brazil, China, Australia, and the USSR. This report found the impact of climate change to be generally favourable' (Nordhaus, 1990*a*). Thus Nordhaus finds that, for the world as a whole, 'our best guess is that $CO_2$-induced climate change will produce a combination of gains and losses, with no strong presumption of substantial net economic damages'.[18]

Furthermore, all this leaves out of account (1) the probable—indeed, inevitable—contribution that will be made by the continued rapid improvements in agriculture and plant technology as a result of genetic engineering, so that even if, on balance, global warming did raise the real costs of achieving given agricultural output by, say, 10 to 20 per cent by the middle of the next century, this is likely to be totally swamped many times over by continued increases in control over plants, possible production of new proteins, techno-

[18] Nordhaus (1990*b*), p. 10. Exactly the same conclusion is reached by Cline, in his survey (Cline, 1990), p. 23.

logical progress in water conservation and irrigation and so on, and (2) the fact that, over the last four decades food production has been rising faster than demand, so that some barely noticeable cut in the rate of growth of agricultural production—if any—does not spell mass starvation (Easterling *et al.*, 1989, p. 92). Famines, as we now know, have invariably been the result of appalling policies, civil strife, and discrimination, rather than acute physical food shortages in any given area.

*Sea-level Rise*

The situation does not change much even if we bring into the picture the other main fairly certain effect of global warming, namely the rise in sea levels. The estimated rise in sea levels has been greatly reduced over recent years. As recently as 1980 it was seriously believed that sea levels might rise as much as 8 metres. In early 1989 the prevailing estimate was down to about 1 metre; in early 1990 it was down to about 65 centimetres by the end of the next century (as in the IPCC report), and current authoritative estimates now put it as low as about 30 centimetres by the end of next century, assuming a 4°C rise in average temperature by then.[19] (If one were to extrapolate trends in these estimates, they would soon be predicting a fall in the sea level, with consequences for many seaside resorts that might be as serious as sea-level rises!) Although alarmists frequently refer to the impact on sea levels resulting from the disintegration of the West Antarctic Ice Sheet and the melting of sea-ice cover and so on, most glaciologists now discount the possibility of the former and there is, as yet, 'no evidence that the Arctic sea-ice cover has changed appreciably over the last two or three decades', a conclusion that has received further confirmation in more recent findings.[20]

But suppose sea-levels did rise appreciably, what would be the economic consequences? Estimates by the United States Environmental Protection Agency for an even greater rise in sea levels (namely 1 metre) are that the cost of protecting US cities by sea walls would be about $100 billion at current prices. Applying a 1.5 per cent per annum compound growth rate to the present

[19] See Solow and Broadus (forthcoming), p. 7; IPCC (1990), p. 1; Mason (1989), p. 431. More recently research carried out in the Geography Department of the University of Edinburgh shows that much smaller rises in the sea level would be associated with a 3°C increase in temperatures. (reported in *The Times* and *The Independent*, 4 January 1991).

[20] Mason (1989), p. 431, and McClaren *et al.* (1990), p. 762. Even back in 1988—which is a long time ago given the speed of downward revision of predictions in this field—it was thought that 'Changes in the mass balance of antarctic ice will probably have little impact on SLR (sea level rise) in the next few centuries . . . Indeed, it is possible that an increase of precipitation over Antarctica due to climate change could act to reduce the rate of SLR.' (See Gjerrit Hekstra, 'Sea-Level Rise: Regional Consequences and Responses', in Rosenberg *et al.* (1989), p. 54. This publication was a report of a conference in June 1988.)

US GNP of about $5.2 trillion would give a GNP by 2090 of $23 trillion, so that as a fraction of GNP in the year 2090 the once-for-all capital cost of the sea walls would be about 0.43 per cent! As a fraction of cumulative GNP over the whole of the next 100 years, during which time the work would have to be carried out, the amounts involved are, of course, totally trivial.

What about the rest of the world? Estimates by William Cline, of the Institute for International Economics, assuming a 1 metre rise in the sea level, and that the costs of sea walls for other threatened coastal cities are comparable to those of the USA, arrive at costs of adaptation, plus valuing the land lost in Bangladesh, of about $2 trillion. By the year 2090 world GNP would be about $115 trillion (assuming the US share remains roughly constant at one-fifth of world GNP), so that the once-for-all capital cost of the sea-level rise would still be only about 2 per cent of one year's GNP, so that as a fraction of cumulative world GNP over the whole period it would still be negligible (Cline, 1989, p. 18). And given that (1) the latest predictions of the rise in the sea level are about half those assumed in these estimates and (2) a given reduction in the estimated sea-level rise implies a more than proportionate reduction in the costs of adaptation or the damage done through land loss,[21] the costs of adaptation and land loss for the world as a whole would be negligible even allowing for a generous margin of error in the above estimates.

Now that may be all very well for the world as a whole but it is not much consolation for the people of Bangladesh, where 20 per cent of the land could be lost under the sea with a 1 metre sea-level rise. True—leaving aside the falling trend in estimates of sea-level rises—but suppose, purely for the sake of illustrating the logic of the choices to be made, that measures to prevent the climate change and the consequent sea-level rise would cost the world community $20 trillion—i.e. ten times as much as the cost of protection against the rising sea level. It would clearly be in the world's interest—and of the Bangladeshis and everybody else concerned—to make some sort of deal such as not incurring the $20 trillion costs that would be needed to prevent the sea level from rising and handing over, say, a quarter of the resulting economy—namely $4 trillion—to the people who would suffer from the sea-level rise. The latter then gain—$4 trillion to carry out work costing only $2 trillion—and the rest of the world still has a net gain of $16 trillion.

In other words, the alternative course of action that is being urged on all sides, namely to prevent the sea level rising at any cost, would mean that the world is being asked, in effect, to incur costs of $20 trillion—or whatever the cost would be—to prevent the Bangladeshis from suffering the effects of the sea-

[21] Cline (1989), p. 26. Of course, as one moves into the even longer term, so that sea-level rises could be much greater, Cline's point about the non-linearity works in the opposite direction—namely, the costs of adaptation would rise more than proportionately.

level rise when there would be a very much cheaper way of sparing them from these effects, and possibly of raising their overall income levels substantially, such as helping them move away from the threatened coastal areas, building dikes (after all, half the Dutch population live below sea level), improving flood control, and, perhaps allowing more of them to emigrate!

During the last two or three decades increased flooding associated with wider fluctuations in the river levels that have nothing to do with climate change has added to the general terrible poverty of Bangladesh, yet the rest of the world has shown no sign of genuine willingness to hand over, in the form of aid, resources commensurate with the task of eradicating that poverty or preventing the existing flooding. So the notion that it should now suddenly be seized by a fit of unprecedented altruism and incur possibly enormous costs to prevent or attenuate GHG emissions rather than accept the far less costly alternatives of adaptation one way or the other is absurdly naïve and unrealistic. If the estimates of the costs involved in significant reductions of $CO_2$ emissions referred to below are anywhere near reality it is clear that the world and the Bangladeshis would be far better off if adaptive policies were taken rather than drastic action to prevent the threatened rise in sea levels. Anyway, since far more land is being lost every year as a result of soil erosion than is likely to be lost through climate change, if the world is seriously concerned about land loss there are policies that could be adopted to reduce it without drastic reductions in world $CO_2$ emissions.

### *Other Effects*

Estimates have been made for other effects of climate change, such as greater need for air-conditioning (offsetting less need for space heating), forest loss, and the sheer disutility for some people of living in a warmer climate (but not for all those people who would like to do so but cannot afford to or are tied to their present locations by other factors). However, these are even more uncertain than those referred to above, and are likely anyway to be less significant.

Of course, the pressure groups or individuals whose *raison d'être* or livelihoods mean they thrive on prophecies of doom will appeal to other ecological scare stories, such as the effect of global warming on the frequency of storms and so on, but, in fact, very few hard results have been produced concerning this effect of global warming and for a very good reason. On the one hand it is true that insofar as the seas become warmer the area over which hurricanes 'breed' will expand. But, on the other hand, storms are correlated with temperature gradients—i.e. the transition between high and low temperatures—so that insofar as the temperature increase is greatest in high latitudes, where it is generally colder, the world-wide temperature gradient will diminish. To calculate the incidence of storms would, therefore, require a far more accurate breakdown by small geographic area of the effects of the climate change than is feasible given current modelling. Storms, like heatwaves or incidence of rainfall, depend very much on more local conditions than can be encompassed in the present state of the art of climate prediction. Hence, it is not surprising that the IPCC scientific working group reported that 'climate models give no consistent indication whether tropical storms will increase or decrease in frequency or intensity as climate changes; neither is there any evidence that this has occurred over the past few decades' (IPCC, 1990, p. 18).

Hence, it seems impossible to escape the conclusion that even under pessimistic assumptions, the annual cost to the world as a whole of global warming associated with a doubling of $CO_2$ concentrations is likely to be almost negligible by comparison with the value of world output over the period in question. However, the annual cost is not a sufficient measure of the marginal cumulative cost of an extra unit of current $CO_2$ emissions, which is what one requires, ideally, for purposes of finding the optimum degree by which emissions should be reduced. In the next section, therefore, we turn to a slightly more detailed economic analysis of the optimal policy to meet the global warming threat.

## 3.5 The Optimum Level of GHG Emissions

### *Outline of the Problem*

Although estimates of the damage that might be done by global warming in some particular future year and the costs that might have to be incurred now to prevent it provide some idea of the sort of choices that have to be made, they are subject to major reservations from a statistical and a conceptual point of view.

As regards the former, in order to estimate the damage that would be done in several decades in the absence of special policies (the 'business as usual' scenario) one would need to be able to project the growth rates of the main countries in the world over the next several decades and, above all, their energy production and consumption technologies, the relative prices of fuels, and so on. Given the total impossibility, in the present state of the art, of making very reliable estimates of these variables for just a few years ahead, the margin of error in predicting over several decades is obviously enormous. And it is these highly uncertain projections that must then be compared with equally uncertain estimates of the lower $CO_2$ emissions resulting from policies to induce society to switch to generally more expensive but less $CO_2$-intensive fuels and the real resource costs of such a substitution. This difference between two very uncertain estimates has then to be translated into corresponding economic effects, which would, in principle, require a general equilibrium model of the world economy in considerable detail, embodying a degree of sophistication incomparably greater than any possessed today in models that attempt merely to predict next year's inflation rate in the UK.

As regards the conceptual limitations on estimates of the kind mentioned above, most of such estimates as are available differ considerably with respect to methodology, assumptions, and time periods, so that it is difficult to compare their results, let alone put them into the form that fits the economic paradigm of a balancing of marginal costs against marginal benefits. For example, they relate to different degrees of $CO_2$-emission reduction over different time periods and from different base 'business as usual' assumptions. Hence, although they provide some idea of the orders of magnitude involved and immediately dispel most of the usual hysteria, they are not adequate for the task of judging exactly how far society ought to go in attempting to reduce GHG emissions. For even if it is accepted that the estimates referred to above suggest that there is no case for taking urgent drastic action at high cost to reduce GHG emissions substantially, it does not follow that there is no case for some action at possibly low cost to achieve some modest reduction in these emissions. Schedules of marginal costs and marginal benefits of emission reductions, taking account of the time dimension of the effects of the emissions, are necessary in order to escape from all-or-nothing choices and to identify exactly how much emission abatement is optimal. However, such schedules are immensely difficult to construct.

The time dimension of the effect of a given reduction in $CO_2$ emissions on the concentration of $CO_2$ in the atmosphere is particularly crucial. For the economic valuation of the damage done by emissions and hence the benefits from any cut in them depends on the time period over which it is achieved and how long it lasts. The more the effects of emissions are delayed the less the present discounted value of the damage. On the other hand, the longer they persist the greater their present discounted value. Hence, snapshot estimates of the damage done in, say, the year 2090 by a doubling of $CO_2$ emissions need to be converted into some estimate of the future damage done over the life of the greenhouse gases that have accumulated and that still persist up to that year, which requires, in principle, some assumptions concerning the time-path of the emissions and the length of life of the GHGs in question, which differ considerably from one GHG to another. Some discount-factor rate must also be introduced, for few people would argue that a dollar's worth of extra consumption in the year 2090 and in subsequent years has the same value as a dollar's worth of extra consumption today.

### *The Nordhaus Model*

Fortunately, as mentioned already, William Nordhaus has succeeded in bringing together the various estimates into a comparable form within this conceptual framework. This is not the place to provide a full description of the Nordhaus model but the following will give the flavour of the approach and his main conclusions (Nordhaus, 1990*a*).

First, the socially optimal level of emissions reductions is, of course, where the marginal costs of reductions equals the marginal damage that would otherwise be done by the extra emissions, through their effect on the climate, throughout their lifetime. The optimality condition in Nordhaus's model may be summarized as follows:

$$g'(E) = DR \qquad (1)$$

where

$g'(E)$ = the marginal cost of reducing emissions;
$R$ = a discount factor (explained below); and
$D$ = the annual damage done by a marginal increase in emissions.

Both $D$ and $R$ encapsulate several variables embodied in a set of equations. $D$ is a function of various parameters, notably the fraction of $CO_2$ emissions that remain in the atmosphere (i.e. as distinct from being absorbed in the oceans or in some other form), the effect on the global temperature in equilibrium resulting from the subsequent rise in $CO_2$ concentrations, and the economic valuation (in terms of percentage of world output) of the damage done by this induced increase in global temperatures.

The 'discount factor', $R$, which plays a crucial part in the calculation, is not just the familiar discount rate or some simple variant of it. It contains both positive and negative elements and assumptions concerning physical as well as economic variables. For what it does is to allow, firstly, for two physical parameters, namely (1) the time-lag between emissions and the subsequent equilibrium rise in temperature (to allow for the 'inertia' caused by the oceans/atmosphere interface) and (2) the duration of the temperature rise (to allow for the length of life of the GHGs). The greater the former the lower would be the present value of the damage and the greater the latter the higher would be the present value. Nordhaus's discount factor also takes account of economic parameters, namely (1) society's pure rate of time preference, (2) the future growth rate of income, and (3) the prevailing real rate of return on capital. What discount rate should be used when dealing with very distant outcomes has been a matter of much debate and raises various philosophical issues, that are also linked to the question of choice under conditions of uncertainty. A fuller discussion of discounting, therefore, is left to a later section. Meanwhile we shall consider the actual Nordhaus results.

*The Main Nordhaus Results*

Since there is obviously scope for major differences of opinion concerning discount rates, growth rates, and the damage that will actually be done by future GHG emissions, single-figure estimates of the gains from any given reduction in emissions would be highly misleading. But Nordhaus's model enables him to convert alternative estimates of the damage done in the future from a doubling of $CO_2$ concentrations (the usual benchmark adopted in most of the studies) into the present value of the future damage done per ton of a marginal increase in current $CO_2$ emissions, given different assumptions as to growth rates and discount rates, and allowing fully for its delayed effects, and the duration of the effects.

In addition he surveys alternative estimates of the costs of reducing emissions of greenhouse gases (in carbon dioxide equivalents) by various means, including reducing CFCs (which is relatively very cheap) and reducing deforestation, which is also very cheap but which can only make a very limited contribution to any programme to reduce greenhouse-gas emissions. After that, reducing such emissions by changing the type of fossil fuel used soon becomes very expensive. By interpolating on the basis of these estimates he is able to construct a marginal cost of GHG emissions to match against the marginal damage done by such emissions resulting from the other exercise explained above. Obviously, the optimum point depends on the particular sets of assumptions adopted including all those mentioned above. The dependence of the socially optimal degree of reduction of emissions on these assumptions is summarized in Nordhaus's conclusions as follows:

> For the low damage function—which includes only identified costs and uses a middle discount rate—we estimate the marginal damage of greenhouse gases to be about \$3 per ton $CO_2$ equivalent. At this marginal damage, the efficient degree of reduction of greenhouse gases is around 10 per cent. This reduction comes largely from the phaseout of the CFCs and from a very small reduction in $CO_2$ emissions. For the medium damage function, which assumes damage from greenhouse warming of 1 per cent of GNP, the cost is reckoned at \$13 per ton $CO_2$; in this case, CFCs are virtually completely phased out, and $CO_2$ emissions are reduced by about 6 per cent. (Nordhaus, 1990*a*)

Nordhaus also gives an estimate for the 'high damage' case, but since even his low-damage case is the one that 'represents the economic costs actually identified in this study (0.25 per cent of total output) along with a moderate discount rate of 1 percentage point above the output growth rate' (Nordhaus, 1990*a*) this seems to be of little practical interest.

My interpretation of the Nordhaus calculations, therefore, is that they confirm the more impressionistic estimates referred to earlier and demonstrate that modification of the $CO_2$ emissions sufficient to slow down significantly the rise in the $CO_2$ concentration and to postpone a doubling of it for several decades would be far more expensive in terms of the real resource costs to society than would be the damages done by a doubling of $CO_2$ emissions. However, Nordhaus shows there is some case for a much more modest reduction in GHG emissions, at least if most of it is achieved by low-cost means, notably the elimination of CFCs (which there may be a case for doing anyway on other grounds, namely the alleged threat to the ozone layer),[22] and prevention of uneconomic deforestation, although a cut in $CO_2$ emissions of the order of about 10 per cent would also be justified.

It follows from this analysis that if taxes on carbon were raised to levels necessary to bring about reductions in GHG emissions of the order of 50 per cent, for which many environmentalists are calling, but which are well beyond the Nordhaus estimates of the optimal reduction, the net losses to the world as a whole could be very large indeed. For the costs of reducing GHG emissions will rise sharply the greater the reduction achieved. For example, estimates of the order of magnitude of the carbon taxes needed to reduce $CO_2$ emissions by 50 per cent usually put the taxes into the region of a few hundred dollars per ton of carbon, which usually translates into taxes of four to five hundred per cent on the net (of tax) price of energy. And estimates along these lines by Whalley and Wigle show taxes of this magnitude leading to net economic welfare losses over the period 1990 to 2030 amounting to about $18 trillion, or about 4 per cent of total world output over the same period. For some areas, such as North America, the loss would be far greater, namely about 10 per cent of GNP (Whalley and Wigle, 1990).

However, the margin of error in estimates of these costs must be substantial. For much will depend on what is done with the revenues. Hence, it is not simply a matter of the welfare loss as measured by the compensating variation of the

[22] This sceptical reference to the ozone-layer threat is based on the fact that although it now seems fairly certain that the ozone layer in the stratosphere is being depleted by CFCs, the ozone concentration in the troposphere seems to have increased, which would help explain why, in fact, there has been no rise in UV (ultra-violet radiation) arriving at the ground in the northern hemisphere. In the Antarctic region, however, the increase in tropospheric ozone may not compensate the seasonal decline in stratospheric ozone, but the level of UV arriving in that region is very much smaller anyway than that arriving in other latitudes.

rise in the tax on energy. Insofar as the object of the operation is not to influence the level of demand in the economy but to change the allocation of resources, the extra revenues—at least from the world point of view—ought to be given back in the form of reductions in other taxes. Hence, to estimate the net loss of welfare requires comparative estimates of the 'deadweight' welfare losses incurred by giving up the former with the welfare gains that might be obtained if the resulting tax revenues are used to reduce taxes on other goods. The real economic welfare cost of such a net shift in the pattern of output might be negligible, and even favourable. No firm *a priori* statement can be made about the welfare cost of a change in tax mix starting from a position which is already sub-optimal on account of the existence of some taxes.

There is a second source of welfare loss that has to be taken into account. This is because what is at issue here is not just a shift in taxes on final output but the imposition (or increase) in a tax on a basic input into the productive system, namely energy. As Bruno and Sachs have shown, in connection with the effects of the oil shocks, a cut in energy inputs can have a significant effect on total output (Bruno and Sachs, 1985, especially chapters 1 and 2). But in that case although the impact of the oil price rise could be analysed as if it were a tax imposed on Western consumers that accrued to oil producers there was no cut in taxes in the latter. So in the context of a carbon tax, insofar as the counterpart tax reductions were to be on taxes on other factor inputs—e.g. some tax on labour income, or a payroll social security tax, or a profit tax—then a shrinking in the economy's productive potential as a result of the reduced inputs of energy could be offset by a stimulus to inputs of other factors of production. Again, it is obvious that the information that would be necessary in order to make even rough estimates of the net outcome for the world as a whole is simply not available.

All this means that it is not possible to reach any firm *prima facie* conclusions about the magnitude of the costs that would be imposed on society by taxes of an order of magnitude needed to reduce GHG emissions by much more than the optimum level or even to accept the Nordhaus estimates as covering all the welfare gains and losses possibilities. Much will depend on the distribution of the taxes and the counterpart transfers, on the time period in question and on the speed with which economies can adapt. It may well be that a model can be constructed showing total real-cost neutrality in the medium- to longer-run equilibrium situation, but a rapid switch in tax patterns would probably mean high costs of disruption and of changes in techniques.

### *Uncertainties*

Of course, every aspect of the problem that one peers into merely reveals a whole new mass of uncertainties. Before going into the uncertainties arising out of the considerations just discussed there are great uncertainties in estimating the costs of reducing $CO_2$ emissions arising out of the variety of estimates of one component of any such estimates, namely the sensitivity of response of $CO_2$ emissions to alternative taxes on carbon, or some corresponding price mechanism disincentive.[23] In a survey of some of the estimates Terry Barker points out that estimates for the UK alone of the tax rates needed to achieve the Toronto target of cutting GHG emissions by 20 per cent below 1988 levels by the year 2005 varied from 41 per cent on coal (and less on other fossil fuels) in Scott Barrett through anything from 123 per cent to 277 per cent on coal (depending on timing assumptions) in Ingham and Ulph up to about 600 per cent in Capros *et al.* (Barker and Lewney, 1991). Depending on the elasticities of response of fossil-fuel use to alternative taxes one would arrive at alternative estimates of the costs to society of this particular method of reducing GHG emissions. These costs are difficult to estimate even without uncertainty as to the elasticities.

One of the reasons for the wide variations in the estimates of the elasticities of total energy use with respect to changes in prices resulting from the imposition of taxes is that, as David Newbery points out, much will depend on the relative price changes of individual fossil fuels and also on the range over which the tax changes in question are to be allowed to vary.[24] For example, it may well be that the elasticity of response will vary greatly according to the size of tax change in question. As he points out, 'One suspects that at a sufficiently high price of carbon, other technologies (e.g. hydrogen produced from nuclear fuel) suddenly become attractive, so that the elasticity suddenly becomes very high at some backstop price'.

Whilst it seems fairly clear, therefore, that very high taxes would be needed to effect significant cuts in GHG emissions, so that if they were introduced too quickly the real adjustment costs of doing so would also be substantial, the margin of error in the estimates is considerable. Much will depend on the type of measures adopted—for example, quantitative restrictions would be far more costly than some price-mechanism policy. The incidence of the tax will also vary enormously according to whether it is imposed on consumption or production of energy. Furthermore, the simplifying assumptions usually made in estimates of the real effects of any reduction in energy inputs, such as the use of conventional production functions, or the assumption of constant returns to

[23] See widely different estimates of the size of carbon tax needed to produce given reductions in emissions in, for example, Barrett (1990), section 2.2.; Whalley and Wigle (1990), p. 5 and passim; Congress of the United States (1990); Grubb (1989), section 5.1.

[24] David Newbery, 'The International Incidence of Carbon Taxes: Comment' (comment on the Whalley and Wigle, 1990, p. 3). The influence of the cross elasticities on the estimated impact of carbon taxes is also clearly brought out in the estimates made by Scott Barrett (1990).

scale, or the use of simple time trends to represent technical progress, could be nowhere near the mark in the real world.[25]

But perhaps the greatest source of uncertainty is the whole area of technological improvements that take the form of energy savings or a switch to forms of fossil-fuel use that are less carbon-intensive, not to mention the use of renewables (solar power, wind power, and so on). So called 'no regret policies' would take the form of trying to encourage the greater use of economically viable technological innovations of this kind. Much is known about some of the technological possibilities, but relatively little is known about the economics of introducing them.[26] Whilst many environmentalists proclaim that there is enormous scope for such economically justifiable energy-saving techniques the question arises why, if that is the case, have they not already been introduced?

There may be perfectly valid answers to this question for there is no doubt that the real world is full of market imperfections. These could include (1) simple lack of information—though there is a limit to the amount of information that it is economically worthwhile any agent trying to get; (2) private discount rate exceeds the social discount rate, so that there may be technologies that would be viable but that do not provide the rapid pay-offs that users might require in this area (e.g. a simple case being the very high pay-off required by householders for house insulation—particularly if the owner does not expect to be able to recoup the capital outlay in the subsequent sale price of the house); (3) liquidity constraints on account of imperfections in the capital market; (4) principal–agent problems—e.g. the people in an organization who are responsible for certain investment decisions are not those who are concerned with economizing in energy operating costs; and, finally, a host of government regulations and subsidies that actually reduce energy efficiency.

However, there is, as yet, not much hard evidence about these and other possible market imperfections affecting energy use.[27] So the problem is to identify those that have impeded their application in this field. But it is important to note that the estimates referred to above of the costs of abatement of GHG emissions might be far greater than the real costs that would follow from economically viable policies to stimulate energy conservation. It could well be that economically viable policies to accelerate the diffusion of knowledge about existing possibilities and accelerate their application could lead to some relatively costless, if limited, abatement of $CO_2$ emissions over the next few years and that, with suitable policies to promote further research and development in this area, as well as to follow up the dissemination and diffusion policies, other gains could be made in subsequent years.

[25] I am particularly indebted to Dr Terry Barker, of Cambridge Econometrics, for information on this point.

[26] A very detailed summary of some of the most important British work in this field is contained in Leach and Nowak (1990), and Barbier *et al.* (1990). See also Fulkerson *et al.* (1990), and Anderson and Bird (1990).

[27] See Leach and Nowak (1990) for an excellent survey of some of the main material available.

Nevertheless, the fact that the developing world is so far behind the advanced industrial countries in energy consumption per head, suggests that it would need more than the widespread adoption of energy saving techniques to prevent a significant increase in worldwide energy consumption and $CO_2$ emissions over the course of the next century. For example, China's carbon emissions already constitute roughly 10 per cent of world total and half of that of the USA. But China's emissions per head are just over one-tenth of those of the USA. Hence, if nobody else increased their carbon emissions at all, and China raised its per capita emissions to half of the USA level, total world emissions would rise by about 40 per cent! Clearly, encouraging people in advanced countries to put the lids on their saucepans when cooking or to insulate the lofts of their houses is not likely to make any impact on emissions in a world in which all the less developed countries (LDCs) will be increasing their emissions on a massive scale.

### *Uncertainty and Choice*

Given the margin of error in estimates of the damage done by global warming, and of the costs of preventing it, particularly if allowance is made for the relatively unquantifiable scope for technical progress in energy efficiency, one is faced with the question of the choices to be adopted under conditions of uncertainty. It is sometimes argued that since the climate-change effect of greenhouse-gas emissions is irreversible in a relevant time period and that it just *might* be catastrophic—although all the evidence set out above is to the contrary—it is urgent that action be taken without delay. This argument is just as false as is the zero-discount argument discussed in the next section. As Arrow and Fisher put it in a classic article in 1974:

> Just because an action is irreversible does not mean that it should not be undertaken. Rather, the effect of irreversibility is to reduce the benefits, which are then balanced against costs in the usual way... Essentially the point is that the expected benefit of an irreversible decision should be adjusted to reflect the loss of options it entails.[28]

If human beings took no action that would have irreversible consequences the human race would have ceased to exist a long time ago!

Up to a point the response to the possibility of climate change can be analysed in terms of the traditional economic analysis of choice under conditions of uncertainty, the key feature of which is the maximization of the expected utility associated with alternative possibilities. A serious outcome with a very low

[28] Arrow and Fisher (1974), pp. 312–19. A very sound outline of some of these issues in relationship to environmental disaster in developing countries is contained in Anderson (1990).

probability could have less weight than a less serious outcome with a high probability.

However, it can be argued that this approach cannot be extended to cover the case of catastrophe, particularly when, in addition, there is no statistical basis for assessing the probabilities to be attached to the outcomes. It is sometimes proposed that 'strong catastrophic risks should, in the limit, not be undertaken at any price' and that risk aversion should justify 'prudence' even if the risks of catastrophe are minimal.[29] Nevertheless, people do not invest time or resources in measures to avoid every minuscule risk that they face, even where the consequences of their failing to do so just might be catastrophic and would also be irreversible. This is obvious in the way people drive! Or in the degree to which they invest in measures to ensure that, for example, their houses never burn down under any circumstances or they are never hit by an out-of-control drunken driver whilst walking along the pavement minding their own business. When Skylab was reported to be out of control recently and certain to fall to earth one knew not where, few people, if any, thought it worthwhile sheltering all day in the nearest underground station although the consequences for them of it falling on their heads would have been very serious indeed and certainly irreversible.

In any case, since it appears that even if nothing is done to reduce GHG emissions the damage by the end of the next century will be far from catastrophic, it is clear that postponing action for a decade or more cannot possibly be the cause of unavoidable catastrophe. The more rational policy in the face of the global-warming threat is to avoid embarking on very costly draconian measures to reduce GHG emissions as soon as possible but to invest now in more research into climate change. If it then transpires, for example, that the probability of serious climate change is, indeed, considerable, then it would become worthwhile incurring greater costs to prevent it. At the same time much more research could be undertaken into ways of reducing energy intensity and GHG emissions per unit of energy use at low cost, through the elimination of market imperfections and the promotion of research into appropriate technologies. This should, of course, be combined with policies of the 'no regret' nature that can already be identified.[30] Indeed, the unknown scope for future technological progress in energy conservation constitutes an offsetting argument to the 'risk of catastrophe' argument. In other words, there are favourable uncertainties as well as unfavourable ones. With more evidence and research one may be better placed to take an informed view of the balance of probabilities and the associated costs and benefits.

[29] See, for example, Collard (1988); Pearce *et al.* (1989) especially pp. 16–17. A recent summary discussion of this issue is in Pearce and Turner (1990), especially pp. 314–19.

[30] See discussion of this issue in Nordhaus (1990*c*), pp. 34 ff.; Manne and Richels (forthcoming), and Cline (1990).

### *Discounting the Future*

In any analysis of the economics of global warming, the crucial role of the time dimension means that estimates of the relative costs and benefits, suitably adjusted for uncertainty where possible, will be very sensitive to the choice of the discount rate. And whilst most economists would probably accept that, for society as a whole, there is no justification for a discount rate that merely reflects 'pure time preference'—i.e. simple impatience, or what Pigou called 'defective telescopic faculty', discounting the future can still be justified on the grounds of diminishing marginal utility of income. That is to say, it may be accepted that the marginal utility of an extra dollar to a rich man will be less than its value to a poor man. Hence, it may be rational to discount the future on the assumption that economic growth will continue so that future societies will be much richer than those of today.[31]

In addition, one must also take account of the rate of return that can be obtained on investment today. Given that it is positive, if one did not discount the future at all—as some extreme environmentalists seem to advocate—the logical implication would be that all resources ought to be turned over to investment and that consumption levels should be reduced to a bare subsistence level. For if the prospect of an extra dollar of consumption in, say, fifty years' time was regarded today as having the same value now as a dollar of consumption today, then it follows that anything greater than one dollar of consumption in the future, say $1.01, would be valued more highly than $1 today. It follows that if giving up one dollar of consumption today one could consume a fraction more than one dollar in the future—however small the fraction—one should make the present sacrifice and invest instead. But clearly that sort of rule would justify cutting consumption to the bone today in order to turn over nearly the whole of our resources to investment, since although it may be difficult to find many more investments that yielded, say, 10 per cent rates of return per annum, it should not be difficult to find investments that yield some infinitesimally small rates of return, even in the British economy.

Such a Stalinist policy of starving the present in order to turn over everything to investment, which would lead to very high growth rates, is obviously not what society wants, or what even the extreme environmentalists would want if they understood the implications of their views on discounting.[32] Nor is it what poor countries, who are not in a position to make much sacrifice of current living standards in the interests of the future, would want. There are good theoretical and empirical grounds for the view that poorer people will apply much higher

[31] A good recent survey of this issue in the context of environmental policy is contained in Pearce and Turner (1990), chs. 14 and 15. A more extensive survey of the more philosophical aspects of this issue is contained in Turner (1988).

[32] This point is made, albeit more diplomatically and technically, in Markandya and Pearce (1988), para. 3.4, p. 30.

discount rates than richer people.[33] Thus, although it may be perfectly true that future generations are not represented in the determination of interest rates and hence the rates of return required on current investment, and might have preferred low rates of discount than those that operate, this is no justification for the complete absence of any discount rate, even if one did not allow for diminishing marginal utility of income and the fact that future generations will be wealthier than those of today.

Even if the 'low discount rate' school of thought does not go quite so far as to advocate a near-zero rate, it is still inconsistent to apply a relatively low rate—say of the order of 4 per cent—on global warming when the discount rate expected in most parts of the world, and particularly in the LDCs, is at least twice this. Given the high discount rate used as a cut-off for investment in general in LDCs, if, instead, a low discount rate were believed to be more appropriate in the interests of giving future generations more of a say in current decisions, there is no reason why all the extra investment should go into preventing global warming. It is reported, for example, that the social rate of return to investment in education in poor countries is around 25 per cent for primary education, and 16 per cent for secondary education. It would appear that if, as a result of using a lower discount rate than currently employed (e.g. in World Bank projects) more investment were to be made in the future welfare of poor countries, reducing world GHG emissions would not come high in the priorities and they could do much better by investment in other forms. Faster economic growth would then increase the world's capacity to switch to less energy-intensive forms of output (as in Japan, France, and increasingly so in other advanced countries) as well as becoming better able to afford action to adapt to such climate change as would eventually come about.

## 3.6 International Negotiations for Reducing GHG Emissions[34]

Although the transnational externality aspect of global warming leads to the conclusion that international action is essential if anything effective is to be done about it, the economic analysis raises the question of whether the game is worth the candle. This is not simply a matter of the apparent excess of the costs of reducing GHGs significantly relative to the damage done by global warming. It is also a matter of the difficulty of reaching international agreement. Even if all countries gained by measures to reduce global warming significantly, it would be very difficult to reach international agreement for reasons set out more fully below. But given that some countries gain and some lose, and by different

[33] Some striking evidence for this is given in Hausman (1979), pp. 33–54.

[34] An extended version of this section is contained in the present writer's chapter, 'Global Warming and International Action: An Economic Perspective', in Hurrell and Kingsbury (forthcoming).

amounts, as a result of global warming or of measures to prevent it, the obstacles in the way of arriving at some optimal collective agreement are enormous.

The above estimates suggest that it will only be optimal for the world as a whole to cut GHG emissions by fairly modest amounts and if the reductions are concentrated on the cheapest forms—such as the elimination of CFCs and of forms of energy use that are not only highly $CO_2$-intensive but are carried to excess as a result of market failure or distortions that can be corrected at little or no cost to society (the 'no regret' policies). Beyond that, the net benefits to the world from far greater cuts in $CO_2$ emissions are likely to be negative so that the gainers could not compensate the losers and still be better off. And even if the net benefits to the world from action on the more drastic scale widely suggested—such as cutting $CO_2$ emissions by about 50 per cent or more—are perceived, rightly or wrongly, to be positive, this would, as argued below, impose such heavy costs on key players in the game that the chances of successful international agreement seem to me to be negligible.

As some commentators, notably Schelling, Skolnikoff, Cline, Grubb, and Richard Cooper have demonstrated, these difficulties are enormous when one takes account of the divergent interests between countries and between different groups within countries, not to mention the scope for everybody to be able to quote scientific evidence on their side.[35] Given all the uncertainties set out above, particularly those concerning the effects on individual countries or regions, it is difficult to imagine any effective international co-operation to take serious action until some of these uncertainties are resolved.

For most countries the optimal policy will be to do nothing and act as free-riders on other countries' abatements, from which they may benefit in more ways than one. For example, the losses incurred by major producers of $CO_2$-intensive fuels have a counterpart terms-of-trade gain for fuel-importing countries, who would find that the ex-tax price of fuel would fall on account of the reduced demand for it.[36] Furthermore, the greater the cut in emissions by other countries the less incentive there is for any given country to cut its own emissions. For the costs of doing so will be unchanged but insofar as global warming is less likely to be serious anyway, the benefits of doing so will be reduced.[37] And some countries might well gain from global warming itself, and so would hope that nobody else does much to stop it.

[35] Cline (1989), p. 48 ff.; Cooper (1985); Grubb (1990); Schelling (1990); Skolnikoff (1989, 1990).

[36] Much would depend, however, on cross-elasticities of substitution between different fossil fuels. For if the different fuels were taxed according to their relative carbon contents, the negative effect on the demand for oil, say, of the tax on oil, could be more than offset by the positive effect on the demand for oil of the relatively greater rise in the price of coal.

[37] The economics can be translated into an exact counterpart to the 'reaction curve' in a Cournot duopoly situation, in which the more a competitor increases output the less is the optimum output of the given firm, since the demand curve for the given firm's output shifts left, thereby reducing the profit maximizing output for the given firm. See Congress of US (1990), p. 57, and Pearson and Smith (1990), pp. 9, 16.

The industrialized countries do not lose much from global warming but, given the scale of their GHG emissions and their consumption of fossil fuels, they would incur heavy costs of significant abatement. By contrast, most other countries are too poor to attach much priority to measures to do so anyway. In particular, significant cuts in $CO_2$ emissions would involve large reductions in $CO_2$-intensive fuels, of which coal is the worst, followed by oil. Hence, countries such as China or India that have large coal resources would lose significantly. Furthermore, these happen to be countries that desperately need to raise their current standards of living. As they do so they will increase their energy use. As Michael Grubb points out, 'if China and India emitted carbon at the same *per capita* level as the US, world emission would be nearly trebled'.[38] The prospects of China or India making sacrifices of current standards of living or immediate growth prospects in order to improve the standards of living of the world in 100 years' time are virtually non-existent. They refused to sign the Montreal protocol on CFCs and, like other developing countries, will no doubt continue to refuse to make far greater sacrifices that would be required to prevent major increases in their GHG emissions except in return for substantial compensation from the industrialized countries that will no doubt not be forthcoming. And the rest of the world should not expect them to act otherwise. Probably the biggest contribution that could be made to curtailing the increase in $CO_2$ emissions in these countries would be more constraint on their rate of population increase.

So one is driven to the conclusion that most of the countries that could afford to do anything about GHG emissions have little incentive to do so and those that may have more incentive to do so from the point of view of the longer-run impact of global warming on their economies cannot afford to do anything about it. Michael Grubb is no doubt correct in concluding, with respect to international agreements to apply quantitative limits on GHG emissions, that 'the idea that a protocol on limiting carbon emissions will be like the Montreal Protocol writ large is an illusion best dispersed before it leads us irretrievably down a blind alley' (Grubb, 1989).

Hence, there seems to be *slightly* more chance of success in pursuing discussions of methods of using the price mechanism in such a way as to leave countries the choice of how far they reduce GHG emissions or, in effect, compensate other countries to do so, in a situation of appropriate incentives. Some form of tradable permits would seem to be the most likely approach. But even this system is open to the objection that the poor countries will just cash in their permits so that, in the end, the rich countries will be doing all the abatement and merely handing over aid to the poor countries disguised in the

[38] Grubb (1989), p.17. Grubb reports that China envisages expanding its coal consumption fivefold by the year 2020, which would add nearly 50% to current world-wide carbon emissions!

form of payments for GHG-emission permits. Since poor countries will discount the future at much higher rates (when you are worried about getting a square meal in the next twenty-four hours you are not very concerned with the carbon concentration in the atmosphere in the year 2090) and also start from relatively very low levels of energy use, their marginal rate of substitution between money and pollution permits will differ so much from that of rich countries that they will presumably sell all their permits for other claims on resources.

Also, some rich countries could accumulate permits that other countries might then be forced to buy back at higher prices at a later date when they have exhausted their own opportunities to reduce GHG emissions cheaply. On the other hand, some form of leased permits—i.e. countries do not buy outright indefinite rights to emit GHGs and have to renew them from time to time—helps mitigate these objections up to a point (Grubb, 1989, especially pp. 33–8).

But pending international agreement, however vaguely and generally defined, it may still make economic sense for individual countries to pursue 'no regret' policies of the type referred to in the previous section. This would be appropriate in any case and certainly appropriate for those countries who, for one reason or another—such as responding to internal political pressures—feel impelled to do something about global warming even if, for the reasons given earlier, it does not make much sense to cut GHG emissions unilaterally. For such countries, the sort of 'no regret' and research policies mentioned above involve little cost and could provide examples and information that would give the right sort of signals to the rest of the world, rather than provide the rest of the world with incentives to do less than they would otherwise have done to reduce GHG emissions.

Such policies are, therefore, much more likely to be implemented than premature attempts to forge international agreements to cut GHG emissions. Such attempts seem to be doomed to failure. And perhaps this is just as well. If there is no rational basis for inflicting relatively heavy burdens on current generations in order that, in 100 years' time, the average income per head be 4.4 times as high as it is now instead of only 4.3 times as high, it is just as well that the chances of imposing such a burden are slim. Alternatively, insofar as the chances of reaching effective international agreement are negligible, it is just as well that there is no real cause for alarm.

## 3.7 Conclusions

The above survey suggests that the damage done by the degree of climate change according to the latest scientific consensus, such as it is, is nothing like as great as is widely believed and certainly not the inevitable global catastrophe scenario hawked around by most environmentalist movements, politicians trying to get some mileage out of the environmental bandwagon, or sections of the media that love scare stories of any kind. There is plenty of time to think and to weigh up the costs and benefits of alternative courses of action. At the same time, it is quite likely that the real costs of measures to cut GHGs are not as awesome as they might seem, provided the measures take the form of some price-mechanism instrument, such as tradable permits or carbon taxes, and provided allowance is made for the offsetting tax reductions that ought to be made elsewhere in the economy.

However, this would depend on avoiding dislocation costs associated with the rapid introduction of high carbon taxes, or their counterpart in high prices on a very limited volume of tradable permits. Thus it seems difficult to avoid the unexciting conclusion that what is needed, in addition to the obvious research into the relevant science, is further research into measures to activate 'no regret' policies, such as those associated with the removal of existing market imperfections that may hamper the introduction of economically viable technologies that economize in energy or in GHG emissions, as well as, perhaps, some modest carbon taxes or tradable-permits scheme that could help stimulate further technological progress in this area. International agreement along these lines would be far more fruitful than attempts to negotiate some share-out of draconian cuts in GHGs, and governments should not let ecological horror stories frighten them into making any moves in that direction.

## Bibliography


Adams, R. *et al.*, (1990), 'Global Climate Change and US Agriculture', *Nature*, 17 May, 345, 219–24.

Anderson, D. and Bird, C. D. (1990), 'The Carbon Accumulation Problem and Technical Progress', draft, September.

Anderson, M. B. (1990), 'Analysing the Costs and Benefits of Natural Disaster Responses in the Context of Development', World Bank Environment Working Paper No. 29, May.

Arrow, K. J. and Fisher, A. C. (1974), 'Environmental Preservation, Uncertainty and Irreversibility', *Quarterly Journal of Economics*, 88, 312–19.

Barbier, E., Burgess, J. C., and Pearce, D. W. (1990), 'Slowing Global Warming', London Environmental Economics Centre, September.

Barker, T. and Lewney, R. (1991), 'A Green Scenario for the UK Economy', in T. Barker (ed.), *Green Futures for Economic Growth*, Cambridge Econometrics.

Barrett, S. (1990), Memorandum to the Select Committee on Energy, 1 May, section 2.2.

Berger, A. (1988), 'Milankovitch Theory and Climate', *Review of Geophysics*, 26(4), 624–57.

Bessemer, L. (1990), 'A Brief History of Climatic Doom', *The Spectator*, 3 March.

Bruno, M. and Sachs, J. (1985), *Economics of Worldwide Stagflation*, Oxford, Basil Blackwell.

Cline, W. R. (1989), 'Political Economy of the Greenhouse Effect', preliminary draft, Washington, D.C., Institute for International Economics, August.

— (1990), 'Economic Stakes of Global Warming in the Very Long Term', draft of November 1990, revision no. 1, Washington, D.C., Institute for International Economics.

Collard, D. (1988), 'Catastrophic Risk: or the Economics of Being Scared' in D. Collard, D. Pearce, and D. Ulph (eds.), *Economics, Growth and Sustainable Environments*, New York, St Martin's Press.

Congress of the United States (1990), *Carbon Charges as a Response to Global Warming: The Effects of Taxing Fossil Fuels*, Washington, D.C., Congressional Budget Office, August.

Cooper, R. (1985), 'International Economic Co-operation: Is It Desirable? Is It Likely?', *Bulletin of the American Academy of Arts and Sciences*, 39(2), 28–32.

Crowley, T. J. (1983), 'The Geologic Record of Climatic Change', *Review of Geophysics*, 21, 828–77.

Easterling, W. E. III, Parry, M., and Crosson, P. (1989), 'Adapting Future Agriculture to Changes in Climate', in N. J. Rosenberg *et al.* (eds.), *Greenhouse Warming: Abatement and Adaptation*, Washington D.C., Resources for the Future.

Ellsaesser, H. W. (1990), 'A Different View of the Climatic Effect of $CO_2$—Updated', *Atmósfera*, 3.

EPA (1988), 'The Potential Effects of Global Climate Change on the United States', draft report to the US Congress by J. B. Smith and D. A. Tirpak (eds.), Washington ,D.C., US Environment Protection Agency.

Fulkerson, W., Judkins, R., and Sanghvi, M. (1990), 'Energy from Fossil Fuels', *Scientific American*, 263(3), September.

Grubb, M. (1989), *The Greenhouse Effect: Negotiating Targets*, The Royal Institute of International Affairs, Section 5.1.

Hausman, J. A. (1979), 'Individual Discount Rates and the Purchase and Utilization of Energy-Using Durables', *Bell Journal of Economics*, 10, 33–54.

Hurrell, A. H. and Kingsbury, B. (eds.) (forthcoming), *The International Politics of the Environment*, Oxford, Oxford University Press.

IPCC (Intergovernmental Panel on Climate Change) (1990), Report Prepared by Working Group I, Policymakers Summary of the Scientific Assessment of Climate Change, June.

Leach, G. and Nowak, Z. (1990), 'Cutting Carbon Dioxide Emissions from Poland and the United Kingdom', Stockholm Environment Institute.

Leggett, J. (ed.) (1990), *Global Warming: The Greenpeace Report*, Oxford, Oxford University Press.

Lindzen, R. S. (1989), 'Greenhouse Warming: Science v. Consensus', in *Proceedings of the Mid-West Energy Conference*, Chicago.

— (forthcoming), 'Some Coolness Concerning Global Warming', *Bulletin of the American Meteorological Society*.

McClaren, A. S., Barry, R. G., and Bourke, R. H. (1990), 'Could Arctic Ice be Thinning?', *Nature*, 28 June, 345.

Manne, A. S. and Richels, R. R. (forthcoming), 'Buying Greenhouse Insurance', in *Global 2100: The Economic Costs of $CO_2$ Emission Limits*.

Markandya, A. and Pearce, D. (1988), 'Environmental Considerations and the Choice of the Discount Rate in Developing Countries', World Bank, Environmental Department Working Paper No. 3, May.

Mason, B. J. (1989), 'The Greenhouse Effect', *Contemporary Physics*, 30(6), 417–32.

Michaels, P. J. (1990), 'The Greenhouse Effect and Global Change; Review and Reappraisal', *International Journal of Environmental Studies*.

Mitchell, J. F. B. (1989), 'The "Greenhouse" Effect and Climate Change', *Review of Geophysics*, February.

Moran, J. M., Morgan, M. D., and Wiersma, J. H. (1986), *Introduction to Environmental Science*, 2nd edn., ch. 9, New York.

Nordhaus, W. D. (1990*a*), 'To Slow or Not to Slow: The Economics of the Greenhouse Effect', draft of February.

— (1990*b*), *Economic Policy Making in the Face of Global Warming*, paper presented to MIT Conference on Energy and the Environment, 9 March.

— (1990*c*), 'Economic Approaches to Greenhouse Warming', paper presented to Conference on Economic Policy Response to Global Warming, Rome, October.

Pearce, D. and Turner, R. K. (1990), *Economics of Natural Resources and the Environment*.

Pearce, D., Markandya, A., and Barbier, E. B. (1989), *Blueprint for a Green Economy*, Earthscan.

Pearson, M. and Smith, S. (1990), *Taxation and Environmental Policy*, Institute for Fiscal Studies, January.

Rosenberg, N. J. *et al.* (1989), *Greenhouse Warming: Abatement and Adaptation*, Washington, D.C., Resources for the Future.

Schelling, T. C. (1983), 'Climatic Change: Implications for Welfare and Policy', in *Changing Climate*, Report of the Carbon Dioxide Assessment Committee, Commission on Physical Sciences, Mathematics, and Resources, National Research Council, Washington, D.C., National Academy Press.

— (1990), 'Global Environmental Forces', in *Energy: Production, Consumption, and Consequences*, Washington, D.C., National Academy Press, 75–84.

— (1990), 'International Burden Sharing and Co-ordination: Prospects for Co-operative Approaches to Global Warming', paper to symposium on 'Economic Responses to Global Warming', Rome, October.

Skolnikoff, E. (1989), 'The Limits of Policy Processes: Responses to Climate Change', mimeo.

— (1990), 'The Policy Gridlock on Global Warming', *Foreign Policy*, 79.

Solow, A. R. (forthcoming, 1991), 'The Nonparametric Analysis of Point Process Data: The Freezing History of Lake Konstanz', *Journal of Climate*.

— and Broadus, J. M. (1989), 'On the Detection of Greenhouse Warming', *Climatic Change*, 15, 449–53.

— and — (forthcoming), 'Global Warming: Quo Vadis?', *Fletcher Forum*.

Turner, R. K. (1988), 'Wetland Conservation: Economics and Ethics', in D. Collard, D. Pearce, and D. Ulph (eds.), *Economics, Growth and Sustainable Environments*, New York, St Martin's Press.

Whalley, J. and Wigle, R. (1990), 'The International Incidence of Carbon Taxes', paper presented to Conference on Economic Responses to Global Warming, Rome, October.

White, R. (1990), 'The Great Climate Debate', *Scientific American*, July, 263(1).

# 4
# Economic Instruments for Environmental Regulation

*T. H. Tietenberg*

## 4.1 Introduction

As recently as a decade ago environmental regulators and lobbying groups with a special interest in environmental protection looked upon the market system as a powerful adversary. That the market unleashed powerful forces was widely recognized and that those forces clearly acted to degrade the environment was widely lamented. Conflict and confrontation became the battle cry for those groups seeking to protect the environment as they set out to block market forces whenever possible.

Among the more enlightened participants in the environmental policy process the air of confrontation and conflict has now begun to recede in many parts of the world. Leading environmental groups and regulators have come to realize that the power of the market can be harnessed and channelled toward the achievement of environmental goals, through an economic incentives approach to regulation. Forward-looking business people have come to appreciate the fact that cost-effective regulation can make them more competitive in the global market-place than regulations which impose higher than necessary control costs.

The change in attitude has been triggered by a recognition that this former adversary, the market, can be turned into a powerful ally. In contrast to the traditional regulatory approach, which makes mandatory particular forms of behaviour or specific technological choices, the economic incentive approach

Tom Tietenberg is Professor of Economics at Colby College, Maine.

allows more flexibility in how the environmental goal is reached. By changing the incentives an individual agent faces, the best private choice can be made to coincide with the best social choice. Rather than relying on the regulatory authority to identify the best course of action, the individual agent can use his or her typically superior information to select the best means of meeting an assigned emission-reduction responsibility. This flexibility achieves environmental goals at lower cost, which, in turn, makes the goals easier to achieve and easier to establish.

One indicator of the growing support for the use of economic incentive approaches for environmental control in the United States is the favourable treatment it has recently received both in the popular business[1] and environmental[2] press. Some public interest environmental organizations have now even adopted economic incentive approaches as a core part of their strategy for protecting the environment.[3]

In response to this support the emissions trading concept has recently been applied to reducing the lead content in petrol, to controlling both ozone depletion and non-point sources of water pollution, and was also prominently featured in the Bush administration proposals for reducing acid rain and smog unveiled in June 1989.

Our knowledge about economic-incentive approaches has grown rapidly in the two decades in which they have received serious analytical attention. Not only have the theoretical models become more focused and the empirical work more detailed, but we have now had over a decade of experience with emissions trading in the US and emission charges in Europe.

As the world community becomes increasingly conscious of both the need to tighten environmental controls and the local economic perils associated with tighter controls in a highly competitive global market-place, it seems a propitious time to stand back and to organize what we have learned about this practical and promising approach to pollution control that may be especially relevant to current circumstances. In this chapter I will draw upon economic theory, empirical studies, and actual experience with implementation to provide a brief overview of some of the major lessons we have learned about two economic-incentive approaches—emissions trading and emission charges—as well as their relationships to the more traditional regulatory policy.[4]

[1] See, for example, Main (1988).

[2] See, for example, Stavins (1989).

[3] See the various issues in Volume XX of the EDF Letter, a report to members of the Environmental Defense Fund.

[4] In the limited space permitted by this paper only a few highlights can be illustrated. All of the details of the proofs and the empirical work can be found in the references listed at the end of the paper. For a comprehensive summary of this work see Tietenberg (1980), Liroff (1980), Bohm and Russell (1985), Tietenberg (1985), Liroff (1986), Dudek and Palmisano (1988), Hahn (1989), Hahn and Hester (1989*a* and 1989*b*), and Tietenberg (1989*b*).

## 4.2 The Policy Context

*Emissions Trading*

Stripped to its bare essentials, the US Clean Air Act[5] relies upon a *command-and-control* approach to controlling pollution. Ambient standards establish the highest allowable concentration of the pollutant in the ambient air for each conventional pollutant. To reach these prescribed ambient standards, emission standards (legal emission ceilings) are imposed on a large number of specific emission points such as stacks, vents, or storage tanks. Following a survey of the technological options of control, the control authority selects a favoured control technology and calculates the amount of emission reduction achievable by that technology as the basis for setting the emission standard. Technologies yielding larger amounts of control (and, hence, supporting more stringent emission standards) are selected for new emitters and for existing emitters in areas where is it very difficult to meet the ambient standard. The responsibility for defining and enforcing these standards is shared in legislatively specified ways between the national government and the various state governments.

The emissions-trading programme attempts to inject more flexibility into the manner in which the objectives of the Clean Air Act are met by allowing sources a much wider range of choice in how they satisfy their legal pollution-control responsibilities than possible in the command-and-control approach. Any source choosing to reduce emissions at any discharge point more than required by its emission standard can apply to the control authority for certification of the excess control as an 'emission reduction credit' (ERC). Defined in terms of a specific amount of a particular pollutant, the certified emissions reduction credit can be used to satisfy emission standards at other (presumably more expensive to control) discharge points controlled by the creating source or it can be sold to other sources. By making these credits transferable, the US Environmental Protection Agency (EPA) has allowed sources to find the cheapest means of satisfying their requirements, even if the cheapest means are under the control of another firm. The ERC is the currency used in emissions trading, while the offset, bubble, emissions banking, and netting policies govern how this currency can be stored and spent.[6]

The *offset policy* requires major new or expanding sources in 'non-attainment' areas (those areas with air quality worse than the ambient standards) to

[5] The US Clean Air Act (42 U.S.C. 7401–642) was first passed in 1955. The central thrust of the approach described in this paragraph was initiated by the Clean Air Act Amendments of 1970 with mid-course corrections provided by the Clean Air Act Amendments of 1977.

[6] The details of this policy can be found in 'Emissions Trading Policy Statement' 51 *Federal Register* 43829 (4 December 1986).

secure sufficient offsetting emission reductions (by acquiring ERCs) from existing firms so that the air is cleaner after their entry or expansion than before.[7] Prior to this policy no new firms were allowed to enter non-attainment areas on the grounds they would interfere with attaining the ambient standards. By introducing the offset policy EPA allowed economic growth to continue while assuring progress toward attainment.

The *bubble policy* receives its unusual name from the fact that it treats multiple emission points controlled by existing emitters (as opposed to those expanding or entering an area for the first time) as if they were enclosed in a bubble. Under this policy only the total emissions of each pollutant leaving the bubble are regulated. While the total leaving the bubble must be not larger than the total permitted by adding up all the corresponding emission standards within the bubble (and in some cases the total must be 20 per cent lower), emitters are free to control some discharge points less than dictated by the corresponding emission standard as long as sufficient compensating ERCs are obtained from other discharge points within the bubble. In essence sources are free to choose the mix of control among the discharge points as long as the overall emission-reduction requirements are satisfied. Multi-plant bubbles are allowed, opening the possibility for trading ERCs among very different kinds of emitters.

*Netting* allows modifying or expanding sources (but not new sources) to escape from the need to meet the requirements of the rather stringent new-source review process (including the need to acquire offsets) so long as any net increase in emissions (counting any ERCs earned elsewhere in the plant) is below an established threshold. Insofar as it allows firms to escape particular regulatory requirements by using ERCs to remain under the threshold which triggers applicability, netting is more properly considered regulatory relief than regulatory reform.

*Emissions banking* allows firms to store certified ERCs for subsequent use in the offset, bubble, or netting programmes or for sale to others.

Although comprehensive data on the effects of the programme do not exist because substantial proportions of it are administered by local areas and no one collects information in a systematic way, some of the major aspects of the experience are clear.[8]

1. The programme has unquestionably and substantially reduced the costs of complying with the requirements of the Clean Air Act. Most estimates place the accumulated capital savings for all components of the programme at over $10 billion. This does not include the recurring savings in operating

[7] Offsets are also required for major modifications in areas which have attained the standards if the modifications jeopardize attainment.

[8] See, for example, Tietenberg (1985), Hahn and Hester (1989*a* and 1989*b*), and Dudek and Palmisano (1988).

cost. On the other hand the programme has not produced the magnitude of cost savings that was anticipated by its strongest proponents at its inception.

2. The level of compliance with the basic provisions of the Clean Air Act has increased. The emissions trading programme increased the possible means for compliance and sources have responded.
3. Somewhere between 7,000 and 12,000 trading transactions have been consummated. Each of these transactions was voluntary and for the participants represented an improvement over the traditional regulatory approach. Several of these transactions involved the introduction of innovative control technologies.
4. The vast majority of emissions trading transactions have involved large pollution sources trading emissions reduction credits either created by excess control of uniformly mixed pollutants (those for which the location of emission is not an important policy concern) or involving facilities in close proximity to one another.
5. Though air quality has certainly improved for most of the covered pollutants, it is virtually impossible to say how much of the improvement can be attributed to the emissions trading programme. The emissions trading programme complements the traditional regulatory approach, rather than replaces it. Therefore, while it can claim to have hastened compliance with the basic provisions of the Act and in some cases to have encouraged improvements beyond the Act, improved air quality resulted from the package taken together, rather than from any specific component.

### *Emissions Charges*

Emission charges are used in both Europe and Japan, though more commonly to control water pollution than air pollution.[9] Currently effluent charges are being used to control water pollution in France, Italy, Germany, and the Netherlands. In both France and the Netherlands the charges are designed to raise revenue for the purpose of funding activities specifically designed to improve water quality.

In Germany dischargers are required to meet minimum standards of waste water treatment for a number of defined pollutants. Simultaneously a fee is levied on every unit of discharge depending on the quantity and noxiousness of the effluent. Dischargers meeting or exceeding state-of-the-art effluent standards have to pay only half the normal rate.

The Italian effluent charge system was mainly designed to encourage polluters to achieve provisional effluent standards as soon as possible. The

[9] See Anderson (1977), Brown and Johnson (1984), Bressers (1988), Vos (1989), Opschoor and Vos (1989), and Sprenger (1989).

charge is nine times higher for firms that do not meet the prescribed standards than for firms that do meet them. This charge system was designed only to facilitate the transition to the prescribed standards so it is scheduled to expire once full compliance has been achieved.[10]

Air-pollution emission charges have been implemented by France and Japan. The French air-pollution charge was designed to encourage the early adoption of pollution-control equipment with the revenues returned to those paying the charge as a subsidy for installing the equipment. In Japan the emission charge is designed to raise revenue to compensate victims of air pollution. The charge rate is determined primarily by the cost of the compensation programme in the previous year and the amount of remaining emissions over which this cost can be applied *pro rata*.

Charges have also been used in Sweden to increase the rate at which consumers would purchase cars equipped with a catalytic converter. Cars not equipped with a catalytic converter were taxed, while new cars equipped with a catalytic converter were subsidized.

While data are limited a few highlights seem clear:

1. Economists typically envisage two types of effluent or emissions charges. The first, an efficiency charge, is designed to produce an efficient outcome by forcing the polluter to compensate completely for all damage caused. The second, a cost-effective charge, is designed to achieve a predefined ambient standard at the lowest possible control cost. In practice, few, if any, implemented programmes fit either of these designs.
2. Despite being designed mainly to raise revenue, effluent charges have typically improved water quality. Though the improvements in most cases have been small, apparently due to the low level at which the effluent charge rate is set, the Netherlands, with its higher effective rates, reports rather large improvements. Air pollution charges typically have not had much effect on air quality because the rates are too low and, in the case of France, most of the revenue is returned to the polluting sources.
3. The revenue from charges is typically earmarked for specific environmental purposes rather than contributed to the general revenue as a means of reducing the reliance on taxes that produce more distortions in resource allocation.
4. The Swedish tax on heavily polluting vehicles and subsidy for new low-polluting vehicles was very successful in introducing low-polluting vehicles into the automobile population at a much faster than normal rate. The policy was not revenue-neutral, however; owing to the success of the programme in altering vehicle choices, the subsidy payments greatly exceeded the tax revenue.

[10] The initial deadline for expiration was 1986, but it has since been postponed.

## 4.3 First Principles

Theory can help us understand the characteristics of these economic approaches in the most favourable circumstances for their use and assist in the process of designing the instruments for maximum effectiveness. Because of the dualistic nature of emission charges and emission-reduction credits,[11] implications about emission charges and emissions trading flow from the same body of theory.

Drawing conclusions about either of these approaches from this type of analysis, however, must be done with care because operational versions typically differ considerably from the idealized versions modelled by the theory. For example, not all trades that would be allowed in an ideal emissions-trading programme are allowed in the current US emissions-trading programme. Similarly the types of emissions charges actually imposed differ considerably from their ideal versions, particularly in the design of the rate structure and the process for adjusting rates over time.

Assuming all participants are cost-minimizers, a 'well-defined' emissions-trading or emission-charge system could cost-effectively allocate the control responsibility for meeting a predefined pollution target among the various pollution sources despite incomplete information on the control possibilities by the regulatory authorities.[12]

The intuition behind this powerful proposition is not difficult to grasp. Cost-minimizing firms seek to minimize the sum of (1) either ERC acquisition costs or payments of emission charges and (2) control costs. Minimization will occur when the marginal cost of control is set equal to the emission reduction credit price or the emission charge. Since all cost-minimizing sources would choose to control until their marginal control costs were equal to the same price or charge, marginal control costs would be equalized across all discharge points, precisely the condition required for cost-effectiveness.[13]

Emission charges could also sustain a cost-effective allocation of the control responsibility for meeting a predefined pollution target, but only if the control authority knew the correct level of the charge to impose or was willing to engage in an iterative trial-and-error process over time to find the correct level.

[11] Under fairly general conditions any allocation of control responsibility achieved by an emissions trading programme could also be achieved by a suitably designed system of emission charges and vice versa.

[12] For the formal demonstration of this proposition see Baumol and Oates (1975), Montgomery (1972), and Tietenberg (1985).

[13] It should be noted that while the allocation is cost-effective, it is not necessarily efficient (the amount of pollution indicated by a benefit–cost comparison). It would only be efficient if the predetermined target happened to coincide with the efficient amount of pollution. Nothing guarantees this outcome.

Emissions trading does not face this problem because the price level is established by the market, not the control authority.[14]

Though derived in the rarified world of theory, the practical importance of this theorem should not be underestimated. Economic-incentive approaches offer a unique opportunity for regulators to solve a fundamental dilemma. The control authorities' desire to allocate the responsibility for control cost-effectively is inevitably frustrated by a lack of information sufficient to achieve this objective. Economic-incentive approaches create a system of incentives in which those who have the best knowledge about control opportunities, the environmental managers for the industries, are encouraged to use that knowledge to achieve environmental objectives at minimum cost. Information barriers do not preclude effective regulation.

What constitutes a 'well-defined' emissions-trading or emission-charge system depends crucially on the attributes of the pollutant being controlled.[15]

To be consistent with a cost-effective allocation of the control responsibility, the policy instruments would have to be defined in different ways for different types of pollutants. Two differentiating characteristics are of particular relevance. Approaches designed to control pollutants which are uniformly mixed in the atmosphere (such as volatile organic compounds, one type of precursor for ozone formation) can be defined simply in terms of a rate of emissions flow per unit time. Economic-incentive approaches sharing this design characteristic are called *emission trades* or *emission charges*.

Instrument design is somewhat more difficult when the pollution target being pursued is defined in terms of concentrations measured at a number of specific receptor locations (such as particulates). In this case the cost-effective trade or charge design must take into account the *location* of the emissions (including injection height) as well as the *magnitude* of emissions. As long as the control authorities can define for each emitter a vector of transfer coefficients, which translate the effect of a unit increase of emissions by that emitter into an increase in concentration at each of the affected receptors, receptor-specific trades or charges can be defined which will allocate the responsibility cost-effectively. The design which is consistent with cost-effectiveness in this context is called an *ambient trade* or an *ambient charge*.

Unfortunately, while the design of the ambient ERC is not very complicated,[16] implementing the markets within which these ERCs would be traded is rather complicated. In particular for each unit of planned emissions an emitter would have to acquire separate ERCs for each affected receptor. When the

[14] See Tietenberg (1988) for a more detailed explanation of this point.

[15] For the technical details supporting this proposition see Montgomery (1972), and Tietenberg (1985).

[16] Each permit allows the holder to degrade the concentration level at the corresponding receptor by one unit.

number of receptors is large, the result is a rather complicated set of transactions. Similarly, establishing the correct rate structure for the charges in this context is particularly difficult because the set of charges which will satisfy the ambient air quality constraints is not unique; even a trial-and-error system would not necessarily result in the correct matrix of ambient charges being put into effect.

As long as markets are competitive and transactions costs are low, the trading benchmark in an emissions trading approach does not affect the ultimate cost-effective allocation of control responsibility. When markets are non-competitive or transactions costs are high, however, the final allocation of control responsibility is affected.[17] Emission charge approaches do not face this problem.

Once the control authority has decided how much pollution of each type will be allowed, it must then decide how to allocate the operating permits among the sources. In theory emission-reduction credits could either be auctioned off, with the sources purchasing them from the control authority at the market-clearing price, or (as in the US programme) created by the sources as surplus reductions over and above a predetermined set of emission standards. (Because this latter approach favours older sources over newer sources, it is known as 'grandfathering'.) The proposition suggests that either approach will ultimately result in a cost-effective allocation of the control responsibility among the various polluters as long as they are all price-takers, transactions costs are low, and ERCs are fully transferable. Any allocation of emission standards in a grandfathered approach is compatible with cost-effectiveness because the after-market in which firms can buy or sell ERCs corrects any problems with the initial allocation. This is a significant finding because it implies that under the right conditions the control authority can use this initial allocation of emissions standards to pursue distributional goals without interfering with cost-effectiveness.

When firms are price-setters rather than price-takers, however, cost-effectiveness will only be achieved if the control authority initially allocates the emission standards so a cost-effective allocation would be achieved even in the absence of any trading. (Implementing this particular allocation would, of course, require regulators to have complete information on control costs for all sources, an unlikely prospect.) In this special case cost-effectiveness would be achieved even in the presence of one or more price-setting firms because no trading would take place, eliminating the possibility of exploiting any market power.

For all other emission-standard assignments an active market would exist, offering the opportunity for price-setting behaviour. The larger is the deviation

[17] See Hahn (1984) for the mathematical treatment of this point. Further discussions can be found in Tietenberg (1985) and Misiolek and Elder (1989).

of the price-setting source's emission standard from its cost-effective allocation, the larger is the deviation of ultimate control costs from the least-cost allocation. When the price-setting source is initially allocated an insufficiently stringent emission standard, it can inflict higher control costs on others by withholding some ERCs from the market. When an excessively stringent emission standard is imposed on a price-setting source, however, it necessarily bears a higher control cost as the means of reducing demand (and, hence, prices) for the ERCs.

Similar problems exist when transactions costs are high. High transactions costs preclude or reduce trading activity by diminishing the gains from trade. When the costs of consummating a transaction exceed its potential gains, the incentive to participate in emissions trading is lost.

## 4.4 Lessons from Empirical Research

A vast majority, though not all, of the relevant empirical studies have found the control costs to be substantially higher with the regulatory command-and-control system than the least-cost means of allocating the control responsibility.

While theory tells us unambiguously that the command-and-control system will not be cost-effective except by coincidence, it cannot tell us the magnitude of the excess costs. The empirical work cited in Table 1 adds the important information that the excess costs are typically very large.[18] This is an important finding because it provides the motivation for introducing a reform programme; the potential social gains (in terms of reduced control cost) from breaking away from the status quo are sufficient to justify the trouble. Although the estimates of the excess costs attributable to a command and control presented in Table 4.1 overstate the cost savings that would be achieved by even an ideal economic incentive approach (a point discussed in more detail below), the general conclusion that the potential cost savings from adopting economic-incentive approaches are large seems accurate even after correcting for overstatement.

Economic-incentive approaches which raise revenue (charges or auction ERC markets) offer an additional benefit—they allow the revenue raised from these policies to substitute for revenue raised in more traditional ways. Whereas it is well known that traditional revenue-raising approaches distort resource allocation, producing inefficiency, economic-incentive approaches enhance efficiency. Some empirical work based on the US economy suggests that

[18] A value of 1.0 in the last column of Table 4.1 would indicate that the traditional regulatory approach was cost-effective. A value of 4.0 would indicate that the traditional regulatory approach results in an allocation of the control responsibility which is four times as expensive as necessary to reach the stipulated pollution target.

**Table 4.1** *Empirical Studies of Air Pollution Control*

| *Study* | *Pollutants covered* | *Geographic area* | *CAC benchmark* | *Ratio of CAC cost to least cost* |
|---|---|---|---|---|
| Atkinson and Lewis | Particulates | St Louis | SIP regulations | 6.00[a] |
| Roach *et al.* | Sulphur dioxide | Four corners in Utah | SIP regulations Colorado, Arizona, and New Mexico | 4.25 |
| Hahn and Noll | Sulphates standards | Los Angeles | California emission | 1.07 |
| Krupnick | Nitrogen dioxide regulations | Baltimore | Proposed RACT | 5.96[b] |
| Seskin *et al.* | Nitrogen dioxide regulations | Chicago | Proposed RACT | 14.40[b] |
| McGartland | Particulates | Baltimore | SIP regulations | 4.18 |
| Spofford | Sulphur Dioxide | Lower Delaware Valley | Uniform percentage regulations | 1.78 |
| | Particulates | Lower Delaware Valley | Uniform percentage regulations | 22.00 |
| Harrison | Airport noise | United States | Mandatory retrofit | 1.72[c] |
| Maloney and Yandle | Hydrocarbons | All domestic DuPont plants | Uniform percentage reduction | 4.15[d] |
| Palmer *et al.* | CFC emissions from non-aerosol applications | United States | Proposed emission standards | 1.96 |

*Notes*:

CAC = command and control, the traditional regulatory approach.

SIP = state implementation plan.

RACT = reasonably available control technologies, a set of standards imposed on existing sources in non-attainment areas.

[a] Based on a 40 μg/m³ at worst receptor.

[b] Based on a short-term, one-hour average of 250 μg/m³.

[c] Because it is a benefit–cost study instead of a cost-effectiveness study, the Harrison comparison of the command-and-control approach with the least-cost allocation involves different benefit levels. Specifically, the benefit levels associated with the least-cost allocation are only 82% of those associated with the command-and-control allocation. To produce cost estimates based on more comparable benefits, as a first approximation the least-cost allocation was divided by 0.82 and the resulting number was compared with the command-and-control cost.

[d] Based on 85% reduction of emissions from all sources.

substituting economic-incentive means of raising revenue for more traditional means could produce significant efficiency gains.[19]

When high degrees of control are necessary, ERC prices or charge levels would be correspondingly high. The financial outlays associated with acquiring ERCs in an auction market or paying charges on uncontrolled emissions would be sufficiently large that sources would typically have lower financial burdens with the traditional command-and-control approach than with these particular economic-incentive approaches. Only a 'grandfathered' trading system would guarantee that sources would be no worse off than under the command-and-control system.[20]

Financial burden is a significant concern in a highly competitive global market-place. Firms bearing large financial burdens would be placed at a competitive disadvantage when forced to compete with firms not bearing those burdens. Their costs would be higher.

From the point of view of the source required to control its emissions, two components of financial burden are significant: (1) control costs and (2) expenditures on permits or emission charges. While only the former represent real resource costs to society as a whole (the latter are merely transferred from one group in society to another), both represent a financial burden to the source. The empirical evidence suggests that when an auction market is used to distribute ERCs (or, equivalently, when all uncontrolled emissions are subject to an emissions charge), the ERC expenditures (charge outlays) would frequently be larger in magnitude than the control costs; the sources would spend more on ERCs (or pay more in charges) than they would on the control equipment. Under the traditional command-and-control system firms make no financial outlays to the government. Although control costs are necessarily higher with the command-and-control system than with an economic-incentive approach, they are not so high as to outweigh the additional financial outlays required in an auction-market permit system (or an emissions-tax system). For this reason existing sources could be expected vehemently to oppose an auction market or emission charges despite their social appeal, unless the revenue derived is used in a manner which is approved by the sources, and the sources with which it competes are required to absorb similar expenses. When environmental policies are not co-ordinated across national boundaries, this latter condition would be particularly difficult to meet.

In the absence of either a politically popular way to use the revenue or assurances that competitors will face similar financial burdens, this political opposition could be substantially reduced by grandfathering. Under

[19] See Terkla (1984).

[20] See Atkinson and Tietenberg (1982, 1984), Hahn (1984), Harrison ( 1983), Krupnick (1986), Lyon (1982), Palmer *et al.*(1980), Roach *et al.* (1981), Seskin *et al.* (1983), and Shapiro and Warhit (1983) for the individual studies, and Tietenberg (1985) for a summary of the evidence.

grandfathering, sources have only to purchase any additional ERCs they may need to meet their assigned emission standard (as opposed to purchasing sufficient ERCs or paying charges to cover all uncontrolled emissions in an auction market). Grandfathering is *de facto* the approach taken in the US emissions-trading programme.

Grandfathering has its disadvantages. Because ERCs become very valuable, especially in the face of stringent air-quality regulations, sources selling emission-reduction credits would be able to command very high prices. By placing heavy restrictions on the amount of emissions, the control authority is creating wealth for existing firms *vis-à-vis* new firms.

Although reserving some ERCs for new firms is possible (by assigning more stringent emission standards than needed to reach attainment and using the 'surplus' air quality to create government-held ERCs), this option is rarely exercised in practice. In the United States, under the offset policy, firms typically have to purchase sufficient ERCs to more than cover all uncontrolled emissions, while existing firms only have to purchase enough to comply with their assigned emission standard. Thus grandfathering imposes a bias against new sources in the sense that their financial burden is greater than that of an otherwise identical existing source, even if the two sources install exactly the same emission-control devices. This new source bias could retard the introduction of new facilities and new technologies by reducing the cost advantage of building new facilities which embody the latest innovations.

While it is clear from theory that larger trading areas offer the opportunities for larger potential cost savings in an emissions-trading programme, some empirical work suggests that substantial savings can be achieved in emissions trading even when the trading areas are rather small.

The point of this finding is *not* that small trading areas are fine; they do retard progress toward the standard. Rather, when political considerations allow only small trading areas or nothing, emissions trading still can play a significant role.

Sometimes political considerations demand a trading area which is smaller than the ideal design. Whether large trading areas are essential for the effective use of this policy is therefore of some relevance. In general, the larger the trading area, the larger would be the potential cost savings due to a wider set of cost-reduction opportunities that would become available. The empirical question is how sensitive the cost estimates are to the size of the trading areas.

One study of utilities found that even allowing a plant to trade among discharge points within that plant could save from 30 to 60 per cent of the costs of complying with new sulphur-oxide-reduction regulations, compared to a situation where no trading whatsoever was permitted.[21] Expanding the trading

[21] ICF, Inc. (1989).

possibilities to other utilities within the same state permitted a further reduction of 20 per cent, while allowing interstate trading permitted another 15 per cent reduction in costs. If this study is replicated in other circumstances, it would appear that even small trading areas offer the opportunity for significant cost reduction.[22]

Although only a few studies of the empirical impact of market power on emissions trading have been accomplished, their results are consistent with a finding that market power does not seem to have a large effect on regional control costs in most realistic situations.[23]

Even in areas having especially stringent controls, the available evidence suggests that price manipulation is not a serious problem. In an auction market the price-setting source reduces its financial burden by purchasing fewer ERCs in order to drive the price down. To compensate for the smaller number of ERCs purchased, the price-setting source must spend more on controlling its own pollution, limiting the gains from price manipulation. Although these actions could have a rather large impact on *regional financial burden*, they would under normal circumstances have a rather small effect on *regional control costs*. Estimates typically suggest that control costs would rise by less than 1 per cent if market power were exercised by one or more firms.

It should not be surprising that price manipulation could have rather dramatic effects on regional financial burden in an auction market, since the cost of *all* ERCs is affected, not merely those purchased by the price-setting source. The perhaps more surprising result is that control costs are quite insensitive to price-setting behaviour. This is due to the fact that the only control-cost change is the net difference between the new larger control burden borne by the price searcher and the correspondingly smaller burden borne by the sources having larger than normal allocations of permits. Only the costs of the marginal units are affected.

Within the class of grandfathered distribution rules, some emission-standard allocations create a larger potential for strategic price behaviour than others. In general the larger the divergence between the control responsibility assigned to the price-searching source by the emission standards and the cost-effective allocation of control responsibility, the larger the potential for market power. When allocated too little responsibility by the control authority, price-searching firms can exercise power on the selling side of the market, and when allocated too much, they can exercise power on the buying side of the market.

According to the existing studies it takes a rather considerable divergence from the cost-effective allocation of control responsibility to produce much

[22] As indicated below, the fact that so many emissions trades have actually taken place within the same plant or among contiguous plants provides some confirmation for this result.

[23] For individual studies see de Lucia (1974), Hahn (1984), Stahl, Bergman, and Mäler (1988), and Maloney and Yandle (1984). For a survey of the evidence see Tietenberg (1985).

difference in regional control costs. In practice the deviations from the least-cost allocation caused by market power pale in comparison to the much larger potential cost reductions achievable by implementing emissions trading.[24]

## 4.5 Lessons from Implementation

Though the number of transactions consummated under the Emissions Trading Program has been large, it has been smaller than expected. Part of this failure to fulfil expectations can be explained as the result of unrealistically inflated expectations. More restrictive regulatory decisions than expected and higher than expected transaction costs also bear some responsibility.

The models used to calculate the potential cost savings were not (and are not) completely adequate guides to reality. The cost functions in these models are invariably *ex ante* cost functions. They implicitly assume that the modelled plant can be built from scratch and can incorporate the best technology. In practice, of course, many existing sources cannot retrofit these technologies and therefore their *ex post* control options are much more limited than implied by the models.

The models also assume all trades are multilateral and are simultaneously consummated, whereas actual trades are usually bilateral and sequential. The distinction is important for non-uniformly mixed pollutants;[25] bilateral trades frequently are constrained by regulatory concerns about decreasing air quality at the site of the acquiring source. Because multilateral trades would typically incorporate compensating reductions coming from other nearby sources, these concerns normally do not arise when trades are multilateral and simultaneous. In essence the models implicitly assume an idealized market process, which is only remotely approximated by actual transactions.

In addition some non-negligible proportion of the expected cost savings recorded by the models for non-uniformly mixed pollutants is attributable to the substantially larger amounts of emissions allowed by the modelled permit equilibrium.[26] For example, the cost estimates imply that the control authority is allowed to arrange the control responsibility in *any* fashion that satisfies the ambient air quality standards. In practice the models allocate more uncontrolled emissions to sources with tall stacks because those emissions can be exported.

[24] Strategic price behaviour is not the only potential source of market-power problems. Firms could conceivably use permit markets to drive competitors out of business. See Misiolek and Elder (1989). For an analysis which concludes that this problem is relatively rare and can be dealt with on a case-by-case basis should it arise, see Tietenberg (1985).

[25] See Tietenberg and Atkinson (1989) for a demonstration that this is an empirically significant point.

[26] This is demonstrated in Atkinson and Tietenberg (1987).

Exported emissions avoid control costs without affecting the readings at the local monitors. That portion of the cost savings estimated by the models in Table 4.1 which is due to allowing increased emissions is not acceptable to regulators. Some recent work has suggested that the benefits received from the additional emission control required by the command-and-control approach may be justified by the net benefits received.[27] The regulatory refusal to allow emission increases was apparently consistent with efficiency,[28] but it was not consistent with the magnitiude of cost savings anticipated by the models.

Certain types of trades assumed permissible by the models are prohibited by actual trading rules. New sources, for example, are not allowed to satisfy the New Source Performance Standards (which imply a particular control technology) by choosing some less stringent control option and making up the difference with acquired emission-reduction credits; they must install the degree of technological control necessary to meet the standard. Typically this is the same technology used by EPA to define the standard in the first place.

A lot of uncertainty is associated with emission-reduction credit transactions since they depend so heavily on administrative action. All trades must be approved by the control authorities. If the authorities are not co-operative or at least consistent, the value of the created emission-reduction credits could be diminished or even destroyed.

For non-uniformly mixed pollutants, trades between geographically separated sources will only be approved after dispersion modelling has been accomplished by the applicants. Not only is this modelling expensive, it frequently ends up raising questions which ultimately lead to the transaction being denied. Few trades requiring this modelling have been consummated.

Trading activity has also been inhibited by the paucity of emission banks. The US system allows states to establish emission banks, but does not require them to do so. As of 1986 only seven of the fifty states had established these banks. For sources in the rest of the states the act of creating emission credits is undervalued because the credits cannot be legally held for future use. The supply of emission-reduction credits is hence less than would be estimated by the models.

The Emissions Trading Program seems to have worked particularly well for trades involving uniformly mixed pollutants and for trades of non-uniformly mixed pollutants involving contiguous discharge points.

[27] See Oates, Portney, and McGartland (1988).

[28] Not all of the cost savings, of course, is due to the capability to increase emissions. The remaining portion of the savings, which is due to taking advantage of opportunities to control a given level of emissions at a lower cost, is still substantial and can be captured by a well-designed permit system which does not allow emissions to increase beyond the command-and-control benchmark. See the calculations in Atkinson and Tietenberg (1987).

It is not surprising that most consummated trades have been internal (where the buyer and seller share a common corporate parent) rather than external. Not only are the uncertainties associated with inter-firm transfers avoided, but most internal trades involve contiguous facilities. Trades between contiguous facilities do not trigger a requirement for dispersion modelling.[29]

It is also not surprising that the plurality of consummated trades involve volatile organic compounds, which are uniformly mixed pollutants. Since dispersion modelling is not required for uniformly mixed pollutants even when the trading sources are somewhat distant from one another, trades involving these pollutants are cheaper to consummate. Additionally emissions trades involving uniformly mixed pollutants do not jeopardize local air quality since the location of the emissions is not a matter of policy consequence.

The establishment of the Emissions Trading Program has encouraged technological progress in pollution control. Although generally the degree of progress has been modest, it has been more dramatic in areas where emission reductions have been sufficiently stringent as to restrict the availability of emission-reduction credits created by more traditional means.[30]

Theory would lead us to expect more technological progress with emissions trading than with a command-and-control policy because it changes the incentives so drastically. Under a command-and-control approach technological changes discovered by the control authority typically lead to more stringent standards (and higher costs) for the sources. Sources have little incentive to innovate and a good deal of incentive to hide potential innovations from the control authority. With emissions trading, on the other hand, innovations allowing excess reductions create saleable emission-reduction credits.

The evidence suggests that the expectations based on this theory have been borne out to a limited degree in the operating programme. The most prominent example of technological change has been the substitution of water-based solvents for solvents containing volatile organic compounds. Though somewhat more expensive, this substitution made economic sense once the programme was introduced.

It should probably not be surprising that the number of new innovations stimulated by the programme is rather small. As long as cheaper ways of creating credits within existing processes (fuel substitution, for example) are available, it would be unreasonable to expect large investments in new technologies with unproven reliabilities. On the other hand as the degree of control rises and the supply of readily available credits dries up, the demand for

[29] The fact that so many trades have taken place between contiguous discharge points serves as confirmation that substantial savings can be achieved even if the geographic boundaries of the trading area are quite restricted.

[30] For more details see Tietenberg (1985), Maleug (1989), and Dudek and Palmisano (1988).

new technologies would be expected to rise as well. This expectation seems to have been borne out in those areas where unusually low air quality or stringent regulatory rules have served to limit the available credits.[31]

This is an important point. Those who fail to consider the dynamic advantages of an economic-incentive approach sometimes suggest that if few credits would be traded, implementing a system of this type has no purpose. In fact it has a substantial purpose—the encouragement of new technologies to meet the increasingly stringent standards.

Introducing the Emissions Trading Program has provided an opportunity to control sources which can reduce emissions relatively cheaply, but which under the traditional policy were under-regulated due to either their financially precarious position or the fact that they were not subject to regulation.[32]

Due to the social distress caused by any resulting unemployment, the control authorities and the courts are understandably reluctant to enforce stringent emission standards against firms which would not be able to pass higher costs on to customers without considerable loss of production. Since many of these sources could control emissions at a lower marginal cost than other sources, their political immunity from control makes regional control costs higher than necessary; other sources have to control their own emissions to a higher degree (at a higher marginal cost) to compensate.

Due to its ability to separate the issue of who pays for the reduction from the issue of which discharge points are to be controlled, the emissions-trading programme provides a way to secure those low cost reductions. The command-and-control policy would assign, as normal, a very low (perhaps zero) emission reduction to any previously unregulated firm. Once emissions trading had been established, however, it would be in the interest of this firm to control emissions further, selling the resulting emission-reduction credits. As long as the revenues from the sale at least covered the cost, this transaction could profit, or at least not hurt, the seller. Because these reductions could be achieved at a lower cost than ratcheting up the degree of control on already heavily controlled sources, non-immune sources would find purchasing the credits cheaper than controlling their own emissions to a higher degree. Everyone benefits from controlling these previously under-regulated sources.

Another unique attribute of an emissions-trading approach is the capability it offers sources for leasing credits.[33]

Leasing offers an enormously useful degree of flexibility which is not available with other policy approaches to pollution control. The usefulness of leasing derives from the fact that some sources, utilities in particular, have

[31] For the experience in California see Dudek and Palmisano (1988).

[32] See Tietenberg (1985).

[33] See Feldman and Raufer (1987) and Tietenberg (1989*a*).

patterns of emission that vary over time while allowable emissions remain constant. In a typical situation, for example, suppose an older utility would, in the absence of control, be emitting heavily. In the normal course of a utility expansion cycle the older plant would subsequently experience substantially reduced emissions when the utility constructed a new plant and shifted a major part of the load away from the older plant to the new plant. Ultimately growth in demand on the system would increase the emissions again for the older plant as its capacity would once again be needed. The implication of this temporal pattern is that during the middle period, as its own emissions fell well below allowable emissions, this utility could lease excess emission credits to another facility, recalling them as its own need rose with demand growth. Indeed one empirical study of the pattern of the utility demand for and supply of acid-rain-reduction credits over time suggests that leasing is a critical component of any cost-effective control strategy, a component that neither the traditional approach nor emission charges can offer.[34]

Leasing also provides a way for about-to-be-retired sources to participate in the reduction programme. Under the traditional approach once the deadline for compliance had been reached the utility would either have to retire the unit early or to install expensive control equipment which would be rendered useless once the unit was retired. By leasing credits for the short period to retirement, the unit could remain in compliance without taking either of those drastic steps; it would, however, be sharing in the cost of installing the extra equipment in the leasing utility. Leased credits facilitate an efficient transition into the new regime of more stringent controls.

Unless the process to determine the level of an effluent or emissions charge includes some automatic means of temporal adjustment, the tendency is for the real rate (adjusted for inflation) to decline over time.[35] This problem is particularly serious in areas with economic growth where increasing real rates would be the desired outcome.

In contrast to emissions trading where ERC prices respond automatically to changing market conditions, emission charges have to be determined by an administrative process. When the function of the charge is to raise revenue for a particular purpose, charge rates will be determined by the costs of achieving that purpose; when the costs of achieving the purpose rise, the level of the charge must rise to secure the additional revenue.[36]

Sometimes that process produces an unintended dynamic. In Japan, for example, the charge is calculated on the basis of the amount of compensation paid to victims of air pollution in the previous year. While the amount of

[34] Feldman and Raufer (1987).

[35] For further information see Vos (1989) and Sprenger (1989).

[36] While it is theoretically possible (depending on the elasticity of demand for pollution abatement) for a rise in the tax to produce less revenue, this has typically not been the case.

compensation has been increasing, the amount of emissions (the base to which the charge is applied) has been decreasing. As a result unexpectedly high charge rates are necessary in order to raise sufficient revenue for the compensation system.

In countries where the tax revenue feeds into the general budget, increases in the level of the charge require a specific administrative act. Evidently it is difficult to raise these rates in practice, since charges have commonly even failed to keep pace with inflation, much less growth in the number of sources. The unintended result is eventual environmental deterioration.

## 4.6 Concluding Comments

Our experience with economic-incentive programmes has demonstrated that they have had, and can continue to have, a positive role in environmental policy in the future. I would submit the issue is no longer *whether* they have a role to play, but rather *what kind* of role they should play. The available experience with operating versions of these programmes allows us to draw some specific conclusions which facilitate defining the boundaries for the optimal use of economic-incentive approaches in general and for distinguishing the emissions-trading and emission-charges approaches in particular.

Emissions trading integrates particularly smoothly into any policy structure which is based either directly (through emission standards) or indirectly (through mandated technology or input limitations) on regulating emissions. In this case emission limitations embedded in the operating licences can serve as the trading benchmark if grandfathering is adopted.

Emissions charges work particularly well when transactions costs associated with bargaining are high. It appears that much of the trading activity in the United States has involved large corporations. Emissions trading is probably not equally applicable to large and small pollution sources. The transaction costs are sufficiently high that only large trades can absorb them without jeopardizing the gains from trade. For this reason charges seem a more appropriate instrument when sources are individually small, but numerous (such as residences or automobiles). Charges also work well as a device for increasing the rate of adoption of new technologies and for raising revenue to subsidize environmentally benign projects.

Emissions trading seems to work especially well for uniformly mixed pollutants. No diffusion modelling is necessary and regulators do not have to worry about trades creating 'hot spots' or localized areas of high pollution concentration. Trades can be on a one-to-one basis.

Because emissions trading allows the issue of who will pay for the control to be separated from who will install the control, it introduces an additional degree of flexibility. This flexibility is particularly important in non-attainment areas since marginal control costs are so high. Sources which would not normally be controlled because they could not afford to implement the controls without going out of business, can be controlled with emissions trading. The revenue derived from the sale of emission-reduction credits can be used to finance the controls, effectively preventing bankruptcy.

Because it is quantity-based, emissions trading also offers a unique possibility for leasing. Leasing is particularly valuable when the temporal pattern of emissions varies across sources. As discussed above this appears generally to be the case with utilities. When a firm plans to shut down one plant in the near future and to build a new one, leasing credits is a vastly superior alternative to the temporary installation of equipment in the old plant which would be useless when the plant was retired. The useful life of this temporary control equipment would be wastefully short.

We have also learned that ERC transactions have higher administrative costs than we previously understood. Regulators must validate every trade. When non-uniformly mixed pollutants are involved, the transactions costs associated with estimating the air-quality effects are particularly high. Delegating responsibility for trade approval to lower levels of government may in principle speed up the approval process, but unless the bureaucrats in the lower level of government support the programme the gain may be negligible.

Emissions trading places more importance on the operating permits and emissions inventories than other approaches. To the extent those are deficient the potential for trades that protect air quality may be lost. Firms which have actual levels of emissions substantially below allowable emissions find themselves with a trading opportunity which, if exploited, could degrade air quality. The trading benchmark has to be defined carefully.

There can be little doubt that the emissions-trading programme in the US has improved upon the command-and-control programme that preceded it. The documented cost savings are large and the flexibility provided has been important. Similarly emissions charges have achieved their own measure of success in Europe. To be sure the programmes are far from perfect, but the flaws should be kept in perspective. In no way should they overshadow the impressive accomplishments. Although economic-incentive approaches lose their Utopian lustre upon closer inspection, they have none the less made a lasting contribution to environmental policy.

The role for economic-incentive approaches should grow in the future if for no other reason than the fact that the international pollution problems which are currently commanding centre-stage fall within the domains where economic-incentive policies have been most successful.[37] Significantly many of the

[37] For an explanation of this point, see Tietenberg (1991).

problems of the future, such as reducing tropospheric ozone, preventing stratospheric ozone depletion, moderating global warming, and increasing acid-rain control, involve pollutants that can be treated as uniformly mixed, facilitating the use of economic incentives. In addition larger trading areas facilitate greater cost reductions than smaller trading areas. This also augers well for the use of emissions trading as part of the strategy to control many future pollution problems because the natural trading areas are all very large indeed. Acid rain, stratospheric ozone depletion, and greenhouse gases could (indeed should!) involve trading areas that transcend national boundaries. For greenhouse and ozone-depletion gases, the trading areas should be global in scope. Finally, it seems clear that the pivotal role of carbon dioxide in global warming may require some fairly drastic changes in energy use, including changes in personal transportation, and ultimately land-use patterns. Some form of charges could play an important role in facilitating this transformation.

We live in an age when the call for tighter environmental controls intensifies with each new discovery of yet another injury modern society is inflicting on the planet. But resistance to additional controls is also growing with the recognition that compliance with each new set of controls is more expensive than the last. While economic-incentive approaches to environmental control offer no panacea, they frequently do offer a practical way to achieve environmental goals more flexibly and at lower cost than more traditional regulatory approaches. That is a compelling virtue.

## Bibliography


Anderson, F. R. *et al.*(1977), *Environmental Improvement through Economic Incentives*, Baltimore, Johns Hopkins University Press for Resources for the Future.

Atkinson, S. E. and Lewis, D. H. (1974), 'A Cost-Effectiveness Analysis of Alternative Air Quality Control Strategies', *Journal of Environmental Economics and Management*, 1, 237–50.

— and Tietenberg, T. H. (1982), 'The Empirical Properties of Two Classes of Designs for Transferable Discharge Permit Markets', *Journal of Environmental Economics and Management*, 9, 101–21.

— and — (1984), 'Approaches for Reaching Ambient Standards in Non-Attainment Areas: Financial Burden and Efficiency Considerations', *Land Economics*, 60, 148–59.

— and — (1987), 'Economic Implications of Emission Trading Rules for Local and Regional Pollutants', *Canadian Journal of Economics*, 20, 370–86.

Baumol, W. J. and Oates, W. E. (1975), *The Theory of Environmental Policy*, Englewood Cliffs, N.J., Prentice-Hall.

Bohm, P. and Russell, C. (1985), 'Comparative Analysis of Alternative Policy Instruments', in A. V. Kneese and J. L. Sweeney (eds.), *Handbook of Natural Resource and Energy Economics*, Vol. 1, Amsterdam, North-Holland, 395–460.

Bressers, H. T. A. (1988), 'A Comparison of the Effectiveness of Incentives and Directives: The Case of Dutch Water Quality Policy', *Policy Studies Review*, 7, 500–18.

Brown, G. M. Jr and Johnson, R. W. (1984), 'Pollution Control by Effluent Charges: It Works in the Federal Republic of Germany, Why Not in the United States?', *Natural Resources Journal*, 24, 929–66.

de Lucia, R. J. (1974), *An Evaluation of Marketable Effluent Permit Systems*, Report No. EPA–600/5–74–030 to the US Environmental Protection Agency (September).

Dudek, D. J. and Palmisano, J. (1988), 'Emissions Trading: Why is this Thoroughbred Hobbled?', *Columbia Journal of Environmental Law*, 13, 217–56.

Feldman, S. L. and Raufer, R. K. (1987), *Emissions Trading and Acid Rain Implementing a Market Approach to Pollution Control*, Totowa, N.J., Rowman & Littlefield.

Hahn, R. W. (1984), 'Market Power and Transferable Property Rights', *Quarterly Journal of Economics*, 99, 753–65.

— (1989), 'Economic Prescriptions for Environmental Problems: How the Patient Followed the Doctor's Orders', *Journal of Economic Perspectives*, 3, 95–114.

— and Noll, R. G. (1982), 'Designing a Market for Tradeable Emission Permits', in W. A. Magat (ed.), *Reform of Environmental Regulation*, Cambridge, Mass., Ballinger.

— and Hester, G. L. (1989*a*), 'Where Did All the Markets Go? An Analysis of EPA's Emission Trading Program', *Yale Journal of Regulation*, 6, 109–53.

— and — (1989*b*), 'Marketable Permits: Lessons from Theory and Practice', *Ecology Law Quarterly*, 16, 361–406.

Harrison, D. Jr (1983), 'Case Study 1: The Regulation of Aircraft Noise', in Thomas C. Schelling (ed.), *Incentives for Environmental Protection*, Cambridge, Mass., MIT Press.

ICF Resources, Inc. (1989), 'Economic, Environmental, and Coal Market Impacts of $SO_2$ Emissions Trading under Alternative Acid Rain Control Proposals', a report prepared for the Regulatory Innovations Staff, USEPA (March).

Krupnick, A. J. (1986), 'Costs of Alternative Policies for the Control of Nitrogen Dioxide in Baltimore', *Journal of Environmental Economics and Management*, 13, 189–97.

Liroff, R. A. (1980), *Air Pollution Offsets: Trading, Selling and Banking*, Washington, D.C., Conservation Foundation.

— (1986), *Reforming Air Pollution Regulation: The Toil and Trouble of EPA's Bubble*, Washington, D.C., Conservation Foundation.

Lyon, R. M. (1982), 'Auctions and Alternative Procedures for Allocating Pollution Rights', *Land Economics*, 58, 16–32.

McGartland, A. M. (1984), 'Marketable Permit Systems for Air Pollution Control: An Empirical Study', Ph.D. dissertation, University of Maryland.

Main, J. (1988), 'Here Comes the Big Cleanup', *Fortune*, 21 November, 102.

Maleug, David A. (1989), 'Emission Trading and the Incentive to Adopt New Pollution Abatement Technology', *Journal of Environmental Economics and Management*, 16, 52–7.

Maloney, M. T. and Yandle, B. (1984), 'Estimation of the Cost of Air Pollution Control Regulation', *Journal of Environmental Economics and Management*, 11, 244–63.

Misiolek, W. S. and Elder, H. W. (1989), 'Exclusionary Manipulation of Markets for Pollution Rights', *Journal of Environmental Economics and Management*, 16, 156–66.

Montgomery, W. D. (1972), 'Markets in Licences and Efficient Pollution Control Programs', *Journal of Economic Theory*, 5, 395–418.

Oates, W. E., Portney, P. R., and McGartland, A. M. (1988), 'The Net Benefits of Incentive-Based Regulation: The Case of Environmental Standard Setting in the Real World', Resources for the Future Working Paper (December).

Opschoor, J. B. and Vos, H. B. (1989), *The Application of Economic Instruments for Environmental Protection in OECD Countries*, Paris, OECD.

Palmer, A. R., Mooz, W. E., Quinn, T. H., and Wolf, K. A. (1980), *Economic Implications of Regulating Chlorofluorocarbon Emissions from Nonaerosol Applications*, Report No. R–2524–EPA prepared for the US Environmental Protection Agency by the Rand Corporation (June).

Roach F., Kolstad, C., Kneese, A. V., Tobin, R., and Williams, M. (1981), 'Alternative Air Quality Policy Options in the Four Corners Region', *Southwestern Review*, 1, 29–58.

Seskin, E. P., Anderson, R. J. Jr, and Reid, R. O. (1983), 'An Empirical Analysis of Economic Strategies for Controlling Air Pollution', *Journal of Environmental Economics and Management*, 10, 112–24.

Shapiro, M. and Warhit, E. (1983) 'Marketable Permits: The Case of Chlorofluorocarbons', *Natural Resource Journal*, **23**, 577–91.

Spofford, W. O. Jr (1984), 'Efficiency Properties of Alternative Source Control Policies for Meeting Ambient Air Quality Standards: An Empirical Application to the Lower Deleware Valley', Discussion Paper D–118, Washington, D.C., Resources for the Future (November).

Sprenger, R. U. (1989), 'Economic Incentives in Environmental Policies: The Case of West Germany', a paper presented at the Symposium on Economic Instruments in Environmental Protection Policies, Stockholm, Sweden (June).

Stahl, I., Bergman, L., and Mäler, K. G. (1988), 'An Experimental Game on Marketable Emission Permits for Hydro-Carbons in the Gothenburg Area', Research Paper No. 6359, Stockholm School of Economics (December).

Stavins, R. N. (1989), 'Harnessing Market Forces to Protect the Environment', *Environment*, **31**, 4–7, 28–35.

Terkla, D. (1984), 'The Efficiency Value of Effluent Tax Revenues', *Journal of Environmental Economics and Management*, 11, 107–23.

Tietenberg, T. H. (1980), 'Transferable Discharge Permits and the Control of Stationary Source Air Pollution: A Survey and Synthesis', *Land Economics*, 56, 391–416.

— (1985), *Emissions Trading: An Exercise in Reforming Pollution Policy*, Washington, D.C., Resources for the Future.

— (1988), *Environmental and Natural Resource Economics*, 2nd edn., Glenview, Ill., Scott, Foresman & Co.

— (1989*a*), 'Acid Rain Reduction Credits', *Challenge*, **32**, 25–9.

— (1989*b*), 'Marketable Permits in the U.S.: A Decade of Experience', in Karl W. Roskamp (ed.), *Public Finance and the Performance of Enterprises*, Detroit, Mich., Wayne State University Press.

Tietenberg, T. H. (1991), 'Managing the Transition: The Potential Role for Economic Incentive Policies', in J. T. Matthews (ed.), *Preserving the Global Environment: The Challenge of Shared Leadership*, New York, W. W. Norton & Co.

— and Atkinson, S. E. (1989), 'Bilateral, Sequential Trading and the Cost-Effectiveness of the Bubble Policy', Colby College Working Paper (August).

Vos, H. B. (1989), 'The Application and Efficiency of Economic Instruments: Experiences in OECD Member Countries', a paper presented at the Symposium on Economic Instruments in Environmental Protection Policies, Stockholm, Sweden (June).

# 5 Valuing Environmental Damage

*Per-Olov Johansson*

## 5.1 Introduction

Most real-world policy changes create conflicts of interest. For example, if a forest which is used as a recreation area is cleared, those owning the forest will gain while those visiting the area or those concerned about an endangered species living there will lose. Nevertheless, a decision must be taken whether or not to cut down the forest. The decision-maker must implicitly or explicitly transform all values to a single 'dimension' to compare them. Then he can decide whether the value of the timber exceeds or falls short of the value of the preserved forest. The economist's way of doing this transformation is by trying to express all values in monetary terms. This is the essence of a social cost–benefit analysis. Once all benefits and costs have been expressed in monetary units, the social profitability of the considered project can be assessed.

Decisions that increase or decrease the degree of environmental damage usually involve effects that are not observable in markets. Most environmental services are unpriced and do not appear as costs to the firm—or individual—undertaking the project in question. In other words, and referring back to the above discussion, the decision-maker imputes a zero value to the

Per-Olov Johansson is Professor at the Stockholm School of Economics. He is grateful to Paul Chen, Michael Hanemann, Nick Hanley, Douglas Hibbs, David Pearce, and V. Kerry Smith for their comments on an earlier version of this paper.

environmental effects unless there is a charge on these effects, or they have an impact on the firm's reputation. This is where the environmental economist comes in. His or her task is to try to measure in monetary units the impact of the project on the environment. Adding these effects to the firm's revenues and costs would ideally indicate the project's profitability to the entire society, ignoring other distortions such as taxes and unemployment.

For a long period of time, however, it was widely believed that it was difficult, if not impossible, to value empirically public goods or 'bads' such as pollution of the air and the water. They were often classified as intangibles. There has, however, been a progressive development during the past two decades, with the result that many goods and services that earlier were classified as intangibles now are classified as measurable. The purpose of this paper is to review the most important parts of the economic theory and measurement of environmental damage. The paper is structured as follows. Section 5.2 introduces the willingness-to-pay concept and money measures such as the compensating variation and the equivalent variation. This section also offers an interpretation of money measures in terms of the outcome of a referendum. Section 5.3 defines the total value of an environmental asset, in order to give the reader an idea of the complexity of the money measures used in recent empirical studies. Sections 5.4 and 5.5 introduce risk or uncertainty and discuss the choice of money measure in a risky world.[1] In section 5.6 three frequently employed methods for the estimation of money measures are introduced. The paper ends with some remarks regarding the limitations of these approaches to decision-making.

## 5.2 Money Measures: An Example

The basic idea of the willingness-to-pay concept can be illustrated by means of a simple example. Suppose that the air quality in a particular area can be improved. Since this improvement is associated with a cost, perhaps for filters and other equipment, the question arises whether the investment is worth its cost. In other words, are people really willing to make the sacrifice the investment represents? By examining the total sum people are willing to pay we get a monetary-benefits measure that can be compared with the investment cost, so that the profitability of the investment can be assessed. An individual's *willingness to pay* is simply the maximum sum of money he is willing to give up to ensure that the suggested project is undertaken. Alternatively, we may

[1]Health effects caused by environmental damage and many of the fundamental theoretical problems in defining (money measures of) welfare changes are addressed in Volume 5 No. 1 of the *Oxford Review of Economic Policy* (1989).

want to enquire the minimum *monetary compensation* the individual needs in order voluntarily to accept that the proposed project is not undertaken. This amount of money makes him as well-off as if the project had actually been undertaken, i.e. compensates him for the 'loss' of the project. Summing over all affected individuals yields the overall or aggregate compensation requirement, just as summing each individual's willingness to pay produces the aggregate or overall willingness to pay. These aggregate sums of money can then be compared to the project's total costs, and the project's social profitability assessed.

Obviously, an individual is not willing to pay—or demands compensation—for *both* improvements and deteriorations in environmental quality. Therefore, one often distinguishes between two concepts, the *compensating variation* and the *equivalent variation*. In the former case, the individual is throughout held at the level of satisfaction or utility he attains in the initial or pre-project situation. Thus, we investigate his willingness to pay for improvements and his compensation claims for deteriorations in environmental quality. The idea behind the equivalent-variation concept is that the individual is held at the level of satisfaction he would attain if a policy change was carried out. Therefore, we investigate the maximum amount he is willing to pay to avoid a deterioration in environmental quality and the minimum compensation he needs to accept that an improvement in environmental quality is not undertaken.

In the above example with an unpriced commodity, there is no difference between the willingness to pay and the *consumer's surplus*. The latter concept is defined as the difference between the willingness to pay and what is actually paid for a policy change. In the case of a private good traded in a perfectly competitive market and whose price rises or falls, the consumer's surplus is simply the area to the left of his demand curve between initial and final prices. (The next section illustrates this further—see Figure 5.1*a*.) Here, it is just noted that a distinction must be made between ordinary or Marshallian demand curves and income compensated or Hicksian demand curves. The former, but not the latter, are 'observable' in the market. The concepts of compensating and equivalent variations are associated with Hicksian demands. See, for example, Johansson (1987) for further discussion.

In closing this section, I would like to put forward an alternative interpretation of the willingness-to-pay concept, an interpretation I have found useful in many contexts. This interpretation is in terms of a referendum. Let us return to the above considered improvement in air quality, and assume that a referendum about the project is undertaken. People are asked to vote yes or no to the project given that it would cost, say, £1,000 per individual. If the majority votes yes, one suspects that the average willingness to pay exceeds £1,000. In fact, if the willingness to pay is symmetrically distributed among the voters, the mean and the median coincide.[2] That is, if the median voter is willing to pay, say, £1,100, this is also the average willingness to pay or the mean. (The median voter is the one for whom it holds that 50 per cent of the voters are willing to pay more and 50 per cent are willing to pay less.) This interpretation highlights the basic idea of the willingness-to-pay concept as well as *cost–benefit analysis* (see, for example, Pearce, 1986). Loosely speaking, the aim is to reveal the people's preferences regarding various proposed projects or policy changes. Whether the people's ranking of two policy alternatives should play an important role or not in decision-making is an issue that is not discussed in this paper.

## 5.3 On the Total Value of a Resource

A typical feature of many environmental resources is that they provide many different values. Following Boyle and Bishop (1985), one may distinguish between four more or less distinct values. First of all, there are *consumptive use values* such as fishing and hunting. Secondly, some resources provide *non-consumptive use values*. For example, some people enjoy bird-watching, while others gain satisfaction from viewing wildlife. Thirdly, a resource may also provide services indirectly through books, movie pictures, television programmes, and so on. Finally, people may derive satisfaction from the pure fact that a habitat or species exists. A change in environmental quality due to, say, pollution of the air may affect the value derived from each of the aforementioned 'commodities'.

Collecting the different cases, the total value, or TV for short, of an environmental asset can be written as

$$\text{TV} = \text{Use Values} + \text{Indirect Services} + \text{Existence Values} \quad (1)$$

where all components are expressed in monetary units. In terms of the compensating variation concept, TV is the minimal sum of money the consumer demands as a compensation in order to be as well-off without the considered asset or resource as he is with it. In terms of the equivalent-variation concept, TV is the consumer's maximal willingness to pay for the resource in question; see the definitions given in section 5.2 above.

Before further discussion of the various components of expression (1), two remarks are in order. First of all, the complications caused by (time and) uncertainty as regards the effects of environmental damage are disregarded here; they will be introduced in sections 5.4 and 5.5. Second, the total value of

[2] Thus, the equivalence does not hold if the distribution is asymmetrical, but for pedagogical reasons, the assumption of a symmetrical distribution is a useful one.

a resource cannot be defined unless the resource is *non-essential*. If life cannot go on in the absence of the resource, it does not make sense to speak of its total value; the loss is unmeasurable or infinitely high. Once we recognize that 'resources' include air to breathe, ozone layers, carbon cycles, ocean functioning, etc. it may seem a bit restrictive to assume that resources are non-essential. Still, if we stick to ('reasonably small') *changes* in 'quality', meaningful money measures can be defined for all kinds of 'resources'.

Environmental damage may affect the use values (including indirect services) derived from an environmental asset through several channels. Three different cases are illustrated in Figure 5.1. Consider first a change in the price of a commodity that is traded in a perfectly competitive market. If environmental damage causes the price of the commodity to increase, the loss of consumer's surplus is given by the shaded area in Figure 5.1*a*, i.e. is measured as an area to the left of a compensated or Hicksian demand curve. If pollution alters several prices, one has to add the change in consumer's surplus in each of the markets.[3]

Many environmental services are provided at a low cost or even free of charge. In some cases this will mean that a service is rationed or congested. Such a case is illustrated in Figure 5.1*b* where the price is fixed below its market-clearing level so that the individual is compelled to consume less than he would if unconstrained. If pollution causes rationing or congestion to increase as in Figure 5.1*b*, the loss of consumer's surplus is given by the shaded area under the compensated or Hicksian demand curve.

Some non-consumptive uses (e.g. bird-watching) and indirect services (e.g. watching a television programme on a nature reserve) may be thought of as public goods. As is seen from Figure 5.1*c*, at the individual level a decrease in the provision of a public good causes an effect similar to the one following from a reduced supply of an unpriced rationed private commodity; the curve in Figure 5.1*c* is interpreted as a (compensated) marginal willingness-to-pay curve. However, at the aggregate level there is a difference, because a change in the provision of a public good affects many individuals (while the change in the private good in Figure 5.1*b* hits a single individual). In other words, we must add areas similar to the one in Figure 5.1*c* across all individuals concerned about the change in the provision of the considered public good.

There is another public-good property of environmental resources that deserves attention. Even if the individual himself does not consume the services provided by the environmental asset under consideration, he may still be concerned about the quality or the existence of the asset. For example, he may derive satisfaction from the pure fact that the asset is available for other people—living now or in the future. Similarly, an individual may take the

[3] See Johansson (1987, chs. 6 and 11) for a full description of the underlying model. Many of the complications considered there are overlooked here in order to simplify the discussion.

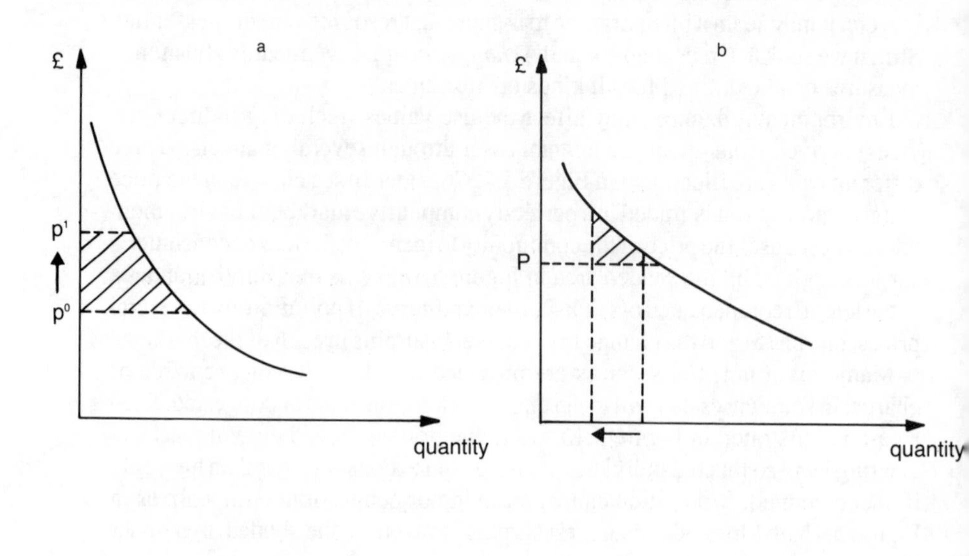


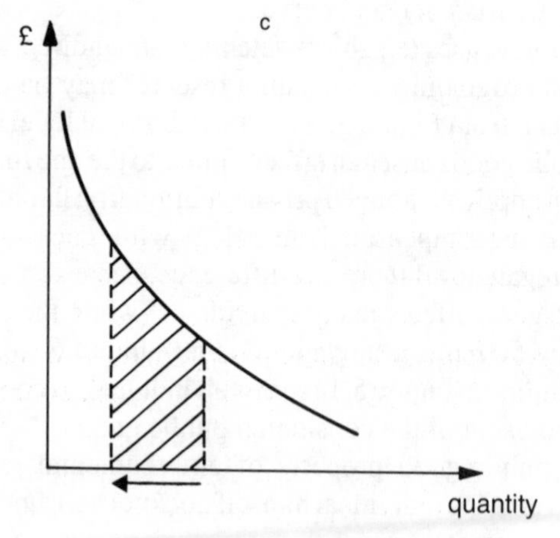


**Figure 5.1** *Compensating Variations associated with (a) A Price Change, (b) A Change in a Ration, and (c) A Change in the Provision of a Public Good.*

position that every habitat or species has a right to exist. Therefore, and for this reason alone, he may derive satisfaction from and be willing to pay for measures taken to preserve endangered species. Boyle and Bishop (1985, p. 13), following Bishop and Heberlein (1984), suggest five altruistic motives for what can be labelled *existence value*:

(1) *Bequest motives*. As Krutilla (1967) argued many years ago, it would appear quite rational to will an endowment of natural amenities as well as private goods and money to one's heirs. The fact that future generations are so often mentioned in debates over natural resources is one indication that their well-being, including their endowments of natural resources, is taken seriously by some present members of society.
(2) *Benevolence towards relatives and friends*. Giving gifts to friends and relatives may be even more common than making bequests of them. Why should such goals not extend to the availability of natural resources?
(3) *Sympathy for people and animals*. Even if one does not plan personally to enjoy a resource or to do so vicariously through friends and relatives, one may still feel sympathy for people adversely affected by environmental deterioration and want to help them. Particularly for living creatures, sympathy may extend beyond humans. The same emotions that lead us to nurse a baby bird or stop to aid a run-over cat or dog may well induce us to pay something to maintain animal populations and ecosystems.
(4) *Environmental linkages*. A better term probably exists here. What we are driving at is the belief that while specific environmental damage such as acidification of Adirondack lakes does not affect one directly, it is symptomatic of more widespread forces that must be stopped before resources of direct importance are also affected. To some extent this may reflect a simple 'you've-got-to-stop-'em-somewhere' philosophy. It may also reflect the view that if 'we' support them in maintaining the environment, 'they' will support us.
(5) *Environmental responsibility*. The opinion is often expressed that those who damage the environment should pay for mitigating or avoiding future damage. In the acid-rain case, there may be a prevalent feeling that if 'my' use of electricity is causing damage to ecosystems elsewhere, then 'I' should pick up part of the costs reducing the damage (Boyle and Bishop, 1985, p. 13).

Even if one does not agree with all the claims and arguments in the above quotation, it reviews some common arguments that are used to motivate the existence-value concept. Given that an existence value is admitted, this value is often modelled by including the stock of the resource as an argument in the utility functions (see Dasgupta, 1982, and Johansson and Löfgren, 1985, for discussions of this issue). In the case of assets such as air and water, one may instead use visibility measures and water-quality indexes respectively. The use of such measures highlights the fact that existence is not always treated as a binary variable. Instead, it is generally assumed that the marginal-existence value is positive but declines with the size of the stock or quality of the resource (although it is not obvious that this holds for all kinds of 'resources', e.g. mosquitoes). This also means that areas under a (compensated) marginal willingness-to-pay curve can be used to assess a change in 'existence value', just as in Figure 5.1*c* above.

In evaluating (1), it should be noted that the overall compensating variation (equivalent variation) is equal to the sum of the changes in compensating variations (equivalent variations) in the 'markets' where prices, quantity constraints, or the supply of public goods changes, i.e. we can add the shaded areas in Figure 5.1*a*–1*c*. This assumes, however, that each change is evaluated subject to all previously considered changes holding utility throughout at its initial level, as is shown in Johansson (1987). The practical implication of this result is that one cannot simply ask a respondent about his willingness to pay for the opportunity to fish in a polluted lake that is cleaned up, then ask about his willingness to pay for the scenic beauty provided by the restored lake, and then sum these amounts and hope to obtain the total value of the lake. Instead, one may proceed by asking for the maximum willingness to pay for fishing, disregarding any scenic values. Next, the respondent is asked for his maximum willingness to pay for the scenic values provided by the lake, subject to what he has paid for the change in fishing. This 'order of integration', just like the reverse or any intermediate 'order of integration', yields the overall compensating variation and hence incorporates the individual's budget constraint. Alternatively, one may simply ask for the total willingness to pay for the improvement in fishing *and* scenic beauty.

## 5.4 Valuation under Uncertainty: Option Value

The model discussed in the previous section is easily interpreted as an intertemporal (discrete time) one. For example, the price change in Figure 5.1*a* can be viewed as referring to a future period or year. Thus, the model can be used to define overall or lifetime consumer-surplus measures. This reinterpretation or generalization of the model causes no particular problems *per se*, but one may question the realism of the underlying perfect-foresight assumption. That is, the assumption that agents know all future prices etc. with certainty.

In a seminal paper Weisbrod (1964) argued that an individual who was unsure of whether he would visit, say, a national park would be willing to pay a sum in excess of his *expected consumer surplus* to ensure that the park would be available:

> To see why, the reader need recognize the existence of people who anticipate purchasing the commodity (visiting the park) at some time in the future, but who, in fact, never will purchase (visit) it. Nevertheless, if these consumers behave as 'economic men' they will be willing to pay something for the option to consume the commodity in the future. This 'option value' should influence the decision of whether or not to close the park and turn it to an alternative use. (Weisbrod, 1964, p. 472)

This argument seemed both novel and intuitively appealing. Nevertheless, there has been much discussion about the precise definition of *option value*. There seem to be at least two different interpretations. The first interpretation links the definition to the idea of a *risk premium* arising from uncertainty as to the future value of the commodity (park) if it were preserved. This view has been advanced by Bishop (1982), Bohm (1975), Cicchetti and Freeman (1971), Freeman (1985), Graham (1981), Plummer and Hartman (1985), and Schmalensee (1972), among others.

A second interpretation of option value focuses on the intertemporal aspects of the problem and the *irreversibility* of any decision to close the park and convert it to alternative uses. By delaying a decision to close down the park one may possibly obtain more information about the uncertain consequences, and information has a value. This option-value concept, here called the *quasi-option value*, was developed by Arrow and Fisher (1974) and Henry (1974). Recently Fisher and Hanemann (1983), Hanemann (1984), and Mäler (1984) have analysed the relationship between the two different definitions of option value. We will consider each definition in turn.

In order to arrive at a definition of (the first interpretation of) option value we must introduce the concepts of expected consumer's surplus and option price. Figure 5.2 is useful as a point of departure in defining these concepts. Consider a park whose future is uncertain; the park is either preserved or damaged by pollution. Thus we consider supply-side uncertainty but we could easily introduce demand-side uncertainty by allowing, for example, income or preferences to be stochastic. In any case, if the park is preserved, the considered individual earns a consumer's surplus equal to the shaded area in Figure 5.2. If the park is destroyed, the consumer's surplus is equal to zero since the services provided by the park are not available at all. The expected consumer surplus or the expected compensating variation is obtained by multiplying the consumer's surplus by the probability that the park is destroyed. This is one possible willingness-to-pay concept in a risky world.

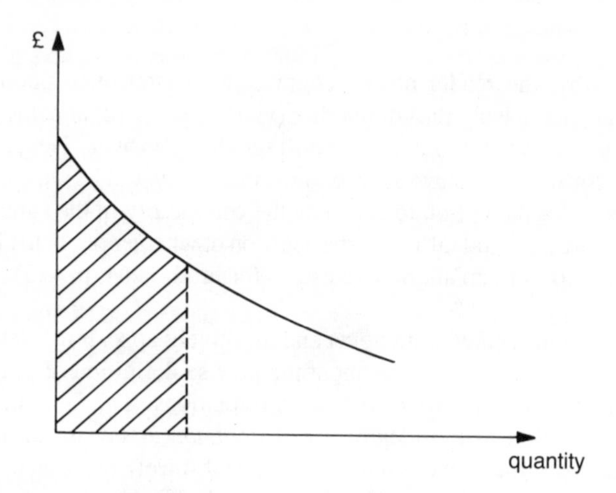


**Figure 5.2** *Consumer's Surplus for a Public Good*

An alternative willingness-to-pay concept is the consumer's option price. This is the maximal sum of money the consumer is willing to pay to ensure that the park is available. Paying this amount and having the park preserved yields him the same utility as he could expect to attain if he does not pay.

Option value is defined as the difference between option price and expected consumer surplus. A common interpretation of the above Weisbrod quotation is that when the supply of and/or demand for the park is uncertain, the expected consumer surplus will underestimate the constant maximum payment (option price) that the consumer is willing to make. The difference, it is argued, arises because the option price, which is non-stochastic or state-independent, measures both the value of retaining an option to consume the good *and* the expected value of actually consuming the good, i.e. the expected consumer surplus. Thus, one would expect the option value to be positive. Furthermore, if the option value is positive, one would know that the expected consumer surplus was an underestimate of the gain of, for example, preserving a national park. This would greatly simplify cost–benefit analysis in cases where an expected consumer-surplus measure, but not option price or option value, is available (at least if the costs fall short of the expected benefits).

I suppose that this result at least in part explains the popularity of the concept of option value. However, if one considers more complicated situations than the one depicted in Figure 5.2, e.g. the case when it is possible to 'stabilize' the supply at some intermediate level, then the expected consumer surplus measure may have the wrong sign. That is, if supply is stabilized at some intermediate level and this causes the consumer's expected utility to increase (decrease), the expected consumer surplus measure may nevertheless indicate that he loses (gains) from the stabilization.[4] The intuitive reason being that the marginal utility of income varies between states, i.e. with the value the supply takes on. Therefore, we have to use different 'weights' when we transform positive and negative compensating variations respectively to units of utility. Thus, for example, if the two compensating variations, i.e. consumer surpluses, are of equal size but of opposite signs, there is no guarantee that the underlying change in expected utility is equal to zero. In turn, this means that the concept of option value becomes questionable or even meaningless; recall that option value is defined as the difference between option price and expected consumer surplus. Thus, option value may be positive, negative, or equal to zero regardless of whether a project is worth while or not and regardless of whether people are risk-averse or not. See Bishop (1988), Helms (1985), and Johansson (1988) for proofs and further discussion.

The conclusion that may seem to follow from this discussion is that option price is the appropriate willingness-to-pay concept under uncertainty (provided, of course, that one accepts the underlying expected-utility hypothesis). Indeed, it has been shown that option price is a sign-preserving money measure, i.e. has the same sign as the underlying change in expected utility. In fact, as is shown in Johansson (1987), option price, or perhaps better, an *ex ante* compensating variation (or equivalent variation), can be used to assess any project or change that affects non-stochastic and/or stochastic prices, quantity constraints, public goods, and incomes. Note that if all variables are non-stochastic, the money measure simply reduces to the one defined by equation (1), while it is a bit more complicated to decompose and interpret in the uncertainty case. Although this holds true at the individual level, it does not necessarily follow that option price is the appropriate benefits measure in an aggregate or social cost–benefit analysis. We will return to the aggregation problem in section 5.7.

## 5.5 Quasi-Option Value

A different concept of option value than the one dealt with thus far has been advanced independently by Arrow and Fisher (1974) and Henry (1974). This concept, labelled *quasi-option value* by Arrow and Fisher (1974), focuses on the intertemporal aspects of development problems. In particular, it is stressed

[4] The stochastic alternative to stabilizing the supply of the public good in Figure 5.2 at some intermediate level is here that the supply either takes on the value zero or unity; one could now think of 'the good' as a quality index.

that environmental decisions concerning the development of resources often involve *irreversible* consequences. This imposes constraints on the range of subsequent actions.

Fisher and Hanemann (1983, p. 3) note that there are at least two ways in which the preservation of natural resources can contribute to human welfare (over and above their contribution to non-material welfare, such as scenic values). Firstly, by preserving plant and animal populations, one conserves genetic information that may, in the future, be useful in some form of economic activity. Secondly, removal of any one species can cause a system to break down because each has evolved a set of characteristics that make it a unique functional part of the system. It may be possible, to some extent, to replace ecosystem services. However, in general, it seems fair to say that some services of ecosystems are non-substitutable.

Let us consider a planner who has to decide how much of a tract of wild land should be developed in each of two periods, where the first period represents 'today' and the second period represents the uncertain future. It is assumed that development is a binary choice, i.e. either develop fully during a period or do not develop at all. Moreover, any development is irreversible.

Two scenarios are introduced regarding the behaviour of uncertainty over time. In the first case, no more information about the stochastic variable becomes available over time. For example, we do not learn whether or not development actually causes the extinction of an endangered species. Therefore, we cannot earn extra benefits by deferring a development decision to the second period. The second scenario assumes that the value taken by the stochastic variable becomes known at the beginning of the second period when we learn whether or not development causes the extinction of the endangered species. It now makes sense to defer a decision to the second period. The increase in expected benefits of not developing the area in the first period, when the planner can delay the decision until uncertainty is resolved instead of taking a decision before uncertainty is resolved, is known as the expected value of perfect information (conditional on no first-period development). This value is called quasi-option value in the literature on environmental economics.

It is possible to correct the inefficiency which follows if decision-makers ignore the possibility of improved information by introducing a tax on development. This tax should be equal to the quasi-option value. Thus, in the simple model considered here we should tax development in order to avoid too much development. However, in some cases, development *per se* may provide information, i.e. the problem may allow for active learning in the sense that the amount and types of information gained depend upon the action taken in the first period. This has been stressed by Freeman (1984) and Miller and Lad (1984). Moreover, as is the case in Viscusi and Zeckhauser's (1976) analysis, some development can provide information regarding whether development is in fact irreversible. These results mean that development decisions involving a quasi-option are not necessarily more conservationist than decisions without the quasi-option. Nevertheless, the literature on quasi-option value hints at an important aspect of decisions involving natural resources. Indeed, Fisher and Hanemann (1986, p. 15) conclude from a numerical example 'that [quasi-] option value can be calculated empirically given appropriate biological, engineering, and economic data and that it may be substantial relative to conventionally estimated benefits'. Unfortunately, there has not yet been a full-scale study aimed at estimating a quasi-option value, but such analyses are probably among the most important and challenging tasks for environmental economists.

## 5.6 Some Practical Methodologies

Several different practical methods, which can be used to measure the willingness to pay for public goods (bads), have been suggested in the literature. This section presents the most frequently used methods (survey techniques, hedonic approaches, and travel-cost methods). Each of these methods has its own weaknesses. However, apart from a few exceptions, no comprehensive discussion of these problems can be undertaken here. Instead the reader is referred to the references given below which provide an extensive discussion of the shortcomings associated with the different methods. Comparisons of methods for valuing environmental commodities can be found in Brookshire *et al.* (1981), Johansson (1987), Johnson *et al.* (1983), Knetsch and Davis (1966), Mäler (1974), Pearce and Markandya (1989), Shapiro and Smith (1981), and Schulze *et al.* (1981).

*Survey Data*

Direct demand-revealing methods for public goods have been suggested and also used by several authors. Roughly speaking these approaches collect preference information by asking the consumers how much they are willing to pay for some change in the provision of a public good or an environmental service, or about the minimum compensation consumers require if the change is not carried out. For example, the following questions may be asked of the respondent:

(CV) Suppose the provision of the public good is increased from A to B. What is the most you would be willing to pay for this increase?

(EV) Suppose that the government refrains from increasing the provision of the public good. What is the minimum compensation you would need in order to be as well-off as after an increase?

The most well-known problem associated with such methods is 'the free-rider problem'. This is as follows: if consumers have to pay on the basis of their stated willingness, they may try to conceal their true willingness to pay in order to qualify for a lower price. On the other hand, if consumers believe that the price (or the tax) charged is unaffected by their response, they may have an incentive to overstate their willingness to pay in order to secure a large supply of the public good.

However, Peter Bohm, in a series of articles, has argued that the free-rider problem can be handled in quite a simple way. The following example is adapted from Bohm (1979). Suppose two large samples of the population are confronted with the task of revealing their true willingness to pay for a public-good project, such as improved environmental quality. If the project were to be carried out, people in the first sample would pay an amount related to their stated willingness to pay. People in the second sample pay nothing or possibly a symbolic sum of money. If the average willingness to pay coincides for the samples, the hypothesis that there are incentives to misrepresent the willingness to pay, so-called strategic bias, is not supported.

If the average willingness to pay differs between the samples, the results can be used to locate an interval in which the true willingness to pay must fall. This is the case at least if people in the first sample, i.e. those paying, have incentives to understate their true willingness to pay while the opposite holds for people in the second sample, i.e. those not paying.

Because of the hypothetical nature of the survey technique, several other potential biases may also occur. The following example is adapted from Schulze *et al.* (1981) who compare six different studies that all use the same survey technique, the contingent bidding survey approach. This technique is characterized by the fact that the valuation is contingent on the specific hypothetical change identified through photographs, brochures, or other means and was first empirically applied by Randall *et al.* (1974). One of the studies, reported in Rowe *et al.* (1980) and assessed in Schulze *et al.* (1981), was the so-called Farmington Experiment, which attempted to establish the economic value of visibility over long distances for Farmington residents and those enjoying recreation at Navajo Reservoir (where visibility was threatened by power-plant emissions).

The interviewee was shown a set of pictures depicting visibility ranges. The pictures were of views in different directions from one location (the San Juan Mountains and Shiprock). A sequence of questions on maximum willingness to pay and minimum compensation was then asked.

For *strategic bias* investigation, the survey instrument was structured so that the individual was told he would have to pay the average bid, not his own. It is difficult for individuals to bid strategically to achieve a specific outcome in such a case. For instance, all previous and future bids must be known. The results also suggested that individuals do not act strategically in order to bias the outcome.

With regard to so-called *information bias*, it was suggested to the individual that his or her bid was not sufficient to keep power-plant emissions at present levels for sustained high-quality ambient air. One-third revised their bids when confronted with the possibility that their bids were insufficient. This result indicates that new information may affect bidding behaviour.

Furthermore, so-called *instrument bias* was addressed in this study. It was observed that the higher the starting bid suggested by the interviewer, the higher the maximum willingness to pay (see below). Also, individuals were willing to pay more when confronted with a payroll tax than with an increase in entrance fees.

These (and other) results reported by Schultze *et al.* (1981) indicate that one must be very careful with both the instrument used for payment and the amount and quality of information given to the interviewee at initiation of the interview. Nevertheless, the Farmington Experiment demonstrated reasonable consistency with other similar studies. Moreover, the detailed comparisons of studies in Schulze *et al.* (1981) and in Cummings *et al.* (1986) suggest that the survey technique yields values that are well within one order of magnitude in accuracy. The reader is also referred to the detailed discussion in Kopp and Smith (1989). It could also be argued that many of the above 'biases' are quite natural. For example, there is no reason to believe that people are indifferent to the choice of payment vehicle, i.e. who pays and how. After all, we know that many people are concerned about distributional issues. Similarly, it is quite natural that the stated willingness to pay for a public good is conditional on the amount and quality of the information provided. This should be no more surprising than the fact that advertising may affect the willingness to pay for a Mercedes Benz. For a recent discussion of many of these and other issues and problems in using the survey technique, the reader is referred to Mitchell and Carson (1989). In particular, they provide a useful evaluation of the taxonomies used to classify biases in the different valuation questions and the state of the art in understanding them.

There are also recent attempts to estimate the willingness to pay for complex policy changes such as those discussed in sections 5.3 and 5.4. For example, Johansson (1989) asked a small sample of Swedes about their willingness to pay for measures taken to save endangered species. The respondents were told that about 300 endangered species—animals, birds, and flowers—are living in Swedish forests. If no measures are taken, e.g. a ban on forestry in some areas and the introduction of soft cutting technologies in other areas, all the considered species may become extinct. Therefore, the respondent was asked to make (once and for all) contributions towards programmes that would save some or all of the species. Four different programmes that would save some or all of the species were suggested. First of all, the respondent was asked about his willingness to pay for a programme which would save 50 per cent of the species. The respondent was then asked to contribute to programmes that would save 75 per cent and 100 per cent of the species, respectively. Finally, the respondent was asked to pay (his option price) for a programme designed in such a way that the probability is 0.5 that the programme saves all species and 0.5 that it saves 50 per cent of the species. It turns out that the reported results are in accordance with the predictions of economic theory. For example, the willingness to pay is an increasing function of the number of species preserved; see Johansson (1989) for details.

In principle, the classification of values discussed in section 5.3 can be used to design simple consistency tests of willingness-to-pay measures. For example, one sample of respondents can be asked to pay for use values while another sample is asked to pay for use values plus existence values. Obviously, if agents behave in accordance with the predictions of economic theory, the average willingness to pay for use values plus existence values should be at least as large as the willingness to pay for use values (*ceteris paribus*).

Unfortunately, the sample of respondents considered in Johansson (1989) was only questioned regarding its total willingness to pay for various programmes aimed at the preservation of endangered species. For this reason, it is not possible to calculate use values and existence values for the individual respondent. However, Table 5.1 reports an attempt to isolate various values provided by a programme which would preserve all 300 endangered species. Each ('paying') respondent was asked to specify why he was willing to contribute to the programme. A few respondents, group 1 in the table, claimed that they would benefit only through use values and indirect services provided by the considered programme. A second small group of respondents, in addition to use values, attributed value to the fact that the programme would give others an opportunity to 'consume' the saved species (benevolence in the table). The third group of respondents in Table 5.1 mentioned both of the aforementioned

**Table 5.1** *Willingness to Pay* as a Function of the Stated Motives for Paying for the Programme*

| *Motive* | *Average WTP* |
|---|---|
| Use values (group 1) | 300 |
| Use values + benevolence (group 2) | 500 |
| Use values + benevolence + sympathy for animals (group 3) | 2,300 |

*Note*: WTP in SEK; a SEK = approx. £0.1.
*Source*: Johansson (1989, p. 44).

motives and also argued that every species has a right to exist (sympathy for animals in the table).

Table 5.1 is based on an extremely low number of observations (4, 5, and 37 observations, respectively; many respondents state combinations of motives that do not fall in any of the 'groups' defined in the table). The results are shown merely to indicate the possibility of using attitude questions to obtain rough estimates of different values/services provided by a natural resource. The ranking of the three willingness-to-pay measures in the table is the one predicted by economic theory, but further investigation involving much larger samples seems to be necessary before one can draw any definite conclusions about the appropriateness of the approach.

Nevertheless, one may question a respondent's ability to locate his maximal willingness to pay for hypothetical complex changes such as the one defined by equation (1) above. One way to simplify for the respondent is to confront him with a starting bid. If he accepts this bid, it is raised, while it is lowered if he does not accept the bid. Such a procedure may help the respondent to locate or at least bound narrowly his maximal willingness to pay. However, as mentioned above, it has been observed that there is a correlation between the starting bid and the reported maximal willingness to pay. An alternative approach, which avoids this problem, is to divide the sample of respondents into subsamples and confront each subsample with a single—'take it or leave it'—bid. For example, subsample 1 is asked if it is willing to pay £10, subsample 2 £20, etc. This approach closely resembles the working of a market. Every day we face such 'take it or leave it' offers in stores; auctions where we have to state our maximal willingness to pay for a commodity, say oranges, are more rare. One expects it to be much simpler for a respondent to accept/reject a bid than to try to locate his maximal willingness to pay. In any case, the resulting yes/no answers can be used to calculate the average willingness to pay using, for example, logit or probit techniques. However, further comparisons between continuous and discrete valuation questions are needed before one can draw any definite conclusions as regards the superiority of one or the other approach. For recent studies involving discrete responses the reader is referred to Bishop and Heberlein (1979), Hanemann (1984, 1990), Johansson and Kriström (1988), and Johansson *et al.* (1990).

### *The Travel-Cost Method*

The services of, say, a recreation site on a fishing stream are usually provided at a low or zero price. However, every user pays a price measured by his travel cost. The user must reasonably find the 'commodity' at least worth the travel cost, while the opposite reasonably holds for the non-user. This insight induced

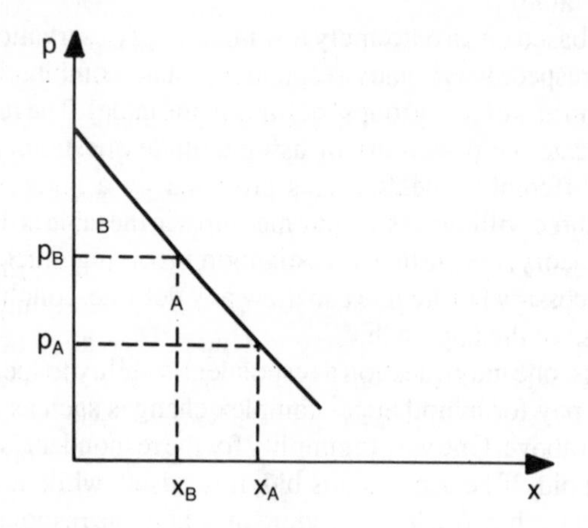


**Figure 5.3** *The Travel-Cost Method*

Hotelling (1947) to suggest the travel-cost method as a basis for valuing environmental services.

The basic idea of the approach is illustrated in Figure 5.3. Suppose for simplicity, that there is a single fishing stream that can be reached by individuals living in the considered area. The number of trips originating from zone *A*, expressed as a percentage of the total population living in the zone, is $x_A$. The average travel cost for these fishing trips is $p_A$. From zone *B*, which is situated further away from the stream than zone *A*, $x_B$ trips *per capita* are recorded. The average travel cost amounts to $p_B$. Given a number of such observations, a distance decay equation for fishing trips, like the one in Figure 5.3, can be estimated with travel costs and, say, socio-economic characteristics as independent variables. Fishermen from zone *A* earn a consumer's surplus equal to area *A* + *B* (multiplied by the number of people living in the zone in order to convert $x_A$ from a proportion to an absolute number). Similarly, multiplying area *B* in the figure by the population in zone *B* gives the consumer's surplus assigned to zone *B*. Summing all zones, one obtains a measure of total consumer surplus, i.e. what is lost if the stream is polluted or otherwise destroyed.

This is the simplest possible (and outdated) version of the travel-cost model. More recent studies usually estimate travel cost demand models with multiple sites taking account of both site and individual characteristics in the estimation of the benefits associated with changes in site attributes. The method is also useful for the estimation of the benefits following the introduction of new recreation sites and for valuing quality changes. However, since it is out of the scope of this paper to review these technical developments, the reader is referred to Kealy and Bishop (1986) and Smith and Desvouges (1985) for further discussion of recent developments.

Smith and Kaoru (1989) analysed 77 US travel-cost recreation-site demand studies in order to try to explain the variation in the benefits estimates across the studies. In an appendix to their study they list 399 different benefits estimates from 35 studies. It turns out that the consumer-surplus estimates range from £0.05 to £150 per trip to a recreational site (in 1967 prices). In part the variation in benefits estimates arises from differences in the theory underlying these demand analyses together with the practical issues of implementing it. In part it reflects 'real' differences, e.g. in type of recreation activities, type of recreation site, availability of substitute sites, etc. For a recent comparison of the travel-cost method and the contingent valuation approach, the reader is referred to Hanley (1989). He applies both approaches to the problem of valuing non-market recreation benefits derived by visitors to the Achray Forest area of the Queen Elizabeth Forest Park in Central Scotland. It turns out that both methods produce annual consumer surpluses of about £160–£180,000 (or £1.1–£1.3 per visitor-day). This might be seen to indicate that the two methods produce similar outcomes. However, Hanley underscores that some fairly strong caveats must be attached to this impression; see Hanley (1989) for details.

The travel-cost method is based on people's actual behaviour and is hence less hypothetical than surveys where one creates a hypothetical market for the considered commodity. Nevertheless, the method has its own shortcomings. All the technical problems one faces when estimating the model will not be discussed here, but are discussed in, for example, Kealy and Bishop (1986) and Smith and Desvousges (1985). What is important to emphasize here is that the method is ill-equipped for handling changes in the provision of public goods. For example, people may attribute an existence value to a recreation area or a fishing stream even if they themselves never travel to the area or the stream in question. This value is not captured by the travel cost method.[5] Thus, the method is quite problematic to use in many important applications in environmental economics.

*Hedonic Prices*

There has been a growing interest in using property values as a source of information on the benefits of controlling environmental disamenities. The idea is that differences in environmental quality variables are reflected in housing

[5] Also note that the (simple) travel-cost method produces an uncompensated, in sharp contrast to an income compensated or Hicksian, money measure.

sale prices. To take the simplest possible example, suppose we consider two houses that are identical in all respects but one, namely that one house, but not the other, is affected by air pollution. Then, the difference in market prices between the two houses should reflect the willingness to pay for better air quality. More generally, the price of a unit of housing can be viewed as a function of a number of characteristics such as housing-structure variables, neighbourhood variables, accessibility variables, and environmental variables. Implicit or hedonic prices for each attribute can be determined by examining housing prices and attribute levels. Therefore, the consumer surplus associated with variations in, for example, environmental quality can be estimated.

Alternatively, one specifies a demand system in terms of an underlying utility function. For example, if air quality is the environmental commodity under consideration, one may include market goods such as housing services and medical services, both of which are related to the environmental commodity air quality. The idea being that air quality in an area affects housing prices as well as expenditures on preventive and medical care associated with the effect of pollution on health. Once such a demand system has been estimated, it is possible (under certain technical conditions) to estimate the change in consumer surplus associated with a change in air quality.

A recent application of this approach is found in Schechter *et al.* (1989). The underlying household survey was based on a stratified, cluster-area probability sample of about 2,000 households in the metropolitan area of Haifa in northern Israel. Using the above indicated approach, the authors find that the average willingness to pay for a 50 per cent improvement in currently perceived air-quality levels is about £12 per year and household (in 1987 prices). The questionnaire also included one question eliciting the willingness to pay in order to achieve a 50 per cent improvement through a reduction of present pollution levels. (A visual stimulus, presenting respondents with photographs depicting a polluted and a clear day in the Haifa area, was provided. The payment vehicle was a municipal tax.) It turns out that this approach produces almost the same average willingness to pay as the aforementioned 'hedonic' approach. Unfortunately, not all studies comparing different methods come up with such consistent results, as will be noted in the next section.

In sum, this subsection has demonstrated that households' aggregate benefits from a public good, say clean air, can be measured indirectly from market data. In the case where property values are available, the property-value approach is of great importance because it is based on people's actual behaviour. (However, see Mäler, 1977, for a critical assessment of the property-value method.) The main drawback of the property-value method is the fact that property values are of no relevance when dealing with many types of public goods, i.e. national parks, endangered species, nationwide acid rains, and so on.

## 5.7 General Problems and Remarks

The purpose of this paper has been to present briefly the economic theory and measurement of environmental damage. In this section, the paper is rounded off by a discussion of some of the general problems one faces when valuing such damage.

Three different methods for valuing environmental damage have been presented. From a purely theoretical point of view, one should obtain the same 'answer', i.e. an identical valuation regardless of which method is used, provided that one and the same money measure (e.g. the compensating variation) is estimated. Nevertheless, studies in which different methods are used and compared do not provide any simple conclusions regarding the appropriateness of the different methods. Some experiments have been successful in the sense that when two or perhaps three methods are used to value the same change, say in air quality, all methods produce approximately the same willingness to pay; see, for example, the study by Hanley (1989) reported in section 5.6. Other studies report unexpectedly large differences between the benefits generated by different valuation methods. Therefore, further work in comparison of the methods is needed before ultimate conclusions can be drawn regarding their relative reliability.

It also turns out that many studies report an unexpectedly large difference between willingness-to-pay measures (WTP) and willingness-to-accept-compensation measures (WTA). There should be a difference, in general, according to economic theory, but it is difficult to explain why one measure (WTA) sometimes produces 5–10 times larger benefits than the other (WTP). For example, in the Israeli study reported in section 5.6, it turned out that the willingness to pay for a 50 per cent improvement in air quality was only about 25 per cent of the compensation needed to accept a 50 per cent worsening in air quality; see Schechter *et al.* (1989) for details.[6] No simple and completely convincing explanation of such large differences is available. An interesting idea put forward by Hanemann (1989), however, is that the substitution possibilities between environmental goods and other goods ('money') play a crucial role. The more difficult it is to replace a loss of environmental goods with other goods, the higher compensation is needed in order for the household to accept the loss. In turn, this tends to create a large difference between the compensation or loss measure and the willingness to pay for more environmental goods. On the other hand, if there is a high degree of substitutability between environmental goods and ordinary market goods, then the

[6] A hedonic price kind of approach was used. The authors also report survey results according to which there is only a marginal difference between WTP and WTA.

compensation measure and willingness to pay should be close in value. Several other possible explanations have been put forward. The reader is referred to Gregory (1986) and Harless (1989) for a detailed discussion of these explanations.

A positive difference between the social benefits and costs of a project, say an improvement in environmental quality, is often interpreted as meaning that gainers are hypothetically able to more than compensate losers. That is, at least hypothetically, all households can gain from such a project. Unfortunately, it has been shown that our benefits measures—compensating and equivalent variations—cannot be given such an interpretation, in general. In fact, the so-called *Boadway paradox* states that gainers may be unable to compensate losers even if the sum of individual compensating variations (equivalent variations) is positive; loosely speaking, the problem is that our money measures overlook that compensation may alter the economy's prices, as was first noted by Boadway (1974); see also Blackorby and Donaldson (1988). Thus, unless losers are actually compensated, one faces a problem of interpretation. To the best of my knowledge, however, it still remains to be investigated whether the Boadway paradox is also a serious problem in the many cases where a project is so small that it leaves most prices more or less unchanged.

The conclusion that may seem to emerge from the discussion in section 5.4 is that option price is the relevant willingness-to-pay concept under uncertainty. Indeed, it can be shown that option price is a sign-preserving money measure, i.e. has the same sign as the underlying change in expected utility following from a policy change. Nevertheless, it has also been shown that option price is the appropriate money measure only if individuals are similar, and risk is collective so that everyone experiences the same state of the world (for example, it rains on everyone and everyone in a particular area is affected by radiation emanating from a nuclear power plant). In other cases, i.e. when individuals are not identical and/or risk is not entirely collective, no simple rules of thumb regarding the appropriate money measure are available. See Graham (1981) for further discussion of this issue.

Recent experiments in which respondents are asked of their willingness to pay for complex policy changes have produced quite promising results, as illustrated in section 5.6. Still, one may question a respondent's ability to grasp fully the general equilibrium consequences of a complicated policy change. An alternative approach is to use a computable general equilibrium model to assess the welfare effects of a policy change. In a recent study, Kokoski and Smith (1987) used such a model of the American economy to evaluate the economic effects of a carbon-dioxide-induced climate change, i.e. the 'greenhouse effect'. Ideally, the advantage of this approach is that it takes care of all the complicated interdependencies between different sectors of the economy, and hence yields the net effect on prices, quantities, etc. of a policy change. Thus, given that ecologists, biologists, and others can provide reasonably good data or guesses on the relationship between economic activity in various sectors and the degree of environmental damage, computable general equilibrium models may provide a new and powerful tool for environmental economics. Even for less developed countries, where one may question the possibility of using surveys, travel costs, or property values for valuing environmental goods, computable general equilibrium models could turn out to be a useful device.

From the above discussion, the reader may get the impression that the present author is quite pessimistic regarding the possibility of valuing environmental commodities from surveys, travel costs, and property values. This is not the case. Rather, the purpose of the discussion has been to identify some important tasks for future research in environmental economics. The valuation methodology has undergone a tremendous development during recent decades and many values that twenty or so years ago were classified as intangibles can now be measured in monetary terms. If development continues in the same rapid way, one would expect many of the remaining problems to be solved within a decade or two.

## Bibliography

Arrow, K. J. and Fisher, A. C. (1974), 'Environmental Preservation, Uncertainty, and Irreversibility', *Quarterly Journal of Economics*, 88, 312–19.

Bishop, R. C. (1982), 'Option Value: An Exposition and Extension', *Land Economics*, 58, 1–15.

— (1988), 'Option Value: Reply', *Land Economics*, 64, 88–93.

— and Heberlein, T. A. (1984), 'Contingent Valuation Methods and Ecosystem Damages from Acid Rain', University of Wisconsin–Madison, Dept. of Agricultural Economics, Staff Paper No. 217.

Blackorby, C. and Donaldson, D. (1988), 'The Case against the Use of the Sum of Compensating Variations in Cost–Benefit Analysis', University of British Columbia, Dept. of Economics, Discussion Paper No. 88–01.

Boadway, R. W. (1974), 'The Welfare Foundations of Cost–Benefit Analysis', *Economic Journal*, 84, 926–39.

Bohm, P. (1975), 'Option Demand and Consumer's Surplus: Comment', *American Economic Review*, 65, 733–6.

— (1979), 'Estimating Willingness to Pay: Why and How?', *Scandinavian Journal of Economics*, 81, 142–53.

Boyle, K. J. and Bishop, R. C. (1985), 'The Total Value of Wildlife Resources: Conceptual and Empirical Issues', invited paper, Association of Environmental and Resource Economists Workshop on Recreational Demand Modeling, Boulder, Colorado, 17–18 May 1985.

Brookshire, D. S., D'Arge, R. C., Schulze, W. D., and Thayer, M. A. (1981), 'Experiments in Valuing Public Goods', in V. K. Smith (ed.), *Advances in Applied Microeconomics*, Vol. 1, Greenwich, Conn., JAI Press.

Cicchetti, C. J. and Freeman, A. M. III (1971), 'Option Demand and Consumer Surplus: Further Comment', *Quarterly Journal of Economics*, 85, 528–39.

Cummings, R. G., Brookshire, D. S., and Schultze, W. D. (1986), *Valuing Public Goods: The Contingent Valuation Method*, Totowa, N.J., Rowman & Allanheld.

Dasgupta, P. S. (1982), *The Control of Resources*, Oxford, Basil Blackwell.

Fisher, A. C. and Hanemann, W. M. (1983), *Endangered Species: The Economics of Irreversible Damage*, Dept. of Agricultural and Resource Economics, University of California, Berkeley.

— and — (1986), 'Option Value and the Extinction of Species', in V. K. Smith (ed.), *Advances in Applied Microeconomics*, Vol. 4, Greenwich, Conn., JAI Press.

Freeman, A. M. III (1984), 'The Quasi-Option Value of Irreversible Development', *Journal of Environmental Economics and Management*, 11, 292–5.

— (1985), 'Supply Uncertainty, Option Price, and Option Value', *Land Economics*, 61, 176–81.

Graham, D. S. (1981), 'Cost–Benefit Analysis under Uncertainty', *American Economic Review*, 71, 715–25.

Gregory, R. (1986), 'Interpreting Measures of Economic Loss: Evidence from Contingent Valuation and Experimental Studies', *Journal of Environmental Economics and Management*, 13, 325–37.

Hanemann, W. M. (1984), *On Reconciling Different Concepts of Option Value*, Dept. of Agricultural and Resource Economics, University of California, Berkeley.

— (1989), 'Willingness-to-Pay and Willingness-to-Accept: How Much Do They Differ?', *American Economic Review*.

— (1990), 'Welfare Evaluations in Contingent Valuation Experiments with Discrete Response Data: Reply', *American Journal of Agricultural Economics*.

Hanley, N. D. (1989), 'Valuing Rural Recreation Benefits: An Empirical Comparison of Two Approaches', *Journal of Agricultural Economics*.

Harless, D. W. (1989), 'More Laboratory Evidence On the Disparity Between Willingness to Pay and Compensation Demanded', *Journal of Economic Behavior and Organisation*, 11, 359–79.

Helms, J. L. (1985), 'Expected Consumer's Surplus and the Welfare Effects of Price Stabilization', *International Economic Review*, 26, 603–17.

Henry, C. (1974), 'Option Values in the Economics of Irreplaceable Assets', *Review of Economic Studies*, Symposium on Economics of Exhaustible Resources, 89–104.

Hotelling, H. (1947), unpublished letter to Director of National Park Service.

Johansson, P. and Kriström, B. (1988), 'Asymmetric and Symmetric Discrete Response Models in Contingent Valuation Experiments', Dept. of Statistics, University of Umeå, mimeo.

Johansson, P.-O. (1987), *The Economic Theory and Measurement of Environmental Benefits*, Cambridge, Cambridge University Press.

— (1988), 'Option Value: Comment', *Land Economics*, 64, 86–7.

— (1989), 'Valuing Public Goods in a Risky World: An Experiment', in Holmer, H. and van Ierland, E. (eds.), *Valuation Methods and Policy Making in Environmental Economics*, Amsterdam, Elsevier.

Johansson, P.-O. and Kriström, B. (1988), 'Measuring Values for Improved Air Quality from Discrete Response Data: Two Experiments', *Journal of Agricultural Economics*, 39, 439–45.

——, and Mäler, K.-G. (1990), 'Welfare Evaluations in Contingent Valuation Experiments with Discrete Response Data: Comment', *American Journal of Agricultural Economics*.

Johansson, P.-O. and Löfgren, K. G. (1985), *The Economics of Forestry and Natural Resources*, Oxford, Basil Blackwell.

Johnson, F. R., Krutilla, J. V., Bowes, M. D., and Wilman, E. A. (1983), *Estimating the Impacts of Forest Management on Recreation Benefits*, Part I: *Methodology*, Part II: *Application with Reference to the White Mountain National Forest* (by F. R. Johnson. and J. V. Krutilla), Multiple Use Forestry Project, Resources for the Future, Washington, D.C.

Kealy, M. J. and Bishop, R. C. (1986), 'Theoretical and Empirical Specification Issues in Travel Cost Demand Studies', *American Journal of Agricultural Economics*, 68, 660–7.

Knetsch, J. L. and Davis, R. K. (1966), 'Comparisons of Methods for Recreation Evaluation', in A. V. Kneese and S. C. Smith (eds.), *Water Research*, Baltimore, Johns Hopkins University Press.

Kokoski, M. F. and Smith, V. K. (1987), 'A General Equilibrium Analysis of Partial-Equilibrium Welfare Measures: The Case of Climate Change', *American Economic Review*, 77, 331–41.

Kopp, R. J. and Smith, V. K. (1989), 'Benefit Estimation Goes to Court: The Case of Natural Resource Damage Assessments', *Journal of Policy Analysis and Management*, forthcoming.

Krutilla, J. A. (1967), 'Conservation Reconsidered', *American Economic Review*, 57, 777–86.

Miller, J. R. and Lad, F. (1984), 'Flexibility, Learning, and Irreversibility in Environmental Decisions: A Bayesian Analysis', *Journal of Environmental Economics and Management*, 11, 161–72.

Mitchell, R. C. and Carson, R. T. (1989), *Using Surveys to Value Public Goods: The Contingent Valuation Method*, Baltimore, Resources for the Future.

Mäler, K. G. (1974), *Environmental Economics: A Theoretical Inquiry*, Baltimore, Johns Hopkins University Press.

— (1977), 'A Note on the Use of Property Values in Estimating Marginal Willingness to Pay for Environmental Quality', *Journal of Environmental Economics and Management*, 4, 355–69.

— (1984), *Risk, Uncertainty and the Environment*, Stockholm, Stockholm School of Economics.

Oxford Review of Economic Policy (1989), *Health*, 5(1).

Pearce, D. W. (1986), *Cost–Benefit Analysis*, London, Macmillan.

— and Markandya, A. (1989), *Environmental Policy Benefits: Monetary Evaluation*, Paris, OECD.

Plummer, M. L. and Hartman, R. C. (1985), 'Option Value: A General Approach', mimeo.

Randall, A., Ives, B., and Eastman, C. (1974), 'Bidding Games for Valuation of Aesthetic Environmental Improvements', *Journal of Environmental Economics and Management*, 1, 132–49.

Rowe, R., D'Arge, R. C., and Brookshire, D. S. (1980), 'An Experiment on the Economic Value of Visibility', *Journal of Environmental Economics and Management*, 7, 1–19.

Schechter, M., Kim, M., and Golan, L. (1989), 'Valuing a Public Good: Direct and Indirect Valuation Approaches to the Measurement of the Benefits from Pollution Abatement', in H. Folmer and E. van Ierland (eds.), *Valuation Methods and Policy Making in Environmental Economics*, Amsterdam, Elsevier.

Schmalensee, R. (1972), 'Option Demand and Consumer's Surplus: Valuing Price Changes under Uncertainty', *American Economic Review*, 62, 813–24.

Schulze, W. D., D'Arge, R. C., and Brookshire, D. S. (1981), 'Valuing Environmental Commodities: Some Recent Experiments', *Land Economics*, 57, 151–72.

Shapiro, P. and Smith, T. (1981), 'Preferences for Non-Market Goods Revealed through Market Demands', in V. K. Smith (ed.), *Advances in Applied Microeconomics*, Vol. 1, Greenwich, Connecticut, JAI Press.

Smith, V. K. (1987), 'Nonuse Values in Benefit Cost Analysis', *Southern Economic Journal*, 54, 19–26.

— Desvousges, W. H. (1985), *Measuring Water Quality Benefits*, Boston, Kluwer Nijhoff.

— Kaoru, Y. (1989), 'Signals or Noise? Explaining the Variation in Recreation Benefit Estimates', mimeo.

Viscusi, W. K. and Zeckhauser, R. J. (1976), 'Environmental Policy Choice under Uncertainty', *Journal of Environmental Economics and Management*, 3, 97–112.

Weisbrod, B. A. (1964), 'Collective-Consumption Services of Individual-Consumption Goods', *Quarterly Journal of Economics*, 78, 471–7.

# 6

# The Problem of Global Environmental Protection

*Scott Barrett*

> Suppose that land is communally owned. Every person has the right to hunt, till, or mine the land. This form of ownership fails to concentrate the cost associated with any person's exercise of his communal right on that person. If a person seeks to maximize the value of his communal rights, he will tend to overhunt and overwork the land because some of the costs of his doing so are borne by others. The stock of game and the richness of the soil will be diminished too quickly. It is conceivable that those who own these rights, i.e. every member of the community, can agree to curtail the rate at which they work the lands if negotiating and policing costs are zero . . . [However,] negotiating costs will be large because it is difficult for many persons to reach a mutually satisfactory agreement, especially when each hold-out has the right to work the land as fast as he pleases. [Furthermore,] even if an agreement among all can be reached, we must yet take account of the costs of policing the agreement, and these may be large, also. (Demsetz, 1967, pp. 354–5)

## 6.1 Introduction

Demsetz's influential paper on the development of private-property rights makes depressing reading for anyone concerned about global common-property resources such as the oceans and atmosphere. Demsetz's view—and it is

Scott Barrett is Assistant Professor in the Faculty of Economics at the London Business School. He wishes gratefully to acknowledge the comments made by David Pearce on an earlier draft of this paper.

one that is shared by many others—is that users of a communally owned resource will fail to come to an agreement on managing the resource even though it is in the interest of all users to co-operate and reduce their rates of use of the resource. The reason is that if this improved situation is attained, every user will earn even higher returns by free-riding on the virtuous behaviour of the remaining co-operators. As a consequence, united action on the part of users can be expected to be unstable; co-operative agreements, even if they are reached, will not persist. The only way out of the common-property dilemma, as Demsetz makes clear, is intervention by '*the* state, *the* courts, or the leaders of *the* community' (emphasis added). In Demsetz's example, the intervention manifests itself in the development of private-property rights to the resource, but the intervention could just as easily involve regulation.

The reason this view is disquieting is that for global common-property resources there is no World Government empowered to intervene for the good of all. To be sure, there do exist international institutions—most notably the United Nations Environment Programme—which have been given the mandate to co-ordinate international environmental protection efforts. But none of these institutions can dictate what is to be done; that requires agreement by the parties concerned. The problem is perhaps best exemplified by the International Whaling Commission (IWC), which was established to conserve whale stocks, but whose best efforts in this regard have been repeatedly foiled. IWC membership is open to any country, and this leaves open the possibility that the whales could be protected for the global good. But any member can object to a majority decision, and hence render that decision meaningless. For example, a 1954 proposal to prohibit the taking of blue whales in the North Pacific was rejected by the only members who hunted blue whales in this ocean—Canada, Japan, the US, and the USSR—and hence did nothing to protect this species. In 1981 the IWC sought to ban the use of the non-explosive harpoon for killing minke whales. The ban was objected to by Brazil, Iceland, Japan, Norway, and the USSR. Since these were the only countries that hunted minke whales, the ban had no effect.[1]

Because national sovereignty must be respected, the problem of conserving global common-property resources is no different from that described by Demsetz. The only way out of the global common-property dilemma is agreement. Yet, just as in the situation Demsetz describes, there are strong incentives for governments not to co-operate, or to defect from an agreement should one be reached. This is the crux of the problem of managing global common property, and what distinguishes this problem from the long-studied one of common-property management under the jurisdictional control of a central authority.

[1] See Lyster (1985).

Attempts to correct global, unidirectional externalities will encounter similar difficulties. Consider the problem where certain activities by one country harm all others. A good example is deforestation of Amazonia by Brazil. The rain forests play a crucial role in the protection of biological diversity and in the functioning of the carbon cycle. When standing, the rain forests serve as habitat to about a half of all wildife species and absorb carbon dioxide, one of the so-called greenhouse gases. When the forests are burned, masses of species can become extinct and substantial quantities of greenhouse gases are emitted. If the rights to generate these externalities are vested in the one country, as indeed they are in the case of Brazilian deforestation, then the others will have to pay this nation to cease its destructive activities. If the externality affected only one other country, then bargaining might be possible; the externalities might be internalized without outside intervention.[2] But in the case of global externalities, all countries except the generator suffer. All sufferers might be willing to bribe the generator to cease its harmful activities. But a contribution by any one country would confer benefits on all others and not just the one making the compensating payment. The others could therefore do better by free-riding. But then so too could the one that contemplated making the payment. Co-operation would again be foiled.[3] Mechanisms exist that can lead countries to reveal their preferences for global public goods truthfully (see, for example, Groves and Ledyard, 1977), and hence for correcting global externalities. But in the absence of a World Government these mechanisms cannot be employed without the consent of the sovereign nations themselves. Every country would be better-off if it agreed to participate in the revelation exercise. But each would do even better if others participated and it did not. All will therefore choose not to participate. The crux of the problem of correcting global externalities, like that of managing global common property, is that global optimality demands global co-operation, and yet the incentives facing individual countries work in the opposite direction.

The theoretical arguments for supposing that co-operation will not develop are compelling. But they can hardly be complete. Co-operation *does* take place and is often codified in international agreements. Some of these are woefully

[2] See Coase (1960). Bargaining has in fact taken place at the bilateral level. A famous example is the Trail Smelter case. The Canadian smelter emitted pollutants that crossed the US border. The case was arbitrated by an international tribunal comprised of an American, a Canadian, and a Belgian. The tribunal found that Canada was liable for damages, and also established emission regulations for the plant. The judicial decisions on this case make fascinating reading. See Trail Smelter Arbitral Tribunal (1939, 1941).

[3] Demsetz (1967, p. 357) argues that in the large numbers case, 'it may be too costly to internalize effects through the market-place'. Elsewhere, Demsetz (1964) argues that it might in fact be optimal for the externality not to be internalized since the costs of internalization should include the costs of transacting the agreement. But even then the free-rider problem would prevail; intervention, were it possible, might still be desired.

ineffective—a famous example being the International Convention for the Regulation of Whaling (1946) which established the IWC. Others do appear to have achieved a great deal. Of these last, the Montreal Protocol on Substances that Deplete the Ozone Layer (1987) seems the most impressive, because it demands that its many signatories undertake substantial reductions in their emissions of ozone-depleting chlorofluorocarbons (CFCs) and halons. Though agreements dealing with unidirectional externalities are rare and almost invariably toothless, there is one—the World Heritage Convention—that at least holds some promise. This agreement places responsibility for safeguarding natural environments like the Serengeti and the Galapagos Islands on a community of nations, and could be invoked to protect the remaining tropical rain forests. There is clearly a need to explore why international co-operation might develop, and what the significance of particular forms of co-operation might be.

To make any progress we will need a basis from which to assess whether co-operation can in fact be expected to achieve much. Contrary to Hardin's (1968) famous allegory of the commons, the absence of co-operation need not lead to tragedy. Section 6.2 discusses some of the parameters that are important in determining the potential gains to co-operation. Having drawn the boundaries, we then consider how we might move closer to the full co-operative solution, the global optimum. Non-co-operation may sometimes wear the disguise of co-operation, and section 6.3 shows that an outcome better than the purely nationalistic one can emerge even where binding agreements are absent. Effective management of global environmental resources does however seem to rely on the more formal institution of international law. Section 6.4 discusses the rudiments of a model that explains why countries would co-operate when the free-rider problem must surely bite, and what international agreements mean for global social welfare and the welfare of citizens of individual countries. Just as failure to co-operate may not lead to tragedy, so co-operation may not buy us very much. Indeed, combining the analysis of the potential gains to co-operation with this model of formal agreements, it can be shown that co-operation is sometimes hardest to obtain when it is most needed.

## 6.2 The Potential Gains to Co-operation

Where a global externality is unidirectional, the country causing the externality will, without a negotiated settlement, ignore the damages its activities impose on other countries. This is the full *non-co-operative* outcome. The full *co-operative* outcome is found by internalizing the externality. Here the country inflicting the externality chooses its actions so as to maximize the net benefits of all countries, including itself. Global net benefits will of course be higher in this case. The difference between the global net benefits for the co-operative and non-co-operative outcomes defines the potential gains to co-operation.

Where the externalities of concern are reciprocal in nature, every country has some incentive to take unilateral action even in the absence of a binding agreement. Furthermore, the strength of this incentive will depend on the actions taken by all other countries. An example of a reciprocal externality is the emission of a global pollutant. If one country reduces its emissions, it will benefit from the improved environmental quality, provided other countries do not increase their emissions so as to fully offset the one country's action. The other countries will benefit partly by being able to increase their emissions somewhat and partly by enjoying a cleaner environment (again, provided their increase in emissions does not entirely offset the one country's extra abatement). The extent of the benefit enjoyed by the conserving country will clearly depend on the actions taken by the other countries, and of course all countries are subject to a similar calculus. It is this interdependence which makes calculation of the potential gains to co-operative management of global common property more difficult. It is better, then, that we work with a specific model.

To fix ideas, reconsider the problem of global pollution. Suppose that the relevant number of countries is $N$. One might think that $N$ would include all the world's countries, but that need not be so, a point we return to later. Let us, however, suppose for simplicity that $N$ does include all countries and that each is identical. Each, therefore, emits the same quantity of a pollutant *ex ante*—that is, before the game is played—and each faces the same abatement cost and benefit functions. The problem is then perfectly symmetric. To simplify the analysis further, assume that the *marginal* abatement cost and benefit functions are linear. Clearly, the marginal-abatement cost schedule for each country must depend on its own abatement level, while each country's marginal-abatement benefit function must depend on *world-wide* abatement.

In the absence of any co-operation, each country will maximize its own net benefits of abatement and in so doing will choose a level of abatement at which its own marginal-abatement cost equals its own marginal-abatement benefit.[4] This is the non-co-operative (Nash equilibrium) solution to this game, and it is shown as abatement level $Q^*$ in Figure 6.1. Were countries to co-operate fully, they would seek to maximize the global net benefits of abatement. Since we have assumed that all countries are identical, the global net benefits of

[4] I am assuming here that every country believes that its choice of an abatement level will not alter the choices of the other countries; that is, I am assuming zero conjectural variations. One can impose positive or negative conjectures, but these assumptions would be *ad hoc*. Alternatively, we could determine a consistent conjectures equilibrium—that is, one in whose neighbourhood every country's conjectures are confirmed by the responses of the other countries. Cornes and Sandler (1983) find that consistent conjectures can lead to even greater overuse of the resource compared with the Nash equilibrium.

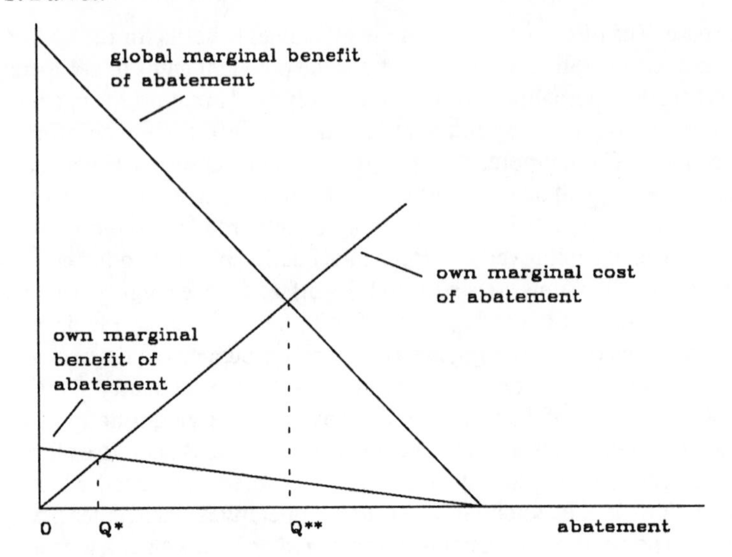


**Figure 6.1** *Graphical Illustration of the Potential Gains to Co-operation*

abatement can be defined as the sum of every country's net benefits of abatement. In maximizing the global net benefits of abatement, each country will choose a level of abatement at which its own marginal costs of abatement equal the global marginal benefits of abatement, or the sum of the marginal-abatement benefits enjoyed by all countries.[5] The full co-operative solution to this game is shown as abatement level $Q^{**}$ in Figure 6.1.

One sees immediately that the full co-operative solution demands greater abatement but, equally, gives to every country a greater net benefit. For a given size of $N$, the difference between $Q^{*}$ and $Q^{**}$ can be shown to depend on the slopes of the marginal-abatement benefit and cost curves. Denote the (absolute value of the) slope of each country's marginal-abatement benefit curve by the letter $b$, and the slope of each country's marginal-abatement cost curve by the letter $c$. Then it can be shown that the discrepancy will tend to be small whenever $c/b$ is either 'large' or 'small' (see Barrett, 1991*a*). The approximate implication of this result is that fairly innocuous pollutants (that is, pollutants for which $b$ is small) that are very costly to control (that is, that have a large $c$) do not cause too great a problem. Nor do extremely hazardous pollutants (that is, pollutants associated with a large $b$) that are cheap to control (that is, pollutants that have a small $c$). In the former case, even collective action will not call for large abatement levels. In the latter, countries will want to abate

[5] This is of course nothing but a restatement of Samuelson's (1954) rule for the optimal provision of public goods. For an alternative presentation of these principles, see Dasgupta's (1982) model of a global fishery.

substantial quantities of emissions unilaterally. The real problem is with pollutants whose marginal-abatement benefit and cost curves are both either steep or flat—that is, hazardous pollutants that are costly to control, and mildly offensive pollutants that can be controlled at little cost. Of these, the former type naturally causes the greatest concern, for the cost of failing to co-operate in this case is very, very high.

Unidirectional and reciprocal externalities are plainly different in their effects. A country has no incentive to abate its emissions if the externality is unidirectional (provided side payments are ruled out), even if the pollutant is highly toxic. Not so if the externality is reciprocal in nature. For then the emitting country will have strong private incentives to control its emissions.

## 6.3 Non-co-operative Environmental Protection

The politics of global environmental protection are not as sterile as the above models would imply. Once we permit alternative strategies to be chosen, widen the choice-sets themselves, and allow motivations other than self-interest (narrowly defined) to guide decision-making, global environmental protection can be enhanced.

### *Supergames*

In the above games, strategies are chosen once, and the games are never repeated. But in the common-property game countries are unavoidably locked in a continuing relationship, and this leaves open the possibility that they may retaliate and hence that co-operative strategies may be countenanced. Suppose then that all countries choose one of two strategies: they either choose the full co-operative abatement level $Q^{**}$ initially, and continue to choose $Q^{**}$ in every future period provided all other countries chose $Q^{**}$ in every previous period; or they choose not to co-operate in any period.[6] Then the co-operative trigger strategy will constitute an equilibrium to this supergame provided the rate of discount is sufficiently low (for then the gains to choosing the non-co-operative strategy will be low, too; see Friedman, 1986). Although this supergame equilibrium entails co-operation, the co-operation is tacit and is enforced by means of a non-co-operative mechanism, retaliation; there is no explicit agreement, no open negotiation.[7]

[6] If countries choose not to co-operate in the initial period, they need not choose $Q^{*}$ in this period. The reason for this is that the optimal non-co-operative abatement level is contingent on the abatement levels chosen by the other countries.

[7] Axelrod's (1984) tournaments of the repeated prisoners' dilemma game suggest that behaviour in the disguise of co-operation may well emerge. Whether his findings carry over to the common-property game with many players, however, is as yet unknown.

One variant of this game involves countries adopting a convention that says that a subset of countries should co-operate in the face of free-riding by the others (see Sugden, 1986). It may, for example, be believed that the industrialized countries should co-operate to reduce emissions of CFCs or greenhouse gases (because it was their emissions that caused the environmental reservoirs to be filled in the first place), and that the poor countries should be allowed to free-ride. In this game, each of the members of the subset could adopt the trigger strategy with respect to the subset, and each of the others could simply choose their optimal non-co-operative responses. This latter possibility may be fragile, because different countries may have different views about which should co-operate and which should not. This ambiguity may help explain why unilateral action to reduce CFC emissions was limited (US Environmental Protection Agency, 1988, p. 30576):

> In 1978 the United States restricted the use of CFCs in aerosols. While several nations adopted similar restrictions (e.g. Sweden, Canada, Norway) and others partially cut back their use (European nations, Japan), there was no widespread movement to follow the United States' lead. Concerns existed then that other nations had failed to act because the United States and a few other nations were making the reductions thought necessary to protect the ozone layer. Similar concerns exist today that unilateral action could result in 'free riding' by some other nations.

It is not obvious how sufferers of a unidirectional externality could punish the offending nation. But so long as the countries are engaged in some form of exchange, potent weapons may be at the sufferers' disposal. The Packwood–Magnuson Amendment to the US Fishery Conservation and Management Act (1976) requires the US government to retaliate whenever foreign nationals compromise the effectiveness of the IWC. An offending nation automatically loses half its allocation of fish products taken from US waters, and if the country refuses to improve its behaviour within a year, its right to fish in US waters is revoked.

*Matching*

In the one-shot common-property game, each country chooses an abatement level and nothing else. There is no reason why a country's choices need be limited in this way. We could, for example, allow countries to choose a 'base' abatement level—that is, a level of abatement which is not explicitly contingent on the abatement levels chosen by other countries—and a 'matching rate'—in our example, a fraction of the sum of all countries' base abatement levels. In effect, countries would then voluntarily subsidize each other's abatement levels. In the original game, one unit of abatement by country $i$ buys country $i$ one unit less of global emission (assuming that the emissions of all other countries are held fixed). In the matching game, one unit of abatement by country $i$ may yield a much greater reduction in global emission. Matching might improve matters—Guttman (1978) shows that under certain conditions matching can sustain the full co-operative solution. But in the management of global common property, matching is rarely invoked. Recently, Norway announced that it would allocate one-tenth of 1 per cent of its GDP each year to a fund on climate change if other industrial countries matched its contribution (on a GDP percentage basis). The offer has yet to be taken up. Environmental groups in the United States have argued that the US should unilaterally surpass the reductions specified in the Montreal Protocol and at the same time impose restrictions on imports of products containing or made with CFCs from countries that fail to agree to make the same reductions. Their plea was rejected by the authorities (US Environmental Protection Agency, 1988, p. 30574).

### *Morality*

In the models discussed thus far, the welfare of every country is assumed to depend solely on its *own* net benefits. An alternative way of looking at the problem is to assume that countries act according to some moral principle which requires that they take stock of the effect their actions have on the welfare of other countries. For example, suppose every country but one reduces its emissions of some global pollutant by at least $x$ tonnes. Let us further suppose that the recalcitrant nation would like all others to reduce their emissions by $y$ tonnes each. Then the leaders of the recalcitrant nation might feel compelled to obey the rule: if $y > x$ then we are morally obligated to reduce our emissions by at least $x$ tonnes. If countries obey this rule, then the free-rider problem can be mitigated (see Sugden, 1984). That moral principles may guide non-co-operative abatement is suggested by the following remarks made by the House of Commons Environment Committee (1984, p. lxxi) in its report recommending that the UK join the Thirty Per Cent Club:[8]

> As our inquiry has progressed the stance of the United Kingdom has become increasingly isolated by its refusal to legislate to reduce $SO_2$ and $NO_x$ emissions. Since our work began three West European countries have joined those already in the 30 per cent club, and several Eastern

[8] The Thirty Per Cent Club consists of the countries that have signed the Protocol to the 1979 Convention on Long-Range Transboundary Air Pollution on the Reduction of Sulphur Emissions or their Transboundary Fluxes by at least 30 Per Cent (1985). The UK has not joined this 'club' but it has committed itself to substantial reductions in sulphur dioxide and nitrogen oxides emissions by agreeing to comply with the European Community Large Combustion Plant Directive.

> European countries have committed themselves to reduce transfrontier emissions by 30 per cent. $SO_2$ emissions in the United Kingdom have indeed fallen by 37 per cent since 1970, but the levels of high-stack emissions which affect remote areas have not fallen. In 1970, when the 37 per cent fall began, we were the largest emitter in Western Europe. In 1984, we are still the largest emitter. $NO_x$ emissions have not fallen. In Western Europe only West Germany deposits more $SO_2$ in other countries than does the United Kingdom, and further significant reductions cannot be achieved by either without controls.

The Committee's concern in this passage lies less with the net benefits to the UK of reducing emissions than with how UK abatement has lagged behind the rest of Europe. Indeed, the Committee's evaluation did not even consider whether the other European countries were abating more simply because it was in their own self-interest to do so. The argument seems to be: 'The other European nations are reducing their emissions, so we should, too.' Compared with the supergame problem, co-operation in this case is not instrumentally important—the Environment Committee did not seek to reduce UK emissions so that others would reduce theirs even further—but intrinsically important. Concerns about fairness have been shown to militate against the free-rider problem in experimental tests (Marwell and Ames, 1981). However, in the next section we shall see that in a bargaining situation, obeying moral principles may serve only to undermine the cause of environmental protection.

## 6.4 Co-operative Environmental Protection

In the absence of co-operation, outcomes better than the full non-co-operative one can sometimes develop, at least in principle. But such instances seem to be rare. Even two close neighbours with strong trading ties can fail to arrive at a preferred solution, as the disagreement between the United States and Canada over the exploitation of the North Pacific fur-seal illustrates. Following an initial conflict between the two nations over the pelagic seal hunt, a Tribunal Arbitration was convened at the request of the two parties (with Great Britain acting for Canada). In late 1893 the Tribunal decided that the United States did not have territorial jurisdiction over the Bering Sea, and hence could not keep Canadian sealing vessels out of these waters. This effectively sanctioned open-access harvesting of the species, and co-operation proved impossible to secure (Paterson and Wilen, 1977, p. 94):

> Following the decision of the Tribunal, the diplomatic efforts of both Great Britain and the United States had been directed to convincing the

> other to reduce its sealing in order to allow the herd to recover from earlier depradations. No agreement could be reached and in 1897 the United States unilaterally forbade its citizens to engage in pelagic sealing in the North Pacific. At the same time quota adjustments were made as the herd diminished in size. So strong was the reaction to the declining herd size and the continued Canadian pelagic hunt that a bill reached the [United States] Senate which called for the complete destruction of the herd. It did not pass.

Better management of the population had to await the signing of the North Pacific Fur Seal Treaty by Great Britain, the United States, Japan, and Russia in 1911—a remarkable agreement that remains in force today.[9] Effective management of global environmental resources seems to demand that countries co-operate openly and put their signatures on international agreements, treaties, and conventions. Explanations for why co-operation of this kind might emerge are offered below.

*International Environmental Agreements*

Consider the following modification to the common-property game described earlier. Suppose a subset of the $N$ identical countries 'collude' by signing an international environmental agreement and that the remaining countries continue to act non-co-operatively. Suppose further that the signatories to the agreement choose their collective abatement level while taking as given the abatement decision functions of the non-signatories, while the latter countries continue to behave atomistically and choose their abatement levels on the assumption that the abatement levels of all other countries are fixed. That is, the signatories act as 'abatement leaders', and the non-signatories as 'abatement followers'. Quite clearly, we would like the number of signatories, the terms of the agreement, and the abatement levels of all non-signatories to be determined jointly. We also require that the agreement itself is stable. A stable agreement is one where non-signatories do not wish to sign the agreement and signatories do not wish to renege on their commitment. Then it can be shown that for identical countries with linear marginal-abatement benefit and cost functions a stable international environmental agreement always exists (Barrett, 1991*a*).

The solution to this problem exhibits many of the features of actual agreements. The net benefits realized by both signatories and non-signatories are higher than in the earlier problem where negotiation was ruled out. What is more, the signatories would like the non-co-operators to sign the agreement. However, non-signatories do better by free-riding.

[9] For legal background on this treaty and its successors, see Lyster (1985).

It is important to emphasize that the agreement is *self-enforcing.* Any signatory that renounces its commitment can reduce its abatement level and hence its costs. However, in pulling out of the agreement, the number of co-operators is reduced and the agreement itself is weakened; the remaining co-operators reduce their abatement levels, too. A signatory will want to pull out of an agreement only if the saving in abatement costs exceeds the resulting loss in benefits. Similarly, a country that joins an agreement will have to abate more and hence incur higher costs. But the very act of joining will strengthen the agreement; the other co-operators will also increase their abatement levels. Joining appears attractive if the resulting increase in benefits realized by the new signatory exceeds the increase in costs that this country must incur in committing itself to the terms of the agreement.

Real treaties are not rewritten with every defection or accession, but mechanisms are at work that have a similar effect. It is common for treaties to come into force only after being ratified by a minimum number of signatories. The Montreal Protocol did not come into force until it had been ratified by at least eleven countries representing at least two-thirds of global consumption of the controlled substances. It is also common for treaties to be reviewed and altered when necessary and often at regular intervals. The Montreal Protocol was renegotiated in June 1990, and was significantly strengthened. That this agreement is self-enforcing is suggested by a comment made by the US Environmental Protection Agency (EPA) (1988, p. 30573):

> EPA judged that the obvious need for broad international adherence to the Protocol counseled against the United States' deviating from the Protocol, because any significant deviation could lessen other countries' motivation to participate.

Self-enforcement is essential in any model of international environmental agreements because nation states cannot be forced to perform their legal obligations. A country can be taken to the International Court of Justice for failing to comply with the terms of a treaty, but only with the defendant's permission. Even then, the disputing countries cannot be forced to comply with the Court's decision.[10]

What are the gains to having international environmental agreements? The answer depends partly on the number of relevant and potential signatories. When $N$ is large, international environmental agreements can achieve very little no matter the number of signatories. The reason, quite simply, is that when $N$ is large, defection or accession by any country has only a negligible effect on the abatement of the other co-operators.

[10] See Lyster (1985) for a discussion of other compliance mechanisms.

Determination of $N$ is not always a trivial matter. Some treaties do not restrict participation, but in these cases many of the signatories may have no effective say in environmental protection. Over 100 countries have signed the 1963 Partial Nuclear Test Ban Treaty, but only a few signatories possess nuclear weapons technology. The 1967 United Nations Treaty on Principles Governing the Activities of States in the Exploration and Use of Outer Space including the Moon and Other Celestial Bodies has been ratified by scores of countries but not by the two with space-technology capabilities—the US and USSR. Other treaties explicitly restrict participation. The Agreement on the Conservation of Polar Bears can only be signed by five circumpolar countries (Canada, Denmark (including Greenland), Norway, the US, and the USSR). To become a signatory to the Antarctic Treaty of 1959 a country must maintain a scientific research station in the Antarctic and be unanimously accepted by existing parties to the agreement. In these cases non-signatories may quite clearly be affected by how the signatories manage the resource. Signatories to the Antarctic Treaty voted recently to allow mineral exploration, despite appeals by non-signatories to designate Antarctica a nature reserve.

In the above model, $N$ was assumed to represent both the number of countries that emit a (uniformly mixed) pollutant into the environment and the number harmed as a consequence. However, for some problems the number of emitters may be less than the number of sufferers (for global pollutants, all countries). When the number of emitters is small, an international environmental agreement signed by a subset of emitters may well have a significant effect on the welfare of these countries. However, the effect on global welfare may still be small because the emitters have no incentive to take into account the welfare losses suffered by non-emitting nations. The appropriate way to account for countries that do not emit the pollutant but nevertheless suffer the consequences of others' emissions is to admit side payments—payments which induce emitting nations to undertake greater abatement but which leave all parties no worse off compared to the situation where side payments are forbidden. We return to the side-payments issue later.

The gains to international co-operation can also be shown to depend on $c$, the slope of each country's marginal-abatement cost curve; and $b$, the (absolute value of the) slope of each country's marginal-abatement benefit curve. For a given size of $N$, the number of signatories to a treaty increases as $c/b$ falls. This suggests that we should expect to observe a large number of signatories (in absolute terms) when $N$ is 'large', the marginal-abatement cost curve is flat, and the marginal-abatement benefit curve steep. However, we already know that when $c/b$ is 'small' the benefit of having an agreement is diminished. It is commonly asserted that treaties signed by a large number of countries accomplish little of substance: 'The greater the number of participants in the formulation of a treaty, the weaker or more ambiguous its provisions are likely to be since they have to reflect compromises making them acceptable to every State involved' (Lyster, 1985, p. 4). This analysis suggests that the reason treaties signed by a large number of countries appear to effect little additional abatement is not that the signatories are heterogeneous—although that may be a contributing factor. Nor is the reason solely that in these cases $N$ is also large. A major insight of the model is that a large subset of $N$ will sign an agreement only when the non-co-operative and full co-operative outcomes are already close.

This latter observation may not seem consistent with all the evidence. The Montreal Protocol, for example, demands of its signatories significant reductions in the production and consumption of the hard CFCs and halons, and about 46 countries have already signed the agreement—a fairly large number by any standard. As Table 6.1 shows, the effect of the agreement on ozone depletion is estimated to be very significant. Percentage ozone depletion is estimated to be reduced from 50 to 2 per cent in 2075 as a result of the agreement. But of course each country has some incentive to take unilateral action in reducing emissions; in doing so all other countries will benefit, but so too will the country taking the action. Furthermore, non-signatories to the agreement may well face an incentive to abate less than they would otherwise for the simple reason that greater abatement on the part of signatories improves the environment for non-signatories as well. Hence it is by no means clear that the agreement necessarily means that the environment and global welfare will be significantly better off, contrary to what the figures in Table 6.1 imply. What the model does suggest is that so many countries would not have committed themselves to the agreement in the first place unless they already intended to take substantial unilateral action. In other words, although the agreement itself may effect only little additional abatement, the very fact that so many countries have signed the agreement suggests that the potential gains to co-operation were in this instance not very great.

**Table 6.1** *Estimates of the Reduction in Percentage Ozone Depletion Effected by the Montreal Protocol*

| *Case* | *2000* | *2025* | *2050* | *2075* |
|---|---|---|---|---|
| No controls | 1.0 | 4.6 | 15.7 | 50.0 |
| Montreal Protocol | 0.8 | 1.5 | 1.9 | 1.9 |

*Source*: US EPA (1988), Table 3, p. 30575.

What does the model predict about the prospects of an agreement being reached on global warming? $N$ will again be large, and this will militate against significant united action. However, in this case $c/b$ will be large, too; the marginal costs of abating carbon-dioxide emissions will rise very steeply as fossil fuels must be substituted for and energy is conserved. This suggests that the number of signatories to an agreement would be small, and that little additional abatement could be effected by co-operation. The tragedy is that in the case of global warming fuller co-operation could potentially result in huge gains in global welfare.[11]

*Leadership*

It is sometimes asserted that countries should, on their own, do more than the non-co-operative solution demands of them. US environmental groups, for example, have argued that the US should have taken greater unilateral action before the Montreal Protocol was drafted, that it should now comply with the terms of the Protocol in advance of the deadlines, and that it should exceed the agreed emission reductions and phase out production and consumption of these chemicals entirely. The House of Commons Energy Committee (1989, p. xvii), in its recent investigation on the greenhouse effect, recommended 'that the UK should . . . consider setting an example to the world by seriously tackling its own emission problems in advance of international action, especially where it is economically prudent to do so'.

We have already seen that such 'unselfish' unilateral actions need not be matched by other countries. The United States, Canada, Sweden, and Norway banned the use of CFCs in non-essential aerosols in the late 1970s, and yet other countries did not reciprocate.[12] Unilateral restrictions on pelagic sealing in the North Pacific by the US were not duplicated by Canada. We have also seen that countries may wish to give in to their moral beliefs and embrace a less insular view of their responsibilities. An important question is whether 'unselfish' unilateral action can be expected to have a positive influence on international negotiations. If one country (or group of countries) abates more than the Nash non-co-operative solution demands, and all others choose the abatement levels that are optimal for them in a non-co-operative setting, will the environment be any better protected when international treaties are later negotiated?

In a two-country analysis, Hoel (1989) shows that the answer depends on whether the unilateral action is taken before agreement is reached and is not contingent on that agreement or whether the action is a commitment to abate more than the negotiated agreement requires. Hoel shows that in the former case, 'unselfish' unilateral action may compromise negotiations and lead, ultimately, to *greater* emissions than would have occurred had both countries

[11] The analysis given here is by necessity over-simplified. For a more detailed analysis, see Barrett (1991*a*).

[12] Reciprocity was certainly not full. The European Community, for example, passed two decisions limiting production capacity of the so-called hard CFCs (CFC-11 and -12) and reducing their use in aerosols by 30%.

behaved 'selfishly'. In the latter case, however, the country's announced commitment to overfulfil its negotiated abatement level can be expected to reduce total emissions.

There is an obvious incentive compatibility problem with this tactic, for the 'unselfish' country could do better by reneging on its commitment (the agreement is therefore *not* self-enforcing). Nevertheless, the analysis shows that the desire by environmentalists and others to reduce total emissions may not be well served by their calls for 'unselfish' unilateral action, a point that the EPA stressed in defending its ozone-depletion policy (1988, p. 30574): 'Unilateral action by the United States would not significantly add to efforts to protect the ozone layer and could even be counter productive by undermining other nations' incentive to participate in the Protocol.'

It is important to note that the US and the European Community announced their intentions to phase out production and consumption of the ozone-depleting chemicals by the end of the century *after* the Montreal Protocol came into force but before renegotiation talks had started. It would be wrong, however, to ascribe these developments simply to 'unselfish' behaviour. After all, the world's largest manufacturer of CFCs, US-based Du Pont, announced its intention to phase out production of CFCs by the end of the century *before* the phase-out decisions were taken by the US and EC. Three days after the EC decided to phase out CFCs, the chairman of the leading European producer of CFCs, ICI, declared that production of CFCs should cease 'as soon after 1998 as is practicable'. Much more is at work here.[13]

### *Efficient Co-operation*

Signatories to an international environmental agreement are assumed to maximize the net benefits accruing to the *group*. This means, among other things, that the marginal-abatement costs of every signatory must be equal; the abatement undertaken by the group must be achieved at minimum total cost.

How realistic is this assumption? In the case of the Montreal Protocol, the assumption is not very wide of the mark. The Protocol imposes on every industrial country signatory an obligation to reduce its production and consumption of CFCs by an equal percentage. This requirement on its own is inefficient because at the margin the costs of complying with the Protocol will surely vary. For example, the UK can apparently meet its obligations by simply prohibiting the use of CFCs in aerosols—an action that is nearly costless. The US banned the use of CFCs in aerosols many years ago, and hence can meet the terms of the Protocol only by instituting more costly measures. However, the Protocol allows limited international *trading* in emission reductions. For any

[13] See Barrett (1991*b*) for an analysis of these developments.

signatory, CFC production through mid-1998 can be 10 per cent, and from mid-1998 onwards 15 per cent, higher than it would have been without trading provided the increase in production by this signatory is offset by a decrease in production by another signatory. Furthermore, trades of consumption (but, strangely, not production) quotas are permitted by the Protocol within the European Community. These provisions will help increase the efficiency of attaining the total emission reduction implicit in the agreement, although they almost certainly do not go far enough.

### *Side Payments*

The equilibrium in the model of international environmental agreements is determined by a concept of stability that prohibits side payments. An important question is whether side payments might effect a Pareto improvement. To investigate this issue, reconsider the concept of stability employed in the model. In equilibrium, non-signatories do better than signatories, but no country can do better by changing its status. Signatories want non-co-operators to sign the agreement, because their net benefits would then increase. But non-signatories do worse by signing. Hence, without compensating payments, non-signatories will not want to sign the agreement. It is in this sense that the agreement is stable.

However, the very fact that signatories do better if non-co-operators sign the agreement suggests that trade might be possible. In particular, it might be possible for signatories to make side payments to a subset of non-co-operators to encourage them to sign the agreement. All might be made better off. It is in fact very easy to show that this can happen, that an international environmental agreement that specifies abatement levels *and* side payments can manage the global common-property resource better than one that prohibits side-payments.

An important feature of the World Heritage Convention is that it does admit side payments. The Convention established a World Heritage Fund that is used to help protect natural environments of 'outstanding universal value'. Each party to the Convention (there are over 90 signatories) is required to provide the Fund every two years with at least 1 per cent of its contribution to the regular budget of UNESCO.[14] In practice this means that the Fund is almost entirely financed by the industrial countries. Clearly, both the industrial and poor countries benefit from the Convention—otherwise they would not have signed it—but the poor countries may not have signed the Convention were it not for the Fund. Though the Fund is small, the mechanism could prove instrumental

[14] The United States and the UK continued to contribute to the Fund even after withdrawing their funding from UNESCO.

in protecting many of the world's remaining natural environments, including the tropical rain forests.

The World Heritage Convention is unique among international environmental agreements for incorporating side payments. But the need for side payments is not unique to the conservation of natural environments and wildlife. It has, for example, become increasingly clear that the success of the Montreal Protocol will ultimately hinge on the accession of non-signatories to the Protocol. Concern has specially been voiced about the need to get the poor countries—and, in particular, China and India—to sign the Protocol. These countries have declared their need for financial assistance, and the issue of setting up a global fund for protecting the ozone layer is likely to dominate discussion at the next meeting of the Protocol's signatories. It would seem to be something that cannot be avoided.

## Bibliography

Axelrod, R. (1984), *The Evolution of Cooperation*, New York, Basic Books.

Barrett, S. (1991*a*), 'The Paradox of International Environmental Agreements', mimeo, London Business School.

— (1991*b*), 'Environmental Regulation for Competitive Advantage', *Business Strategy Review*, forthcoming.

Coase, R. H. (1960), 'The Problem of Social Cost', *Journal of Law and Economics*, 3, 1–44.

Cornes, R. and Sandler, T. (1983), 'On Commons and Tragedies', *American Economic Review*, 73, 787–92.

Dasgupta, P. (1982), *The Control of Resources*, Cambridge, Mass., Harvard University Press.

Demsetz, H. (1964), 'The Exchange and Enforcement of Property Rights', *Journal of Law and Economics*, 7, 11–26.

— (1967), 'Toward a Theory of Property Rights', *American Economic Review*, 57, 347–59.

Friedman, J. W. (1986), *Game Theory with Applications to Economics*, Oxford, Oxford University Press.

Groves, T. and Ledyard, J. (1977), 'Optimal Allocation of Public Goods: A Solution to the "Free Rider" Problem', *Econometrica*, 45, 783–809.

Guttman, J. M. (1978), 'Understanding Collective Action: Matching Behavior', *American Economic Review Papers and Proceedings*, 68, 251–5.

Hardin, G. (1968), 'The Tragedy of the Commons', *Science*, 162, 1243–8.

Hoel, M. (1989), 'Global Environmental Problems: The Effects of Unilateral Actions Taken by One Country', Working Paper No. 11, Department of Economics, University of Oslo.

House of Commons Energy Committee (1989), *Energy Policy Implications of the Greenhouse Effect*, Vol. 1, London, HMSO.

House of Commons Environment Committee (1984), *Acid Rain*, Vol. 1, London, HMSO.
Lyster, S. (1985), *International Wildlife Law*, Cambridge, Grotius.
Marwell, G. E. and Ames, R. E. (1981), 'Economists Free Ride, Does Anyone Else?', *Journal of Public Economics*, 15, 295–310.
Paterson, D. G. and Wilen, J. (1977), 'Depletion and Diplomacy: The North Pacific Seal Hunt, 1886–1910', *Research in Economic History*, 2, 81–139.
Samuelson, P. (1954), 'The Pure Theory of Public Expenditure', *Review of Economics and Statistics*, 36, 387–9.
Sugden, R. (1984), 'Reciprocity: The Supply of Public Goods through Voluntary Contributions', *Economic Journal*, 94, 772–87.
— (1986), *The Economics of Rights, Co-operation and Welfare*, Oxford, Basil Blackwell.
Trail Smelter Arbitral Tribunal (1939), 'Decision', *American Journal of International Law*, 33, 182–212.
— (1941), 'Decision', *American Journal of International Law*, 35, 684–736.
US Environmental Protection Agency (1988), 'Protection of Stratospheric Ozone; Final Rule', *Federal Register*, 53, 30566–602.

# 7
# International Environmental Problems

*Karl-Göran Mäler*

## 7.1 Introduction

Man-made borders are completely arbitrary from the point of view of the biosphere. There is no reason that environmental disturbances should be confined by human definitions of areas of jurisdiction. But that means that the 'environmental problem area' will in general not be identical to the area of jurisdiction and control and there is as a result no single authority with the right to control and decide on a solution to the problem. One may therefore expect lack of co-ordination and inefficiency whenever the area of jurisdiction differs from the area of environmental concern. In no other field is this as apparent as in the field of international environmental problems. As there is no international or multinational 'government' that can enforce international environmental policy, these problems must be solved by voluntary agreements among the countries concerned, and as some countries may lose from an agreement, it is scarcely surprising that effective international co-operation is lacking. In spite of this, a number of international treaties have been agreed upon, treaties that perhaps do not aim to solve the environmental problems directly but have

Karl-Göran Mäler is Professor at the Stockholm School of Economics. This chapter was written while he was a visiting professor at the World Bank. He would like to express his appreciation to the Bank for giving him excellent opportunities for research. He is also obliged to David Pearce for detailed comments on an earlier draft. He adds that neither the World Bank nor David Pearce should be blamed for remaining shortcomings.

as their main objective the creation of an atmosphere conducive to further discussions and negotiations.

Building on the work of Landsberg and Russel (1971) the following taxonomy of international environmental relations is proposed. First, let us differentiate between the various kinds of environmental relations: there are physical relations, that is when a pollutant moves across a border through rivers, currents in seas, or by winds in the atmosphere. Second, there is the human transport of wastes across international borders. Even if a particular transport is accepted by both the sending and the receiving country, it may be that the transport is not compatible with sustainable development. Moreover, there is the hazard of accidental discharges. Third, there are non-physical relations that arise because individuals in one country may be concerned with environmental resources in another country. For example, there are many individuals in Europe and North America who are concerned with the preservation of the African elephants and are willing to sacrifice part of their present consumption in order to guarantee their survival. Fourth, there are the economic side-effects that arise because of environmental policies, in particular effects through the international trade. A second dimension which must be kept in mind in discussing international environmental problems is where the sources of pollution or resource loss are, and who are the sufferers of the damage done.

The classical case is the *unidirectional externality*, exemplified by upstream polluting countries and downstream suffering countries. This case can be divided into the many-victim case, when many countries are affected negatively by the externality, and the one-victim case, where only one country is damaged. This differentiation is important for the economic analysis, given the incentives to 'free-ride'. Much of the analysis in this paper deals with this problem. Furthermore, there is the differentiation between the case with one source and the case with many sources. In the latter case, there is the important question on how abatement costs should be shared and how control measures should be allocated among countries in a cost-efficient way.

The next main case is *regional reciprocal externalities*, in which a group of countries is both the source and victim of an environmental problem. Acid rain in Europe is one example of such a regional problem.

Finally, we have the case of *global environmental problems*, which affect most of the countries of the earth in one way or another. Here it is useful to separate out three sub-cases. The first deals with environmental problems in which one or a few countries are the sources of the problem but all or almost all countries are suffering from the problem. Excessive hunting of whales is carried out by only a couple of countries, but the threat of extinction of some of the species is a cost that will be carried by all mankind. It is quite similar to unidirectional externalities but with the difference that almost all countries will be hurt (including the countries causing the problem). The second case deals with the opposite situation, when almost all countries on earth contribute to the degradation of the environment but only a few countries are hurt. Finally, we have the case of global commons, when all countries contribute to the problem and all countries are also victimized. This use of the term 'global commons' is not the usual one. The established interpretation of global commons is in legal terms, covering resources such as the deep seas, or the Antarctic, or the radiation spectrum. This taxonomy is, however, based on the economic analysis of incentives to economize with resources, and from that point of view, biodiversity, global climate, the common biosphere are all very similar to the deep seas or the radiation spectrum.

We can display this taxonomy in the matrix shown in Table 7.1. This classification is founded in the economic analysis of incentive problems and not in the legal status of the various situations.

In this paper, we concentrate on physical relations and on unidirectional externalities and regional reciprocal externalities. Global environmental problems are discussed in Scott Barrett's chapter in this book. However, from an analytical point of view, global commons have very much in common with regional reciprocal externalities.

Two questions will be addressed: (1) what are the incentives to co-operate? and (2) how should institutions be designed in order to promote co-operation to achieve economic efficiency?

In the remaining sections of this chapter physical and non-physical transnational problems will be discussed. Although the two remaining issues in the matrix—waste transport and economic side-effects—are important as parts in the network of international environmental relations, they will not be dealt with further.

## 7.2 International Treaties

International co-operation on environmental issues was in its early stage mainly concerned with the preservation of species. A few treaties on damage from oil spills and on the use of nuclear power were also signed. There were also some agreements on pollution of rivers. After the Stockholm Conference of 1972 the situation changed. At the conference decisions were made to establish the United Nations Environment Programme (UNEP), to ensure that different UN organizations (FAO, UNESCO, etc.) should include environmental considerations in their operations, and to adopt a number of recommendations on international co-operation. In particular, paragraph 21 in the Stockholm Declaration dealt explicitly with transboundary pollution problems. That paragraph states that 'States have . . . responsibility to ensure that activities

**Table 7.1** *A Matrix of International Environmental Problems*

| | *Global externality* | | | *Regional reciprocal externality* | *Unidirectional externality* | |
|---|---|---|---|---|---|---|
| | *Many sources few victims* | *Many victims few sources* | *Common property* | | *One victim* | *Several victims* |
| Physical | | | | | | |
| Non-physical | | | | | | |
| Waste transport | | | | | | |
| Economic side-effects | | | | | | |

within their jurisdiction or control do not cause damage to the environment of other States or of areas beyond the limits of national jurisdiction.'

This paragraph has guided and will probably continue to guide international co-operation on environmental problems. It can be interpreted as a defence for the polluter-pays principle, meaning that the one who is causing an environmental problem has the responsibility to take the necessary measures to eliminate the problem and bear the full cost for these measures.

The polluter-pays principle or 'PPP' was adopted by the OECD countries in 1972 mainly as a guideline for domestic environmental policies. The main reasons for adopting PPP were the following. First, it was argued that PPP was a necessary condition for economic efficiency. Any attempt to subsidize pollution abatement would lead to biased incentives and therefore to distortions in the domestic economy. Thus, PPP can be defended on this account. Second, if we take the long-run technical development into account, it seems that the case for PPP is even stronger, as companies are rewarded by developing better and less expensive abatement technologies. Third, it was argued that the application of PPP would not create unintended distortions in foreign trade, as the exporter would have to absorb the total social cost for the product he is selling.

These arguments deal solely with the application of PPP to domestic environmental policy. It is, however, a very short step to extend the application of PPP to international environmental problems, i.e. that polluting countries should bear the cost of controlling the transboundary pollution emanating from them. This application also has a superficial mark of fairness, which probably lies at the bottom of the popularity of the polluter-pays principle. On the basis of the Stockholm Declaration, a large number of conventions, protocols, and agreements (about eighty) have been signed. Among these are such global treaties as the Law of the Sea (1982), the convention on trade in endangered species, and the Vienna convention on protection of the ozone layer (1985). A number of regional treaties have also been signed, for example conventions on the Baltic Sea and the North Sea, which regulate the form of co-operation between the countries involved. There are also treaties on the use of rivers such as the Rhine (1986) and the Niger (1980). Within the European Community, there are several very specific agreements and directives.

Most of these conventions have the character of a framework, in which countries can agree on particular methods for co-operation. The Vienna convention on the protection of the ozone layer is of this nature, as is the 1979 Geneva convention on long-range transport of pollutants. Pursuant to these conventions, there are special protocols that regulate the obligations of the signatory countries, for example the 1987 Montreal protocol of the ozone convention, which regulates nations' responsibilities to reduce the use and emission of chlorofluorocarbons (CFCs). Another example is the protocol

(1985) to reduce emissions of sulphur by 30 per cent and a protocol on the control of nitrogen emissions. We will come back to a discussion of these two protocols later. Most of these conventions are not legally binding but should be seen as moral obligations on the part of the signatories.

All these conventions presume the polluter-pays principle. However, OECD (1981) has recognized that the PPP may not be applicable in all cases of international environmental problems. In fact, in an analysis of the role of international financial transfers in solving transboundary pollution problems, OECD wrote, 'A willingness on the part of countries to give and to accept such compensation is an extremely important aspect of transfrontier pollution problems, since it often will be difficult, particularly in existing situations, to negotiate an efficient solution without such payments.' Obviously, what OECD must have had in mind is that in some cases, PPP must be abandoned in favour of 'VPP'—the victim-pays principle. We will analyse this concept in later sections. For the present it is important to recognize that the application of VPP in international agreements on transboundary pollution problems is not necessarily contradictory to the application of PPP in domestic environmental policy. It may then happen that the government of a downstream country finds it beneficial to pay the government of an upstream country to reduce the pollution of a river and that the upstream government accepts the payment, but applies PPP to the domestic companies that are polluting the river. It is in this sense that we will interpret PPP and VPP in the international context—as transfers between governments.

## 7.3 Unidirectional Externalities

We will distinguish three cases of unidirectional externalities. The first is the classic case where there is an upstream country, 1, that pollutes a river running into a downstream country, 2. Here we have a standard case of bargaining between two parties. In the second case, there are many downstream countries that are harmed by the pollution dumped into the river. In the third case there are many polluting countries. The interesting difference between the three cases is that in the second, downstream countries have the incentive to be free-riders, hoping that the other downstream countries will solve the pollution problem for them. In the third, there is the problem of allocating abatement measures among the sources in a cost-efficient way. These two latter issues will, however, only be illustrated with respect to regional reciprocal externalities.

### *One Upstream and One Downstream Country*

Let $E$ stand for the emission of a pollutant in the river in the upstream country. For concreteness, let us assume that $E$ is the amount of degradable organic material discharged. The upstream country—country 1—can reduce that discharge by applying sewage treatment, controlling pulp-mills, etc. Assume that the original discharge is $E_0$, so that the amount of discharge reduction is $R = E_0 - E$. Let the cost of reducing the discharge be given by a cost function $C = C(R)$.

The cost will naturally increase with the amount of reduction, but it is also natural to assume that the *marginal cost* will increase, as it will in general be more expensive to control the discharge of one more unit when the waste stream is already much controlled.

The discharge of organic wastes will consume free oxygen in the river, with detrimental effects to the downstream country. The downstream country is experiencing environmental damage which can be expressed as a monetary damage function $D = D(E)$.

From this formulation it follows that the benefits to the downstream country from reducing the discharge with $R$ is given by

$$B(R) = D(E_0) - D(E_0 - R).$$

We assume that $B(R)$ is increasing in the amount of waste reduction but that the marginal benefit is decreasing. This corresponds to the case when a marginal improvement in the water quality has a higher value when the river is highly polluted than when it is quite clean. It should be noted that this assumption is not always satisfied. Let us assume that the river is so polluted that it is an open sewer. A marginal improvement of the river would not change the appearance of the river or bring back natural ecological systems, and in this case it seems natural to assume that the marginal benefits are zero. This corresponds to the case when there are non-convexities in the feasibility set.[1] For this discussion, we will, however, retain the assumption of convexity, that is that the marginal benefits decrease with pollution control. We can now draw the marginal-reduction (or abatement) cost curve and the marginal-benefit curve in a diagram (Figure 7.1).

Let us now assume that (1) both countries know the abatement-cost function and the damage-cost function in each country, (2) there are no transaction costs, (3) the original distribution of property rights is well defined, (4) the pollution of the river can be seen in isolation from other international relations, and (5) the change in the distribution of the rights between the countries will not change the abatement-cost or the damage-cost functions. Most often the original distribution of rights is not determined by any convention or binding international law, but is based on traditions giving the upstream country the

[1] For a discussion of the existence and importance of non-convexities in connection with negative externalities, see Starret (1972) and Baumol and Bradford (1972).

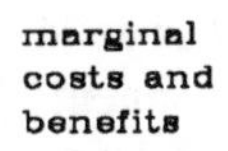


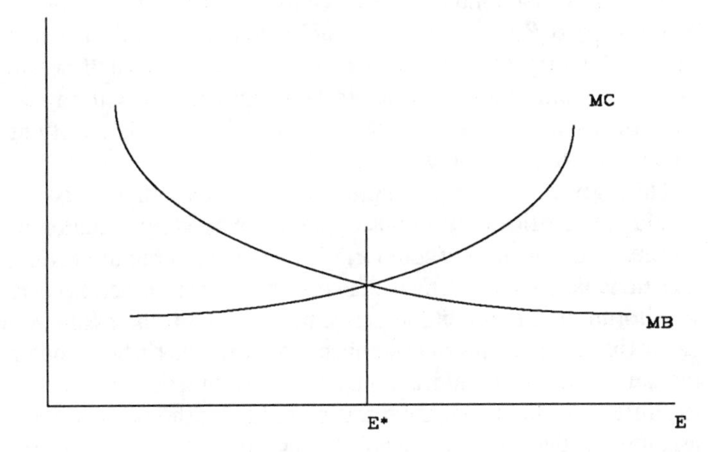


**Figure 7.1**

right to pollute. Assumption (4) is made in order to prevent the possibility that an agreement on the river can prejudice agreements with other countries or with the same country on other common problems. Assumption (5) is the standard assumption made in discussing the Coase theorem.[2]

In this situation, the Coase theorem guarantees that an agreement will be reached by which country 1 voluntarily restricts its discharges to $E^*$. If country 1 has the initial right to pollute the river, country 2 will cover the abatement costs to 1 and will bear the residual damage costs. If 2 has the initial right to a clean river, the agreement would mean that 1 covers the abatement costs and compensates 2 for the residual damage.

In order to understand this diagram better and to prepare for later analysis, let us reformulate this result in terms of non-co-operative game theory. As before, let $B(R)$ be the benefit function for the downstream country, and assume that the downstream country pays a side-payment, $\$S$, to the upstream country. The pay-off for the downstream country is therefore $NB_2 = B(R) - S$. The pay-off for the upstream country is then $NB_1 = S - C(R)$. Assume that the negotiations between the two countries take place in the following way: both countries make offers $(R_1, S_1)$ and $(R_2, S_2)$, meaning that the upstream country offers to reduce its discharge with $R_1$ if it is paid $S_1$, and the downstream country offers to pay $S_2$ if the upstream country reduces the discharges with $R_2$. If the two offers are such that either $S_2 - C(R_2) \geq S_1 - C(R_1)$ (that is the offer from the downstream

[2] It is interesting to note that Coase himself does not think this assumption about the absence of income effects is necessary. See Coase (1988).

country is as good for the upstream country as the upstream country's offer) or $B(R_1) - S_1 \geq B(R_2) - S_2$ (that is the offer from the upstream country is as good for the downstream country as its own offer), there will be an agreement. Otherwise both countries are left in the initial situation with pay-off zero. It can be shown that there are a large number of equilibria satisfying the above game—see Appendix 1.

Thus, given the five assumptions stated above, there exist equilibria that would entail efficient solutions of the transboundary pollution problem. The problem is the richness of equilibria. However, the assumptions made above are questionable. First of all, there may be substantial transaction costs involved in monitoring and enforcing an agreement. Second, the assumption that both parties have perfect information on the cost functions in both countries is hardly realistic. Insufficient information on the cost functions may create incentives to bluff in order to improve the gains to the home country. Finally, the assumption that one can regard this environmental problem in isolation is generally wrong. If the upstream country has the right to pollute, then the Coase theorem would dictate the victim-pays principle, something that may not be acceptable to the downstream country in view of its prejudicing effect on the negotiations with a third country. These three problems must be addressed in order to make a serious economic analysis of the unidirectional externality possible. Appendix 2 analyses these problems formally. It is possible to secure an efficient outcome to bargains when incomplete information prevails since incentives exist for both countries to tell the truth. However, the conditions necessary for this result to hold are very restrictive, and attention needs to be paid to the design of incentive structures for the avoidance of cheating. One such structure is the *mutual-compensation principle*.[3]

### *The Mutual-Compensation Principle*

The mutual-compensation principle, as well as the other that will be reviewed here, is based on the existence of an international agency whose objective is to create an environment fostering co-operation among the countries. We will here only look at the economic environment, although it is quite clear that other aspects may be equally or more important. The objective for the agency is thus to establish an economic environment through economic incentives for the involved countries to reveal correctly their abatement costs and their estimated benefits from pollution control and thereby encourage them to co-operate. However, one should note that we now have to some extent left the approach that characterized our previous analysis of the bargaining problem. There we looked at what could be accomplished with completely *voluntary* agreements,

[3] This principle is a special case of the Groves'mechanism (Groves, 1973), but was independently discovered by Smets (1973) in the OECD discussions on transboundary pollution probems.

while we now assume the existence of an international agency and that countries are willing to endow this agency with some powers of taxing the member countries. We should of course have tried to establish this agency as an outcome of negotiations between the interested countries. We have selected the much simpler solution of assuming that countries already have agreed to establish co-operation in the field, and the problem we will address is what policies the agency should adopt in order to induce countries to behave in a certain way. Moreover, in view of the result obtained in Appendix 2 concerning incomplete information, it may be argued that the case of unidirectional externality with only two countries involved is not the best area for the application of mechanisms that induce countries to reveal correct information. This is probably a correct criticism and the main reason why the mutual-compensation principle is discussed here is the simplicity offered by the analysis of only two countries.

With this interpretation of the agency, the analysis of these economic incentives is an application of the theory of compatibility of different incentives. Groves's mechanism (Grove, 1973) is one of the earliest attempts rigorously to analyse incentives in public decision-making. We can interpret the international agency as a government (although with very limited power) and the two countries as the citizens. The problem for the government is to make a decision on the control of pollutants so that the resulting outcome is Pareto-efficient. In order to do that, the government (or the agency) needs information from the citizens on their valuation of the pollutants. The citizens (or the countries) send messages to the government, and on the basis of these messages, the government pays or taxes the citizens and makes the decision on pollution abatement. Appendix 3 makes this abstract scheme more concrete. It should be pointed out, however, that the existence of the international agency must be agreed upon, and one should enlarge the appropriate game so as to include agreements on the agency, its objectives, and its instruments. This has, however, not been done in the literature, and we will not pursue that question further. Appendix 3 investigates the analytics of the mutual-compensation principle. The discussion of different mechanisms which would make truth-telling profitable indicate that the problems of incomplete information may not be that severe, if they exist at all. We will come back to these issues when discussing reciprocal externalities. However, there is another information problem that should be addressed. We have tacitly assumed that it is possible to monitor the waste reductions and that both countries would agree on the amount of actual waste discharged into the river. This is patently not so in very many cases. In fact, many international treaties have their origin in the need to monitor the actual flow of wastes. The EMEP—Environmental Monitoring and Evaluation Program—was set up by the ECE (the United Nations Economic Commission for Europe) as a protocol under the Geneva convention, to monitor the emissions of sulphur oxides and of other pollutants. Important though the monitoring problem is, we will leave it for now and come back to it in connection with the analysis of reciprocal externalities. When there are many source countries, special problems arise in connection with the question of how the reduction of waste discharges should be allocated among them. Similarly, if there are many downstream countries, the problem of cost-sharing will also arise. Moreover, in this case the downstream countries have strong incentives to be free-riders, hoping that other downstream countries will 'buy' a better environment for them. These problems will also be encountered in connection with the problems of regional reciprocal externalities and discussion is deferred until then.

### *The Victim-Pays Principle*

It seems to be clear from the discussion that a necessary condition for an effective agreement between the two countries involved in a unidirectional externality is that the victim-pays principle is upheld. However, the applications of this principle are very rare in reality. There may be several reasons for this, but two merit a more detailed discussion. The first has to do with the prejudicing effect of accepting the victim-pays principle. If a country has to deal with two or more countries on transboundary pollution issues, or deal with the same country on several such issues, then too fast an acceptance of the victim-pays principle in the negotiations on one of these issues may give the country a reputation as a 'weak' negotiator. In view of this, it may pay for the country to insist rather stubbornly on the polluter-pays principle in the negotiations on the first issues in order to gain the reputation of being a tough negotiator. This kind of situation has been illustrated in game theory by the so-called chain-store paradox.[4] It is also much discussed in the literature on time-consistent macroeconomic planning. In a way, the situation reflects the situation where there is true uncertainty about the benefit function of waste reductions in the downstream country, and where an agreement will give information on the true nature of this function.

Another factor is that countries exist and develop in a web of international relations. Two countries with a transboundary pollution problem will have a large number of links other than the flow of pollutants from one of the countries to the other. They are probably trading with each other, they operate on the same international capital market, they have mutual or antagonistic goals in foreign policies, people from one country visit the other as tourists, etc. The negotiations

[4] The chain-store paradox was discovered by Selten and discussed in Friedman (1986). It illustrates the choices available to a chain store in order to prevent newcomers from taking its business. A perfect equilibrium in the model would require that the chain store should play 'soft', letting the newcomers enter the market, a result which is counter-intuitive.

on the transboundary pollution problem will obviously reflect all these other relations and the repercussion of the negotiations on environmental issues on these relations will of course be taken into account. One country may want to make concessions in order to improve friendly neighbourhood relations and thereby achieve advantages in other areas of mutual interest.

Krutilla (1966, 1968) studied the economics of the Columbia river treaty. This treaty between the United States and Canada, although not on transfrontier pollution problems, illustrates these points. The Columbia river is a joint Canadian–American river and there were plans to develop that resource into hydro-power generation and flood protection. It was thought that the best way of accomplishing that would be through co-operation between the two countries. In 1961 this materialized in the Columbia treaty.

Krutilla found that (1) 'there seems little to commend it in terms of realizing, through co-operation, economies unavailable to each riparian independently' and (2) 'there is a demonstrable gain to Canada from the Columbia River Treaty, but there is no similar net gain to the United States'. In fact, Krutilla's analysis suggested a gain of about $225 million to $275 million to Canada and a loss equal to about $250 million to $375 million to the US. Moreover, the treaty did not achieve an overall economically efficient outcome. Why did the United States accept the treaty? There were several reasons for this, but one of the more important is given in the following quotation from one of the American negotiators:

> we were anxious that this agreement operate to progressively reduce power costs in British Columbia; firstly and obviously because if there was going to be an agreement it had to operate in that direction for the Canadians; secondly we regard Canada as a partner in the free world, and its growth, its economic growth, as being important to the United States.[5]

Thus, an important treaty on the use of an international river was accepted in spite of the fact that the downstream country subsidized the development in the upstream country, although there were no legal or purely economic reasons to do that. The most important motivation seems to have been that in the long run the downstream country would benefit from a strong economic development in the upstream country.

Kneese's study (1988) on US–Mexican rivers reaches the same conclusions. He looked in particular at the 1973 agreement (Minute 242 of the International Water and Boundary Commission) on desalinization of the Colorado river as it crosses the Mexican–American border.

[5] Statement made by Ivan B. White, Deputy Assistant Secretary of State, in Hearings before the Committee on Foreign Relations, United States Senate, 87th Cong., 1 Sess., 8 March 1964. The quotation is from Krutilla (1968).

Mainly through consumptive use of relatively pure water in the upper basins of the river, the salinity in the downstream areas has increased substantially. In the early 1960s the salinity grew dramatically because of increased use of the water for irrigation in Wellton-Mohawk district. Mexico complained about the bad quality of water delivered by the USA which resulted eventually in a pledge by the Nixon administration to undertake several measures among which the most important and most costly was the construction of a desalinization plant at Yuma, Arizona where the Colorado river crosses the border. The US Congress approved essentially the entire package.

There are several interesting features of this programme. First, the administration chose a very costly solution to reduce the salinity in the river. The main reason for the increase in salinity in the 1960s was the expansion of irrigation in the Wellton-Mohawk district, an expansion that came about through large federal subsidies. According to Kneese, a reduction of the irrigated acreage in the Wellton-Mohawk district might even produce positive benefits besides the reduction in the salinity of the river. Thus it would have been possible to achieve the desired salinity reduction at very small or even negative cost. Why did the administration choose a much more costly way? The answer is local politics and the way water politics had developed in the South West. Moreover, the international aspects of the salinity made it possible: 'to argue successfully that reducing and controlling the salinity in the Colorado was a national obligation, the states were able to shift the cost to the national taxpayer.'

Second, why did the United States want to enter an agreement with Mexico in such a way that the visible benefits accrued to Mexico and the high costs were borne by the United States? The outcome was in accordance with the polluter-pays principle, but as we have argued above, there is no direct role for PPP in this context. The answer, according to Kneese, is that there were non-visible benefits to the US from desalinization of the water in the Colorado river. Kneese goes on to say:

> Indeed, as long as all interested parties have something of value to trade, and as long as national self-interest is the primary motive force in international affairs, as I believe it is, this broad trading process seems to be the only sure path to international agreements. This may be especially true in the situation that characterizes the salinity problem.

Kneese illustrates this conclusion with the 1939–44 negotiations over the Colorado and the Rio Grande, in which the US agreed to deliver a large quantity of water in the Colorado to Mexico. One reason was that the US wanted to cultivate good relations with Mexico during the Second World War. Another reason was that the situation in the Rio Grande was the opposite of the previous case. Here most of the water in the lower parts originates in Mexico. Therefore, it was possible to make trade-offs between the two rivers in addition to trade-offs between water and other valuable services. The 1973 agreement on the Colorado can be seen in the same light. The US wanted to cultivate more favourable relations with Latin American countries. Moreover, there is the speculation that it had something to do with the discovery of Mexican oil.

Krutilla's and Kneese's studies reveal that at least along the US–Canada and the US–Mexico borders, agreements on water and water quality have involved 'trades' in areas other than the rather restricted area defined by the environmental resource. The important point is that there have been trades, although they may not be directly visible. One could therefore argue that, even if it seems superficially that the polluter-pays principle has been adhered to, the victim-pays principle has been applied, although the payment has not been in cash but in kind, and made in such a way that it may be difficult or impossible to register it.

What are the implications of these findings for the analysis of international environmental problems by using game theory? One first implication is that neither national nor local governments always behave rationally. The choice of a very costly scheme to reduce the salinity in Colorado shows this convincingly. Game theory, on the other hand, is based on extreme rationality of the players. One should therefore not expect game theory to produce realistic predictions of negotiation processes. However, game theory can identify incentives that the various countries have to agree. Even if it cannot predict accurately how the countries will react to these incentives, it is an important step by itself that such incentives are identified. This is probably the most important contribution we should expect from game-theoretical analysis of international environmental problems. Furthermore, another implication is that side-payments do not appear to be common, if by side-payments we mean transferable utility. In the discussion in the previous section we have applied the assumption of transferable utility (this was the essential reason why the Harsanyi–Selten approach yielded an efficient outcome, see Appendix 2). We should model these negotiation games as games without transferable utility. However, much less is known about such games, which is also the reason that we will continue to make the apparently unrealistic but very simplifying assumption that utility is transferable.

## 7.4 Regional Reciprocal Externalities

Regional reciprocal externalities exist when there is a common property resource with free access for many countries. The North Sea as a fishery is such an example, the European atmosphere used for waste disposal is another example. Whenever there is a common property resource with free access, one should suspect that it is being over-used. The reason is simply that each user will extend his use as far as is beneficial for him, without regard for the consequences to other users. Suppose that the net benefit from using a common property resource to an individual country $i$ is $NB_i = h_i(x_i, \Sigma x_j)$, where $x_i$ is the $i$'th country's use of the resource (harvest of fish in the North Sea, emission of sulphur in the European atmosphere, etc.) while $\Sigma x_i$ is the total use of the resource (the total harvest of fish, the total emission of sulphur, etc). It is reasonable to assume $h$ is increasing in its first argument but decreasing in its second argument. Each country will in its self-interest maximize $NB_i$, and a necessary condition for this is

$$\delta NB_i/\delta x_i = h_{i,1}' + h_{i,2}' = 0,$$

that is the sum of the partial derivatives should be equal to zero. When each country does this, the result will be a Nash equilibrium[6] $x_i^*$, $i = 1, \ldots, n$.

The Pareto-efficient outcome (if we assume that countries can make side payments to each other) is defined by Maximize $\Sigma NB_i$.

The necessary conditions for a maximum of the sum of net benefits can be written

$$h_{i,1}' + \Sigma_j h_{j,2}' = 0.$$

If the $h$-function is concave in its first argument, it follows that each country will use more of the common property resource in the Nash equilibrium than in the Pareto-efficient outcome. Thus, countries that are not bound by an agreement, will tend to harvest more fish than is efficient and they tend to emit more pollutants to the atmosphere than is efficient.

Before illustrating these general points with a more detailed discussion of one particular case of reciprocal externalities, it is worth while pointing out that there are indeed two different problems that show up in connection with reciprocal externalities. The first is the problem of cost-efficiency. As all countries are contributing to the environmental problem, the measures necessary to reduce the problem must be allocated among the countries, and one way would be to look for the least expensive way of allocating the measures. Note that in the case of unidirectional externalities, the problem of cost-efficiency will be there as soon as two or more countries are polluting the environment of

[6] Note that we have made no assumption that the $h$ function is separable. Runge, in an often cited article (1981) argues that whenever costs (or benefits) are not separable, one has to use a quite different paradigm—the problem is to co-ordinate the actions of the agents and one has therefore to change the pay-offs. This is nonsense and it is disturbing that an article that demonstrates such loose thinking has been so much cited.

a downstream or downwind country or countries. To the extent that the following analysis deals with cost-effective approaches, it is also relevant for these unidirectional externality situations. The second is the problem of incentives to participate in agreements. All will gain from being free-riders, hoping that the other countries will undertake abatement measures. This problem will also arise in connection with unidirectional externalities whenever there is more than one country that is damaged from a transboundary problem. Therefore, the following analysis on the free-rider aspects will be relevant also for those cases of unidirectional externalities with many downstream or downwind countries.

### *The Acid-Rain Game—A Short-Run Model*

In order to illustrate these points, we will use the simulations in Mäler (1989*b*) on the use of the European atmosphere as a dump for sulphur oxides. It has been well known for at least twenty years that such emissions will contribute to acid rains with detrimental effects on ground and surface water and on forests. However, it is also known that nitrogen oxides contribute to acid rains. We will, for simplicity leave nitrogen out of the discussion. The reader can easily imagine the qualitative changes that would be necessary to accommodate emissions of other substances.

Although it may seem that European problems of acid rain are rather special, the constructs and analysis that will be presented in this section have a much wider application. The problems of global warming and the emissions of greenhouse gases have essentially the same economic nature and the discussion on sulphur emissions will throw light on this larger issue.

Sulphur oxides are emitted when fossil fuels are burnt and in some industrial processes. In the atmosphere, the oxides are oxidized into sulphates, which can be transported by winds for very long distances. Ultimately, they are removed from the atmosphere by rain—wet deposition, and by contact with plants, surface water, etc.—dry deposition. In either case, the deposition of the sulphates will increase the acidity of the surface water, the top soil, etc. and will have detrimental environmental effects.

As the winds blow in various directions, this is a case of a reciprocal externality, although because some winds are more prevailing than others, the situation is not completely symmetric. Some countries are more upwind than others and some are more downwind. The extent to which a country is a net receiver of sulphates is given by a transport model. In this case of sulphur, the annual transport between countries can be described in terms of a matrix $A$ with co-efficients $a_{i}j$ indicating the amount of sulphur deposited in country $j$ from the emission of one ton of sulphur in country $i$. As most of the sulphur emitted in a country will be deposited in the same country, the diagonal elements of the transport matrix will in general be large compared with the non-diagonal elements.

Let us assume there is for each country a well-defined cost function for reducing sulphur emissions and a well-defined damage function from the deposition of sulphur. If a country is acting rationally, and if it is not bound by international agreements, it will emit sulphur to the point where the marginal abatement cost equals the marginal damage cost. The marginal damage cost from domestic emissions is equal to the marginal damage cost from sulphur depositions multiplied by the proportion of the deposition that originates from domestic sources. Thus, country *i* emits sulphur until

$$C_i'(E_i) = a_{i,i} \; D'_i(Q_i)$$

where $E_i$ is the emission in country *i*, $C'$ the marginal abatement cost, $Q_i$ the deposition and $D'$ the marginal damage cost from further deposition of sulphur (for details, see Appendix 4).

This condition describes the Nash non-co-operative equilibrium that would be the outcome from the interplay of rational countries that are not bound to take into account the effects of their emissions on other countries. However, this Nash non-co-operative equilibrium will not correspond to a collectively rational outcome. A collectively rational outcome would be a situation where the total net gains to all countries is maximized and would correspond to the following necessary condition:

$$C_i'(E_i) = \Sigma_j a_{i,j} D_j'(Q_j).$$

This condition says that the marginal-abatement cost in each country should be equal to the marginal damage in all countries that are affected by the emissions.

In order to use this model for illustrative purposes, the unknown cost and damage functions must be numerically specified and a relevant transport model must be found. Within the European Monitoring and Evaluation Programme (EMEP) a transport model has been estimated and used for producing 'sulphur budgets' for Europe.[7] The matrix *A* above has been estimated on the basis of the sulphur budgets for 1980–5. Cost of abatement functions have been estimated by IIASA,[8] and although these estimated abatement functions have some serious drawbacks, they have been used for this application. There are no available consistent estimates of damage functions from acid rain. In order to overcome this problem, the following procedure was followed.

[7] See The Norwegian Meteorological Institute (1987).
[8] See Amann and Kornai (1987).

We assume that 1984 was a year when the emissions of sulphur in Europe could be characterized as a Nash equilibrium. This assumption implies that if we know $a_i j$ and the marginal abatement cost $C_i'$ we would be able to calculate the marginal damage cost $D_i'$. Thus all required information for a calibration of the marginal damage cost $D'$ in 1984 exists. If we finally make the assumption that the marginal damage costs are constant and independent of the amount of deposition, the whole model can be calibrated numerically. It should be stressed that the damage-function estimate so obtained is quite different from the concept used previously. It may be interpreted as the revealed preferences of the governments for reductions in emissions of sulphur. Because of this procedure of calibrating the damage functions and the model, all numerical results should be interpreted with caution. The simulations do not purport to give numerical predictions but only qualitative insights into the problem of regional reciprocal externalities.

By using the calibrated model, different co-operative outcomes can be illustrated. One possible outcome is achieved if the sum of the net benefits over all European countries is maximized. This will be called the full co-operative solution. The consequences for some countries of this solution are summarized in Table 7.2.

One can first note that substantial gains of over 6 billion Deutschmarks can be made from co-operation. Moreover, in view of the calibration procedure, it is certain that the gains are understated in Table 7.1. The full co-operative solution requires an average reduction of sulphur emissions in Europe of almost 40 per cent, more than that corresponding to the protocol to the convention on long-range pollutants on sulphur emission reductions, the so-called 'Thirty Per

**Table 7.2** *Net Benefits from the Full Co-operative Solution*

| *Country* | *Emission reduction (%)* | *Net benefit (million Deutschmarks)* |
|---|---|---|
| Czechoslovakia | 75 | 152 |
| Finland | 14 | –2 |
| GDR | 80 | 11 |
| FRG | 86 | 328 |
| Poland | 27 | 599 |
| Sweden | 4 | 606 |
| Soviet Union | 2 | 1,505 |
| United Kingdom | 81 | –336 |
| Europe | 39 | 6,290 |

*Note*: The IIASA cost functions are expressed in Deutschmarks, and we have kept that currency in these simulations.

Cent Club'. More interestingly, the net benefits from co-operation are very unevenly distributed among the countries. Some countries will even experience losses from co-operation. This is mainly due to the geographic location of these countries, some are more upwind than others so that they will not have as big net benefits as those countries that are more downwind. An extreme case is provided by the United Kingdom, which is very much upwind, and therefore would have to abate its emissions quite a lot, while not benefiting from the abatement in other countries. Sweden is an example of a downwind country, having to reduce emissions by only 4 per cent, and making substantial net benefits. The USSR is a special case because it is large and very little of its substantial emissions affects other European countries.

Why should the United Kingdom be willing to sign an agreement by which it would lose more than 300 million Deutschmarks? We are obviously back to the earlier issue of the polluter-pays principle versus victim-pays principle. The only reason the UK would be willing to accept this burden is by expecting to gain something in some other arena. Let us stick to the assumption that it is possible to measure this other gain in Deutschmarks—that is, assume that the transferable utility can be measured in this currency. Then the UK needs a gain worth more than 300 million Deutschmarks in order to sign the full co-operative agreement. In fact, in the full solution, four countries (Finland, Italy, Spain, and the UK) would experience losses that must be compensated in order to induce these countries to sign the agreement. However, the net benefits in the rest of Europe would be more than sufficient to cover their losses.

The situation is, however, more complicated, because if the United Kingdom does not sign the agreement, while the other countries do, the UK will benefit from the reduction of emissions in the rest of Europe, while not bearing any burden. It may pay the UK to become a free-rider. Let us assume that all the four countries that would experience losses decide not to sign an agreement but that the rest of Europe decides to go ahead and maximize their total net benefit. The result is shown in Table 7.3.

Not only have the losses for the four countries disappeared but they have even turned into substantial gains. These are the gains from being a free-rider—enjoying the benefits from the co-operation among other countries without having to make any sacrifices. However, these free-rider gains can be achieved by all countries. By defecting, Sweden, could achieve a gain, although only a very small one as Sweden does not have to abate much of its emissions in the full co-operative solution. Similarly for every other country—they all stand to gain by not signing the agreement, hoping that the rest of Europe will co-operate. The outcome will obviously be that there will be no agreement that includes all European countries. The free-rider incentives in this model are so pervasive that we should not expect a full co-operative solution to emerge. Why it is necessary to include the words 'in this model' we shall soon see.

**Table 7.3** *Net Benefit from Coalition Formation*

| *Country* | *Emission reduction (%)* | *Net benefit (million Deutschmarks)* |
|---|---|---|
| *Co-operating countries* | | |
| Czeckoslovakia | 75 | 125 |
| GDR | 80 | –47 |
| FRG | 86 | 78 |
| Poland | 27 | 544 |
| Sweden | 3 | 478 |
| Soviet Union | | 1,372 |
| Total for co-operating Europe | 37 | 4,933 |
| *Defecting countries* | | |
| Italy | | 150 |
| United Kingdom | | 87 |
| Total | | 247 |
| Total for Europe | 28 | 5,180 |

Note that exactly the same mechanism will be working in the case of unidirectional externalities when there is more than one country receiving pollution from other countries and the downwind countries have to compensate the upwind countries.

### *A Long-Run Model*

Before continuing, it is of some interest to note the rather simplifying assumptions that have implicitly been made on the acidification processes in the discussion of the short-run model. We have assumed that it is the *annual* deposition of sulphur that matters and that each year starts afresh. In reality, there is an *accumulation* of sulphur in surface waters, ground water, and soil, which will only slowly disappear because of leaching or because of the buffering capacity of the environment. Thus, current deposition will have detrimental environmental effects not only now but also far into the future. The speed at which sulphur is removed from the environment depends on the media. A stream with low pH[9] may recover quite fast because of the replenishment of the water. For a lake, it may take a much longer time and still longer for ground

[9] pH is a measure of the acidity of a solution. The lower the pH-level is, the more acid is the solution. A neutral solution has pH-level of 7. Lakes in Scandinavia that have turned acid because of sulphur and nitrogen emissions may have levels as low as 4–5.

water and the soil. In order to simplify, let us assume that there is a fixed amount per hectare of sulphur that the environment can assimilate. This amount is known as the 'critical load', and is defined as 'a quantitative estimate of the exposure to one or more pollutants below which significant harmful effects on specified sensitive elements of the environment do not occur according to present knowledge' (Nilsson, 1986).

In order to take critical loads into account, one can construct a model[10] that makes the annual change in the accumulated sulphur in the environment equal to the annual deposition minus the assimilative capacity of the environment. In view of the definition of critical loads, it seems possible to interpret this assimilative capacity as the critical load. Thus, the stock of sulphur will change over time reflecting both the deposition and the removal of sulphur. It is then natural to assume that the annual damage from sulphur is a function of the stock of sulphur and not of the annual deposition. In this way, the situation can be modelled as a dynamic game, in which each country tries to minimize its present value of future abatement costs and damage costs.

In dynamic games of this type, it is important to differentiate between different kinds of strategies, depending on the information structure. If no country expects new information on what the other countries are doing in emission abatement or on the deposition in their own country, then each country will formulate an abatement policy that it will follow for ever. In this case we have 'open-loop' strategies. If each country expects to be able at each moment of time to get correct information on the deposition in its own country, then the country can formulate a strategy such that the actual emission abatement at any point of time depends on this deposition. In this case we have a 'closed-loop' or 'feedback' strategy.

One can show that if the strategies are restricted to open-loop strategies, there exists a unique Nash non-co-operative equilibrium. Moreover, the equilibrium strategies are such that the emissions will in the long run approach the levels that are compatible with the critical loads. Thus, if countries are not receiving more information than they have now, we should expect a long-run equilibrium such that the stock of sulphur in the environment will not grow further.

However, it is a rather strong assumption that countries will not get any more information on emissions and depositions. Therefore, a more realistic equilibrium should take as its base the use of closed-loop strategies. Countries would adjust their emissions according to the information available on the stock of sulphur in the environment. What kind of adjustments of the emissions would constitute an equilibrium in closed-loop strategies? There exist an infinite number of different equilibria in closed-loop strategies. However, one can show that there exists at least one perfect equilibrium that would correspond to

[10] For details, see Mäler (1989*b*) where a model for a differential game is constructed and analysed.

countries choosing co-operating strategies if side-payments are allowed to compensate the countries that would lose from using such strategies. In principle, these equilibrium closed-loop strategies supporting co-operation are very close to the trigger strategies discussed in the theory of repeated games. If a country discovers that the stock of sulphur increases more than would correspond to co-operation, the country would break the co-operation with the result that all countries would be punished, including the defecting country. It can be shown that this threat is sufficient to make it unprofitable to break co-operative agreements.

Moreover, it can also be shown that, in the long run, these co-operative strategies imply emissions that would be compatible with the critical loads. Thus in the long run, the emissions in a co-operative equilibrium and in an open-loop non-co-operative equilibrium will be the same. However, the convergence toward the critical-load emissions are faster with the co-operative strategies and the resulting stock of sulphur will be smaller.

Thus, analysing the incentives from a dynamic point of view seems to change the conclusions reached earlier significantly. First of all, the conclusion that there is a need for international transfers remains. Unless countries that are losing from co-operation are compensated, no co-operation with them will be established. Second, given this compensation, there are in the long run incentives for the countries to co-operate, and even if there are incentives to be a free-rider, these incentives will gradually diminish when the horizon goes to infinity. Third, in the long run, emissions will be adjusted in such a way as to become compatible with the critical loads.

### *Cost-Efficiency*

The previous discussion suggests that an optimal co-operative policy could be approximated by a policy that would see to it that the emissions are reduced fast to levels consistent with critical loads. Thus international negotiations on reducing sulphur emissions should proceed in such a way to ensure that the depositions eventually correspond to the critical loads. The question is how to design international institutions that can manage agreements on these issues.

Before discussing this it may be a good time to take stock of the results reached so far. The numerical estimates that have been presented in Tables 7.1 and 7.2 are of course not worth more than the assumptions that were used to produce them. The numbers should therefore not be taken literally. However, together with the qualitative analysis on repeated games and dynamic games, they do represent some real and valuable conclusions, namely:

1. the net benefits from co-operation will in general be very unevenly distributed among the countries in a region with reciprocal environmental

externalities. This implies that there is a need for a compensation system in order to redistribute the gains from co-operation in a way that is fair and gives countries incentives to co-operate;
2. in the short run, countries will have strong incentives to be free-riders;
3. in the long run, countries will try to maintain co-operation because they are expecting losses exceeding the short-run benefits from defecting from the agreement;
4. in the long run, optimal co-operative solutions will tend towards a steady state in which the annual deposition will correspond to the critical loads; and
5. monitoring the performance of the agreement can be made through monitoring of depositions, until reliable technologies for monitoring emissions are available.

Let us now see whether it would be possible to construct a concrete institution that would produce incentives to co-operate so as to reach approximately the full co-operative solution. We shall look at two different issues: (1) the cost-efficiency of different ways of reducing the depositions, and (2) different institutional arrangements to induce countries to limit their sulphur emissions.

Suppose that there is an agreement among European countries to reduce the emissions of sulphur oxides and that the objective is ultimately to reduce the deposition of sulphur to levels corresponding to the critical loads. This can be done in many ways. A first, but unsatisfactory attempt, has been made through the protocol on 30 per cent uniform reduction of emissions. It is unsatisfactory in many ways, one being that not all countries (UK and Poland are the notable exceptions) have signed the protocol, another being that 30 per cent reduction is not enough (we saw in the simulations earlier that even in a static setting, an average reduction of about 40 per cent is warranted, although this is not enough to satisfy the critical-load requirements). However, there is another way that is of concern here, namely the cost-effectiveness of such a solution.

Using the same notation as above, we can define cost-efficiency as the emissions reductions $R_i$ necessary in each country $i$ to reduce the depositions in each country to the critical load level in least expensive way possible. Mathematically, this can be formulated as

$$\text{Minimize } \Sigma_i C_i(R_i) = C^I$$

subject to

$$\Sigma_j a_{ij} R_j \geq Q_{oi} - Q_i^c, \; i = 1, \ldots, n,$$

where the right-hand side is the necessary deposition reductions to achieve the critical loads.

In contrast to this, the agreed reduction on sulphur emissions is formulated as an emission reduction uniform for all signatory states. This will henceforth be called the 'club solution'. If we are trying to reach the critical loads by a club solution, we would

$$\text{Minimize } \Sigma_i C(R_i) = C^2$$

subject to

$$\Sigma_j a_{ij} R_j \geq Q_{oi} - Q_i^c, R_i / E_i = \theta, i = 1, \ldots, n$$

where $q$ is the variable representing the uniform emission reduction. The solution to this problem determines the proportional emission reduction $k$ and the country reductions $R_i$ necessary to meet the requirement that the depositions do not exceed the critical loads in the least expensive way.

Obviously, this solution will yield a higher total cost than the previous one, as we have restricted the reductions more in the second problem than in the first. Thus we know that $C^1 \leq C^2$.

It would be interesting to know whether the difference between $C^1$ and $C^2$ is 'big' or 'small'. If it is small, we might be satisfied with the club solution as it is easier to manage and gives a superficial sense of fairness.

By using the same transport model and the same cost functions as before,[11] the solutions to these two problems were computed. It turned out that the club solution would cost 76 per cent more than the cost-efficient solution. Furthermore, the club solution would reduce the total emissions in Europe by 88 per cent while the cost-efficient solution would reduce the emissions by 63 per cent. Thus, in order to reach the targets set by the critical loads, the club solution would require an 'Eighty-Eight Per Cent Club' to be formed. The computations indicate quite clearly that the club strategy with uniform emission reductions is very expensive.

However, it may happen that the cost of achieving the cost-effective solution is very unevenly distributed among the participating countries, which would necessitate transfers among the countries. In fact, this is not so and, moreover, if each country accepts the targets set by the critical loads, formal co-operation may not even be necessary! In order to see this, let us therefore assume that each individual country strives for a deposition in its own country that does not exceed the critical load. We can then define the Nash non-co-operative equilibrium as such a pattern of emission reductions, that no country would gain

[11] In fact, a number of countries have been excluded from the simulations because of the unsatisfactory estimates of cost functions available. It turned out that if Albania, Ireland, Norway, Portugal, Turkey, and the Soviet Union were included, emission reductions far outside the domain of the cost functions were needed. For more details on the simulations see Mäler and Olsson (1990).

by deviating from its equilibrium emission reduction as long as the other countries follow their equilibrium strategies. More formally, the Nash equilibrium is defined by

$$\text{Minimize } C_j(R_j)$$

subject to

$$\Sigma a_{j,i} R^* + a_{j'j} R_j \geq Q_{oj} - Q_j^c, \quad = 1, \ldots, n$$

where $R_i^*$ is the equilibrium reduction for country *i*.

It follows that if the transport matrix *A* has an inverse, the Nash equilibrium is given by

$$E^* = A^{-1}(Q_o - Q^c).$$

However, if the matrix *A* has a non-negative inverse, the cost-effective solution is

$$E = A^{-1}(Q_o - Q^c),$$

the same solution. In practice, *A* does not have a non-negative inverse and the Nash solution would yield a 1 per cent higher cost than the cost-effective solution. Thus, if countries accept the objective of reducing emissions so that the deposition in their own countries equals the critical load, they will accomplish this by themselves, without the need to have a formal agreement. Obviously, this result depends on the very peculiar shape of the marginal-damage cost function underlying these models. We have, in fact, assumed that the marginal-damage cost is infinite for depositions exceeding the critical load and zero below that load. It is hardly likely that countries believe such valuations. Also note that in the previous model of the acid-rain problems as a differential game, we did not need such an extreme assumption.

The main conclusion to be drawn from this exercise is that substantial cost savings can be achieved if international agreements are suitably designed. We will therefore in the next sections look at two types of agreements that will achieve efficiency or near efficiency.

It should finally be stressed that the importance of cost-efficiency is as relevant for unidirectional externalities with many upstream or upwind countries, and in fact the same kind of analysis carried out above could and should be performed as soon as gains can be expected from choosing a more cost-effective strategy.

*Taxation of Sulphur Export*

Suppose that the countries involved agree on the following:

1. To establish a European Acidification Fund (EAF) with the purpose of giving participating countries a platform for discussions and negotiations and to manage any agreement that will result, including the collection of taxes, redistribution of tax revenues, and responsibility for the necessary monitoring of emissions. As before, EAF could also be charged with the duty of finding and funding economically and environmentally viable projects which would otherwise not be undertaken.
2. A transport model for sulphur oxides and nitrogen oxides in Europe.[12]
3. A scheme for redistributing a proportion of the tax revenues in order to compensate countries that would otherwise lose and to achieve a fair distribution of the gains from the co-operation.
4. A tax rate which will be applied on the airborne export of sulphur from one signatory country to all other signatory countries. The export of sulphur will be determined by the actual emissions and the transport model.
5. Finance for mutually beneficial environmental projects. As market failures can be expected to be pervasive in East Europe, it may be desirable for EAF to fund some pollution abatement activities in this part of Europe, abatement that otherwise would not come about.

It is clear that a tax system such as the one proposed above will not achieve a first-best optimum, as it will not differentiate between exports to countries with high marginal-damage cost and countries with low damage cost. In a first-best policy one should differentiate the tax rate between different exporters. However, such a differentiation would create not only practical problems but also obstacles to reaching an agreement. Moreover, as we will soon see, the gains from going to the first-best optimum seem to be marginal. Therefore, the proposal is one of a uniform tax rate, independent of the exporting country.

By using the numerically calibrated short-run model discussed previously, it is possible to find the effects of different tax rates. In Table 7.4, the simulations with a tax rate of 4 Deutschmarks per kilogram sulphur exported are shown for a sample of countries.

It is extraordinary how close this second-best solution is to the first-best solution in Table 7.2. The total benefit from the full co-operative solution is 6,290 million Deutchmarks while the uniform-tax solution would yield a total benefit only about 1 per cent lower. Not only the aggregate benefit but also the *distribution* of emission reductions and country-specific net benefits are very

[12] The EMEP model that has been used previously in this article is an example of such a transport model. In light of recent finding on the emissions of sulphates from the North Sea due to decay of algae, it seems that existing models may need some revision.

**Table 7.4** *Effects of a Tax Equal to 4 DM/kg Sulphur Exported*

| *Country* | *Emission reductions (%)* | *Net benefits* | *Tax payments* | *Net benefits–taxes* |
|---|---|---|---|---|
| Czechoslovakia | 75 | 147 | 585 | –438 |
| GDR | 80 | –11 | 374 | –385 |
| FRG | 81 | 363 | 332 | 32 |
| Poland | 30 | 530 | 1,495 | –965 |
| Sweden | 4 | 580 | 114 | 466 |
| Soviet Union | 2 | 1,508 | 234 | 1,274 |
| United Kingdom | 79 | –326 | 133 | –546 |
| Europe | 38 | 6,213 | 7,067 | –856 |

similar between the full co-operative solution and the uniform-tax solution. On the basis of these results, it is possible to feel comfortable with this second-best solution.

The total tax payments would be about 7 billion Deutchmarks (DM), exceeding the total net benefits by about 850 million DM. Thus, EAF needs to use this 850 million DM from the tax revenue to compensate the losing countries, but would still end up with a net revenue corresponding to the total net benefit from the emission reductions.

The difficult problems with the proposed scheme have to do with the distribution of the net tax revenues (net after compensating the losers) among the participating countries, the incentives to reveal the objective cost- and damage-functions, and the problem of monitoring the emissions. Given that the latter problems can be solved, the first problem could be attacked by trying to reach an agreement in which the Nash bargaining solution is achieved. That would mean that with the Nash non-co-operative solution as a threat point, the total net benefits would be shared equally among the participating countries. One can doubt whether such a solution will be reached in reality as countries differ substantially in size and importance. It would be surprising if a small country with small emissions would be able to secure for itself as much as France, Poland, or the United Kingdom. However, we do not have to determine the outcome of this bargaining process here. The important point is that there will be a substantial gain that must be distributed.

The other problems are more demanding. Both have to do with the revelation of information necessary for a fruitful co-operation. Let us start by assuming that emissions can be monitored perfectly but countries can give false information on their true abatement and damage cost.

The first thing to note is that in contrast to the unidirectional externality with only one downstream and one upstream country, we can no longer expect that truth-telling to be an equilibrium strategy. In fact, because of the incentives to be a free-rider, there will be no equilibrium in which all countries are giving correct information.

Secondly, as long as countries agree to the tax solution, the information they supply is only used for calculating the tax rate. Irrespective of the rate, we can be quite sure that the resulting allocation of emission reduction is cost-effective. We therefore know that whatever the outcome will be, it will be cost-effective. The problem is, however, that the tax rate may be too high or too low to support emission reductions that would maximize the total net benefit. Moreover, incorrect information may distort the negotiations.

We could think of applying the mutual-compensation principle in this situation in order to induce participating states to give correct revelation of abatement- and damage-cost. We have already seen that this principle will generate a surplus that must be disposed of. However, this is not a significant problem in this application, because as we will soon see, there are some investments that would not come about automatically and which would enhance the welfare of the European countries and which the EAF should finance. A more important objection is that the mutual-compensation principle would destroy the simplicity, both of the export tax solution and the solution based on tradable permits, to be discussed in the next section.

The second problem is perhaps even more important, because if emissions cannot be monitored, countries would have strong incentives to violate the agreement. However, as has already been pointed out, technical development may eventually permit satellite monitoring of the transboundary flux of pollutants. Meanwhile, statistical analysis of the actual deposition, together with information on the transport model and the actual weather conditions, may give indications on violations of the agreement.

### *Tradable Export Permits*

Instead of taxing the export of sulphur from one country to other signatory states, the agreement could establish export quotas for sulphur for each country and in order to make the scheme efficient, the quotas or export permits would be made transferable between countries. The export of sulphur would be determined exactly as in the tax solution by the use of a transport model. Assume that the countries involved agree on the following:

1. To establish a European Acidification Fund (EAF) with the purpose of giving participating countries a platform for discussions and negotiations and to manage any agreement that will result, including the determination of export permits for each country, and the responsibility for the necessary

monitoring of emissions. Moreover, EAF could also be charged with the duty of finding and funding economically and environmentally viable projects which would otherwise not have been undertaken.
2. A transport model for sulphur oxides and nitrogen oxides in Europe.
3. The rules for using funds available to EAF.
4. The total amount of export of sulphur from one participating country to other co-operating countries.
5. Calculations of the 'weights', i.e. the export shares of each country.
6. Auction of initial permits, either to governments or to organizations in participating countries, or agreement on other ways of distributing the initial rights.
7. If further reductions of sulphur are judged desirable, EAF buys permits at market prices.
8. As before, finance for mutual beneficial environmental projects.

Obviously, this proposal is very similar to that for a sulphur export tax. In fact, given that the total amount of sulphur export between the participating states is set equal to the amount potentially achieved in the tax solution, the allocation of exports will be the same in the two proposals (assuming that informational and monitoring problems can be neglected). Moreover, the price on permits will in equilibrium be equal to the tax rate.

If the allocative properties are the same, what are then the differences between the two approaches? First, if costs and benefits are not known with certainty, there will be allocative differences. This follows from Weitzman's (1974) analysis of prices versus quantities as regulatory instruments. If a tax is chosen as a regulatory instrument, uncertainty in the cost of abatement functions may have as a consequence that the actual export will significantly exceed the optimal export. If the marginal benefit function is inelastic, it follows that the cost from too much sulphur being transported between countries would be large. This conclusion is strengthened if the marginal cost of abatement function is elastic as, in that case, small changes in the tax will cause large changes in abatement. Thus, with elastic marginal abatement cost functions and inelastic marginal benefit functions, a tax solution may cause large *ex post* costs. If, on the other hand, a permit system is chosen, the total amount of sulphur exported is fixed. However, if the marginal-abatement cost functions are inelastic, a small error in determining the total amount controlled may cause large variations in abatement cost. Thus, the relative slopes of the marginal-abatement cost curves and the marginal-benefit curves are important for deciding which approach is to be preferred.

Second, the tax proposal has the advantage that it will generate revenues for EAF, revenues that are needed to compensate the losers and to finance other abatement measures that are deemed desirable. A permit system may be designed to raise the same amount of money, if the permits are valid only for a limited time, and if they are auctioned off regularly. Then the permit system will be identical to a tax system under full information. However, it is possible to design the permit system differently. If the initial distribution of rights is determined in some other way, for example as a proportion to the initial sulphur export, no revenues will be raised. In that case, the compensation to the losers must be made through the distribution of initial rights. One possibility would be that countries that are expected to have negative expected net benefits would be given permits equal to their initial exports, while the other countries would be given permits as a fixed uniform proportion of their intitial exports ('grandfathering'). In this case, no country would lose, and an efficient outcome could still be expected. Under these circumstances EAF would not raise any money, but it would not need any funds for compensation either. However, as we will come back to, such an EAF would need some financial means in order to increase cost-efficiency.

Third, the two approaches differ with respect to incentives to cheat. With a tax system, it is in the interest of each country to understate the actual emissions, and with imperfect monitoring, countries will probably try to make gains by giving biased reports. With a tradable-permit system, countries still have incentives to cheat. If cheating becomes pervasive, however, the demand for permits will go down and so will the equilibrium price on permits, thereby reducing the incentives to cheat.[13] Thus, the tradable-permit system has a self-regulating mechanism that makes cheating less profitable than in a system with a tax as a regulatory instrument.

### *Cost-Efficiency and Market Failures*

We have several times pointed to the need for taking into account various forms of market failures. In regional environmental problems, and perhaps much more so in global environmental problems, countries with different economic systems have to deal with each other. As the economic systems differ, there will be unexploited trades between different economic systems that can be of interest for an agreement on environmental issues. In Europe, the controls of the markets for capital and foreign exchange in Eastern Europe provide an example of this. Because of these controls the real cost of capital is higher in Eastern Europe than in the West and the cost of buying West European technology is higher because the exchange rate is lower in the West than in the East. Thus, pollution abatement in Eastern Europe may be less expensive if it is undertaken and financed by organizations in Western Europe. The European Acidification Fund can therefore potentially play an important role in initiating

[13] Andreasson (1989) has rigorously studied these interesting characteristics of taxes and tradable permits.

and financing pollution-abatement projects in Eastern Europe. The reason why EAF should do this is not to 'help' the East Europeans, but to promote the interests of all EAF countries by exploiting less expensive measures to improve the environment.

One should be aware of some rather difficult problems that seem to be inherent in a scheme like this. These problems have to do with the possibility for the receiving country to react to the proposed measure. In Figure 7.2 the marginal cost of abatement is drawn together with the marginal-benefit curve in the receiving country.

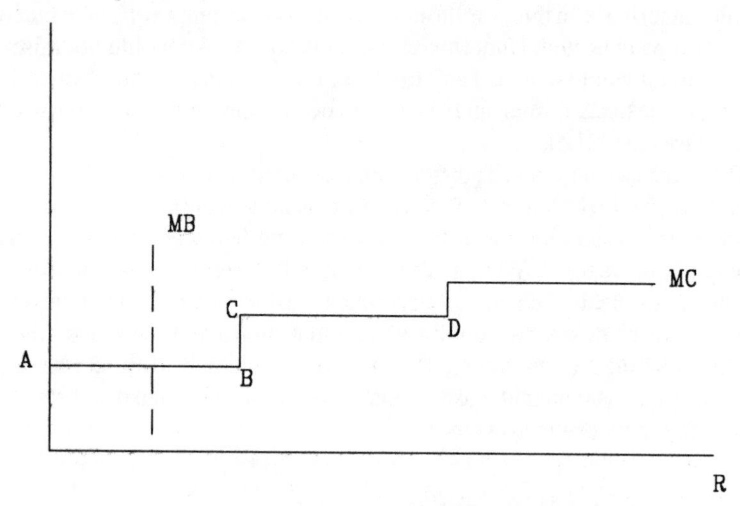


**Figure 7.2** *Marginal-Abatement Cost and Marginal-Damage Cost in a Country Receiving Environmental Aid*

Here we have assumed that the *MC*-curve has a staircase shape with each step representing a particular abatement measure. We have also assumed that the marginal-benefit curve is inelastic, so that the existing abatement is $R^*$. Let us assume now that Western countries decide to finance the measures represented by the step *CD* in the diagram. With the given marginal-benefit function, it is profitable for the receiving country to stop abatement altogether, because the foreign financed abatement alone will reduce the emissions with more than $R^*$. Of course, this problem of perverse incentives can be solved, at least in the short run. The best way is probably to introduce conditions in the contracts that guarantee satisfactory monitoring. However, in the long run, when the country is developing its industry, it may become difficult and even impossible to keep track of which abatement measures that have not come about because of the measure *CD*.

## 7.5 Global Issues

*Physical Externalities*

Global physical externalities are, from an analytical point of view, very similar to regional reciprocal externalities. The emissions of chlorofluorocarbons or CFCs is a good example. The CFCs will, irrespective of where they are released in the atmosphere, reduce the ozone in the troposphere, and thereby create health hazards through increased ultraviolet radiation. From an economic analytical point of view, this situation is almost identical to the situation with acid rains, discussed in the previous section. Barrett's discussion of the Montreal convention in this book shows that the same incentive problems to create effective co-operation exist for international control of CFC emission as do for managing sulphur emissions.

The increases in the emission of greenhouse gases, primarily carbon dioxide but also methane, CFCs, and di-nitrogen oxide are, from an economic theoretical perspective, also very similar to the sulphur and nitrogen emissions in Europe.[14] However, one can suspect that the variation in net gains from any actions to reduce global warming will be much greater compared with the case of acid rains in Europe. Therefore, it seems necessary to develop the idea of side-payments into new institutional frameworks much further in order to get the much needed global co-operation on reducing the threats to global climate.

One other aspect merits mentioning. Although climatologists agree that the greenhouse effect is real and that global average temperature will rise over the next 100 years, they are very uncertain about quantitative predictions and in particular about the spatial distribution and the timing of the warming.[15] Moreover, the consequences in terms of sea-level rise, precipitation, agricultural productivity, etc. are very uncertain. Therefore, any action taken today to reduce the emission of greenhouse gases (including measures to increase the absorption of $CO_2$ by afforestation) will have very uncertain consequences. On the other hand, any change in the global temperature will have irreversible consequences, although we cannot predict these consequences with a high degree of precision. Thus, we are facing a situation in which the 'no-action' means continued accumulation of greenhouse gases and irreversible changes in the global environment, while any action to reduce the accumulation of greenhouse gases will have consequences that are not, at least in their spatial and time dimensions, well known. The description of this decision-making

[14] For an overview of the current views on global warming and the greenhouse effect, see Houghton and Woodwell (1989).

[15] See Beardsley (1989) for an illustration of the wide estimates of the warming rising from different assumptions on cloud formation and heat absorption in the oceans.

problem obviously calls for a 'Bayesian approach',[16] that is an approach by which we take into account both the irreversibility of the changes and the possible forthcoming of new information on the consequences from global warming. In the theory of 'quasi-option values', as developed by Arrow and Fisher (1974) and Henry (1974),[17] it has been shown that a rational decision-maker should be cautious, not commiting himself to 'too many' irreversible changes. The loose phrase 'too many' can be made quite precise in the theory, but it is not necessary to go into any details here. The main point is that even if the expected future damage from global warming is quite small (i.e. less than the expected cost of reducing $CO_2$ emissions), it may still be desirable to take action to reduce the irreversible consequences from the change in the climate. Thus, even if there is considerable uncertainty about the future climate, one can argue convincingly that in spite of (or perhaps because of) this uncertainty, action should be taken today to reduce the release of greenhouse gases in order to prevent 'too many' irreversible changes.

*Non-Physical Effects*

There are many good examples of global environmental interdependencies that are not based on physical interactions between different countries or regions of the world. The threat to some old Egyptian temples from the flooding of Lake Nasser created a willingness on the part of Europeans and North Americans to pay for the removal of the temples to non-flooded areas. The preservation of the cultural heritage is thus an example of an international externality that does not correspond to any physical flows between countries. Similarly, the general concern for preservation of biological diversity and in particular for whales, elephants, rhinos, etc., is an example of an externality that extends across national boundaries without any associated flows of materials from one country to another. In contrast to the pollution cases, discussed in previous sections, we here have cases of services that one country can but is not necessarily induced to provide to the rest of the world.

It is important to understand the nature of these services and we will therefore discuss one such service—that of *preserving biodiversity*—in some detail. As the tropical rainforests represent the greatest biological variation and as these forests are seriously threatened today, it is natural that the discussion focuses on the preservation of these forests. The values of biological diversity to mankind are of different kinds. First of all, many species are used for various purposes—food, clothing, transport, fuel, pets, medicine, hydrological control, etc. It is difficult to overestimate the importance of these *use-values*, not only

[16] For an excellent introduction to Bayesian decision-making, see Raiffa (1968).

[17] See Mäler (1989*c*) and (1989*d*) for an attempt to create a more general theory on these issues.

for single species but also for complete ecological systems.[18] For many species and ecological systems, these use-values can only be attributed to the people using the corresponding resources. Thus, it is mainly the people in Amazonia that gain from the control of the hydrological cycle that the tropical forests in that area provide. Most of these use-values are therefore local or regional. The role for the global carbon cycle played by these forests is perhaps an example of use-values of a global nature.

Many of the species existing in a tropical rain-forest have no use-value today, but may in the future become important preconditions for new medicines, new hybrids of grains, or for other human activities. However, we do not know which species will generate use-values in the future. On the other hand, we do know that the extinction of a species today will for all future time be irreversible. Therefore, the extinction of a species means that we have reduced our future options with respect to the use of environmental resources. The value of keeping these options—the option value—may sometimes be quite important.[19] The option value may be interpreted as the conditional expected value of future information, given that the species is preserved. This value cannot in general be assumed to go to any particular group. As the value will be realized only in the future in activities unknown today, it will have the character of a global public good. Thus, the private incentives to preserve biological diversity will not in general reflect appropriately the option values.

In particular, it can be expected that people in countries outside the tropics may have great interest in preserving species. Moreover, this interest is strengthened by *existence values* or *preservation values*. These values represent the values that people associate with the preservation of biological diversity without expecting that they ever will be able to obtain direct use values. The total value from preservation of biological diversity is thus equal to the sum of use values, option values, and preservation values. Of these terms, the use values are most often concentrated in the area where the species are to be found. Option values and preservation values can on the other hand arise all over the earth. They have the character of *global public goods*.

However, there are no institutional arrangements which would enable people to express their willingness to pay for preserving biodiversity at the present. In a way, the situation is similar to the situation of acid rains in Europe. The net gains from the preservation of biodiversity is very much dispersed among nations and there are strong incentives to behave as a free-rider for some nations. However, because of the irreversibility of species extinction, these

[18] For a more precise definition of use values see Carson and Mitchell (1989) or Mäler (1989*d*). For an interesting discussion of use values from preserved biodiversity see Wilson (1988) and McNeely *et al.* (1989, forthcoming).

[19] See Fisher and Hanemann (1986) for an interesting study of the option value of keeping a special variety of Mexican rye.

incentives are moderated. A country which does not co-operate in the preservation of a species knows that the result from its behaviour may be irrevocable, and that will reduce the incentives to act as a free-rider. The problem is to design the international institutions that would encourage the needed co-operation.

One approach, which to some extent already has been tested, is the *debt-for-nature swaps*. Such swaps are defined as the purchase of developing country debt at a discounted value in the secondary debt market, and cancelling the debt in return for environment-related action on part of the debtor nation (Hansen, 1988). These measures can probably only make marginal contributions to the preservation of the tropical rain forests. One reason is the incentive problems arising from the public-good aspect of the preservation. Another, and perhaps more important, is the problem of creating the right incentives in the debtor countries. We have here a similar problem to the one discussed in connection with the European Acidification Fund and its relation with Eastern Europe. Unless the swap is tied to some national measure of preservation which can be monitored, there is no reason to assume that the swap will make any contributions to the preservation of forests.

Other measures such as buying land in the developing world have the same problems. The scale will be too small because of the incentive problems and the result may not be satisfactory if the country can exploit other areas instead.

There seem to be two different but not necessarily mutually exclusive routes which can be followed. The first is to help these countries to make *policy reforms* including the institution of private property rights to land. It has been shown that much of the present destruction of tropical forests is due to badly designed property rights and to macroeconomic policy measures.[20] In general, policy reforms will improve the overall efficiency of the economies and should be desirable, even without positive environmental side-effects. Therefore, one can hope that the World Bank and various donor countries will be able to convince developing nations that it is in their interest to reform their main economic institutions.

The second route is to try to accomplish global agreements on the greenhouse effect. Such agreements may involve a *tradable emission permit*, similar to what was discussed for acid rains in Europe. Preservation of tropical forests should in such a system generate the right to increases in the initial allocation of permits. As such permits can be sold, the preservation of tropical forests therefore means export revenues, and investments in tropical forests may become quite profitable in some countries. Of course, to accomplish such agreements and to develop the necessary monitoring and enforcing organizations may prove to be very difficult.

[20] See Warford and Schramm (1987) for a collection of studies that discusses the role of policy failures for environmental degradation and Binswanger (1989) for a discussion of land titles and taxes for deforestation in Brazil.

## 7.6 Concluding Comments

We have seen that there are many different kinds of international environmental problem, and an attempt to classify them was given in section 7.1. In the paper, only four problem types are analysed—the unidirectional externality case, the regional reciprocal externality case, the global physical externality case, and the global non-physical externality case. The following main conclusions emerge from the analysis:

1. There will be many situations where the victim-pays principle, or transfers from the country whose environment has been degraded to the country that causes the degradation, will be necessary in order to achieve an efficient solution.
2. Quite often, these transfers will take the form of concessions in other areas in which the countries have common interests and not of financial transfers.
3. In the case of several 'upstream' countries causing damage or regional reciprocal externalities, substantial gains can be made by searching for, and implementing, a cost-efficient allocation of abatement among the upstream countries compared to agreements on uniform reductions.
4. In the case of several 'downstream' countries or regional reciprocal externalities, there will in the short run be strong incentives for the countries experiencing environmental damage to be free-riders. In the long run, however, the incentives to be a free-rider will diminish because the temporary gains from being a free-rider will not be sufficient to compensate for the long-run losses if co-operation breaks down.
5. In the case of acid rain, the optimal strategy consists of reducing the emissions over time in such a way that they ultimately become compatible with the sulphur-deposition pattern that would not lead to long-term damage, that is the critical loads.
6. The emission reductions can be achieved by various economic instruments such as export taxes or tradable export quotas. In both these cases cost-efficiency will be achieved.
7. The global problems discussed—mainly the greenhouse effect and the preservation of biological diversity—are very similar from an analytical point of view to the regional reciprocal externality case, and one should expect the same kind of incentive structures.
8. Both the extinction of species and global warming involve irreversible changes. The possibility of more information forthcoming in the future should make us more cautious about accepting such irreversibilities.
9. Much of the reduction in biological diversity is due to badly designed macroeconomic policies and to badly designed property rights. By policy reforms which would improve the overall efficiency of the economies,

much can be accomplished to preserve species.

10. Global agreements based on internationally tradable permits to emit greenhouse gases can make preservation of tropical forests profitable.

## Appendix 1 Unidirectional Externalities

Assume that the downstream country has made the offer $(R_2, S_2)$. The best reply to this offer from the upstream country is given by the solution to the following problem:

$$\text{Maximize } S - C(R)$$

subject to

$$B(R) - S \geq B(R_2) - S_2.$$

The solution to this problem entails that $R_1 = R^*$, i.e. the efficient amount of pollution control and

$$S_1 = B(R^*) - B(R_2) - S_2.$$

If $S_1 - C(R_1) \geq 0$, then $(S_1, R^*)$ is the best reply from the upstream country, otherwise it is (0,0). Notice that the condition $S_1 - C(R^*) \geq 0$ can be written

$$B(R^*) - C(R^*) \geq B(R_2) - S_2.$$

Thus the condition $S_1 - C(R^*) \geq 0$ is satisfied unless the downstream country's bid is such that the downstream country asks for more than the maximum possible gain.

In the same way it can be seen that if the upstream country offers $(R_1, S_1)$, the best reply from the downstream country is $(R^*, S_2)$, where $S_2$ is defined by

$$S_2 = S_1 - C(R^1) + C(R^*)$$

if $B(R^*) - S_2 \geq 0$, and otherwise zero. The latter happens if the upstream country's offer implies that its gain would be greater than the maximum gain to be shared.

Thus, all Nash non-co-operative equilibria are in the set

$$\{(R^*, S); B(R^*) \geq S \geq C(R^*)\}$$

and the set of equilibrium pay-offs is given by

$$\{(NB_1, NB_2); NB_1 + NB_2 = B(R^*) - C(R^*)\}.$$

Thus we would end up with embarrassingly many equilibria. Each equilibrium will be efficient (because $R = R^*$). If we assume that the two countries have identical bargaining power one could apply the Nash bargaining solution. This predicts that the outcome of the game would be such that the product of the gains is maximized.[21] It turns out this solution entails that the total gains $B(R^*) - C(R^*)$ from the co-operation will be divided equally between the two countries, so that $S = 1/2\{B(R^*)+C(E^*)\}$ and $NB_1 = NB_2 = \{B(R^*) - C(R^*)\}/2$.

## Appendix 2 Incomplete Information

Assume that the downstream country reveals incorrect information. Instead of revealing the true benefit function $B(R)$, it states that the damage-cost function is $B(R,l)$, where $l$ is a parameter reflecting the degree of misrepresentation. Let $l = 0$ correspond to truth-telling and let us for the moment assume that the upstream country is honest and gives the correct information on abatement costs. Will the downstream country have an incentive to choose $l$ different from zero? That depends on the profit-sharing rules. Assume that it has been agreed that the downstream country pays the actual abatement costs. Then it is easy to see that it is in the interest of the downstream country to declare publicly the true damage costs, as the net benefits to the downstream country would be

$$B(R,0) - C(R).$$

In this case, the whole benefit from co-operation is being collected by the downstream country. In the opposite case, when the upstream country has to compensate the downstream country, it obviously pays for the downstream country to overstate the damage cost, i.e. the need for compensation. In the former case, when all the benefits go to the country that can lie, there are no incentives to lie. When the benefits go to the honest country, the other country has incentives to misrepresent its costs. The result is simply that if the total benefits can be internalized to a country, then that country has no incentive to mis-state the costs. The question arises whether it is possible to internalize the total gains to both countries in such a way that *both* of them have incentives to

[21] The Nash bargaining solution is based on a couple of axioms which seem to be quite reasonable; see Friedman (1986) for a discussion of these. The Nash solution is the combination of abatement $R$ and transfer $S$ that maximizes the product of the net gains to the two countries.

tell the truth. This the source of much discussion, especially in the OECD in the early 1970s, on how to construct international institutions that would reduce or eliminate these incentives. We will come back shortly to these constructions.

The situation can be analysed by using the approach developed by Harsanyi and Selten.[22] This approach takes as it starting point the following intellectual construction. Each country selects an agent for each possible cost or benefit function. Then an agent is selected from each of the two countries randomly and the probability for an agent to be selected is known in both countries. Then the game is played by the selected agents and it is a game with complete information. Given the cost and benefit functions these agents represent, the outcome will be efficient (but not necessarily efficient relative to the true cost and benefit functions). Given the probabilities for the selection of agents, the countries can calculate the expected net benefits from the game. Harsanyi and Selten have shown that given some reasonable assumptions, the outcome of the game will be the unique vector of pollution controls and side-payments that maximizes the Nash product

$$\Pi_k ENB_1^{\sigma_k} \Pi_l ENB_2^{\mu_l}$$

over $S_k,l$, where $\sigma_k$ is the probability that agent $k$ will be selected in the upstream country and $\mu_l$ is the probability that agent $l$ will be selected in the downstream country. If one maximizes this product, one will obtain the following necessary conditions for a maximum:

$$\Sigma_{i\mu i}\{S_{k,i} - C(R_{k,i}, k)\} = \Sigma_j \sigma_j \{B(R_{j,l}, l) - S_{j,l}\}.$$

The left-hand side is the expected pay-off to agent $k$ of the upstream country. The right-hand side is equal to the expected pay-off to agent $l$ of the downstream country. The right-hand side is independent of $k$, which means that all agents of the upstream country will have the same expected pay-off, including the agent that represents truth-telling. Thus the upstream country does not stand to gain from not revealing the true abatement cost. In the same way, it can be concluded that the downstream country will not gain from not revealing the true benefit function (or damage cost function). Thus neither the upstream nor the downstream country will, in the Harsanyi–Selten equilibrium, cheat. Both will reveal the true information. Therefore, the outcome of the negotiations will be efficient, that is it will maximize benefits minus costs. The reason for this rather startling result is the existence of the lump sum transfers $S_{k,l}$ and the fact that

[22] Harsanyi developed the general theory of games with incomplete information in Harsanyi (1967–8). Building on that, Harsanyi and Selten (1972) developed an extension of the Nash bargaining solution to determine the outcome for bargaining under incomplete information. Similar results have been obtained by others following different routes. See, for example, Binmore (1987).

both countries have linear utility functions. If the downstream country cheats by announcing too high a damage cost and therefore too high a benefit from discharge reduction, the result will be a larger than efficient reduction of the discharges and the downstream country will benefit from that. But the Harsanyi–Selten axioms will completely offset this gain by increasing the transfer to the upstream country.

The importance and relevance of this analysis depend of course on the belief one has in the basic axioms underlying the Harsanyi–Selten approach. The most doubtful assumption is perhaps that the probabilities $\sigma_k$ and $\mu_l$ are common knowledge.

## Appendix 3 The Mutual-Compensation Principle

Let the stated cost function for the upstream country be, as before, $C(R, k)$, where $k = 0$ corresponds to truth-telling. As before, let $B(R, l)$ be the benefit function in the downstream country with $l = 0$ representing the true damage function. Let $R^*_{k,l}$, be the discharge that maximizes

$$B(R, l) - C(R, k).$$

We will assume that each country reports to the international agency the benefit and cost functions and that the agency on the basis of this information calculates $R^*_{k,l}$. Then the agency determines transfers $t_i$ $(i = 1,2)$ to the countries according to the following formulas:

$$t_1 = B(R^*_{k,l}, l) - C(R_{k,l}, k) + H_1(l)$$
$$t_2 = -C(R^*_{k,l}, k) + H_2(k).$$

The functions $H_1(l)$ and $H_2(k)$ are arbitrary, except that $H_1$ must not depend on the chosen strategy of country 1 and $H_2$ must not depend on the chosen strategy of country 2. The transfer to country 1 depends only on $k$ through the influence on $R^*$. Similarly the transfer to country 2 depends also only on $l$ through the effect on $R^*$. The only way a country can possibly gain from lying is through the effects on the agreed amount of waste discharges. However, one can easily see that no country can gain anything from lying, even if the other country is lying. For country 1, for example, the gains from truth telling would be

$$-C(R^*_{0,1}, 0) + B(R^*_{01}, l) + H_1(l) = \max_R\{ B(R, l) - C(R, 0)\} + H_1(l) \geq$$
$$\geq B(R^*_{k,l}, l) - C(R^*_{k,l}) + H_1(l).$$

But the last line is the gain from reporting $k$ instead of 0. Thus, independently of what strategy the downstream country chooses, it is best for the upstream country to tell the truth. In the same way, one can show that it is alway beneficial to the downstream country to tell the truth, irrespective of what the upstream country does. We will, therefore, with the proposed mechanism end up in an equilibrium in which both countries are using dominant strategies, which correspond to truth-telling.

The Groves mechanism has two serious drawbacks. The first drawback is that it is based on separability in the benefits in the two countries. In the case we have discussed, neither the cost of abatement nor the environmental-damage cost depends on the income levels in the two countries. If, however, the pollution is a serious threat to the downstream country, and the cost of abating it in the upstream country is significant, it is quite possible that the transfers involved in the application of the mechanism may change the valuations. If that happens, the Groves mechanism no longer works. However, this is perhaps a less severe drawback as, in most cases, these unidirectional externalities will be quite small compared with the total GNP.

The other drawback is more serious. Let us compute the total net transfer generated by the mechanism. It is

$$t_1 + t_2 = B(R_{0,0}^*, 0) - C(R_{0,0}^*, 0) + H_1 + H_2.$$

If $H_1$ and $H_2$ are zero, then the total transfers would be equal to the total maximum gain from co-operation. But that is impossible, because that would mean that the countries would receive this gain twice. The transfers $H_1$ and $H_2$ must therefore be negative in order to make the mechanism satisfy the overall budget constraint. In fact, they must sum to minus the total gain in order to make the net transfers equal to zero. It can be shown that it is impossible in general to design the transfers in such a way that they will add to zero and still induce truth-telling. However, it is possible to design the $H_1$ and $H_2$ functions in such a way that the overall budget surplus (or deficit) is close to zero.

Remember that the benefit function is defined as

$$B(R, l) = D(E_o, l) - D(E_o - R, l).$$

Let $\alpha$ be a positive number less than one and let the transfers to the upstream country be

$$t_1 = \alpha D(E_o, l) - D(E_o - R, l).$$

This would correspond to the situation where $H_1 = -(1-\alpha)D(E_o, l)$ and $H_2 = A$ ($A$ is a fixed amount). It is easily seen that it is still beneficial to the upstream country to report the true cost function and for the downstream country to report the true damage-cost function. The net benefits to the two countries are now

$$NB_1 = \alpha D(E_o, 0) - D(E_o - R^*_{0,0}, 0) - C(R^*_{0,0}, 0)$$
$$NB_2 = D(E_o, 0) - D(E_o - R^*_{0,0}, 0) - C(R^*_{0,0}, 0) + A.$$

These transfers would generate incentives to both countries to tell the truth. The sum of the transfers is

$$t_1 + t_2 = \{B(R^*_{0,0}, 0) - C(R^*_{0,0}, 0)\} - (1-\alpha)D(E_o, 0) + A.$$

If the agency has an estimate of the total net benefit from co-operation, it could choose $\alpha$ and A in such a way that, roughly, the budget will balance. If for example, A is set equal to zero, then $\alpha$ can be determined in such a way that country 1 will not gain anything and the whole net benefit goes to the downstream country. If, on the other hand, A is chosen negatively, then $\alpha$ can be chosen so that even the upstream country will benefit. As the agency does not know the true benefit and cost functions with certainty, it cannot calculate $\alpha$ and $A$ with high precision. However, it seems to be possible to reduce the problems with the budget balance substantially. Note, however, that both $\alpha$ and $A$ must be determined before the scheme starts to operate, so that no country stands to gain from manipulating these variables. That means that the countries in a pre-play must determine the distribution of the net gains in a way satisfactory to both.

Instead of looking for an equilibrium in dominating strategies as in the Groves mechanism, we could look for a Nash equilibrium. The difference is that in an equilibrium in dominating strategies, a strategy choice of one player is the best choice regardless of what the other player chooses, while in a Nash equilibrium, an equilibrium strategy is the best choice for the player only if the other players are using their equilibrium strategies. It is possible to show that one can design mechanisms that in a Nash equilibrium would implement efficient outcomes.[23] However, there is a serious conceptual problem with the Nash equilibrium solution when it is applied in this game of incomplete information. As no player knows the pay-offs of the other player, no one can calculate his Nash equilibrium strategy! The solution to this is to look for a Bayesian solution. In fact, this was exactly what we did above when we applied the Harsanyi–Selten framework to the negotiations between the two countries.

If the countries are very risk-averse, we could imagine that they would be choosing their maximin strategies, that is they are maximizing the worst outcome. It is possible to show that transfers can be designed in such a way that

[23] See Laffont and Maskin (1982).

truth-telling is a maximin strategy so that the outcome would be a Pareto-efficient discharge reduction.[24]

## Appendix 4 The Acid-Rain Model

Let $E_i$ be the emission of sulphur in country $i$ and let $E$ be the corresponding vector $[E_1, E_2, \ldots, E_n]^T$ ($^T$ denotes the transpose) of sulphur emissions. Let the deposition of sulphur in country $j$ be $Q_j$ and the corresponding vector $Q = [Q_1, \ldots, Q_n]$. Then we have

$$Q = AE$$

or

$$Q_i = \sum_{j=1}^{n} a_{i,j} E_j,\ i = 1, \ldots, n.$$

Let the cost of reducing sulphur emissions in country $i$ be

$$C_i = C_i(E_i)$$

and the monetary damage from the deposition $Q_j$ be[25]

$$D_j = D_j(Q_j).$$

If the initial deposition is $Q_{oj}$, then the benefit to country $j$ from having the deposition reduced to $Q_j$ is

$$D_j(Q_{oj}) - D_j(Q_j).$$

A Nash equilibrium is now defined as an emission vector $E'$ such that for each $i$, $E_i'$ maximizes

$$NB_i = D_i(Q_{oi}) - D_i(Q_i) - C_i(E_i)$$

[24] See Mäler (1974) and Green and Laffont (1980).

[25] Note that this assumes that the annual damage is a function of annual deposition. This is a highly critical but somewhat unrealistic assumption. This is the reason why the model has been named a short-run model.

subject to

$$Q_i = \Sigma_j \alpha_{ij} E_j.$$

Thus, in the Nash equilibrium, each country is maximizing its own benefit without regard for the consequences in other countries. A necessary condition for a maximum is that

$$C_i' = -a_{ij} D_i',$$

for all $i$, that is the marginal-abatement cost equals the marginal-damage cost times the proportion of the country's own emissions that is deposited in the home country.

## Bibliography

Amann M. and Kornai, G. (1987), 'Cost Functions for Controlling $SO_2$ Emissions in Europe', Working Paper, May, WP–87–06,5 IIASA.
Andreasson, I.-M. (1988), *Costs of Controls on Farmers' Use of Nitrogen*, Stockholm School of Economics, Stockholm.
Arrow, K. I. and Fisher, A. C. (1974), 'Environmental Preservation, Uncertainty and Irreversibility', *Quarterly Journal of Economics*, 88.
Baumol, W. J. and Bradford, D. F. (1972), 'Detrimental Externalities and Non-Convexity of the Production Set', *Economica*, 39.
Beardsley, T. (1989), 'Not so Hot', *Scientific American*, November.
Binmore, K. (1987), 'Nash Bargaining and Incomplete Information', in K. Binmore and P. Dasgupta (eds.), *The Economics of Bargaining*, Oxford, Basil Blackwell.
Binswanger, H. (1989), 'Brazilian Policies that Encourage Deforestation in the Amazon', Environment Department Working Paper No. 16, The World Bank, Washington, D.C.
Carson, R. T. and Mitchell, R. C. (1989), *Using Surveys to Value Public Goods: The Contingent Valuation Method*, Resources for the Future.
Coase, R. H. (1988), *The Firm, the Market and the Law*, Chicago, University of Chicago Press.
Fisher, A. C. and Hanemann, W. M. (1986), 'Option Value and the Extinction of Species', *Advances in Applied Micro-Economics*, 4.
Friedman J. (1986), *Game Theory with Applications to Economics*, New York.
Green, J. R. and Laffont, J.-J. (1980), *Incentives in Public Decision-Making*, Amsterdam, North-Holland.
Groves, T. (1973), 'Incentives in Teams', *Econometrica*, 41.
Hansen, S. (1988), 'Debt for Nature Swaps: Overview and Discussion of Key Issues', Environment Department Working Paper, The World Bank, Washington D.C.
Harsanyi, J. C. (1967–8), 'Games with Incomplete Information Played by "Bayesian" Players', Parts I–III, *Management Science*, 14, 159–82, 320–34, 486–502.

Harsanyi, J. C. and Selten, R. (1972), 'A Generalised Nash Solution for Two Person Bargaining Games with Incomplete Information', *Management Science*, 18.

Henry, C. (1974), 'Investment Decision under Uncertainty: The Irreversibility Effect', *American Economic Review*, 64(6).

Houghton, R. A. and Woodwell, G. M. (1989), 'Global Climatic Change', *Scientific American*, April.

Kneese, A. V. (1988), 'Environmental Stress and Political Conflicts: Salinity in the Colorado River', paper presented at conference December 1988 at the Royal Swedish Academy of Sciences, Stockholm.

Krutilla, J. (1966), 'The International Columbia River Treaty: An Economic Evaluation', in A. V. Kneese and S. Smith (eds.), *Water Research*, Baltimore, Johns Hopkins University Press.

— (1968), *The Columbia River Treaty: A Study in the Economics of International River Basin Development*, Baltimore, Johns Hopkins University Press.

Laffont, J.-J. and Maskin, E. (1982), 'The Theory of Incentives: an Overview', in W. Hildenbrand (ed.), *Advances in Economic Theory*, Cambridge, Cambridge University Press.

Landsberg H. H. and Russel, C. S. (1971), 'International Environmental Problems—a Taxonomy', *Science*, 172, 25 June.

McNeely, J. A., Miller, K. R., Reid, W. V., and Mittermeier, R. A. (forthcoming), *Conserving the World's Biological Diversity*, IUCN, WRI and WWP–US, Washington, D.C.

Mäler, K.-G. (1974), *Environmental Economics—A Theoretical Inquiry*, Baltimore, The Johns Hopkins University Press.

— (1989*a*), 'The Acid Rain Game', in H. Folmer and E. van Ierland (eds.), *Valuation Methods and Policy Making in Environmental Economics*, Amsterdam, Elsevier.

— (1989*b*), 'The Acid Rain Game 2', paper presented at the workshop on Economic Analysis and Environmental Toxicology, Noordwijkerout, May.

— (1989*c*), *Risk and Environment*, Research Paper 6390, Stockholm School of Economics.

— (1989*d*), *Environmental Resources, Risk and Bayesian Decision Rules*, Research Paper 6391, Stockholm School of Economics.

— and Olsson, C. (1989), 'The Cost-Effectiveness of Different Solutions to the European Sulphur Problem', forthcoming in *European Journal of Agriculture Economics*.

Nilsson, J. (ed.) (1986), 'Critical Loads for Nitrogen and Sulphur', The Nordic Council of Ministers, Report 1986: 11, Copenhagen.

The Norwegian Meteorological Institute (1987), Sulphur Budgets for Europe for 1979, 1980, 1981, 1982, 1983, 1984, and 1985 EMEP/MSC–W Not 4/87.

OECD (1981), *Transfrontier Pollution and the Role of States*, Paris, OECD.

Olsson, C. (1988), 'The Cost-Effectiveness of Different Strategies Aimed at Reducing the Amount of Sulphur Deposition in Europe', Research Report 261, EFI Stockholm School of Economics.

Raiffa, H. (1968), *Decision Analysis: Introductory Lectures on Choices under Uncertainty*, New York, Random House.

Runge, C. F. (1981), 'Common Property Externalities: Isolation, Assurance and Resource Depletion in a Traditional Grazing Context', *American Journal of Agricultural Economics*.
Smets, H. (1973), *The Mutual Compensation Principle*, Paris, OECD.
Starret, D. (1972), 'Fundamental Non-Convexities in the Theory of Externalities', *Journal of Economic Theory*.
Warford, J. and Schramm, G. (eds.) (1987), *The Annals of Regional Science*, November 1987.
Weitzman, M. (1974), 'Prices vs Quantities', *Review of Economic Studies*, 90.

# 8
# The Regulation of Oceanic Resources: An Examination of the International Community's Record in the Regulation of One Global Resource

*Timothy M. Swanson*

## 8.1 Introduction

The regulation of oceanic resources is of particular interest for environmental policymaking because of the long history of attempts at the international management of this resource. Its resources were probably the first for which management was attempted on an international basis, and there is now at least 100 years' experience of such regulation to review. For example, the first attempts at regulating the oceanic fur-seal trade occurred during the latter half of the nineteenth century.

This history is important because the outcome of each of these numerous attempts has, in general, been an unhappy one. The abject failure of some fisheries commissions to achieve agreed quotas, after years and even decades of negotiations, is perhaps the most eggregious example; the failure of the United Nations Law of the Sea Convention to secure acceptance of its Deep Seabed Mining Regime is probably the most recent. In application, these failures have resulted in many of the subject resources being exploited to near exhaustion. There has been a complete collapse of a number of commercial fisheries, e.g. the California sardine and the Atlantic halibut; the Antarctic whaling industry exhausted one species after another of the great whales in those waters. Stellar's sea-cow has been rendered entirely extinct through over-exploitation.

Timothy Swanson is a Lecturer in the Faculty of Law and the Department of Economics, University College London.

Where the approach to regulation was based on liability rather than quotas, the regimes have failed just as completely. For example, liability regimes have been completely avoided by the use of 'flags of convenience', which are flown by a substantial proportion of the world's shipping fleet. The *Torrey Canyon* and the *Amoco Cadiz* are two well-known examples of Liberian tankers which generated substantial externalities, on the shores of Cornwall and Brittany respectively.

After a 400-year experiment in the joint management of oceanic resources, the accumulated experience has resulted in the jettisoning of this approach. In an almost universal shift of orientation, the vast majority of the ocean's resources were translated from international to domestic resources. In the latter part of the 1970s the international community acted to 'enclose the oceans', by way of the parallel proclamations of individual 200-mile exclusive economic zones. These actions brought over a third of the oceans, and over 90 per cent of known oceanic resources, within individual state control. Therefore the ultimate consequences of the complete failure of these regimes was avoided by the existence of this alternative for oceanic resources; the 400-year-long experiment with the oceans as a global commons has come to an end in the 'safety net' of private property rights.[1]

This 'privatisation' option is unavailable for many of today's international environmental problems. The technology to enclose the other global commons (the ozone layer, the atmosphere, biodiversity) is not going to appear for quite a while. Joint management is probably the sole option for regulating these resources into the foreseeable future.

This paper examines the reasons for the failure of international resource management as it pertained to the ocean's resources over the last century. It is both a theoretical undertaking, by placing the issue of international resource regulation into the framework of a multilateral bargaining problem, and an empirical investigation, by the application of this framework to the experiences of the various regulatory attempts involving oceanic resources. It commences with a brief introduction to the idea of the ocean as a global resource in section 8.2. It then undertakes an investigation of the difficulties of joint management of international resources under existing international law in section 8.3. In sections 8.4 and 8.5, the comparative costliness of different approaches to joint

[1] It is not the case that the 'enclosure of the oceans' has completely resolved the problems of joint management of resources. Substantial externalities continue to exist, with regard to migratory resources such as tuna and whales for instance. However, the joint management problem has had its quality altered substantially none the less. This is because the resources involved are now jointly managed by a relatively small number of clearly identified interested parties, rather than the whole of the peoples of the planet. The former is a significant contracting problem involving the necessary agreement between a small number of identified parties; the latter is a pure 'collective choice' problem which is nearly impossible to resolve under existing institutions.

management of global resources is considered. In section 8.6, all of this is illustrated by reference to the history of attempts to manage the oceanic resources.

The experience with the regulation of oceanic resources indicates that, even when the stakes are high and the managed solution is obvious, international co-operation is not necessarily forthcoming. The reasons why international regulation has been so problematic (even more so than its counterpart, domestic regulation) must be carefully investigated and analysed. Otherwise, we will have little possibility of performing better with regard to the next century's global resources than we did with the last.

## 8.2 The Ocean as a Global Resource

The earliest history of oceanic use did not indicate the direction which the regulation of this resource would ultimately take. In fact, the earliest users attempted to place substantial claims to property rights to the resources of the oceans. For example, in the fifteenth century Sweden and Denmark claimed the Baltic and Norwegian Seas; Venice claimed sovereign rights in the Adriatic; and Britain claimed sovereign rights in something it called the 'British' seas. An extreme example of such claims at that time was the papal decree in 1493 which divided the use of the Atlantic Ocean between Portugal and Spain.

Of course, such vast empires of oceanic real estate were not destined to stand the test of time, primarily because the oceans were the only means of communication between many parts of the world at that time. The trading states argued strongly for the absence of sovereignty over any of the high seas, in order that they might be maintained free for the use of all states for purposes of navigation. The main proponent of this debate was the Dutch East Indies Company and its advocate Hugo Grotius, ironically known as the 'father of modern international law'. Grotius published *Mare Liberum* in the first decade of the seventeenth century, in which he argued the case for maintaining the seas as *res nullius*, i.e. a thing that belongs to no one.

> The vagrant waters of the sea are . . . necessarily free. The right of occupation rests upon the fact that most things become exhausted by promiscuous use and that appropriation consequently is the condition of their utility to human beings. But this is not the case with the sea; it can be exhausted neither by navigation nor by fishing, that is to say neither of the two ways which it can be used. (Grotius, 1608)

Thus, Grotius argued (much as would a present-day economist) that the primary justification for property rights is the creation of the correct incentives for the use of scarce resources; however, Grotius was obviously wrong in arguing that there was no foreseeable scarcity in oceanic resources.

Nevertheless, Grotius' arguments held sway and most of the claims to sovereign seas were dropped in the seventeenth century. The state of the oceans was universally recognized by that time as one of open access. The only navigable waters for which absolute ownership was claimed were those which were actually supervised by a cannon battery, and only to the extent that the waters were within the range of that cannon. Since the range of the very best cannon at that time was something less than three miles, and to avoid the necessity of continuous cannon postings along the state's shorelines, it came to be agreed that the 'cannonshot doctrine' should apply to all states; that is, all states were vested with sovereign rights in three miles of 'territorial waters' (because they had the right to place a cannon on shore and defend it). Otherwise, the remainder of the oceans and their resources were to remain open access in nature.

This was in general the state of the law regarding the seas until about mid-way through the twentieth century, when the enclosure of the seas commenced. In 1942, the first step toward the enclosure of the oceans was taken by the United Kingdom and Venezuela, when they entered into a Treaty relating to the Submarine Resources of the Gulf of Paria. This was a very tentative step toward enclosure, as it did not consist of a claim of rights by either state; the two states simply drew a line between them (the UK on behalf of Trinidad) and then stated that neither claimed any rights on the other side of that line. Since the two states were the only ones bordering directly on those waters, the treaty constituted an implicit partition of the resource between them. The fact that no state raised an objection to this method of partition laid the groundwork for the future enclosure of the oceans.

Shortly afterwards, in 1945, the US issued the Truman Proclamation asserting sovereignty over the resources of the 'continental shelf': an ambiguous term which created a claim to property rights to resources located in some places more than 200 miles from the nation's shores. The idea of unilaterally extending state sovereignty immediately caught on. On the west coast of Latin America these states seized the opportunity to claim rights in the resources off their shores; however, for these states little or no continental shelf exists (and so neither do the resources appurtenant to a shelf), they instead claimed rights in a designated breadth of oceanic waters and the resources within them. There are important fisheries off the coast of Latin America, which reside primarily within the Humboldt Current, which brings nutrients up from the Antarctic. The maximum breadth of the Humboldt Current was believed to be about 200 miles, and so this was the extent of the Latin American claims, i.e. 200-mile bands of sovereign territorial seas.

There was much controversy about claims of 200-mile bands of sovereignty, primarily due to the impacts of these zones on navigation once again. Ultimately, the rights in the oceans were 'unbundled' to resolve these disputes. In a series of international conferences, commencing with the Geneva conference in 1958 and concluding with the United Nations Conference on the Law of the Sea III (UNCLOS III) in 1982, conventions were developed which vested states bordering on the oceans with much greater jurisdiction, control, and sovereignty over various bands of resources within the previously open-access oceans. The enclosure of the oceans, to the extent that it currently exists, was concluded in just under twenty-five years.[2]

The current regime governing the oceanic resources, under the United Nations Convention on the Law of the Sea, appears generally as follows. First, the convention provides that all bordering states have near complete sovereignty in a 12-mile band of 'territorial seas'; the sole significant exception being the requirement of free navigation in those seas. With absolute sovereignty comes the duty to regulate those resources to provide for the safe and efficient use of them.

Secondly, the convention provides that all states shall have sovereign rights in the continental shelf and its resources (subject to the same exception) to a minimum distance of 200 miles and a maximum of 350 miles from the shores. Thirdly, the specific rights in the ocean's resources includes a 200-mile band of waters bordering the state. In this 'exclusive economic zone', the state has the exclusive right to 'explore and exploit, conserve, and manage' the living and non-living resources. A subsidiary right is the right to regulate the zone for the protection and conservation of the marine environment, i.e. pollution control (LOSC, Art. 56).

Although the United Nations Law of the Sea Convention (LOSC) is not yet in force, most states have already asserted and recognized the enclosure of the oceans along these lines. Most of these claims occurred in a short period in the late 1970s. In 1987, seventy-four states had claimed 200-mile exclusive economic zones, and a further fifteen states had claimed 200-mile exclusive fishery zones. This enclosure has transferred some 36 per cent of the ocean's surface area, 90 per cent of its commercial fisheries, and 87 per cent of its known oil reserves from international to domestic control. The sole significant asset left in the international domain is the deep sea, whose most important uses are for seabed mining (not now commercially viable) and waste disposal. The remainder of the sea's resources were translated into domestic resources.

[2] The United Nations Convention on the Law of the Sea is not yet in force. It has been subject to significant non-acceptances itself, as will be discussed in section 8.6. None the less, many of its terms have been substantially accepted in international practice, and have thereby been rendered 'customary international law'.

Between the time of Grotius' tract (about 1510) and the Treaty of the Gulf of Paria (1942), the regulation of oceanic resources was a wholly international affair. Here was a resource that was susceptible to 'property rights' management that was subjected instead to various joint management regimes under international law. The examination of the comparative costliness of this system of resource management is the task of this paper. Section 8.3 is a general theory of the costliness of existing international regulation, while sections 8.4 and 8.5 compare the costliness of methods of joint management. Section 8.6 discusses this theory in the context of the international community's experiences with oceanic resource regulation.

## 8.3 A General Theory of International Regulatory Failures

It is the thesis of this paper that the failures of international law in regulating oceanic resources have been entirely predictable because they are derived from the peculiar combination of both the nature of the problem (the regulation of open-access resources) and the nature of the process which has been applied to its resolution (multilateral contracting). In essence, the nature of problem and process together generate predictably high 'bargaining costs', which prevent the gains from joint management from being achieved.

The costliness of contracting in this context is attributable to three factors. First, there is the nature of 'international resources'. These are generally *open-access* resources available to the entire international community for use, which therefore require the co-operation of all users (existing and potential) for resolution. Secondly, there is the nature of 'international lawmaking'; the *contractual* nature of international law requires that each state find the proposed convention to be in its own interest before acceptance is possible. Thirdly, another facet of international lawmaking is its multilateral character; this makes the possibility of *sequential acceptance* (as opposed to simultaneous commitment) a real possibility, which generates a system of incentives which runs contrary to agreement.

These next two sections develop the reasons why these three factors result in predictable regulatory failures. This section will investigate the capability of regulation to operate effectively in the presence of all three of the factors above. In section 8.4, the third assumption (regarding sequential acceptance) is dropped, and then the comparative costliness of international contracting in either situation is examined in section 8.5. The final section of the paper analyses both approaches in the context of the regulation of oceanic resources.

## *International Law as a Multilateral Bargaining Problem*

The peculiar difficulties of international resource agreements may be conceptualized as 'multilateral bargaining problems'. A 'bargaining problem' is a situation in which a joint gain is clearly achievable by virtue of co-ordinated action, but it is not realizable until agreement is reached on how such a gain should be distributed. In the context of an international resource agreement, the gain from joint management would result from the implementation of the aggregate optimal rate of use of the resource, and the issue of distribution concerns the allocation of 'shares' in the international resource once joint management is achieved.

Bargaining problems of a bilateral nature can be difficult and costly to resolve, but where many parties are involved ('multilateral contracting') the problem is raised to a higher order of difficulty; such joint management problems have been discussed under the rubric of 'collective choice problems' in the domestic context (Olsen, 1972). This is because multilateral contracting affords the possibility of sequential acceptances. That is, in bilateral contracting, there are only two options: the parties are either in a state of disagreement or agreement; the potential for gain from agreement provides the impetus for movement from the former state to the latter.[3] In multilateral contract, there is the added possibility that some subset of the necessary parties will agree to the standard while some other subgroup will not. It is this third option which generates the distinct set of problems associated with international resource conventions.

## *The Impact of Sequential Acceptance—Free-Riding*

The international lawmaking process generally operates as follows.[4] First, there is an international conference on the subject at which a text is agreed and published. Second, the text, or 'convention', is then left open for signature and ratification, usually for several months or years. Third, the text comes into

[3] In the bilateral case, it is believed that each party's share is determined in accordance with its relative cost of disagreement. That is, the benefits from agreement will be valued differently by different parties, resulting in differing degrees of 'impatience' concerning delayed agreement. (Such patience may be translated into individual discount factors that in turn determine each party's share of the realizable gain.) So long as the parties remain in disagreement, this impatience takes its toll and encourages the parties to find the indicated basis for an agreement. See Rubinstein (1988).

[4] There are in fact a number of different pathways to making international laws: treaties (or conventions), international treaty organizations (such as the United Nations), and custom (the universal observance of a particular standard or rule). This paper will emphasize the first, as it is only this manner of lawmaking, in the international context, which can ultimately address the problems of holdouts in international resource lawmaking.

effect for ratifying states once a sufficient number (as indicated in the text of the convention) have ratified. Fourth, the convention remains open for subsequent acceptance by other states, should they choose to later 'accede' to the laws. Therefore, the entire process is usually geared to the non-contemporaneous acceptance of the convention's standards.

Sequential acceptance essentially affords the possibility for the bargaining problem to continue in existence even after the agreement has been signed by some of the necessary parties.[5] The terms of the international resource convention will prescribe an initial standard which will expressly or implicitly determine the distribution of the relative shares of the gain from co-ordinated usage. The effect of 'holdouts' is primarily redistributive; that is, a holdout reallocates shares away from those parties which have agreed the standard and towards itself. Therefore, in the context of sequential acceptances, international resource conventions afford the possibility of continuing the bargaining process (and hence its costliness) even after the terms of the convention have been established (by their acceptance by some subgroup of users).

The essentially redistributive effect of sequential acceptance of international resource convention standards is easily illustrated. This would be analogous to the situation in which any subgroup of users of an open-access resource were to undertake unilateral restraint. Consider a fishery, for example, which is being depleted through competitive harvesting. If a number of the fishing vessels undertook voluntary restrictions on their catches, there would not necessarily be any effect on the aggregate level of the use of the resource, as the unconstrained harvesters could simply absorb the surplus stocks made available by the others' constraints. On the other hand, in this scenario there would be significant redistributive effects.[6]

[5] Although agreement exists in name, where sequential acceptance is allowed there is the option to continue to disagree over 'shares' even after the convention is 'agreed' by some parties. This means, in effect, that the terms of the management standard are being written into stone *before* the bargaining problem is solved. The costliness of proceeding in this fashion arises from the continued wastage of the resource while some necessary parties remain outside of the agreement on account of disputes over shares. This problem and approach will be deemed *ex post* bargaining throughout the remainder of this paper.

[6] This assumption is fully applicable in the case of a pure open-access resource, such as a fishery. In the case of other 'global' resources it is possible for one state to abstain from harvesting and to realize some gain from such abstemption. This would be the case with regard to the lower atmosphere, for example, in many instances. In addition, several contiguous states might abstain from the use of such a resource and thus confer benefits on one another which could not be completely appropriated by other more distant non-conforming states. All of these possibilities merely evidence the empirically valid assertion that many international resource conventions in fact embrace numerous distinct resources within their terms. The assumption underlying the analysis of this paper is that each physically distinct resource logically requires its own administrative mechanism for efficient usage, and therefore the one resource/one convention assumption is not a 'special case' in this sense.

Figure 8.1 presents the depiction of the open-access resource problem with partial adherence to a co-ordinating standard (which prescribes some reduced aggregate rate of access to the resource). Assume that the users of the resource initially attain Point B via competitive rent-seeking behaviour; that is, each user pursues individual maximization with reference only to the aggregate stock of the resource available, and without reference to the potential impacts on other users. This manner of optimization will indeed lead the users to reach Point B, the point of zero rents and over-exploitation of the resource.[7]

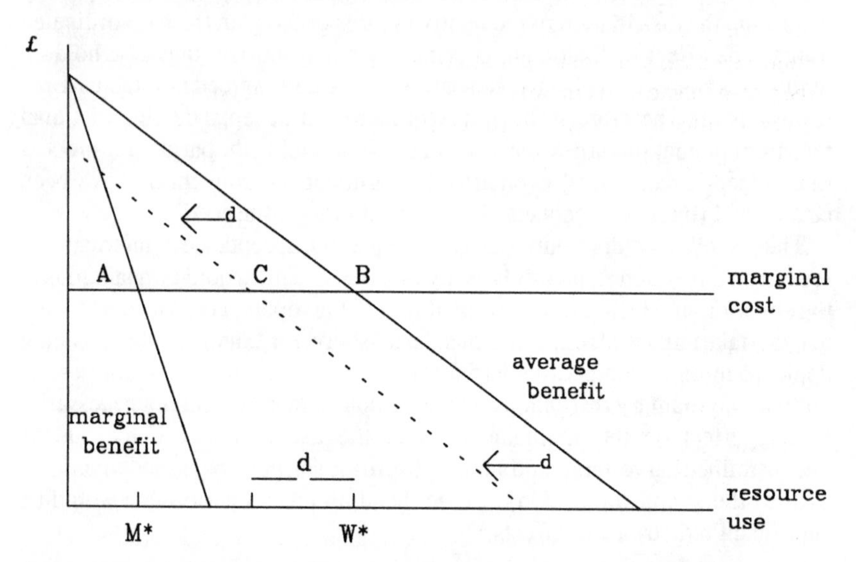


**Figure 8.1** *Impact of Unilateral Restraint by Subgroup of Users of Resource*

Assume now that some subset of these users undertake a binding constraint on their use of the resource, what will be the impact of this action? There would be no positive impact on the resource, but there will be a substantial redistribu-

[7] This implies the application of a particular simplifying assumption, viz. that there is absolutely no capacity to co-ordinate behaviour in the use of the resource in whole or in part. This would indeed be the case if the resource were widely diffuse (i.e. no single state had more than a small fraction of the resource that it was able to affect) and if the number of states undertaking the activity which affects the resource is very large. The classic example of such a resource is an 'open access' fishery. See Cheung (1970). However, where either of these assumptions is relaxed, then there is the possibility that some lesser form of over-utilization might occur, i.e. that some degree of 'co-ordination' in use might occur by reason of the recognition of individual/group impact on the resource. In any case, barring the existence of a 'fully co-ordinating multilateral agreement' involving all users, existing and potential, there will be excessive degradation of the resource.

tive impact. If the constrained parties were to fix their joint harvest to an amount (*d*) as represented in the above diagram, then the average benefit curve would shift in (horizontally) for the remaining unconstrained users to a corresponding extent (as indicated by the dashed line in the diagram). These unconstrained users would then expand individual production to reach Point C, which when added to *d* returns the resource harvest to Point B, the unconstrained result.

Thus, a subgroup of users operating under the regulatory constraint has no more immediate effect on the resource than would no constraint at all. This is because the fundamental problem relates to the incentives to exploit the resource to the point of zero rents, so long as a group of unconstrained users continues making unrestricted access to the resource. Voluntary constraints on the part of some users merely transfer their share of the resource rents to those users who decline to assume the constraints.[8]

The combination of 'open-access resource' and 'sequential acceptance' is the source of the 'free-rider problem' which is inherent in all attempts to contract in this manner with regard to the use of an international resource. The resulting system of incentives is such that the first-best option in multilateral contract bargaining will always be the pursuit of unconstrained maximization while other users assume binding constraint. This is an example of the general problem of *opportunism in contracting* when appropriable rents exist (Williamson, 1980).

The problem of opportunism, or free-riding, may be depicted in a simple bilateral 'game' which shows the consequences for each player given the actions of the other. In this scenario, each player has the choice of accepting or not accepting the proposed constraint, where universal acceptance will produce the jointly maximized outcome (M*) and total non-acceptance will result in the wastage of the result, an inferior result (W*). All players would do better under M* than W*, if the same choices were made by all, but the possibility of non-contemporaneous acceptance makes the choice more complicated. This is because the individual first-best result is to 'not accept' the constraint while the other player 'accepts'; in this case, the unconstrained player receives, say, 0.75W* while the constrained receives only 0.25W*. This is the appropriable rent available from acting opportunistically.

[8] A more technical paper on this problem is Hoel (1989).

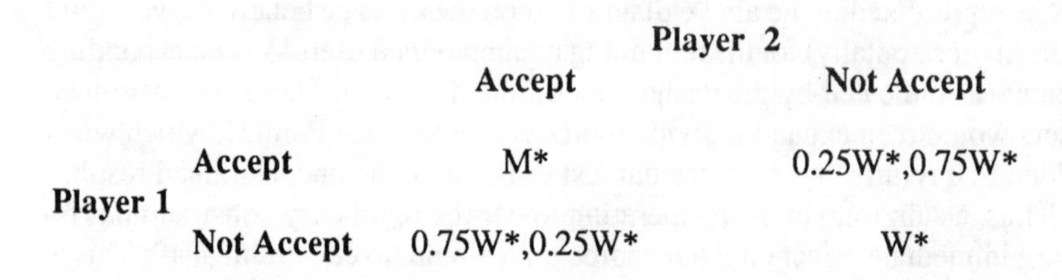

| | | Player 2 | |
|---|---|---|---|
| | | **Accept** | **Not Accept** |
| **Player 1** | **Accept** | M* | 0.25W*,0.75W* |
| | **Not Accept** | 0.75W*,0.25W* | W* |

**Figure 8.2** *Opportunism and the Incentives to Non-acceptance*

The incentive structure within this framework is such that the continued wastage of the resource is inevitable. Individual incentives exist which drive the international community away from agreement.

It is the facet of sequential acceptance which might at first be attributed with the responsibility for these incentives to disagreement. Sequential acceptance by itself makes available the possibility of an individually preferred outcome to M*. Where this option is available, the predictable result is non-acceptance by some necessary party and the continued wastage of the resource: W*. It is for this reason that most economists advocate the adoption of *ex ante* bargaining and simultaneous acceptance as the solution to these international contracting problems; for example, see Mäler's chapter in this volume.

In addition, it is worth noting that the incentives to non-acceptance actually increase when the context is altered from two parties to many. This is because the incentives to free-ride, in this framework, actually increase with *each* successive acceptance. The transfer of one more user from the unconstrained group to the constrained makes available more of the resource for the remaining holdouts. These states actually face an increasing opportunity cost from acceptance of the standard. Therefore, multilateral contracting with sequential acceptance increases the incentive to free-ride on other users' unilateral restraint; it makes the possibility of moving ultimately to the jointly managed outcome even more costly (for individual states) and hence more unlikely (Barrett, 1989).

### *An Alternative Source of Holdouts—Heterogeneous Parties*

What motivates an individual state to become a holdout? One possibility, described above, is opportunism, but this fails to indicate why some states are and others are not holdouts. There is no distinctive trait which determines the capacity to receive 'free-rider rents'. Any state which is successful at being other than first to assume the constraint is able to appropriate a larger share of the resource rents. In fact, the last state to hold out would have the capacity to command the entirety of the gains from agreement in return for its accession. Within this analysis, it is difficult to understand why *any* states would elect to accept a binding standard.[9]

Opportunistic behaviour is not the sole motivating force behind the holdout problem, however. Another predictable source of holdouts is the rational reaction of diversely situated parties to a proposed uniform standard.[10] In short, any proposed standard, no matter how uniformly presented, will have widely varying impacts. This is because states are heterogeneous in the availability of substitutes for the common resource, as well as (to some extent) the cost of accessing the resource. There will be a spectrum of costliness related to any proposed constraint. Many states will find that the constraint is not binding at all; some will find it severely binding. Those states which find the constraint non-binding will see the potential benefit to co-ordination, with none of the cost; those which find it binding will find it necessary to weigh the costs of the constraint against the benefits of co-ordination. Many of these will, of necessity, find that the costs will outweigh the benefits.

The difference in the set of incentives facing two parties may once again be illustrated in a simple 'game' matrix. In this case it will be assumed that Player 1 incurs a higher costliness from immediate acceptance of the constraint than does Player 2, and/or receives a greater benefit from non-acceptance. Therefore, it could be assumed that with heterogeneous parties the comparative costliness of acceptance might be very different, and this could be indicated by the relative 'shares' that would be received in either state: universal agreement or universal disagreement.

[9] That is, the above theory explains why it is the case that, *given* the fact that certain states undertake unilateral restraint, the remaining states find it in their interests to free-ride on the first movers. It is more difficult to explain why, given the creation of this incentive structure, any state would choose to engage in unilateral restraint. There are two plausible explanations. First, some states are willing to invest in the creation of 'customary international law', which will evolve norms over time that will ultimately bind all states. That is, despite the initial assumption that all international law is purely contractual in nature, in fact much of it is evolved in the convention-making and -observing process. In a field in which there is no true legislature to enunciate rules, these conventions are often the closest substitutes, even though they remain largely ineffective by reason of holdouts for many years. Therefore, if it is believed that unanimity is impossible to get via *ex ante* bargaining, then it is rational to proceed in this way. Secondly, there has been little or no experience with true *ex ante* bargaining in lawmaking. The ideal of uniform standards in lawmaking has been so strong that, up to the very recent past, the possibility of engaging in this manner of bargaining has never been recognized. Thus, the only option has been *ex post* bargaining until very recently, the 1987 protocol on the reduction of substances harmful to the ozone layer being the first example of an international resource agreement applying non-uniform standards.

[10] This is known as 'adverse selection' in the insurance economics literature. It is the predictable result of any attempt to pool heterogeneous parties within the ambit of a uniform 'price'; those whose individual characteristics make the uniform price a net cost opt out, while those whose characteristics make the price a benefit stay in (Rothschild and Stiglitz, 1976).

| | | Player 2 | |
|---|---|---|---|
| | | **Accept** | **Not Accept** |
| **Player 1** | **Accept** | 0.25M*,0.75M* | 0.50W*,0.50W* |
| | **Not Accept** | 0.95W*,0.05W* | 0.75W*,0.25W* |

**Figure 8.3** *Heterogeneity and the Incentives to Non-acceptance*

In Figure 8.3, the situation is depicted where Player 1 is far more reliant on the current situation than is Player 2 (perhaps on account of heavy investments attuned to the current usage rates of the resource). In this scenario, if there is total non-acceptance of the standard, Player 1 benefits disproportionately from that fact, and also suffers disproportionately from movement to total acceptance of a new standard.

The capacity of a given standard to divide the group of users into two sets is illustrated by the entries in the matrix. The 'natural' bias in the two states' preferences makes it likely that the two will prefer different outcomes. In short, Player 1 above would prefer 'non-acceptance' if its share in that situation (0.75W*) were greater than its expected share under an efficient management regime (0.25M*). Player 2 on the other hand has a natural tendency toward 'acceptance'; its expected pay-off from efficient management of the resource (0.75M*) clearly exceeds its current pay-off under non-acceptance (0.25W*). Therefore, the proposal of this standard, no matter how uniformly presented, will have the effect of dividing the users into two groups: those receiving net benefits and those receiving net burdens from its acceptance.

This matrix also illustrates the interaction between heterogeneity and opportunism. For example, a state which is biased towards non-acceptance would receive substantial benefits from others' acceptances and would then perceive these benefits as an opportunity cost of acceptance as well. Conversely, a state naturally inclined to acceptance would see a dramatic increase in its relative share if it did free-ride (a doubling from 0.25W* to 0.50W*) but this would still remain far below its expected return from efficient management (0.75M*). Thus, opportunistic benefits magnify the benefits for those naturally inclined to reject the standard, while they appear as wasteful opportunism to those inclined to acceptance.[11] Therefore, the nature of the holdout behaviour is not an objective matter; it is dependent upon the perspective of the party.

[11] The generalized version of these problems is set forth in the Appendix to this paper.

*The Nature of Alternative Solutions to the Holdout Problem*

Therefore, there are two potentially very different sources of holdouts in international resource contracting. One is the set of incentives to act opportunistically with regard to any constraint for which sequential acceptance is a possibility; these incentives are depicted in Figure 8.2 above. The other is the wholly reasonable reaction of diversely situated states to a proposed uniform standard; these incentives are depicted in Figure 8.3.

The nature of the solution to the holdout problem is also very different, depending on the ultimate source of the problem. Holdouts sourced in heterogeneity require side-payments in order to equalize shares; individual incentives based in share redistribution are the necessary basis for agreement. Holdouts sourced in opportunism, on the other hand, must be convinced of their incapacity to procure side-payments by means of their recalcitrance; incentives based in the firm refusal of share redistribution are the necessary basis for agreement.

These two solutions may be demonstrated by reference to Figures 8.2 and 8.3. With regard to holdouts sourced in opportunism, as depicted in Figure 8.2, the efficient solution is readily obtained once the option of 'asymmetric pairing' (i.e. the simultaneous play of opposing strategies) is removed; this is the means by which changes in the law in domestic regimes are effected. This may be accomplished by placing a 'ban' on the choice of non-acceptance, while specifying a date on which all states will move simultaneously (or not at all) to that new equilibrium. The requirement of simultaneity removes the jointly dominated, but individually profitable, strategies from consideration (Schotter, 1986).[12]

On the other hand, the required approach to the problem of state heterogeneity is *ex ante* bargaining and redistribution. Under this scenario, the states benefiting from efficient regulation must share their benefits with those disproportionately burdened in order to secure the latter's agreement to the change. In Figure 8.3, this would require that Player 2 transfer some of its gain to Player 1 in return for agreement; for example, Player 2 might agree to transfer 0.25M* to Player 1 (as compensation for its disporportionate burden), resulting in a joint pay-off to agreement of 0.50M*,0.50M* (see chapters by Mäler and Barrett in this volume).

It is very difficult to regulate international resources through either of these methods. First, regarding the use of uniform 'bans', there is literally no global

[12] If all states had not agreed to movement to the new position by the proposed date, then no such movement would occur. If no movement occurred, then the states which had refused to accept the new standard would not benefit from their non-acceptance, and they would see that their continued refusal would only contribute to the continued wastage of the resource (to their own detriment). In this way movements occurring simultaneously would remove the free-rider rents which would accrue otherwise.

resource for which all states are similarly situated; the heterogeneity of states is too great to allow for this.[13] On account of this it is always necessary to attempt to ascertain individual burdens. Since it is not possible to force parties to contract with regard to a global resource, the 'domestic' solution of declaring an activity illegal is largely ineffective given heterogeneous parties.[14]

Second, it is virtually impossible to segregate entirely between the effects of heterogeneity and opportunism. At one level, it is usually very difficult to determine where the recalcitrant state's desire for compensation leaves off, and its pursuit of free-rider rents sets in. As developed in Figure 8.3, a state inclined to non-acceptance will see the benefits derived from others' acceptances as another cost of compliance; therefore, this state's 'reservation price' may come to embody *both* transfers sourced in differential burden and in opportunism.[15]

Third, and more fundamentally, it is sometimes the case that the distinction between 'compensable burden' and 'free-rider rent' is not very clearcut. The information is not always available to separate between the two different motives; even the logical distinction between the two becomes confused given the dependence of current individual costliness upon choices that the state itself made much earlier (regarding sunken investments and courses of development). In the context of Figure 8.3, this indicates that the 'natural bias' in a party's pay-offs is in fact dependent upon prior choices made regarding the use of a resource, e.g. whether to invest in more or less intensive use. Then those

[13] States differ widely in geographical, economical, and cultural terms. One example: the so-called 'value of life', i.e. the amount of money which the typical individual requires to undertake a small risk of life endangerment in the UK is estimated to be about $1,000,000. The same figure is found to be between $5–50 million in the US. And, in a country as different from these two as, say, China, that figure would be an amount several orders of magnitude different. This is a fundamentally important example because the costliness of risk is of crucial importance in determining the correct level of many sorts of environmentally harmful activity. In the US, for example, the primary costs of ozone depletion are estimated to lie in an increased incidence of skin cancers by about 10–20,000 per year. The costliness of activities to reduce this risk, such as the substitution of more expensive chemicals for CFCs, would be considered very differently in the US than it would be in, for example, China or India. Therefore, different costliness of uniform standards are implicit in just about every international standard which concerns health impacts.

[14] Of course, the assumption of 'voluntary contracting' could be relaxed. There are two directions to consider. One is contracting by force; this is the idea of the necessity of a Hobbesian prince for the solution of problems of collective action. The other is the attempted removal of the benefits of holding out, by imposing sanctions on non-participants. This latter method has been used quite frequently by the US in regard to marine resources, especially with regard to marine mammals. The same costliness accrues in this case as in any manner of *ex post* bargaining, and it will be considered more fully in section 8.5.

[15] The 'reservation price' of a contracting party is the minimum amount which that party would be willing to accept in return for its participation in the transaction. The entire point of this paper is that this 'price' is an elusive quantity to determine in the context of multilateral bargaining, because in this context the result of non-participation can be *gains* rather than losses. This possibility muddies the entire concept of reservation price, rendering it difficult to ascertain objectively the compensation to which a party is entitled.

who have recently been investing heavily in an inefficiently utilized resource are those with the largest claims for compensation. In that case some sort of arbitrary judgement must usually be taken concerning the point in time at which previously reasonable non-acceptance becomes transformed into an act of opportunism.[16]

These last two points are the primary contributors to the costliness of *ex ante* bargaining. The indivisibility of compensable burden and opportunistic rents means that there is no objective basis for agreeing the 'scientifically correct' shares. In addition, the fuzziness of the line separating the two categories of costliness results in excessive demands on the resource. Each state's price of agreement usually includes a component of both; hence, the aggregate shares often add up to more than the carrying capacity of the resource. These difficulties are at the core of the costliness of *ex ante* bargaining, and they will be elaborated upon in section 8.4.

Between these two 'purist' solutions (of imposed bans or *ex ante* bargains) lies a third range of possibilities. These result from the combination of uniform standards and sequential acceptance. When this combination exists, the states perceiving the standard as a net benefit will accept it immediately, while those perceiving it as a net burden will not. For the latter group of states the option of 'tailoring' the agreement to their individual characteristics remains open, despite the uniformity of the standard. That is, through *ex post* redistributions it is possible for these states to receive a very different allocation of the resource than that which is set forth under the terms of the governing convention. The bargaining problem, consisting of tailoring individual shares to individual characteristics, is resolved in this situation via *ex post* redistributions (i.e. after the convention has come into existence) rather than *ex ante* bargaining. This is the method of *ex post* bargaining which is used to regulate many global resources today.

## 8.4 Reasons for the Failure of *Ex Ante* Bargaining

The failure to agree enforceable shares *ex ante* implies the adoption of the sequential acceptance mechanism for attempting to achieve the jointly managed solution. This in turn implies substantial redistribution of shares through the mechanism of free-riding on others' unilateral restraint. Ultimately, this method of *ex post* bargaining over shares may also lead to universal agreement;

[16] In international law, this manner of evolving international standards by means of incomplete contracting is known as the creation of 'customary law'. This sort of law comes into being by reason of being the accepted practice of the majority of states on a given matter; however, it can never be applied (or 'opposed') to a state that makes consistent objections to its applicability (Akehurst, 1987).

however, it entails its own costliness during the period in which holdouts exist. The comparative costliness of these two manners of solving the bargaining problem is discussed in section 8.5, and a comparison of these two methods in the context of oceanic resources is the subject of section 8.6. In this section, the specific reasons for the costliness of *ex ante* bargaining are surveyed. That is, why is it that these bargaining problems cannot be solved by agreeing prior transfers between the necessary parties in order to secure agreement?

*Characteristics of a binding resource management agreement.* The fundamental problem to resolve in international resource law is how to create an optimal management agreement which is concrete, universally binding, and enforceable. This requires that the contract contain each of the following elements:

1. concrete individual shares;
2. of an optimal aggregate usage level;
3. together with a monitoring system for share enforcement; and
4. sanctions to deter evasion of the monitoring system.

These are the necessary characteristics of a binding agreement, i.e. one that is concrete and enforceable. *In addition, in order to secure a universally binding agreement, it will be necessary to to construct the terms of the agreement in such a manner that it induces simultaneous acceptance by each and every state.*

This is the precise implication of an *ex ante* bargaining procedure; that is, the object of *ex ante* bargaining should be to achieve the *simultaneous* movement of all potential users to the co-ordinated equilibrium, by constructing an agreement in such a way as to create the incentives for this move. This is a difficult task to comprehend in the context of a single instrument; this section investigates the difficulties involved in solving all four parts of the *ex ante* bargaining problem. They will be considered in reverse order.

### *Sanctions: The Necessity of Self-Enforcing Conventions*

One source of contractual costliness is the necessity of a self-enforcing contract. In the international context, there is no overarching authority in place for the enforcement of bargains, as there is in the case of domestic contracts (i.e. the judiciary and the police). This does *not* imply that such contracts are unenforceable; it merely implies that enforcement must be supplied as part of the contract, since it is not automatically supplied elsewhere. This means that the contractual terms must not only induce agreement at the time that the bargain is struck; these terms must also induce performance of the agreement throughout its life as well.

Most contracts in private relations are in fact of this nature. It is prohibitively costly to access the governmentally supplied enforcement mechanism, so enforcement must be provided on a private basis to supplement the public mechanism (Williamson, 1986). This is often done by providing for third-party mediators, or by making contracts within the framework of a repeating relationship. To the extent that these private contractual mechanisms are successful, this success is attributable to the existence of reciprocal sunk investments in the relationship. Sunk investments are any expenditures which will only yield a return through the performance of the terms of the contract. They are the 'bonds' provided to assure performance of the agreement. To the extent that all parties have roughly equivalent bonds riding on the performance of the original bargain, the freedom to engage in unilateral restructuring of that contract is limited.

This means that an international resource agreement must not only determine shares of resource use, but also that such shares must be allocated over a certain period of time and bonds instituted for the enforcement of this bargain. Otherwise, changed conditions will alter individual perceptions of the distribution of the benefits and burdens of co-ordination, and the agreement will collapse. Therefore, the bargaining problem in the international resource context is further complicated by the addition of this dynamic dimension to the negotiations over resource shares.

### *Implementing a Credible International Monitoring System*

A monitoring system is a fundamental component of a system of joint management. The resolution of the bargaining problem has little impact unless the performance of the agreement is observable. Each party receives its 'implicit return' from personally forgoing the opportunistic strategy by means of observing that all other parties are reciprocating. Without monitoring, the parties to the contract are returned to the prisoner's dilemma.

One of the fundamental problems with international law has been its reliance upon state self-implementation of international obligations. This manner of monitoring is doomed to failure, not because states are necessarily opportunistic but because there is no observable return to self-enforcement. The return to enforcement must come from observing other states' enforcement efforts, i.e. international monitoring.

### *Determining Optimal Aggregate Use*

The determination of the optimal aggregate level of use is problematic because it becomes easily intertwined with the issue of share determination. For example, those parties desiring larger shares often do so through the mechanism of arguing for a *pro rata* share of a larger aggregate quota, thereby implying that the burden of optimal management will be left to fall upon other states. This argument for individualized treatment often takes the form of the presentation of 'scientific evidence' supporting a high level of aggregate use; then those supporting lower aggregate rates of access may be made to absorb the majority of the impact of the position which they are supporting. Therefore, there exist incentives to distort the objectivity of the process even at the level of determining aggregate usage.

*Determining Individual Shares*

This is the core of the regulatory problem. There are no obvious or easily calculated methods for determining individual shares, and the confusion between burdens and opportunism renders the bargaining even more difficult. This section considers why several possible 'focal point' solutions fail to work well in solving the bargaining problem in the international resource context.

*The problem of uniform share allocations.* One means of solving the distributional problem would be to use the 'rule of equal treatment' to allocate equal shares in the global resource to all states. It has been argued by some that this rule appeals to 'the sense of fairness', especially in regard to the use of international resources (Young, 1989). This principle is in wide usage in the formulation of most international resource conventions.[17]

But it is a singularly unhelpful approach, as is any approach which attempts to treat unequals equally in a contractual context. The construction of a contract must take into consideration the incentives its terms create for its own acceptance; otherwise, it is doomed to failure. Uniform standards ignore the fact that the 'sense of fairness' is not shared by all (certainly not by those affected unequally) and this results in the predictable failure of the regulatory mechanism, because international resource regulation requires the agreement of all potential users.

Importantly, these concepts of fairness have been developed within an entirely different institutional environment. In the domestic context, the multilateral bargaining problem no longer arises because a distinct layer of institutions has evolved to deal with multilateral contract situations. Domestically, contract has been largely relegated to the bilateral spheres of activity, and multilateral contracting has been largely managed through 'political' processes, such as representative government and majority voting. These addi-

[17] Many if not most international conventions propose 'equal shares' of access for the various users. See, for example, Young (1989) for the argument that the allocation of 'equal shares' within such regimes appeals to the sense of fairness. Many times this 'equal share' is equal to zero, i.e. a ban on use. See, for example, Birnie (1985) on the ban on commercial whaling operations under International Whaling Convention, and Glennon (1990) on whether the ivory trade 'ban' was effective in conserving the African elephant.

tional institutions provide the means by which heterogeneous parties may be pooled within a contract with a uniform set of standards. To apply 'senses of fairness' acquired within the domestic context to the international is counter-productive because the latter has evolved ways of dealing with these problems which the former has not.

*The problem of allocation under objective criteria.* In theory it should be possible to ascertain *objectively* the individual cost of compliance. But this is a very difficult task to accomplish in a multilateral setting. Such a determination is usually unnecessary in bilateral bargaining, where it is possible instead to rely on the individual's 'reservation price', viz. the user's own subjective determination of its individual costliness of acceptance. The costs from otherwise remaining in the (unco-ordinated) state of disagreement create incentives for truthful revelation in that context. This is of course not the case in multilateral contracting. The 'costs of disagreement' in this context are often the 'benefits from free-riding' on others' restraint, if sequential acceptance occurs. Therefore, in multilateral contract, there is little incentive for the state truthfully to reveal its perceived costs.

In fact, the holdout state itself might not be aware of the true source of its recalcitrance in this situation; when sequential adoption occurs, the two phenomena, individual costliness and free-rider benefits, will be necessarily interrelated. As a sequence of states curtail the use of a resource (or potential users abstain), the holdout will increase its rate of access in pursuit of rents. This increased rate of usage will, however, simply increase the costliness to this state of future accession to the agreement. Thus, differential dependence on the resource is itself a symptom of the pursuit of 'holdout rents'.

This leaves two avenues for the allocation of shares in the resource after co-ordination. The first is to attempt an 'objective' (or scientific) determination of the relative costliness of accession. To a large extent this is merely a reformulation of the initial task (of securing some basis of agreement on shares) by means of involving a group of third-party intervenors. In the international regulation context the reference to scientific criteria usually leads to pitched battles along these lines, as each state then arms itself with its own 'expert testimony' as to its individual burden. Even if a scientific consensus is developed, there is no reason why any one state must necessarily submit to that tide of opinion, especially as it can usually be predicted that the consensus was developed with the backing of those states whose interests are advanced by that particular perspective.

A variant on this theme is the establishment of a 'scientific committee' under the international regulatory mechanism, whose recommendations as to shares are vested with some presumption of validity. In these regimes the fundamental battles are then waged in regard to the manner by which appointments to the scientific committee are occasioned.[18]

*The problem of allocation by prior appropriation.* Alternatively, the individual shares of the resource could be determined by reference to some point in time; that is, shares can be frozen by reference to use at that time. Such entitlements procured through first use are known in the domestic context as rights by 'prior appropriation'.

Although the principle of 'prior appropriation' has been used quite extensively with regard to common resources in the domestic context (e.g. oil pools, minerals, water, wildlife, etc.), it has been demonstrated that this doctrine results in the same wastage in that context that can be anticipated to occur in the global context. Prior appropriation as a legal regime is hugely inefficient with regard to the exploitation of domestic open-access resources (e.g. oil pools) and it has resulted in the complete dissipation of the resource rents in the form of wasteful over-capitalization in these industries (e.g. domestic fisheries) (Libecap, 1989).

*The problem of paying the polluter.* Furthermore, it makes even less sense to create a general system of incentives to encourage investment in international resources in this way. An international resource management system which is constructed so as to compensate disproportionate investments in the appropriation of some global resources will have the effect of encouraging those investments with regard to other international resources. That is, the dynamic efficiency of 'paying the polluter' is doubtful. It will, perhaps, result in a binding universal agreement with regard to one global resource only at the expense of encouraging further the over-exploitation of other such resources.

This range of problems regarding the determination of individual shares is the fundamental problem of *ex ante* bargaining. There is no obvious criterion for determining shares under an international resource agreement. Yet, shares must be determined on an acceptable basis in order to acquire universal agreement. It is the resolution of this paradox which is at the base of the fundamental costliness of *ex ante* bargaining.

## 8.5 The Costliness of *Ex Post* Bargaining

The allocation of concrete shares of an international resource and the construction of a mechanism for their enforcement is no small task. The costliness of the bargaining to accomplish this would not be inconsequential in any case. Nevertheless, there are good reasons to prefer an *ex ante* bargaining solution to

[18] The introduction of representative voting and majority voting at the scientific commission level were probably the first tentative steps toward the introduction of the crucial elements of representative government at the international level.

an *ex post* one. First, the *ex post* solution implies delayed co-ordination in the use of the international resource. This is an irretrievable deadweight loss. In addition, it is possible that the continued over-exploitation of the resource may result in an additional loss by reason of its extinction. With regard to most natural resources, once exploitation has reached a certain level, the resource cannot be retrieved. This implies additional losses regarding future 'options' and generations.[19]

Another reason to prefer the *ex ante* solution concerns the external effects of *ex post* redistributions on other international regulatory regimes. These redistributions are often undertaken in the form of express disagreements and the refusal to sign or ratify the convention. More often, however, these redistributions occur in the context of tacit disagreements which do not, in writing, appear to rise to the level of total non-acceptance, but in practice have the same effect. These forms of tacit disagreement are often countenanced in the pursuit of nominal 'consensus', but do a great deal of harm to both the administration and the reputation of international resource regimes.

Each of these forms of disagreement, express and tacit, addresses the same *ex post* bargaining problem; that is, each is a method used to enable individual states to appropriate greater shares of the resource than would be allowed under the terms of the agreement. Non-acceptance of the treaty, via failure to sign, ratify or accede, is of course the classic form of holdout. Equally damaging is the party that formally accepts the treaty, but makes a significant reservation with regard to its use of the resource.[20] The lack of concreteness in convention language is often argued to be necessary for consensus, but this also renders the convention largely unenforceable against any state.[21] Finally, the acceptance of the convention in all respects *de jure*, while (owing to severe monitoring problems) the state continues use without regard to its international obligations *de facto* has the same impact as each of the preceding practices.[22]

These acknowledged inefficiencies of international resource lawmaking are various manifestations of the costliness of the solution to the 'bargaining problem' in this context. That is, all of these difficulties in international law are traceable to the problem of agreeing on the distribution of the gains realized by

[19] See Pearce and Turner (1990).

[20] The 'right of reservation-consensus' tradeoff is also recognized in the literature. See Zemanek (1983).

[21] There is a substantial international law literature discussing the 'concreteness-consensus' trade-off. See, for example, Monnier (1975), and Jenks (1965).

[22] For example, this is the case in regard to the Elephant Ivory Management Quota System adopted under the Convention on International Trade in Endangered Species. Although about 30 of the 33 range states are parties to this convention, only about half of these states even met their obligations to establish a quota under the system in the years 1986 and 1987. Of these, only four or five were established in conformance with the system guidelines. In fact, there was virtually no adherence to the system although it was almost universally subscribed. See Barbier *et al.* (1990).

agreement; a state which feels aggrieved about its allocated share of the resource under the convention standard has available to it any of these options for the unilateral appropriation of additional shares of the resource. One of the fundamental costs of this system of *ex post* 'bargaining' is that 'agreed' laws are subject to unilateral restructuring; hence the perception that international agreements have little substance is perpetuated.

Therefore, there are fundamentally sound reasons to prefer a system of *ex ante* bargaining concerning international resource regimes as opposed to the *ex post* form that has developed. Of course, an *ex ante* system would itself not be costless; the preceding section indicated that there would be substantial costliness involved in solving the bargaining problem on this basis. However, the costliness of bargaining over shares exists, whether accomplished on an *ex ante* or an *ex post* basis, while the benefits to co-ordinating usage of the resource are achieved earlier in the former case. In essence, international resource agreements are an example of the 'shrinking cake' bargaining game, where the parties lose for ever the benefits from agreement when it is deferred (Rubinstein, 1988). In this framework, it will always be more efficient to pursue the *ex ante* approach.

## 8.6 The Regulation of Oceanic Resources

During their open-access period, the regulation of oceanic resources had to occur through joint international management. Dozens of such regimes were attempted; there is only one notable success story. Most times the regimes failed for the reasons discussed above; that is, in general, the problem was one of holdouts continuing to over-exploit the resource.

The purpose of this section is to illustrate the theory developed above, by reference to the myriad of examples of such bargaining problems. The first part will demonstrate the occurrence of *ex post* bargaining with regard to oceanic resources; the next will detail the difficulties with attempts at *ex ante* bargaining.

### Ex Post *Bargaining regarding Oceanic Resources*

The theory developed in section 8.3 stated that there are four different avenues by which *ex post* redistributions can occur, even after a convention has been adopted for the regulation of an international resource: (1) non-signatories; (2) reservations; (3) textual ambiguity; and (4) non-implementation.

*Non-signatories*. The collapse of international regulatory regimes by reason of the refusal of users to accept the standards of the convention has occurred widely. Most recently, the United Nations Law of the Sea Convention, developed through twenty-five years of continuous negotiations, failed to gain wide acceptance. Although open for signature since 1982, it has still failed to obtain sufficient acceptances (sixty states) to come into effect. Amongst the significant non-signatories are the Federal Republic of Germany, the United Kingdom, and the United States. In fact, even though 159 states signed the convention within its two-year signature period, as of 1987 only thirty-two had ratified.

The primary reason that this convention has failed to secure the acceptance of these important signatories is its provisions for regulating the one area of the oceans which are retained exclusively in international jurisdiction, i.e. the deep seabed. The vast majority of states declared this region the 'common heritage of mankind', and the LOSC provides that any working of this region is to proceed through an international body known as the Enterprise, or its licensees (LOSC, Art. 134 ff.). This provision proved unacceptable to most of the developed states (including the non-signatories listed above), whose firms had already invested over $250 million in the development of deep seabed technology and exploration.

An eleventh-hour attempt to save the Law of the Sea Convention was launched in 1982, by the adoption of a compromise resolution which vested exclusive rights to seabed areas of up to 150,000 square miles in each of eight 'pioneer investors' for a period of eight years. Obviously, this was a last ditch attempt at some true *ex ante* bargaining, but the offer was declined; the seabed-mining states instead entered into a reciprocating states regime under which they recognized one another's claims to certain areas of the seabed.

This was perhaps one of the most recent, and most famous, incidents in a long line of international regime failures. The very first attempt at regulation of oceanic resources was subject to the same difficulty. In the latter part of the nineteenth century, the taking of fur-seals at sea by US and Russian fleets had resulted in the near decimation of this species; in about 1885, these two states agreed to undertake the unilateral restraint of forbidding their fleets from taking fur-seals at sea. The response was immediate; Canadian and Japanese sealers swarmed into Alaskan and Siberian waters, respectively. In 1893 the US and the UK (for Canada) finally agreed a ban on all pelagic (at sea) sealing, which of course only opened that part of the seas to Japanese exploitation as well. By the turn of the century, the fur-seal populations were reduced to a small proportion of their original size, and Japanese sealers had appropriated a much greater share of the harvest by reason of the unilateral restraint of the other sealers.

In general, the history of the international fisheries commissions was rendered an unhappy one by the appearance of the long-distance trawlers on the scene in the 1960s. This entry by a few states with large factory-sized ships rendered nascent agreements by territorial states unworkable in a large number of regulated fisheries: the Inter-American Tropical Tuna Commission; the International Commission for the Northwest Atlantic Fisheries; and the International Pacific Halibut Commission are examples. In fact, the last-named commission had, through forty years of co-operation between the US and Canada, just achieved maximum sustainable yields when the large trawlers arrived on the scene. The trawlers tended to be from one of a few states (Japan, USSR, Korea, either Germany) at that time, but the identity was of little consequence. The arrival of these trawlers was predictable, as the unilateral restraint of bordering states began to pay off in higher yields; these large ships were simply the technologically determined manifestation of the fisheries free-riders under these circumstances.

All of these fisheries were hugely overfished in the period leading up to enclosure. Although the world-wide fish harvest remained roughly stable during this period (at about 68 million tonnes), this was being achieved primarily by substituting less-demanded species for overfished ones; for example, the world-wide catch of haddock had been reduced from 910,000 tonnes to 240,000 tonnes in the decade of the 1970s (FAO, 1985). In addition, many fisheries have made substantial recoveries in the period after enclosure (Keen, 1988). For example, the Pacific halibut catch has increased from 13,500 tonnes to 34,400 tonnes between 1976 and 1988. Effective regulation of many of these resources is now occurring.

*Reservations.* The taking of a reservation or objection is simply the means by which an existing member of a regulatory commission is allowed to opt out individually with regard to a proposed regulation. Such reservations occur predictably when the negotiations over shares have concluded unhappily for a particular state.

An example of the use of a right of reservation in order to redistribute shares is the short-lived regime of the Northeast Atlantic Fisheries Commission (NEAFC). During the years 1974–6, when it was apparent that the herring fishery was under tremendous pressure, this commission adopted four different quotas in order to regulate the resource. The first quota was adopted (under the prevailing code of majority rule) by a vote of 9 to 2, but the two states in the minority simply took reservations and ignored the quotas. The next quota was passed by a vote of 8 to 3, but only two of the three objecting states took official reservations. The penultimate quota was actually passed by consensus, and no reservations occurred. The final quota, before enclosure occurred, was passed by a vote of 7 to 2, with both objecting states taking reservations. The sum total of this regulation was that, in three years of regulation constituted of scientific fact-finding and continuous negotiations, a set of binding quotas were only in effect for six months. The stocks of herring sufferred accordingly; the sustainable harvest recommended by the scientific committee fell from 310,000 tonnes in 1974 to zero in 1976 (Underdahl, 1980).

*Non-implementation.* Perhaps the most notorious of all holdouts are the so-called 'flags of convenience' states in international shipping. A flag of convenience is, in effect, a state which is not adequately regulating its fleet of registered ships. All such states are non-signatories of the High Seas Convention, which requires genuine links between a ship-owner and the registering state (in order to provide that state with jurisdiction over that person and his assets). In addition, many of these states, even though signatories to a number of conventions regarding safety standards at sea, implement a lax and ineffective regulatory regime. The offering of registration to non-resident owners together with the implied laxity of safety standards allows these states to appropriate a disproportionate share of the shipping trade, and consequently the registration fees which are attached.[23] Liberia, Panama, and Cyprus are all flag-of-convenience states, and they together represent about 25 per cent of the world's registered shipping tonnage.

The oceanic resources which are over-exploited as a result are the waters and shorelines which are polluted as the consequence of potentially avoidable tanker accidents. The ship-owners do, of course, have incentives to undertake sufficient safety measures to protect the value of their vessels, but they have little regard for the potential losses inflicted upon others by reason of the loss of one of their vessels. As exemplified by the *Torrey Canyon*, the *Amoco Cadiz*, or the recent Alaskan oil spill, these external effects can in fact be quite substantial; perhaps, far greater than the value of the vessel itself. The clean-up cost in Alaska was in excess of $2 billion. Therefore, the protection of these third parties (to tanker accidents) requires the international regulation of the resource, and the appearance of flag-of-convenience states is the predictable response to the development of such regulations. These states are simply acquiring the holdout rents from lax implementation of the various navigational safety conventions; they are the unavoidable consequence of the failure to create an adequate international monitoring scheme.

The impact of these holdouts on the resource is observable from the differential accident rates experienced by the various flag states. For example, between 1980 and 1983 flags of convenience accounted for only 27 per cent of shipping tonnage but for 37 per cent of all lost tonnage. In 1985, the serious accident rate per tonnage was 2 per cent for Panama and 0.7 per cent for Cyprus (both flag of convenience states), the corresponding rate for the other large shipping countries (Japan, UK, USSR) was well under 0.1 per cent for each (IMO, 1987). In sum, nearly a third of the world's shipping tonnage was being regulated by regimes whose accident experience rate was 10–20 times that of the other major shipping states (Churchill and Lowe, 1988).

[23] Recently, the UK shipping fleet threatened to defect *en masse* on the grounds that UK implementation of international shipping standards resulted in a £1,500 per day cost differential between themselves and their flag-of-convenience competitors.

Non-implementation is a far more pervasive phenomenon in international regulation than is indicated by even this one fairly spectacular example, but by its nature it is not that readily observable. Where agreements are made, but enforcement is left in the hands of each of the individual states on the high seas, there is little reason to expect that their terms are honoured. An example of this would be the International Whaling Commission which established Antarctic whaling quotas for thirty years, which went largely ignored. The same is true of many of the fisheries commissions; the Inter American Tropical Tuna Commission went on setting annual quotas after the entry of numerous long-distance fishing states, even though the declining stocks clearly indicated that these quotas were being ignored (Keen, 1988). In short, although the evidence is sparse, it is apparent that strict self-implementation of the terms of an international resource convention is the exception rather than the rule.

*Ambiguity*. The ambiguity of the terms of an international resource convention can allow for *ex post* redistributions, by permitting a wide range of interpretations to be given to the shares implied by the agreement. Sometimes it is the case that a convention is rendered a nullity by reason of overly vague language. For example, the initial Convention on the Continental Shelf failed to achieve agreement on the delimitation of the shelf (which is an ambiguous concept in itself) and settled instead on vesting full sovereignty in the adjacent submarine lands 'to where the depth of the superjacent waters admits of the exploitation of the natural resources of the area'. This was not the vesting of property rights in an international resource, which is a viable approach to regulating previously open-access resources; it was simply the enshrining of the resource's open-access status. The convention was so ambiguous that it became a non-statement. This is often the case with the language of international law texts, which frequently broadly admonish states to behave properly and do right.

Another form of ambiguity is the 'loophole'; a purposefully inserted ambiguity whose initial intent was perhaps narrow, but whose interpretation can be extended so as to swallow up the whole of the restrictions in the text. A good example of such a loophole is the 'scientific whaling' exception in the International Whaling Convention. Because the convention was intended to regulate the more significant commerical whaling sector, it exempted the scientific takings from its regulatory requirements on the assumption that such removals were too insignificant to affect stocks. When the commercial whalers were subjected to zero quotas by the commission in 1984, suddenly a new and substantial scientific whaling industry sprang up; Japan gave notice of the taking of 800 whales under this exception and Iceland gave notice of the taking of 400 immediately after the moratorium was introduced.

Similarly, when the US and Canada had achieved success in their regulation of the Pacific halibut fishery after forty years of management, the USSR and

Japan sent long-distance trawlers into the waters. When it was unanimously agreed that the halibut fishery was already operating at full capacity, the two new entrants agreed to fish outside of halibut waters and to 'abstain' from halibut fishing when in those waters. The 'abstention' loophole allowed the long-distance trawlers into the halibut fishery, and the US/Canadian harvest of halibut collapsed over the next fifteen years (to a third of its previous volume) until the fishery was enclosed and the interlopers ejected.

In sum, these are all examples of the ineffectiveness of agreeing regulations, which are then subject to unilateral *ex post* restructuring. The deterioration of these resources under these regimes was evidence enough of the inefficacy of this approach.

### Ex Ante *Bargaining regarding Oceanic Resources*

*Ex ante* bargaining regarding oceanic resources requires the satisfactory accomplishment of the four tasks: (1) the determination of aggregate optimal use of the resource; (2) the determination of individual shares of that aggregate quota; (3) the implementation of an international monitoring scheme; and (4) the creation of sanctions to deter opportunistic share appropriation. The agreement to this regime must be universal and simultaneous to have effect *ex ante*, if at all.

*Optimal aggregate quotas.* The primary difficulty here, as indicated above, is the willingness of states to advocate some far-reaching scientific evidence as a means of staking their claim to a greater individual share of the agreed quota. That is, if a state asserts that a far greater harvest is optimal, then, even if its share is the same as the other users, its computed off-take for itself will exceed that computed by the others. This device is used quite routinely. For example, in 1975 the scientific commission of NEAFC stated that the sustainable harvest of Norwegian cod did not exceed 510,000 tonnes, while the USSR attended the negotiations armed with its own scientific estimates of a potential off-take of 1,165,000 tonnes.

More recently, the most heated battles on this issue have centred on whether there should be any off-take whatsoever. The most sordid example of politics entering the scientists' laboratory occurs in the context of the International Whaling Commission's Scientific Committee. This is the committee which recommends aggregate quotas to the IWC, and it is constituted of delegates of each of the member states (Birnie, 1985). This framework has resulted in an open competition between whaling states and conservation organizations in the acquisition of the most delegates to the scientific commission (Holt and Gulland, 1982). The initial volleys were hurled by the conservation organizations, who packed the commission with pro-moratorium delegates elected from new member states such as Seychelles, Belize, St Lucia, St Vincent, and even land-locked Switzerland. Japan countered by securing the entry of new whaling states, Korea and Peru, and by attempting to buy back the support of the delegate from the Seychelles. Obviously, it will remain difficult to achieve a meaningful scientific consensus on the whaling issue in the context of such political (and other) manoeuvring. This is not meant to imply that there is no place for politics in the regulation of international resources; it is meant to point out the difficulty of segregating the political forum from the scientific.

*Individual shares.* The first hurdle to agreeing individual shares is the problem of unilateral restraint. Such restraints muddy the waters again and again regarding the allocation of shares in oceanic resources. This is because unilateral restraints encourage new entrants, who therefore demand a share corresponding to their new investment in the industry, while the states who exercised restraint desire a reward for their unilateral action and a penalty for the opportunists. Obviously, these share demands will sum to more than 100 per cent of the aggregate quota.

There are numerous examples of this phenomenon; nearly as many examples as there are over-exploited resources. The short history of the North East Atlantic Fishing Commission is again disproportionately colourful. For example, in the deliberations of the NEAFC discussed above, the twelve different parties broke down into three readily identifiable camps: those states arguing that the individual quotas failed to give enough weight to 'historical rights' (Poland, Sweden, Russia); those arguing that the individual quotas failed to give enough weight to 'industry problems' (Denmark); and those arguing that the overall quota must be kept low irrespective of individual demands (UK, Norway). The first group is simply those states which have been exercising unilateral restraint of late, and demanding that quotas take that into account. The second group, Denmark, was the opportunist in this case; it was stuck with heavy new sunk investments in North Sea fishing capital. The third group was the group that expected to benefit most from the new 200-mile EEZ proposed under the LOSC; that is, they were the future owners of the property that NEAFC was then regulating. The agreed overall quota was 400,000 tonnes, while the sum of the individual shares demanded in this round was 572,000 tonnes; this latter figure was greater than the total estimated biomass of the fishery in that year. Ultimately, the states caved in to Denmark's demands (giving it a 42 per cent share of the fishery, higher even than its recent catches).

The next year's negotiations were even more interesting. From the outset, the states that had practised unilateral restraint were out to punish Denmark for its opportunism. They pushed uncompromisingly for individual quotas which would require the greatest sacrifice from the big users: Denmark, Norway, and Iceland. Their argument rings familiar; it was that those primarily responsible for the deteriorating state of the fishery should bear the brunt of the cutbacks required to protect the resource. The proposed quota required that 92 per cent of the cutbacks fall on these 'big users'. The measure was passed by a predictable margin (8 to 3), and then, just as predictably, ignored by the minority. The 'enacted quota' was for 254,000 tonnes while the actual harvest was 365,000 tonnes; the share captured by Denmark in that year actually increased by almost 33 per cent over the previous year, when the other states had totally capitulated to Denmark's demands.

Another example of the perverse impact of unilateral restraint is the dilemma now faced by Japan in regard to its whaling fleet. When the Antarctic whaling industry had taken its toll to the extent that binding constraints were finally being introduced by the IWC, many of the then-existing whaling states decided to exit a no longer very profitable industry. Under the Whaling Convention, the individual quotas actually attached to existing ships, not states; so, when the UK and Netherlands left the industry in the 1960s, they sold their fleets with attached quotas to the Japanese. Thus, the Japanese did not expand opportunistically into newly available whaling waters; they purchased the property rights to do so. It was in fact the departing states who received rents in this transaction. Ten years after their exit, several of these same states are at the centre of the movement to eliminate the industry altogether, to the profound dismay of the Japanese, who have paid for most of the world's whaling ships and quotas. It is difficult to agree unanimously on individual quotas when starting from such profoundly different positions.

This same scenario is threatening to present itself with regard to purse-seine tuna fishing. The US fleet has been exercising unilateral restraint in regard to this practice in order to protect the incidentally harmed porpoise populations. The other fleets are profiting at the expense of the US, and expanding their investments in and shares of the tuna catch; the unilateral restraint taken by the US will not aid in the ultimate determination of shares in the regulation of these resources. It will be difficult to distinguish between legitimate claims for compensation and previous opportunism.[24]

The other significant problem in agreeing individual shares arises with the necessity of side-payments for optimal *ex ante* management. Although it may be the most efficient way to proceed, the direct transfer of sums of money in return for shares is an infrequent event. The one example is the Japanese acquisition of whaling quotas, which did not work out too happily. More often, the states insist on receiving their individual shares directly by working the resource, and this is a source of much conflict.

The one happy exception to this rule is also the oldest existing international regulatory regime. The pelagic sealing conventions were discussed earlier, and

[24] These resources will have to be managed by international regulation, even after enclosure, because of their highly migratory nature. Tuna continuously migrate, commencing from the Antarctic and moving up along the west coast of the Americas.

the saga of the fur-seal was left at the turn of the twentieth century in a state of complete disorder. Shortly thereafter, in 1913, the four sealing states (US, Canada, USSR, and Japan) entered into a treaty whereby the exclusive rights to harvest Pacific fur-seals were vested in the US and USSR, while all four parties agreed to enforce a ban on pelagic sealing. Therefore, sealing could only occur on the lands of the US and the USSR, thereby preventing other states from gaining access to the forgone seal harvest. In return, Canada and Japan received 15 per cent each of the returns from the seal harvest, and participated equally in determining the aggregate annual quota. This international resource regime was a success for seventy years, while all of the other oceanic resource regimes were floundering.

*Monitoring*. The requirement of monitoring is self-evident, yet it is something which has been only slowly introduced throughout the realm of international law. The first attempt to introduce international monitoring occurred in the context of the International Whaling Commission. The International Observor Scheme was adopted in London in 1963, and provided that each whaling ship was to have on board a monitor in the employ of the commission. The only problem with this scheme was the time that it took to implement. After thirty years of non-implementation of quotas, the monitoring scheme was finally adopted (Elliot, 1979). Then, even after adoption, it required another ten years before the whaling states would actually accept observors on board; the monitoring scheme was not implemented until the 1973–4 whaling season.

The only other oceanic regulatory system which provides third-party monitoring concerns shipping safety standards. Such monitoring was recently introduced under the terms of the Law of the Sea Convention. In essence, even if ultimate regulatory authority remains with the 'flag state'; the new regime allows 'port states' (i.e. those states receiving cargos from these ships) to engage in arrest of those ships which they have reason to believe are not in compliance with international safety regulations.

A 1982 Memorandum of Understanding among fourteen Western European states goes even further. Under this agreement, each of these states undertakes to engage in random inspections of a full 25 per cent of all ships visiting its ports for non-compliance with international safety regulations, irrespective of the status of its flag state with regard to these regimes. If any ship is found not to be in compliance with these regulations, it will not be allowed to proceed prior to remedying the defect. Therefore, there are rapid steps currently being taken in order to remedy the defects in the prior system of international regulation regarding shipping standards; soon, the value of a flag of convenience will be quite low. In fact, Liberia (the leading flag of convenience) has lost 35 per cent of its fleet in the past decade.

*Sanctions*. Part and parcel of the requirement of monitoring is the necessity of sanctions; it makes little difference if a violation is detected, if it remains unpunished. The one system of true international sanctions lies in the system of 'strict liability' for oil spills under the International Convention for Civil Liability for Oil Pollution Damage of 1969. This system provides for liability, without showing fault, for any damages caused to the territory of a contracting state.

There is one very significant problem with this convention; it (and its companion convention, the International Oil Compensation Fund) entirely misallocate the responsibility for insuring (and thus taking preventive measures) against such spills. Under the combined terms of these conventions, the ship-owner has responsibility for the first (approximately) £10 million, the oil companies have responsibility for the next (approximately) £4 million, and the victims themselves have the responsibility for the residual harm. In addition, if the spill is the result of an 'act of God', the convention absolves the ship-owner of liability altogether. Obviously, this regime places a lot of the responsibility for spill prevention with totally unequipped victims; the strict liability convention must place the full responsibility for avoiding the full amount of the harm with those capable of preventing it.

The other means of invoking sanctions is the implementation of retaliatory domestic legislation. The US has enacted numerous pieces of legislation with the object of supporting international regulatory regimes. For example, the 1972 Marine Mammal Protection Act prohibits the importation of marine mammal products from states whose harvesting is inconsistent with an international regime. Even more generally, the Pelly Amendment to the Fisherman's Protective Act bans the importation of fish products from any country whose nationals fish in a manner that diminishes the effectiveness of any international conservation programme. Similarly, the 1979 Packwood Amendment to the Fisheries Conservation and Management Act, disallows fishing in the US 200-mile EEZ to any state acting to diminish the effectiveness of an international fisheries conservation programme or an international programme to protect endangered species.

True international sanctions, in the sense of bonds instituted in order to assure compliance, have yet to be implemented. But, then, most of the requirements of effective international resource regulation are similarly situated.

## 8.7 Conclusion

The regulation of oceanic resources has been fraught with failure over its 100-year history. To a large extent, these failures have been the predictable result of the interaction of problem and process, the problem being one of the regulation of common resources, and the process being that of international lawmaking.

Although these failures were, for the most part, the predictable consequence of the use of an *expost* bargaining procedure for acquiring universal acceptance, this does not mean to imply that these failures are easily remediable. As the analysis of this paper shows, the substitution of *ex ante* bargaining for *ex post* will itself be a problematic affair; where it has been attempted in tentative measures, it has usually proved impossible to achieve.

Luckily, with regard to oceanic resources, there was the safety net of private property rights to fall into. With regard to the future's international resource regulation problems, it is unlikely that we will be so lucky. It will soon be crucial to learn the solutions to these bargaining problems.

## Appendix General Multilateral Bargaining Problem with Sequential Acceptance

Assume that there is a common resource for which a uniform standard (e.g. a uniform rate of access: $S$ units per state per year) has been proposed in the context of an international resource convention. The present value of the flow of net benefit to any individual state ($B_i$) from the international resource is a function of the rate of harvest by the $i$th user ($x$), and the rate of harvest by all other users ($y$). Therefore, the perceived net benefit of the convention is a function of the expected flows of benefits from the resource under the alternative scenarios of acceptance and non-acceptance of the convention standard.

*State Decision Problem regarding Acceptance of Convention Standard*

Accept if:

$$B_i[\, x(y,S),\, y(x,S)\,] \;\geq\; B_i[\, x^d(y),\, y(x^d,S)\,] \tag{1}$$

where:

$B_i$ is the net benefit to state $i$ of flow of resource (value of flow less cost of access)

$S$ is the uniform standard (rate of access)

$x$ is the optimal rate of use by state $i$ under constrained maximization (constraint $S$)

$x^d$ is the optimal rate of use by state $i$ under unconstrained maximization

$y$ is the rate of use of the resource by other states (also a function of $x$ or $x^d$ and $S$).

This decision problem states that there will be one present value of benefits to state *i* given state *i*'s acceptance of the standard (with *i* receiving a flow of benefits corresponding to the acceptance of constrained maximization) and another value resulting from state *i*'s non-acceptance of the standard (with *i* receiving a flow of benefits corresponding to unconstrained maximization). Each state must decide to accept or not based upon the relative net benefits arising out of these two possible scenarios.

What will be the effect of a proposed standard *S* (which operates as a uniform constraint on the per period access to the resource)? Consider the introduction of a standard as equivalent to a change in the previous constraint (which previously was non-binding on any state) to one which is now binding on a large number of the states. Total differentiation of the above expression with regard to *S* presents the following decision problem facing a state after the introduction of the new binding standard:[25]

For dS, accept the new constraint if:

$$[dB_i/dx\ dx/dS\ /\ dB_i/dx^d\ dx^d/dy\ dy/dS + dB_i/dy\ dy/dx\ dx/dS) + dB_i/dy\ \ dy(x)/dS - dB_i/dy\ \ dy(x^d)/dS] > 0 \qquad (2)$$

This expression may be considered as four separate terms, each having a different effect on the incentives to agreement; those terms are:

*Term 1: Individual Bindingness of Constraint*

$dB_i/dx\ dx/dS$
( < 0 for all, to varying degrees )

*Term 2: Opportunity Cost of Acceptance—Forgone Free-Riding*

$-\ dB_i/dx^d\ dx^d/dy\ dy/dS$
( < 0 with sequential acceptance )

*Term 3: Losses from Unilateral Acceptance—Others Free-Riding*

$dB_i/dy\ dy/dx\ dx/dS$
( < 0 with sequential acceptance )

[25] These are the impacts of acceptance of the standard under the conjecture of competitive harvesting of the resource. That is, these terms result if it is assumed that the resource will be exploited either to the point of zero rents (if joint management fails) or to the agreed aggregate quota (if joint management succeeds).

*Term 4: Impact on Others' Acceptance of Standard*

$$dB_i/dy \;\; dy(x)/dS - dB_i/dy \;\; dy(x^a)/dS$$
(< 0 with sequential acceptance)

Consider the prospects for universal acceptance of the convention standard under the regime of sequential acceptance. Given the expectation that some states will undertake unilateral restraint, the incentives for the individual states contemplating whether to accept the standard are all running against acceptance. Term 1 represents the individualized costliness of moving unilaterally from unconstrained to constrained optimization in response to the uniform standard.[26] Term 2 represents the forgone free-rider's rents, available if others undertake unilateral restraint. Term 3 represents the loss of the same rents when they are conferred upon others, if unilateral restraint is undertaken while others free-ride. Term 4 represents the impact of unilateral restraint on the decision-making processes of other states, concerning whether to accept the constraint or not. Even this term is negative under sequential acceptance, as each act of unilateral constraint simply increases the opportunity costs for those states from the acceptance of the constraint.

Contracting is possible despite this problem of opportunism. All that is required is the *simultaneous* movement to the jointly managed, and hence jointly optimal, position. If the parties' expectations were geared to the belief that any move that occurred would happen simultaneously, then many of the incentives to non-acceptance would be negated. In essence, the requirement of simultaneity removes the free-rider strategy from the menu of choice for the parties; there would be no reason to believe that other parties would ever exercise unilateral restraint with regard to the resource, so there is no expectation of being able to profit from such action. In the above schematic, terms 2 and 3 would then become zero in value, because the option of free-riding would be removed.

Then the parties are presented with only the two options: the inefficient unmanaged position or the efficient managed position. Terms 1 and 4 would then equal the state's expected share of the joint gains from contracting to manage the resource optimally; that is, these would represent the benefits flowing to the individual state from the simultaneous movement to the optimal management of the resource.

[26] Since states vary in their individual endowments, technological capacities and sunken investments, the costliness of a uniform constraint can be realistically assumed to be variant across the user states.

## Bibliography


Akehurst, M. (1987), *A Modern Introduction to International Law*, London, Unwin, sixth edn.

Barbier, E., Burgess, J., Swanson, T., and Pearce, D. (1990), *Elephants, Economics and Ivory*, London, Earthscan.

Barrett, S. (1989), 'On the Nature and Significance of International Environmental Agreements', mimeo, London Business School.

Binmore, K. and Dasgupta, P. (1988), *The Economics of Bargaining*, London, Blackwell.

Birnie, P. (1985), *International Regulation of Whaling: From Conservation of Whaling to Conservation of Whales*, London, Oceana Publications, Vols. I and II.

Brown, G. (ed.) (1982), *The Economics of Ocean Resources*, Seattle, University of Washington Press.

Cheung, S. (1970), 'The Structure of a Contract and the Theory of a Non-Exclusive Resource', *Journal of Law and Economics*, 12, 49–70.

Churchill, R. and Lowe, V. (1988), *The Law of the Sea*, Manchester, Manchester University Press, second edn.

Eckert, R. (1979), *The Enclosure of Ocean Resources*, Stanford, Hoover Press.

Elliot, G. (1979), 'The Failure of the International Whaling Commission', *Marine Policy*, **3**, 147–59.

FAO (1985), *World Catch Statistics*, Rome, Food and Agriculture Organization.

Glennon, M. (1990), 'Has International Law Failed the Elephant?', *American Journal of International Law*, 1.

Grotius, H. (1608), *Mare Liberum*.

Gulland, J. and Holt, S. (1982), 'Viewpoint: The Organisation of Scientific Commissions', *Marine Policy*, 6, 54–5.

Harrison, R. (1985), 'The Offshore Petroleum Industry', *Introduction to Marine Affairs*, International Maritime Organisation.

Hirschleifer, J. (1982), 'Evolutionary Models in Law and Economics', *Research in Law and Economics*, 4, 1–66.

Hoel, M. (1989), 'Global Environmental Problems: The Effects of Unilateral Actions', Discussion Paper, Oslo University Department of Economics, May 1989.

Jenks (1965), 'Unanimity, the Veto, Weighted Voting, Special and Simple Majorities and Consensus as Modes of Decision in International Organisation', in R. Jennings (ed.), *Cambridge Essays in International Law; Essay in Honour of Lord McNair*, Cambridge, Cambridge University Press.

Johnston, D. (1981), *The Environmental Law of the Sea*, Berlin, E. Schmidt.

Keen, E. (1988), *Ownership and Productivity of Marine Fishery Resources*, Virginia, McDonald.

Libecap, G. (1989), *Contracting for Property Rights*, Cambridge, Cambridge University Press.

Mäler, K.-G. (1989), 'The Acid Rain Game 2', paper presented at the workshop on Economic Analysis and Environmental Toxicology, Noordwijkerout.

Monnier (1975), 'Observations sur quelques tendencies récentes en matière de formation de la volonté sur le plan multilateral', *Annuaire Suisse de droit international*, **31**, 31–58.

Ogley, R. (1984), *Internationalising the Seabed*, Aldershot, Gower.

Olsen, M. (1970), *Logic of Collective Action*, New York, Schocken.

Pearce, D. and Turner, K. (1990), *Economics of Natural Resources and the Environment*, Hemel Hempstead, Harvester Wheatsheaf.

Pearson, C. (1975), *International Marine Environment Policy*, Baltimore, Johns Hopkins University Press.

Rothschild, M. and Stiglitz, J. (1976), 'Equilibrium in Competitive Insurance Markets', *Quarterly Journal of Economics*, 90(4), 629–49.

Rubinstein, A. (1988), 'Perfect Equilibrium in a Bargaining Model', in K. Binmore and P. Dasgupta, *The Economics of Bargaining*, London, Blackwell.

Sanger, C. (1986), *Ordering the Oceans*, London, Zed.

Schmidhauser, J. and Totten, G. (eds.) (1978), *The Whaling Issue in US–Japan Relations*, Boulder, Westview.

Schotter, A. (1986), *The Economics of Institutions*, Cambridge, Cambridge University Press.

Underdahl, A. (1980), *The Politics of International Fisheries Management*, Oslo, Universitetsforlagt.

Van Dyke, J. (ed.) (1985), *Consensus and Confrontation, The US and the Law of the Sea Convention*, Honolulu, East–West Institute.

Williamson, O. (1979), 'Transactions Cost Economics, The Governance of Contractual Relations', *Journal of Law and Economics*, 22, 3–61.

— (1983), 'Credible Commitments, Using Hostages to Support Exchange', *American Economic Review*, 73(4), 519–40.

— (1986), *The Economic Institutions of Capitalism*, London, Free Press.

Young, O. (1989), 'The Politics of International Regime Formation: Managing Natural Resources and the Environment', *International Organisation*, 43(3), 1–37.

Zemanek, K. (1983), 'Majority Rule and Consensus Technique in Law-Making Diplomacy', in R. MacDonald and D. Johnston (eds.).

# 9
# An Economic Approach to Saving the Tropical Forests

*David Pearce*

## 9.1 The Issue

The fate of the tropical forests is currently an issue of major international concern. Television and film images of burning forests as they are cleared for agriculture, road building, timber extraction, and industrial development abound. Most of the appeals to 'save the rain forest' are emotionally directed and aim to raise funds to secure outright protection, especially where indigenous peoples are present, or to assist with sustainable uses of the forests. While such campaigns are wholly understandable and generally justifiable, there are other pressure points in the world economic system which promise greater efficacy of action. By and large, these involve demonstrating to governments and international agencies, in the rich and poor world alike, that tropical forests have economic values when they are conserved and utilized sustainably. Moreover, these economic values could be significantly greater than the alleged 'development' values derived by destroying these unique assets. The purpose of this paper is to outline an approach to the economic valuation of tropical forests and to illustrate it with examples of the kinds of anti-conservation bias that exist in prevailing systems of economic incentives.

David Pearce is Professor of Economics at University College London; Associate Director of the London Environmental Economics Centre; and Special Adviser to the Secretary of State for the Environment.

He is indebted to Simon Rietbergen, Ed Barbier, Jeff Sayer, and Jack Ruitenbeek for comments on an earlier version of this paper; to Bernadette Gutierrez for the estimate of Amazonian GDP; and to Dieter Helm for valuable editorial comments.

There are various land-use options for tropical forests. They can be 'left alone'. If no human use of the forest land is permitted at all, we might refer to this land-use option as *preservation*. Maintaining the forest stock in broadly its original state but allowing human use of it can be defined as *conservation*. There will be a broad spectrum of conservation options. Limited selective logging might be permitted with subsequent natural or managed regeneration of the removed timber. Forest products, such as latex or rattan, might be 'harvested' without removing timber stock. Agricultural clearance on a 'shifting cultivation' might be practised with full regeneration of the forest being allowed as a new plot is exploited. Some experts would not regard shifting cultivation as a conservation option: the terminology is not universally agreed. But the basic idea remains that conservation involves use without there being significant destruction of the forest ecosystem. Above all, any use option that produces *irreversible* effects is not a conservation use of the land. 'Development' options would then include clearance for agricultural use without any intent of securing regeneration, clear-felling of timber without regeneration, removal of the forest for use of the land for infrastructure, e.g. a road or mining or industrial development. By and large, development options preclude the regeneration of the forest because of damage to forest soils arising from the development programme's use of the land. This is not inevitable, but it is very likely.

## 9.2 The Rate of Deforestation

Global concern about the rate of tropical deforestation accelerated in the 1980s. Data for all types of forest are approximate. Different sources use different definitions of 'tropical forest' and different definitions of 'deforestation', but annual rates of deforestation at the end of the 1980s appear to be somewhere between 14 and 17 million hectares per annum (Table 9.1). Depending on how forest area is defined, this rate of deforestation may be some 1.8–2.2 per cent of the remaining area of tropical forest (taken to be some 8 million $km^2$, or 800 million hectares). Although comparisons are difficult because of changing definitions, deforestation rates may have been running at far less, around 0.6 per cent per annum, in the late 1970s.

The focus of attention on tropical forests has arisen because of the sheer diversity of functions which they serve, the uniqueness of primary forest in evolutionary and ecological terms, and the accelerating threat to their existence. In the briefest of terms, tropical forests are the homeland of many indigenous peoples, some practising shifting cultivation; they provide the habitat for extensive fauna and flora (biodiversity), which are valued in themselves, and are valued for educational, crop-breeding, and medicinal purposes; they supply hardwood timber, and other forest products such as fruit, nuts, latex, rattans, meat, honey, resins, oils, etc; they provide a recreational facility (e.g. 'ecotourism'); they protect watersheds in terms of water retention, flow regulation water pollution, and organic nutrient cleansing; they act as a store of carbon dioxide so that, while no net gains in the flow of carbon dioxide accrue to climax forests, carbon dioxide is released, and a cost ensues, if deforestation occurs, while forests also fix carbon in secondary forests and in reforested areas; and finally they also provide a possible regional microclimatic function.

**Table 9.1** *Rates of Tropical Deforestation, 1980s (million hectares p.a., closed forest only)*

| | *Late 1970s*[a] | *Mid-1980s*[b] | *Late 1980s*[c] |
|---|---|---|---|
| S. America | 2.67 | 9.65[d] | 6.65 |
| C. America | 1.01 | 1.07 | 1.03 |
| Africa | 1.02 | 1.06 | 1.58 |
| Asia | 1.82 | 3.10 | 4.25 |
| Oceania | 0.02 | 0.02 | 0.35 |
| Total | 6.54 | 14.90 | 13.86 |
| Adjusted Total[e] | n.a | 15.29 | 14.22 |
| % of remaining forest | 0.6 | n.a. | 1.8–2.1 |

*Notes and Sources*:

[a] Late 1970s data for the 34 countries covered in Myers (1989*a*) from Food and Agriculture Organization (1981).

[b] Various years to 1986, taken from World Resources Institute (1990), Table 19.1. In turn, the estimates are based on FAO sources, including an update for some countries of the 1981 estimates, and some individual sources. *Note that the estimates cover closed forests only.* Closed forests refer to dense forests in which grass cover is small or non-existent due to low light penetration through the forest canopy.

[c] Myers (1989*a*). Myers' estimates cover 34 countries accounting for 97.3 per cent of the extent of tropical forest in 1989.

[d] This figure appears out of line with other estimates and is accounted for mainly by a single country—Brazil. Whereas Myers estimates 5 million hectare p.a. loss for Brazil in 1989, the World Resources Institute figure for the mid-1980s is some 8 million hectare p.a. for closed-forest loss.

[e] Myers estimates that 40 other countries with small tropical forests suffered deforestation rates totalling 0.36 million hectare p.a in 1989. We have 'grossed up' the World Resources Institute figures by the same factor (14.22/13.86) to ensure comparability.

*All* these functions are *economic* functions because they contribute to human welfare either directly or indirectly.[1] The issue to be addressed is how to determine the 'total economic value' of a tropical forest. The issue is important because decisions about the use of tropical forest land are currently made in the context of an imperfect understanding of the total functions of the forest. Even if the functions are broadly understood, only some of them enter into the economic calculus that determines land use. In particular, the *direct-use values* (timber, agricultural land) dominate land-use decisions and the wider environmental values are neglected. The resulting *asymmetry of values* explains much deforestation and its analysis indicates some policy instruments for better forest management.

## 9.3 Total Economic Value

One approach to decision-making about tropical forest use is the *cost–benefit approach* (CBA). Under CBA, decisions to 'develop' a tropical forest would have to demonstrate that the net benefits from development exceed the net benefits from 'conservation'. Development here is taken to mean some use of the forest that would be inconsistent with retention of the forest in at least approximately its natural state. Conservation could have two dimensions: preservation, which would be formally equivalent to outright non-use of the resource, and conservation which would involve limited uses of the forest consistent with retention of natural forest. The definitions are necessarily fuzzy. Some people would argue, for example, that ecotourism is not consistent with sustainable conservation, others that it may be. Accepting the lack of precise lines of differentiation, the CBA rule would be to develop if and only if the development benefits minus the development costs are greater than the benefits of conservation minus the costs of conservation. Put another way, the development benefits minus both the development costs and the net conservation benefits must be positive.

It is not sufficient, therefore, for the net benefits of development to be positive. The forgone net benefits of conservation must also be subtracted from net development benefits.[2]

Typically, development benefits and costs can be fairly readily calculated because there are attendant cash flows. Timber production, for example, tends to be for commercial markets and market prices are observable. Conservation

[1] 'Economic' is not to be confused with 'financial' or 'commercial'. Anything contributing to human welfare is deemed to be an economic function, and the flow of services may or may not have a cash flow associated with it. In the case of tropical forests most functions do not have evident cash flows.

[2] See Pearce (1989), pp. 11–27, and Pearce and Turner (1989), ch. 20.

benefits, on the other hand, are a mix of associated cash flows and 'non-market' benefits. This fact imparts two biases. The first is that the components with associated cash flows are made to appear more 'real' than those without such cash flows. There is 'misplaced concreteness' and decisions are likely to be biased in favour of the development option because conservation benefits are not readily calculable. The second bias follows from the first. Unless incentives are devised whereby the non-market benefits are 'internalized' into the land-use choice mechanism, conservation benefits will automatically be downgraded. Very simply, those who stand to gain from, say, timber extraction or agricultural clearance cannot consume the non-marketed benefits. This 'asymmetry of values' imparts a considerable bias in favour of the development option.

Conservation benefits are measured by the *total economic value* of the tropical forest. Total economic value (TEV) for a tropical forest is explained in Table 9.2. TEV comprises *use* and *non-use values*. Conservation is consistent with some sustainable uses of the forest, including sustainable timber harvesting.

**Table 9.2** *Total Economic Value (Use Value and Non-use Value) in the Tropical Forest Context*

| | *Use value* | | + *Non-use value* |
|---|---|---|---|
| *(1)* | *(2)* | *(3)* | *(4)* |
| Direct value | + Indirect value | + Option value | + Existence value |
| Sustainable timber | | | |
| Non-timber products | Nutrient cycling | Future uses as per (1) and (2) | Forests as object of intrinsic value, as bequest, as a gift to others, as a responsibility (stewardship). Includes cultural and heritage values. |
| Recreation | Watershed protection | | |
| Medicine | Air-pollution reduction | | |
| Plant genetics | Micro-climate | | |
| Education | | | |
| Human habitat | | | |

*Direct*-use values are fairly straightforward in concept but are not necessarily easy to measure in economic terms. Thus minor forest products' output should be measurable from market and survey data, but the value of medicinal plants is extremely difficult to measure. *Indirect* values correspond to the ecologist's concept of 'ecological functions' and are discussed further below.

*Option values* relate to the amount that individuals would be willing to pay to conserve a tropical forest for future use. That is, no use is made of it now but use may be made of it in the future. Option value is thus like an insurance premium to ensure the supply of something the availability of which would otherwise be uncertain. While there can be no presumption that option value is positive it is likely to be so in the current context.[3]

*Existence* value relates to valuations of the environmental asset unrelated either to current or optional use. Its intuitive basis is easy to understand because a great many people reveal their willingness to pay for the existence of environmental assets through wildlife and other environmental charities but without taking part in the direct use of the wildlife through recreation. To some extent, this willingness to pay may represent 'vicarious' consumption, i.e. consumption of wildlife videos and TV programmes, but studies suggest that this is a weak explanation for existence value. Empirical measures of existence value, obtained through questionnaire approaches (the contingent valuation method), suggest that existence value can be a substantial component of total economic value. This finding is even more pronounced where the asset is unique,[4] suggesting high potential existence values for tropical forests and especially for luxuriant moist forests.

From Table 9.2, then, total economic value can be expressed as:

$$\text{TEV} = \text{Direct-use value} + \text{Indirect-use value} + \text{Option value} + \text{Existence value}$$

It is important to note that the components of TEV cannot simply be aggregated. There are trade-offs between different types of use value and between direct- and indirect-use values. In practice, then, the TEV approach has to be used with care. We address each component of TEV in turn.

[3] The literature on option value is extensive. See Bishop (1982); Freeman (1985); Plummer (1986); Johansson (1988); Bishop (1988). The sign of option value is indeterminate but may be expected to be positive if the future demand for the asset in question (the tropical-forest function in this case) is certain, and the supply is uncertain.

[4] Brookshire *et al.* (1983); Brookshire *et al.* (1985); Schulze (1983).

## 9.4 Direct-Use Values in the Tropical Forest

Direct-use values may be classified broadly in terms of timber and non-timber uses. Non-timber products include fruits, nuts, rattan, latex, resins, honey, and wildmeat.

### *Timber*

Logging for timber *can* be consistent with conservation if the timber management regime practises sustainable forestry. Sustainable forestry consistent with leaving the original ecosystem broadly intact effectively requires natural forest management, i.e. selective cutting combined with natural regeneration. Traditionally, natural management regimes have been regarded as loss-making unless certain conditions are met. These are: that biological growth rates are very high; that stumpage prices (i.e. log prices) are high; that management is effective and at minimum cost; and finally that the discount rate is low compared to typical commercial and even official government levels.[5]

This bias explains the general absence of sustainable natural management systems in tropical forestry.[6] Inefficiency arising from governmental interference is of considerable importance as far as non-sustainable management is concerned. Thus, the treatment of forest taxation has encouraged rapid depletion as investors engage in rent-seeking caused by inadequate and low taxation.[7]

Table 9.3 shows some estimates of the financial profitability of different forestry systems in Indonesia. Six regimes are compared. TPI is a selective cutting system in which only the largest commercial trees (over 50 cm diameter at breast height) are taken. The management of TPI systems is crucial since careless selective cutting can damage the residual stock, reducing future harvests. In its ideal form, however, it is a sustainable system. CHR is 'complete harvesting and regeneration', i.e. harvesting all merchantable trees, followed by natural or enriched regeneration. INTD is an intensive dipterocarp system based on the idea of heavily managed plantations on clear-felled land.[8] PULP refers to plantations of fast-growing species for pulp. SAWT refers to saw-timber plantations at ten and twenty years rotations respectively. Environmen-

[5] See Leslie (1987).

[6] A detailed survey of tropical moist forest management systems concluded that only one-tenth of 1% of the 828 million hectares of productive forest is under sustained-yield management. See Poore (1989), ch. 7.

[7] See, for example, Repetto and Gillis (1988).

[8] Dipterocarps are a family of exceptionally tall tropical trees, with over 600 species. They grow only in south-east Asia and are highly prized by loggers for being well grained, hard, and durable.

tally, it seems reasonable to rank TPI above CHR.[9] INTD is an untried system which may or may not be environmentally better than CHR. SAWT and PULP are both *prima facie* environmentally undesirable since they are typically based on uniform plantings of non-indigenous species on cleared land. However, such plantations on currently unforested land could be important for 'carbon-fixing' purposes (see below).

**Table 9.3** *Comparative Financial Profitability of Forest Management Systems in Indonesia (Net Present Value: 1986 US$/Hectare)*

| *Regime* | *Discount Rate (%)* | | |
|---|---|---|---|
| | *5* | *6* | *10* |
| TPI | 2705 | 2409 | 2177 |
| CHR | 2690 | 2593 | 2553 |
| INTD | | 2746 | 2203 |
| PULP | | 2926 | 2562 |
| SAW20 | | 2419 | 2278 |
| SAW10 | | 2165 | 2130 |

*Source*: Pearce (1987). The base data come from Sedjo (1987*a* and *b*). The NPVs include revenues from the initial harvest of the standing stock.

Table 9.3 suggests that, on financial grounds, rapid-growth plantations for pulp production are most desirable at an interest rate of 6 per cent, and are equally ranked first at a 10 per cent interest rate. Of the systems involving the least 'management', the selective cutting system is not favoured except at the low discount rate of 5 per cent. Typically, rates of discount used for project appraisal in developing countries are 10 per cent and above. Table 9.3 therefore bears out the general presumption that natural management systems based on selective cutting are unprofitable compared to managed intensive systems and, perhaps, clearer-cutting systems with some natural regeneration. There are many caveats to this conclusion, however. First, the results are likely to be location-specific. Second, they relate to *financial* profitability and not to *economic* worth. An economic assessment would allow for 'shadow' pricing, i.e. a valuation procedure that reflects the worth of the investment to the economy as a whole rather than to a forest concessionaire.[10] Third, the discount rate is seen to be crucial. Shadow pricing may dictate a lower rate depending on the nature of the rationale for discounting.[11] None the less, a direct appeal

[9] For the view that sustained forest management should be based on clear-cutting and the maximization of biomass use, see Hartshorn *et al.* (1987). The analysis tends to assume that market conditions are right, i.e. that timber production takes place near to markets.

[10] Leslie (1987) suggests that shadow pricing will favour the more natural management systems.

[11] See Markandya and Pearce (1988).

to timber benefits is clearly a risky argument for defending the sustainable use of tropical forests.

*Non-Timber Products*

Non-timber products can be important sources of revenue. In Indonesia, for example, exports of non-timber forest products rose from $17 million in 1973 to $154 million in 1985, comprising 12 per cent of forest export earnings.[12] They rose to $238 million in 1987.[13] Exports of rattan alone were $80 million in 1985. Tropical forests also supply essential oils such as camphor, cinnamon, clove, and nutmeg, a trade worth some $1 billion per annum,[14] although most of the output of these products comes from plantations. It cannot be assumed that non-timber product exploitation is itself free from environmental damage. The management record for many non-timber products is hardly better than that for tropical timber.[15] Analysis of fruit and latex yields in a 1 hectare plot of Peruvian Amazonian rain forest suggests that non-timber product revenues may actually *exceed* timber revenues.[16] The results are shown in Table 9.4.

**Table 9.4** *Timber and Non-Timber Revenues in a Peruvian Rain Forest (Equitos) (Net Present Value at 5 per cent: US$ per hectare)*

| | | |
|---|---|---|
| | Fruit and latex | 6330 |
| plus | Selective logging | 490 |
| | Total | 6820 |
| | Clear-felling timber | 1000 |

*Source*: Peters *et al.* (1989).

The implication of Table 9.4 is that tropical-forest conservation might be achieved by simple appeal to financial profitability. It is likely that much forest is unnecessarily damaged because of a failure to investigate alternative management regimes for alternative 'crops'. But there are several dangers in extrapolating from a 1 hectare plot to entire forests. First, markets for non-timber products are very unlikely to be that big. As production of non-timber products expands so their prices are likely to fall. Second, the Peruvian case considers a plot of land near to markets, whereas the major part of the tropical-

[12] See Pearce *et al.* (1990), ch. 5.
[13] de Beer and McDermott (1989).
[14] See Myers (1983).
[15] We are indebted to Simon Rietbergen for this point.
[16] See Peters *et al.* (1989).

forest area will be distant from the market-place, affecting transport costs. The analysis also raises an important question: if it is *privately* profitable to exploit forests for non-timber products, why is greater use not made of them for this purpose? Put another way, why does the exercise of market forces not produce this result ?

The answer to this question reveals some of the most important policy implications for conserving tropical forests. A great deal of deforestation would be avoided if markets were allowed to function more efficiently. It is because of direct government interference that the price signals are distorted, making timber extraction and, more importantly, clearance (usually by fire) for agriculture profitable. Clearly, allowing market forces alone to operate will not solve the problem since market prices themselves fail to reflect full social costs. None the less, getting government underpricing of resource use corrected is important. The forms taken by this interference are well established and have included, in the case of Brazil:[17] tax credits whereby the costs of 'investment' in forest-land clearance for cattle ranching can be offset against income tax; subsidized credit for crops and livestock development; the building of road infrastructure to establish political boundaries.

The empirical relevance of these factors may already have been revealed. Rates of deforestation in the Amazon appear to have slowed in the final few years of the 1980s, coincident with (1) the ending of many of the clearance subsidies and (2) the effective termination of the federal road-building programme. Equally important in the bias towards clearance is the status of land tenure. Forest dwellers frequently have no secure rights to the land, so that outsiders can readily establish rights through clearance. Indeed, in many cases, clearance of the land is a prerequisite for claiming land rights.[18] In the event of competition for rights, the agricultural colonists invariably win. Security of land tenure for indigenous peoples may be one of the most important ways of conserving tropical forests. Conferring security of tenure on colonists, however, acts like a magnet for outsiders to clear land for agriculture.

The social undesirability of forest clearance for ranching is revealed by the fact that, without subsidies, Brazilian beef-cattle ranching revenues cover only about one-third of the costs of setting up the ranches, as Table 9.5 shows.[19] The subsidy system explains why what is privately profitable is socially unprofitable. The combined costs of tax credits, subsidized credit, and the forgone timber revenues from forest destruction is estimated to have been $4.8 billion between 1966 and 1983.

[17] See Mahar (1989); Binswanger (1989); Repetto and Gillis (1988).
[18] See Southgate *et al.* (1989).
[19] See Browder (1988*a* and *b*).

**Table 9.5** *Cost Structure of Typical Beef Cattle Ranch: Brazilian Amazon (US $ per hectare over 5-year period, 1984 prices)*

| | | *(% total)* |
|---|---|---|
| *Capital Investment* | | |
| Land cost | 31.7 | (13.1) |
| Forest clearance | 66.0 | (27.3) |
| Pasture planting | 26.4 | |
| Fencing | 19.4 | |
| Cattle acquisition | 90.9 | (37.6) |
| Other | 7.4 | |
| TOTAL | 241.8 | (100.0) |
| *Operating Costs* | | |
| Labour | 26.2 | (15.1) |
| Herd maintenance | 21.0 | |
| Pasture maintenance | 47.3 | (27.3) |
| Infrastructure | 74.3 | (42.9) |
| Other | 4.2 | |
| TOTAL | 173.0 | (100.0) |
| Total cost | 414.8 | |
| Total revenue | 112.5 | |
| Revenue as % of costs | 27.1 | |

*Source*: Browder (1988*b*).

Government interference is not always a prime cause of deforestation. In Africa, for example, it is frequently government *inaction* that allows others to exploit forests unsustainably.

## *Ecotourism Values*

Tropical forests are increasingly attracting tourists searching for adventure and/or nature appreciation. Ecotourism promises to be a major development, comparable to the existing substantial revenues earned in African countries from wildlife viewing and game drives. European package 'explorer' holidays to the Peruvian Amazon, for example, cost around £1,500 ($2,300) per person for twenty days.[20] In Costa Rica, Ecuador, Philippines, and Thailand, tourism

[20] One company advertises a tour with a two-day excursion into Amazonia, the excursion costing $250 extra on a basic charge of $2,300. As a very rough guide, therefore, each 'visitor day' could be worth $125 as a gross value, and less as value-added.

ranks among the top five industries and brings in more foreign exchange than timber and timber-product exports.[21] Thus, Costa Rica earned $138 million in what was mainly nature-based tourism in 1986. Tourists arriving in Manaus, in Amazonas state, increased from 12,000 in 1983 to 70,000 in 1988. Tourism is expected to be the largest single source of income in Amazonas state in the 1990s.[22] The tourism potential of Central America[23] and Latin America[24] remains largely untapped. Self-evidently, tourism to these countries cannot all be credited to forested areas, but some unquestionably is. Additionally, tourism brings its own external costs in a variety of forms, including pollution and over-exposure of wildlife to tourist vehicles.

One study suggests tentative values for tourist benefits in the Korup Forest in Cameroon.[25] On the basis of assumptions about visit rates from both tourists and researchers, annual net income to Cameroon once visitor rates have stabilized is put at £117,000 (around $180,000). Clearly, the potential for ecotourism depends on the availability of infrastructure (transport, accommodation) and thus some countries are unlikely to be able to develop this aspect of forest use.

### *Uses of Wild Flora and Fauna*

Tropical forests act as the habitat for an enormous variety of species. Meat production from wild animals in Peru amounted to some 13,000 tonnes in 1976,[26] while fish and game comprise around 80–5 per cent of all animal protein intake in the lowland Amazon region outside urban centres. Legal exports of hides and skins from Peru amounted to 5 million and 0.5 million units respectively between 1965 and 1976.[27] The trade in live animals is significant and, sadly, non-sustainable due to excessive exploitation. As with tourism, there are frequently fine distinctions between what is and is not sustainable.

Tropical forests act as the source of genetic material for modern food crops. Cross-breeding with wild varieties is essential to resist diseases and pests. One authority suggests that such cross-breeding has already saved sugarcane, banana, and cocoa crops from major damage.[28] Tropical forests also house many insects that are the natural enemies of plant-damaging pests, and plant chemicals that are used as insecticides. No reliable estimates of willingness to

[21] See Gradwohl and Greenberg (1988), pp. 66–7.
[22] Quoted in Dogse (1989).
[23] See Leonard (1987).
[24] See Dourojeanni (1985).
[25] Ruitenbeek (1989).
[26] Dourojeanni (1985), p. 420.
[27] Dourojeanni (1985), p. 423.
[28] Myers (1983).

pay for tropical-forest genetic material are available, and the informational needs for securing such estimates may be substantial relative to what exists in codified form.[29] Certainly, a valuation exercise should not be confused with simply looking at the value of the final product.

The valuation problem is also formidable in respect of the pharmaceutical use of tropical-forest species. There is a 1 in 4 chance that the initial base materials for prescribed drugs have their origins in tropical forests.[30] But calculations of the market value of the prescriptions bought for such drugs is not an estimate of the value of the plant used to manufacture the drug. A number of estimates of the market value of plant-based drugs have been made.[31] But what is required is the price which drug manufacturers would be willing to pay for the plant material, plus a measure of consumers' net gains from such drugs relative to a substitute. The role of substitutes for plant-based drugs is thus crucial. Many modern drug manufacturers tend to focus more on the production of synthetic drugs using recent advances in molecular biology and biotechnology.[32] Put another way, their willingness to pay for retention of tropical forests as repositories of potential pharmaceuticals could be very low.

One study has approached the value of genetic information in the Korup Rainforest, Cameroon by assuming that the value of patents can be applied to a 'guesstimated' number of research discoveries in the forest area.[33] Assuming 10 such discoveries per year and an average patent value of £5,000 ($8,000), annual benefits could be £50,000 ($80,000), of which Cameroon would, of course, capture only a fraction.

## 9.5 Indirect-Use Values

The ecological functions of tropical forests are many. Valuation procedures tend to be focused on either 'damage done' or 'cost of replacement'. Thus, removal of a tropical forest that protects a watershed can result in soil erosion, downstream sedimentation, and increased floods. The damage done would then be a measure of the value of the watershed protection function since such damage would be avoided by conserving the forest. Alternatively, if the damage occurs, the expenditure on reconstituting the affected area would be a measure of the protection function. If the damage cannot be reconstituted, it may be

[29] See Brown (1986).

[30] Farnsworth and Morris (1976).

[31] Notably, Farnsworth and Soejarto (1985). A figure of some $8 billion is quoted as the value of prescribed plant-based drugs for the USA. Principe calculates a figure for all OECD countries of $43 billion in 1985, including over-the-counter drugs. See Principe (1987).

[32] See Principe (1987).

[33] Ruitenbeek (1989).

necessary to invest in replacing the protection function. However, replacement-cost approaches need to be used with caution. Implicitly, they assume it is *worth while* to make the replacement, i.e. that the benefits from replacement exceed the costs of replacement. But replacements costs are being used to *value* the benefits of replacement, a procedure which automatically produces benefit–cost ratios of unity.

### *Watershed Effects*

The nature and extent of losses of ecological functions from deforestation are disputed. Hamilton and King (1983) provide a survey of claimed *watershed* effects and the empirical evidence for their existence, but others dispute their assessment.[34] Table 9.6 summarizes Hamilton and King's survey. An issue of

**Table 9.6** *Hamilton and King's Assessment of Ecological Impacts of Tropical Deforestation*

| *Impact* | *Assessment* |
|---|---|
| Reduced rainfall | No evidence to support this claim. Possible exception of Amazon rain forest recycling[a] if permanent and large-scale deforestation occurs. Fog and cloud forests do increase rainfall. |
| Reduced water supplies, floods | Claim based on idea of forests as a reduced 'sponge'—taking in water in wet season and releasing slowly in dry season.[b] Forests more like 'pumps'. Cutting tends to *increase* water supply. But *conversion* to agriculture can lower water tables and reduce dry-season river flow. |
| Soil erosion and sedimentation | Both effects result from conversion to agricultural systems that themselves are unstable. Traditional *shifting agriculture* is not implicated in such damage but modern slash-and-burn techniques ('forest farming') are unstable. |

*Notes*: [a] See Salati *et al.* (1979). [b] Myers (1983) espouses the sponge analogy.

importance is that ecological impacts depend upon the *use* to which deforested land is put, i.e. the nature of the agricultural system if conversion is to agriculture, the nature of the logging regime, and so on. The argument is that

[34] Hamilton and King (1983). For a contrasting view see Myers (1983).

forests are not unique in their watershed protection functions, and hence deforestation *per se* does not produce adverse effects. Rather it is the nature of the succeeding *land use* that matters. In theory it is perfectly possible for forest clearance to have limited or negligible watershed effects, e.g. through allowing soils to secure a cover of grasses and shrubs. In reality, the forest clearer is often the same agent that subsequently uses the forest soils in an environmentally damaging way, e.g. for cattle ranching or agriculture.

Ruitenbeek estimates the value of forest protection for inshore fisheries in the Korup region of Cameroon.[35] This comes to some £3.8 million in present value terms (at 8 per cent discount rate). Flood control benefits are similarly estimated at £1.6 million.

### *Nutrient Cycling*

Tropical-forest systems involve complex nutrient cycles. The nutrients in question include calcium, magnesium, and potassium which are 'bound' to soil and water, and elements such as nitrogen which are interchanged with the atmosphere. All the elements are distributed between the soil and the biomass (not, as frequently stated, in the biomass alone) but biomass removal can often reveal poor quality concentrations of remaining nutrients in the soil. Litterfall is thus critical in cycling these nutrients through rapid decomposition and take-up through mycorrhizal associations. The carbon and sulphur cycles are considered separately below.

The significance of nutrient cycling for the *valuation* problem is twofold. First, disturbance of the forest system releases the nutrients into aquatic systems. In tropical forests drainage water into the aquatic system is typically low in nutrients. Deforestation and, more generally, opening of the canopy causes a nutrient outflow which itself can give rise to pollution of river and coastal ecosystems.[36] Second, and far more significant, however, the outflow of nutrients arising from deforestation means that the productive capacity of the previously forested area is seriously reduced. Forest soils are low in nutrients and this explains why cleared forest land will often sustain only limited livestock and crop production without substantial additions of artificial fertilizer. In short, 'nutrient lock-up' tends to impose an irreversibility on the spectrum of land uses subsequent to deforestation.

### *Carbon Cycling and the Greenhouse Effect*

In the process of photosynthesis, *growing* forests 'fix' carbon dioxide and give off oxygen. *Once grown*, forests no longer accumulate carbon from the

[35] Ruitenbeek (1989).
[36] See Furtado and Ruddle (1986); Furtado (1978).

atmosphere. Mature forests are said to be in a state of (approximate) 'carbon equilibrium', i.e. they release as much $CO_2$ as they absorb. (The northern hemisphere's temperate and boreal forests may actually exhibit a slight net fixation of carbon, but tropical forests may safely be regarded as being in carbon equilibrium if they are mature, as would be the case for the remaining primary forest.) But while the rate of carbon exchange with the atmosphere is zero for mature tropical forests, these forests 'lock-up' or 'sequester' carbon as a stock. This distinction is important since it means that *deforestation* will release $CO_2$ into the atmosphere and thus contribute to the 'greenhouse effect'. Indeed, deforestation releases other greenhouse gases such as methane. Tropical forests are major stores of carbon and hence the use made of tropical forest land, and of the timber on the land, is an important factor in global warming.

It is important to distinguish what it is that is being valued when talking of the 'carbon-fixing value' of a tropical forest. The context is best viewed as one of the costs and benefits of alternative land use. Consider two basic options, to conserve tropical forest and to clear it for agriculture.

By conserving a mature carbon-equilibrium forest, any carbon release associated with the alternative land use (agriculture) is avoided, and hence the damage associated with that carbon release is avoided. It is legitimate, then, to speak of the forest as having a 'carbon credit' equal to the avoided damage.

By clearing the forest for agriculture, deforestation occurs and carbon (and other pollutant) releases occur. The damage associated with that carbon release is therefore a 'carbon debit' to that particular forest land use.

However, it is not legitimate both to ascribe a credit to the conservation option *and* a debit to the clearance option. That would be double-counting since the credit and debit are the obverses of each other. Either conservation is credited with damage avoided, or the agriculture option is debited with the damage done by deforestation.

A further complication is that the credit or debit depends on how the timber is removed, how it is subsequently used, and how the deforested land is subsequently managed.[37] Clearance by burning will be associated with a 'total' release of $CO_2$, i.e. there are no offsetting credits in terms of the use made of the timber. But if the land is subsequently managed in such a way that carbon is once again fixed, for example by grassland, then that rate of fixation has to be offset against the loss of carbon from deforestation. Typically, forests contain 20–100 times more carbon per unit of area than agricultural lands. Thus the offset due to subsequent land use will be far from sufficient to offset totally the loss from deforestation through clearance. The same goes for any 'down-

[37] We are indebted to Jack Ruitenbeek for assistance in clarifying the argument in this section. Much of the literature on the 'carbon value' of tropical forests is misleading in that it fails to take account of (1) uses of the timber culled from deforestation, and (2) the subsequent land use. For an exercise in calculating carbon credits for *temperate* forests see Pearce (1991).

stream' reappearance of carbon: by far the greater part of released carbon goes into the atmosphere.

If the forest is clear-felled and all the timber is used to make long-lived wood products (housing timbers, furniture, for example) then the act of deforestation may cause very little carbon release because the carbon remains 'locked up' in the timber products. This is 'product carbon offset'. Subsequent land use may then fix some carbon, so that the overall effect of deforestation on carbon release could be very small, zero, or even, possibly, negative. This second kind of offset is 'land-use carbon offset'.

In fact, taking a global view, most deforestation occurs through direct clearance or incidental damage. The early 1980 estimates of deforestation suggested that some 11.1m ha.p.a of tropical forest were being lost. Of this, 7.3m ha.p.a were being cleared directly for agriculture, usually by burning, and a further 3.8m ha.p.a. were cleared for some combination of agriculture and fuel-wood. *Selective* logging took place on a further 4.4m ha.p.a and, while selective logging is, in principle, consistent with regeneration (and hence little change in the carbon store over time) in practice it tends to be associated with extensive damage to the remaining tree stocks and hence produces carbon release.[38] While the extent of net carbon release will be location-specific, in terms of the overall rate of deforestation it is fair to suggest that there is little 'product carbon offset' to the carbon releases caused by deforestation. Both the 'land-use offset' and the 'product offset' tend to be allowed for in the better studies of carbon release.[39]

Taking the various offsets into account, carbon emissions for 1980 due to deforestation have been estimated to lie somewhere in the range $0.4 - 2.5 \times 10^{15}$g, i.e. 0.4 – 2.5 gigatonnes per annum ($10^{15}$g = 1 billion metric tonnes = 1 gigatonne),[40] with a mean figure of 1.8 gigatonnes per annum. This compares with fossil fuel $CO_2$ releases of 5.3 gigatonnes in 1984. Of this total of 7.1 gigatonnes around half remains in the atmosphere, the rest being absorbed by the oceans and other sinks, making a net accretion of some 3.6 gigatonnes in the atmosphere. Tropical deforestation may therefore be contributing about 25 per cent of $CO_2$ emissions which, in turn, contribute perhaps half of the total greenhouse gases. Tropical deforestation would therefore contribute some 10–13 per cent of all greenhouse-gas emissions.

More recent estimates suggest that global deforestation may have increased and carbon released could be some 2–3 gigatonnes per annum.[41]

Two issues arise: (1) what 'carbon credit' should be given to tropical forests for their contribution to avoiding the global warming impacts of deforestation,

[38] See World Resources Institute (1988) and Repetto (1990).

[39] e.g. Houghton (1990*a*).

[40] Houghton *et al.* (1985) and Houghton (1990*a*).

[41] Houghton (1990*a*).

i.e. what is the carbon credit to conservation and hence the carbon debit to clearance, and (2) what contribution could *afforestation* make to containing the greenhouse effect?

*Carbon Credits.* In line with the 'damage avoided' approach to valuation, a tropical forest should be credited with the value of global warming damage avoided by its conservation. Some monetary estimates of global-warming damage exist, and they suggest that the damage done, mainly in terms of sea-level rise, could be some $13 per tonne of carbon (1989 prices).[42]

Table 9.7 shows some recent estimates of rates of deforestation and the resulting carbon releases for a single year, 1989. Most of the carbon release from deforestation occurs in the first five years. Focusing on a single year therefore understates the total carbon loss since release occurs beyond the single year. But the analysis helps to illustrate the orders of magnitude of cost involved.

**Table 9.7** *Deforestation Rates and Carbon Release, 1989*

| *Country* | *Rate of deforestation (million ha)* | *Carbon release (m tC)* | *Carbon release/ deforestation (tC/ha)* |
|---|---|---|---|
| Brazil | 5.0 | 454 | 90.8 |
| Indonesia | 1.2 | 124 | 103.3 |
| Vietnam | 0.35 | 36 | 102.9 |
| Bolivia | 0.15 | 14 | 93.3 |
| Guyanas | 0.05 | 4 | 80.0 |
| 34 Countries | 13.86 | 1,398 | 100.9 |

*Source*: Adapted from Houghton (1990*b*).

Table 9.7 indicates that, on average, deforestation of one hectare of land contributes some 100 tonnes carbon to the atmosphere in a single year. At some $13 per tonne damage, it follows that deforestation causes damage at a rate of some $1,300 per hectare. In reality, the damage is higher than this because of the fact that carbon release continues after one year.

*The Carbon Value of Afforestation.* Sedjo (1989) has suggested that 1 hectare of new forest on good sites in the Pacific Northwest and southern United States could sequester some 6 x $10^6$g C per annum (6 tonnes).[43] If, hypothetically, afforestation programmes were designed to take up, say, 3 gigatonnes of the 3.6 gigatonnes net accretion of carbon, then some 470 million hectares of new

[42] See Nordhaus (1990).
[43] Sedjo (1989).

plantation would be needed, or around 10 per cent of the current area of forest in the world. Given the obvious problems of such a massive land-take for forestry, effort might be better devoted to raising existing standing-crop biomass. The figures suggest that it would be necessary to raise crop biomass by 50 per cent.

Myers suggests that a working mean sequestration rate of 10 tonnes of carbon per hectare per annum is appropriate for tropical forests,[44] making the required hectarage of afforestation around some 300 million hectares. At 10 tonnes per hectare per annum, the carbon credit would be some $130 per hectare per annum.

### *Sulphur Cycling*

The nature of sulphur cycling in tropical forests appears to be imperfectly understood. Some authorities have suggested that tropical forests contribute to acid rain.[45] Others regard tropical forests as net 'scrubbers' of sulphur.

### *Conclusions on Indirect-Use Value*

There is uncertainty about the precise nature of tropical-forest ecological functions. But it is clear that the forests generate positive economic value in this respect, for example in terms of watershed protection. Moreover, given the uncertainty about what forests do and how those functions interact with mankind's welfare, it is inconsistent with risk-averse behaviour to deforest. Deforestation of closed-canopy primary forest is effectively irreversible. It is a long process to re-establish climax systems (systems which have reached ecological equilibrium and do not change in nature), although many secondary forests (forests that regrow after initial deforestation) are thought to have biological diversity approximating that of climax systems. Rational behaviour under uncertainty would dictate a very cautious attitude to deforestation.

## 9.6 Non-Use Benefits: Existence Value

The final category of value is non-use value, the value attached to tropical forests simply to ensure that they exist. The motivations for existence value need not concern us unduly.[46] Efforts to estimate existence value are based on

[44] Myers (1989*b*).

[45] Clark *et al.* (1980). See also Herrera (1985).

[46] Although some economists express a concern that such valuations may be 'counter-preferential', i.e. inconsistent with individuals' preferences in the same way that acts of duty or obligation are counter-preferential. If so, there may be implications for the underlying structure of the welfare economics used to evaluate 'resource worth'. See Brookshire *et al.* (1986).

*contingent valuation* studies which essentially use a 'willingness to pay' questionnaire approach. No study has been carried out for tropical forests, but Table 9.8 reports estimates of average annual values per person taken from mid-1980s contingent valuation studies for selected animal species and natural amenities. While the studies are limited in number, there is a consistency about the values. The animal values cluster in the $5–8 range, with American national symbols—the grizzly bear and the bald eagle—in the $10–15 range. The Grand Canyon similarly has a high valuation as a piece of major national heritage, compared to the value of cleaning up a river.

Could such values be 'borrowed' for tropical forests? They are unique assets, but they are (generally) not in the countries of rich nations. Allowing for this 'distance' between valuer and the object of value (which applies to the blue

**Table 9.8** *Non-Use Values for Unique Natural Assets*

| *Asset* | | *Value per adult ($ mid 1980s)* |
|---|---|---|
| Animal Species | | |
| | Bald eagle | 11 |
| | Emerald shiner | 4 |
| | Grizzly bear | 15 |
| | Bighorn sheep | 7 |
| | Whooping crane | 1 |
| | Blue whale | 8 |
| | Bottlenose dolphin | 6 |
| | California sea otter | 7 |
| | Northern elephant seal | 7 |
| Natural Amenities | | |
| | Water quality (S. Platte river basin) | 4 |
| | Visibility (Grand Canyon) | 22 |

*Source*: Samples *et al.* (1986).

whale as well), and the substantial worldwide interest in tropical deforestation, a figure of $8 per adult per annum would seem very conservative. Allowing for valuations by just the richest nations of the world with some 400 million adults (Western Europe, North America, Australasia), the valuation would be some $3.2 billion per annum.

The opportunity cost of forest conservation is the 'development' benefits forgone. As we have seen, these may not in fact be greater than the benefits of sustainable use of tropical forests. But in order to assess the back-of-the-envelope guesstimate of existence value, one might look at the developmental uses of tropical forests to see what benefits accrue. If we take Amazonia as an example, the entire GNP of 'classical' Amazonia is about 6 per cent of Brazil's GNP. In 1986 Brazil's GNP was some $200 billion. Thus Amazonia contributed around $12 billion. On the assumption that each adult person in wealthy countries of the world would be willing to contribute $8 per annum to an 'Amazon Conservation Fund', the resulting $3.2 billion would enable the people responsible for more than 25 per cent of the economic output of Amazonia to be compensated for ceasing their activities.

## 9.7 Conclusions

The concept of total economic value offers a comprehensive framework within which to value tropical forests. Total economic value comprises use values, option values, and existence values. Direct-use values include timber and non-timber products and ecotourism. Indirect-use values include the ecological functions of tropical forests: their watershed protection and mineral cycling functions. Existence value relates to the value of the forest 'in itself', unrelated to any use. All these values are 'of' people. The total-economic-value approach is totally anthropomorphic. It does not deny other rationales for conserving tropical forests based on 'rights' in nature. Yet it may not be necessary to resort to such moral arguments. Economic arguments alone could well be sufficient to justify a dramatic reduction in deforestation.

There is some evidence that use values alone favour forest conservation. Clearance for livestock agriculture in particular appears to have no financial rationale. Its existence depends on substantial subsidies which themselves introduce major economic distortions. Alternative uses to timber, based on minor forest products, appear to give higher financial rates of return than timber in some areas. Markets fail to allocate forests to their 'best' uses because of inefficiency in government intervention, notably subsidization and the absence of secure tenure for small farmers. The recreational use of tropical forests is only now beginning to be realized.

Indirect-use values must be estimated. As yet, little effort has been made to value these indirect functions. As we have seen, some of them are disputed, but there is no question that deforestation followed by unsuitable land use causes significant damage. Additionally, tropical forests should be given 'carbon credits' for their role in containing the greenhouse effect. For existing forests the credit would relate to avoided damage by not developing, i.e the benefit of conservation. This might total some $1,000 per hectare for a single year, with perhaps similar benefits for about five years. For new forests, values might be of the order of $130 per hectare per annum.

Existence values could be substantial and might easily dominate the use and indirect values. That would be consistent with other findings in the total-economic-valuation literature. On the assumption that the Amazon forest is valued at an average of $8 per adult in the advanced economies of the world (only), existence value could readily amount to $3 billion, or a quarter of the entire GDP contribution of classic Amazonia to Brazil's GDP, inclusive of mineral extraction, timber, and agriculture.

## Bibliography


Binswanger, H. (1989), 'Brazilian Policies that Encourage Deforestation in the Amazon', Working Paper No. 16, Environment Department, World Bank, Washington, D.C.

Bishop, R. C. (1982), 'Option Value: an Exposition and Extension', *Land Economics*, 58(1), 1–15.

— (1988), 'Option Value: Reply', *Land Economics*, 64, 88–93.

Brookshire, D., Eubanks, L., and Randall, A. (1983), 'Estimating Option Prices and Existence Values for Wildlife Resources', *Land Economics*, 59, 1–15.

Brookshire, D., Eubanks, L., and Sorg, C. (1986), 'Existence Values and Normative Economics: Implications for Valuing Water Resources', *Water Resources Research*, 22(11), 1509–18.

Brookshire, D., Schulze, W., and Thayer, M. (1985), 'Some Unusual Aspects of Valuing a Unique Natural Resource', Department of Economics, University of Wyoming.

Browder, J. (1988*a*), 'The Social Costs of Rain Forest Destruction: a Critique and Economic Analysis of the "Hamburger Debate"', *Interciencia*, 13(2).

— (1988*b*), 'Public Policy and Deforestation in the Brazilian Amazon', in R. Repetto and M. Gillis (eds.), *Public Policies and the Misuse of Forest Resources*, Cambridge, Cambridge University Press, 247–97.

Brown, G. (1986), 'Preserving Endangered Species and Other Biological Resources', *The Science of the Total Environment*, 56, 89–97.

Clark, H. L. *et al.* (1980), 'Acid Rain in the Venezuelan Amazon', in J. I. Furtado (ed.), *Tropical Ecology and Development*, Kuala Lumpur, 683–5.

de Beer, J. and McDermott, M. (1989), 'The Economic Value of Non-Timber Forest Products in South-East Asia', International Union for the Conservation of Nature, Netherlands Commitee, Amsterdam.

Dogse, P. (1989), 'Sustainable Tropical Rain Forest Management: Some Economic Considerations', paper prepared for the Division of Ecological Sciences, UNESCO, Paris.

Dourojeanni, M. J. (1985), 'Over-Exploited and Under-Used Animals in the Amazon Region', in G. Prance and T. Lovejoy (eds.), *Key Environments: Amazonia*, Oxford, Pergamon, 419–33.

Farnsworth, N. and Morris, R. (1976), 'Higher Plants—the Sleeping Giant of Drug Development', *American Journal of Pharmacy*, 147(2), 46–52.

Farnsworth, N. and Soejarto, D. (1985), 'Potential Consequence of Plant Extinction in the United States on the Current and Future Availability of Prescription Drugs', *Economic Botany*, 39(3), 231–40.

Food and Agriculture Organization (1981), *Tropical Forest Resources*, Rome.
Freeman, A. M. (1985), 'Supply Uncertainty, Option Price and Option Value', *Land Economics*, 61,176–81.
Furtado, J. I. (1978), 'The Status and Future of the Tropical Moist Forest in Southeast Asia', in C. MacAndrews and L. S. Chia (eds.), *Developing Economies in South East Asia and the Environment*, Singapore, McGraw-Hill, 73–119.
— and Ruddle, K. (1986), 'The Future of Tropical Forests', in N. Polunin (ed.), *Ecosystem Theory and Application*, Wiley, 145–71.
Gradwohl, J. and Greenberg, R. (1988), *Saving the Tropical Forests*, London, Earthscan.
Hamilton, L. and King, P. (1983), *Tropical Forested Watersheds: Hydrologic and Soils Response to Major Uses or Conversions*, Boulder, Westview Press.
Hartshorn, G., Simeone, R., and Tosi, J. (1987), 'Sustained Yield Management of Tropical Forests: A Synopsis of the Palcazu Development Project in the Central Selva of the Peruvian Amazon', Tropical Science Center, San Jose, Costa Rica.
Herrera, R. (1985), 'Nutrient Cycling in Amazonian Forests', in G. Prance and T. Lovejoy (eds.), *Key Environments: Amazonia*, Oxford, Pergamon, 95–105.
Houghton, R. (1990*a*), 'The Future Role of Tropical Forests in Affecting the Carbon Dioxide Concentration of the Atmosphere', *Ambio*, 19(4), 204–9.
— (1990*b*), 'Emissions of Greenhouse Gases', in N. Myers, *Deforestation Rates in Tropical Forests and their Climatic Implications*, London, Friends of the Earth.
— Boone, R. D., Melillo, J. M., *et al.* (1985), 'Net Flux of Carbon Dioxide From Tropical Forests in 1980', *Nature*, 316, 617–20.
Johansson, P.-O. (1988), 'On the Properties of Supply-Side Option Value', *Land Economics*, 64, 86–7.
Leonard, H. J. (1987), *Natural Resources and Economic Development in Central America*, New Brunswick, Transaction Books.
Leslie, A. J. (1987), 'A Second Look at the Economics of Natural Management Systems in Tropical Mixed Forests', *Unasylva*, 39(155), 46–58.
Mahar, D. (1989), 'Government Policies and Deforestation in Brazil's Amazon Region', Washington, D.C., World Bank.
Markandya, A. and Pearce, D. W. (1988), 'Environmental Considerations and the Choice of Discount Rate in Developing Countries', Working Paper No. 3, Environment Department, World Bank, Washington, D.C.
Myers, N. (1983), 'Tropical Moist Forests: Over-Exploited and Under-Utilized?', *Forest Ecology and Management*, 6, 59–79.
— (1989*a*), *Deforestation Rates in Tropical Forests and their Climatic Implications*, London, Friends of the Earth.
— (1989*b*), 'The Greenhouse Effect: A Tropical Forestry Response', *Biomass*, 18.
Nordhaus, W. (1990), 'To Slow or Not to Slow: The Economics of the Greenhouse Effect', mimeo, Department of Economics, Yale University.
Pearce, D. W. (1987), 'Forest Policy in Indonesia', memorandum, World Bank.
— (1989), 'Economic Incentives and Renewable Natural Resource Management', in OECD, *Renewable Natural Resources: Economic Incentives for Improved Management*, OECD, Paris, 11–27.
— (1991), 'Assessing the Returns to the Economy and to Society from Investment in Forestry', in (UK) Forestry Commission, *Forestry Expansion*, Edinburgh.

Pearce, D. W., Barbier, E. and Markandya, A. (1990), *Sustainable Development: Economics and Environment in the Third World*, London, Edward Elgar.

— and Turner, R. K. (1989), *Economics of Natural Resources and the Environment*, London, Harvester-Wheatsheaf, and Baltimore, Johns Hopkins University Press, ch. 20.

Peters, C., Gentry, A., and Mendelsohn, R. (1989), 'Valuation of an Amazonian Rainforest', *Nature*, 339, 655–6.

Plummer, M. (1986), 'Supply Uncertainty, Option Price and Option Value', *Land Economics*, 62, 313–18.

Poore, D. (1989), *No Timber without Trees: Sustainability in the Tropical Forest*, London, Earthscan.

Principe, P. (1987), *The Economic Value of Biological Diversity among Medicinal Plants*, OECD, Paris.

Repetto, R. (1990), 'Deforestation in the Tropics', *Scientific American*, 262(4), 36–42.

— and Gillis, M. (eds.) (1988), *Public Policies and the Misuse of Forest Resources*, Cambridge, Cambridge University Press.

Ruitenbeek, J. (1989), *Social Cost–Benefit Analysis of the Korup Project, Cameroon*, London, World Wide Fund for Nature.

Salati, E. *et al.* (1979), 'Recycling of Water in the Amazon Basin: An Isotopic Study', *Water Resources Research*, 15, 1250–8.

Samples, K., Gowen, M., and Dixon, J. (1986), 'The Validity of the Contingent Valuation Method for Estimating Non-Use Components of Preservation Values for Unique Natural Resources', paper presented to the American Agricultural Economics Association, Reno, Nevada.

Schulze, W. (1983), 'Economic Benefits of Preserving Visibility in the National Parklands of the Southwest', *Natural Resources Journal*, 23, 149–73.

Sedjo, R. (1987*a*), 'The Economics of Natural and Plantation Forests in Indonesia', mimeo, Resources for the Future, Washington, D.C.

— (1987*b*), 'Incentives and Distortions in Indonesian Forest Policy', mimeo, Resources for the Future, Washington, D.C.

— (1989), 'Forests to Offset the Greenhouse Effect', *Journal of Forestry*, 87, 12–14.

Southgate, D., Sierra, R., and Brown, L. (1989), *The Causes of Tropical Deforestation in Ecuador: A Statistical Analysis*, London Environmental Economics Centre, LEEC Paper 89–09.

World Resources Institute (1988), *World Resources 1988–1989*, New York, Basic Books, 71.

— (1990), *World Resources 1990–1991*, Oxford, Oxford University Press.

# 10
# Domestic Energy Conservation: Environmental Objectives and Market Failures

*Vanessa Brechling*
*Dieter Helm*
*Stephen Smith*

## 10.1 Introduction

Energy-pricing measures, such as the introduction of a 'carbon tax', are likely to be an important component in any credible policy to reduce energy use to an extent sufficient to achieve the various environmental targets now being discussed. However, the use of pricing measures alone is unlikely to be desirable, for three, linked, reasons.

First, the level of taxation on energy that would be necessary to achieve substantial reductions in energy use would be unprecedented. Despite the extensive real-price variation experienced over the past two decades, a wide range of uncertainty still surrounds estimates of the overall price elasticity of demand for energy.[1] However, a general consensus still exists that the elasticity is low, especially in the short run, and the tax rates necessary to induce large changes in behaviour correspondingly high.

Second, the distributional effects of high energy taxes constitute a significant obstacle to the introduction of such taxes at the appropriate levels. Recent estimates (Johnson, McKay, and Smith, 1990) of the distributional impact of higher taxes on domestic energy consumption show that the additional tax paid

Vanessa Brechling is a research officer at the Institute for Fiscal Studies (IFS). Dieter Helm is Fellow in Economics at New College, Oxford, and a research associate of IFS. Stephen Smith is Senior Lecturer in Environmental Economics at University College, London, and Deputy Director of IFS. They are grateful to Ed Criswick and George Henderson for advice, but acknowledge their own responsibility for all errors.

[1] See, e.g., Hunt and Manning (1989 ) for a survey of recent estimates for the UK.

would be only very weakly related to income; the additional tax paid by the poorest quintile of the population would be about two-thirds of the additional tax paid by the richest quintile, yet the richest quintile have, on average, ten times the income of the poorest. Moreover, the consumption responses would be greatest amongst poorer households; a 15 per cent energy tax would reduce the consumption of energy by the poorest quintile by 10 per cent, but the richest quintile would hardly reduce their consumption at all.

Third, while reductions in domestic energy consumption under the stimulus of higher prices might be most efficiently achieved through a combination of energy-efficiency investments and simple reductions in energy consumption (i.e. substitution towards non-energy spending), a number of reasons can be identified for believing that there may be various obstacles or 'market failures' preventing efficient levels of such investments being undertaken by some groups of the population. The existence of these market failures, especially if they are correlated with distributional factors, would tend to increase the costs of reducing energy demands through price measures.

Measures to encourage the take-up of energy-efficiency investments are therefore likely to be of importance in energy and environmental policies, whether in conjunction with energy-pricing policies or alone.[2] Indeed, to the extent that such policies can succeed in removing sources of market failure at low cost, they may even constitute 'no regrets' policy measures—in other words, measures that would be desirable in themselves, regardless of the future costs of greenhouse-gas and acid-rain emissions. Given the enormous range of uncertainty about the future environmental costs of current energy use, policies that yield benefits regardless of the magnitude of future environmental costs clearly have substantial attractions.

In this paper, we set out a framework for assessing the factors underlying individual consumers' decisions regarding investments in energy saving in domestic buildings, and for identifying the importance of possible sources of market failure, which policy measures might seek to correct. Section 10.2 sets out a theoretical framework describing the factors influencing domestic conservation decisions, and shows the relationship between energy prices and investments, and between investments and subsequent energy consumption. Section 10.3 describes the evidence on the scope for cost-effective energy-efficiency investments, and considers the extent to which they account for all relevant costs and benefits. Section 10.4 considers reasons why cost-effective energy investments might not be undertaken by some households; here the discussion is organized around certain sorts of 'market failure' in conservation. Section 10.5 describes the scope of past and current policies towards domestic energy efficiency, and assesses the extent to which they have addressed the

[2] See House of Commons Energy Committee (1989).

sources of market failure identified in Section 10.4. Section 10.6 concludes the paper with an assessment of current policy, and some suggestions for improvement.

## 10.2 Domestic Conservation Decisions

The main focus of the paper is on the actions households can take to prevent energy loss from existing energy-using activities, principally domestic space and water heating. The range of possible measures includes the installation of loft insulation, cavity-wall insulation, double glazing, draught-proofing, and the lagging of hot-water tanks. In each case, the measures have the character of investments; money spent on them in one year yields benefits over a number of subsequent years.

In addition, although we do not consider them in detail in this paper, there are certain other actions to reduce energy use that can be taken. Existing energy-using capital equipment may be replaced with new, more thermally efficient, equipment. As with insulation measures, the decision has the character of an investment decision, in this case complicated by the scrapping of earlier equipment. Changes in behaviour patterns may also reduce energy needs. These may range from the trivial, such as minor adjustments to lighting levels or ambient temperatures, to major rescheduling of domestic and business activity, such as changes in working hours to maximize the use of daylight.

The demand both for energy and for conservation investments is a derived demand (Barnett, 1986); consumers seek energy services, in the forms of heat, light, or power, from a combination of energy inputs (electricity, gas, etc.) and capital investments (appliances, insulation, etc.).

The cost to a particular household of obtaining any given level of energy services is thus given by the price of energy inputs, and by the efficiency with which these are converted into energy services. A reduction in the price of energy inputs, or an increase in energy efficiency, will both reduce the cost of energy services. Indeed, we can see that there is likely to be a close parallel between changes in energy efficiency and changes in the price of energy inputs. A reduction in the energy price would be expected to reduce the cost of achieving any given level of energy services, but spending on energy inputs by any particular household would be unlikely to fall by this amount. Some of the benefit to households of a lower price for energy inputs would be likely to be taken in the form of increased consumption of energy services (and the purchase of larger quantities of energy inputs); depending on the price elasticity of demand for energy services, expenditure on energy inputs used could fall, rise, or remain unchanged.

Similar effects should be expected from a change in energy efficiency; if energy efficiency rises, the cost of achieving any given standard of energy services will fall, and households may choose to consume more. Use of energy inputs may fall, but is unlikely to fall by as much as would be the case if the level of energy services used remained constant. A guide to the likely balance between the effect of greater energy efficiency on the quantity of energy inputs used and on the standard of energy services consumed is given by the price elasticity of demand for energy; the lower this is, the more likely it is that improvements in energy efficiency will result in reductions in the demand for energy inputs.

## 10.3 Calculation of Cost-Effectiveness in Energy-Efficient Investments

Technical measurements of the housing stock, and of the impact that various energy-efficiency measures would have on the energy inputs required to maintain current levels of heating etc., have formed the basis for a number of studies of the scope for energy savings through domestic energy-efficiency measures (e.g. Pezzey, 1984; Henderson and Shorrock, 1990). Broadly speaking, these studies have been concerned with two different types of estimate of the scope for energy savings. First, technical measurements alone have been used to estimate the energy savings that could be achieved, if all technically feasible energy-efficiency measures were implemented. Second, technical measurements and cost data have been combined, along with assumptions about the appropriate investment decision rule, to estimate the scope for energy savings through cost-effective energy-efficiency measures. These measures are the subset of technically feasible measures which would contribute worthwhile (profitable) investments, given specific assumptions about the cost of the investment, and the future course of energy prices.

The estimates of the scope for energy savings through cost-effective energy-efficiency investments, in particular, provide a useful yardstick by which to assess the extent of actual take-up of energy-efficiency measures (Table 10.1). To the extent that the various assumptions made in the calculation of cost-effectiveness are appropriate, and actual take-up of energy-efficiency investment falls short of full take-up of all cost-effective measures, obvious questions are raised about the efficiency of household decision-making, and the possibility of market failures in the market for conservation products.

In this section, therefore, we examine the basis for the estimates of the scope for cost-effective energy-efficiency investments in the UK housing stock, and consider to what extent the apparent discrepancy between the estimated 'cost-effective' level of investment and actual investment take-up can be explained by features of the calculation of the cost-effective level, such as, for example,

**Table 10.1** *Percentage Take-Up of Energy-Efficiency Measures, 1989*

| *Type of insulation* | *Country as a whole* | | *Local authority tenants* | |
|---|---|---|---|---|
| | *Partial* | *Full* | *Partial* | *Full* |
| Loft insulation | 89 | 44 | 90 | 32 |
| Draught-proofing | 37 | 10 | 38 | 10 |
| Cavity-wall insulation | | 22 | | 18 |
| Double glazing | 47 | 19 | 15 | 5 |
| Tank insulation | 95 | 11 | 91 | 9 |
| Central heating | | 78 | | 70 |

*Source*: Henderson and Shorrock (1989)
*Note*: The figures above represent percentages of the potential housing stock that is amenable to the specific insulation measure.

the omission of transactions costs. In the next section, we examine the market failures and other reasons that could explain why genuinely cost-effective measures have not been undertaken by individual households.

### *Methods of Calculation*

The starting point for the estimates of the scope for cost-effective energy-efficiency measures is experimental measurement of the impact of each of the range of possible measures on the energy inputs required to maintain room temperatures, water temperature, and other services provided by energy at given levels. Clearly, the impact of energy-efficiency measures will be a function of characteristics of the property and of the baseline pattern of energy use; in addition, the impact of one measure is unlikely to be independent of whichever other measures have been adopted. The extent of technically feasible savings can thus be calculated for a typical property, or, making assumptions about how the potential for energy savings is related to the characteristics of individual properties, for a representative sample of properties such as those surveyed by the English House Condition Survey.

Further assumptions are then required to identify cost-efficient energy-saving investments—costs for the investment, prices for energy (to value the future energy savings), and an appropriate decision rule to weigh up costs and benefits in different time periods. The issues involved in the choice of an investment decision rule are familiar, and in practice the net present value rule has been generally accepted in most calculations of cost-effectiveness. This discounts future costs and benefits by a pre-determined discount rate, to yield a figure for the present value of the future net benefits from the investment, which can be compared with the initial investment outlay. The net present value (NPV) of the investment is thus given by

$$NPV_o = -C_o + \sum_{t=1}^{N} S_t \, [P_t/(1+r)^t] \tag{2}$$

where $S$ is the reduction per period in the amount of energy required to provide the current level of energy services, $p$ is the expected real price of energy in each period, $C_o$ is the initial outlay, $r$ is the discount rate, and $N$ is the decision-maker's planning horizon or the lifetime of the investment.

Whilst in principle all investments with positive net present value are worth undertaking, a measure of the 'degree' of cost-effectiveness of each different investment can be obtained by dividing the net present value by the initial capital cost, giving the net present value per unit of capital cost, $NPV/K$.

**Table 10.2** *Net Present Value per unit of Capital Cost, for Various Energy-Efficiency Measures*

| *Type of insulation measure* | *NPV/K* | |
|---|---|---|
| | *Gas heating* | *Electric heating* |
| Loft insulation | | |
| —an increase from 0–100mm | 3.3 | 7.2 |
| Internal wall-cavity insulation | 1.8 | 4.7 |
| Double glazing | | |
| Entire house | –0.6 | –0.4 |
| Downstairs only | –0.5 | –0.2 |
| Hot-water tank insulation | | |
| —keeping water at 60°C | 16.0 | 51.0 |

*Source*: Derived from estimates in Pezzey (1984).

Illustrations of the cost-effectiveness of a range of energy-efficiency investments in a typical private dwelling, based on calculations in Pezzey (1984), are shown in Table 10.2. It is clear that there are large differences in the cost-effectiveness per unit of capital of the various energy-efficiency investments shown, ranging from large gains per unit of investment from insulation of the hot-water tank, to small net losses from the installation of double glazing. The gains are sensitive to the type of fuel used for heating, and are in general greater where electric heating is used than where heating is by gas.

How appropriate are the assumptions made in calculating the net present value of different energy-efficiency measures as a measure of the full set of costs and benefits which an individual decision-maker would wish to take into account? We consider each of the elements of the net present value calculation in turn.

### *Initial Cost*

Calculations of the cost-effectiveness of energy-efficiency investments which include within the initial outlay only the 'purchased' items—materials and contractors' services—will omit two important sources of cost, which may be perceived, quite reasonably, by households as reasons not to undertake certain investments.

The first group of omitted costs are costs of inconvenience and incidental damage that households may experience in having certain types of energy-efficiency measure installed—the loss of amenity during installation, and the costs of 'making good' incidental damage caused, including any re-wallpapering, repainting, or cleaning that may be necessary.

Secondly, most measurements of cost do not take into account the DIY costs of labour. This is justified by Pezzey (1984) on the grounds that it is very difficult to measure the cost to an individual of the time and trouble involved in DIY projects. Of course, some may gain utility from installing the measures themselves. Others will find the task so onerous that no amount of savings will convince them that it is a good idea. However, although the spectrum of costs ranges widely, this is no reason for such costs to be ignored. The conventional method of dealing with a problem such as this is to use an opportunity-cost method of costing labour time. This could be either applied to an average wage rate or the cost of hiring a contractor to do the work. Pezzey uses both DIY figures exclusive of labour costs and contractors' costs figures to calculate the *NPV/K*. The calculation for contractors' costs is used here, as it incorporates both the hiring of a contractor and one possible method of applying an opportunity cost to DIY estimates. It should, however, be noted that even this may understate the DIY labour costs; hiring a contractor to undertake works still requires the householder to bear the costs of co-ordination and supervision, which may be considerable.

### *Future Reductions in Energy Use*

The calculation of the impact of any given energy-efficiency measure on future energy use, assuming a constant level of energy services, requires the application of complex physical data and relationships, derived in laboratory conditions, to actual situations. In practice, the calculations cannot possibly take into account all of the precise house-specific factors that will effect the level of energy required to achieve a given standard of energy services. These include whether the house has central heating, the material that the house is made of, and the extent of existing energy-conservation measures.

Most energy-saving investments display diminishing returns. For example, the rate of return to each additional centimetre of loft insulation decreases quite sharply. Figures from Pezzey (1984) show that the net present value of investment in loft insulation per unit of capital (*NPV/K*) is equal to £8.60 when insulation is increased from zero to 100mm, but if there is already 25mm of insulation, adding 100mm will yield a *NPV/K* of £2.40, and if there is already 50mm, the *NPV/K* is only £0.801.[3]

Some measures also have diminishing returns with respect to an increase in the uptake of other energy-efficient goods; the net present value of one measure is affected by what other measures are also taken. Some measures are complementary, increasing the level of energy savings when combined, whilst others detract from each other's effectiveness, causing the level of energy savings to decrease with the uptake of another measure. An example of where measures are complementary is wall insulation combined with loft insulation in a house that does not heat the upstairs. The measure that is applied first will increase the heating level upstairs and cause more energy savings attributable to the second measure than that measure would cause alone. An example where two investments detract from each other is hot-water tank insulation and loft insulation. The uptake of tank insulation will lower the amount of savings from loft insulation, as less heat is able to escape from the tank which lowers the level of heat in the house and reduces the savings from loft insulation.

In addition, whether a measure is cost-effective in a particular application will also depend on the characteristics of the particular household's consumption of energy services. A household with more members or whose members are home for more of the day will, other things being equal, tend to have higher energy demands, as will households with higher incomes, and households whose members have a preference for warmer ambient temperatures etc. These households will then tend to be able to make greater savings from the installation of energy-efficiency measures than those with lower energy demands, and more measures will appear to them to be cost-effective.

Finally, these calculations assume that the level of energy services consumed is kept constant, and households take all of the benefits in the form of monetary savings from reduced fuel use. In practice, this assumption is unlikely to be accurate. Many households will increase their consumption of energy services, and hence the monetary savings will therefore not be as great as the *NPV/K* method suggests.[4] Of course, the household's utility level will increase with the

[3] These figures assume electric-powered centrally heated homes.

[4] In an examination by the Social Policy Research Unit of a low-income target scheme of energy conservation, only 21 per cent of the residents in the scheme actually reduced expenditure on energy with the uptake of the insulation measures; 70 per cent spent exactly the same amount on delivered energy, hence increasing their consumption of energy services; and 9 per cent increased their expenditure (Hutton *et al.*, 1985).

greater consumption of energy services, and in theory should be higher than if all benefits had been taken in the form of reduced energy consumption.[5] Nevertheless, benefits in terms of increased comfort etc. may not appear to the household in the same manner as lower utility bills and may in practice be treated differently in any assessment of overall benefits.

### *Future Energy Prices*

The issue of the price of energy is contentious, as it is not easy to forecast future energy prices, which in turn affect the level of savings attainable by the investment. The Building Research Establishment (BRE) calculations made by Pezzey (1984) quote two values for the *NPV/K* figure of each investment, one assuming no increase in fuel prices and the other assuming a 3 per cent rise. The estimates reported above are based on the first of these assumptions. Recent events display how difficult it is to make these assumptions and they should be considered to have quite a large margin of error. The possibility of a sustained low level of energy prices for a period of many years cannot for example be ruled out, and would have major implications for the cost-effectiveness of energy-efficiency measures.

Uncertainty about the rate of return on energy-efficiency investment, due to uncertainty about future energy prices, could lead to households requiring a higher rate of return, or some 'risk premium', before they were prepared to undertake the investment. This, too, is typically not reflected in the calculation of 'cost-effectiveness'.

### *Discount Rate*

The final area for consideration is the discount rate. The conventional discount rate used is a real rate of 5 per cent, which indicates a willingness to postpone benefits from this period to next period so long as they increase at the rate of 5 per cent. This assumption has received much criticism from some economists, who claim that the individual discount rate is actually much higher than the social discount rate, as individuals are more myopic than policy-makers (note that it can equally be argued that politicians, who rarely spend more than a decade in office, may be more concerned with short-run payoffs than the long run, while heads of families may be concerned about a much longer period of time possibly including future generations). Hausman (1979) calculates an average individual discount rate of 26.4 per cent, which varies inversely with income. A higher discount rate implies that a shorter payback period is necessary for investments.

[5] On the basis of a revealed-preference argument.

## 10.4 Sources of Market Failure in Energy Efficiency

The calculations described in the previous section demonstrate the potential for reducing domestic energy use through investments in energy saving, and they also show the extent to which households have failed to invest in energy-efficiency measures which would appear to be cost-effective for them to undertake. The calculations do not, however, reveal why particular households have failed to make cost-effective energy-saving investments, and therefore provide only limited guidance as to the form which should be taken by public policy interventions to improve take-up. Understanding why the decentralized market system fails to lead to apparently beneficial outcomes—in other words, identifying the sources of market failure—is an essential preliminary to devising forms of intervention targeted at the underlying problems, and most likely to improve matters without excessive cost.

In this section we attempt to set out the various forms of market failure which could account for incomplete take-up of potentially beneficial investments in energy efficiency.[6] Broadly speaking, the relevant market failures can be analysed under four headings.

*Information.* Some consumers may fail to undertake cost-effective measures because they are poorly informed about the technological possibilities for energy-efficiency investments, and about the likely impact of such investments on their fuel and costs. This general statement has a number of separate aspects.

The first may simply be the adequate dissemination of existing information about the general properties of the various possible measures, and their impact on the thermal efficiency of dwellings in general. Some of this information may be technical and not easily communicated to the layman. However, in general, this aspect of informational market failures is perhaps the most likely to be resolved through the efforts of market participants; suppliers have an obvious self-interest in advertising and communicating information as long as the gains from greater information exceed the dissemination costs.

A second aspect of the information problem is that to make appropriate decisions, consumers need not merely general information about the properties of energy-efficiency measures in 'typical' applications or laboratory conditions, but also information enabling them to assess the cost-effectiveness of such measures in their own individual circumstances. The gains from undertaking energy-efficiency investments will depend on the physical characteristics of the property and the pattern of individual energy use, and precise calculations

[6] See also on this Jochem and Gruber (1990).

of the likely gains will be complex, and normally beyond the capability of individual householders.

A third, and more intractable, information problem is that the asymmetry of information between buyers and sellers of appliances and insulation materials could give rise to adverse selection in the range of appliances and materials on offer. Purchases of energy-efficiency goods are in general one-off transactions, and consumers therefore do not gain experience of the various competing products on offer through repeated purchase. If this means that consumers are unable to make an adequate assessment of the merits of competing products before purchase, and if the production of fuel-efficient goods is more expensive than the production of fuel-inefficient goods, the competitive process is likely to tend to drive out fuel-efficient products from the range offered by the market. The additional expense involved in manufacturing such products will not be warranted by the additional sales that can be achieved by improving fuel-efficiency, since consumers are insufficiently aware of the relative merits of different products to identify and choose those resulting in the greatest gains in energy efficiency.

The implications of this process are rather more general than the incomplete take-up of apparently beneficial energy-efficiency measures—although the risk of encountering 'cowboy' double-glazing contractors and the like is likely to be part of the story behind incomplete take-up. It is possible that, beyond this, the asymmetry between buyers and sellers could result in an inadequate pace of development of the fuel-efficiency characteristics of goods; if consumers are unlikely to be able to value improvements in fuel efficiency properly, firms will devote inadequate resources to research and development to extend and improve the range of available energy-efficiency measures. The adverse selection problem could thus affect the scale of cost-effective measures, as well as the extent to which they are taken up.

*Non-optimization.* Even if consumers are fully informed about the potential benefits from energy-efficiency investments, they may fail to make appropriate decisions based on the information they possess.

One aspect of this may be that consumers may use inappropriate decision rules for weighing up costs and benefits in different time periods. The estimates of cost-effective energy-saving investments discussed in the previous section use the net present value of the investment as a criterion for identifying worthwhile projects. Alternative decision rules, including some widely used in commercial investment appraisal, could lead to different judgements about cost effectiveness. Thus, for example, use of the 'payback period' of an investment (i.e. the period of time before the costs of an investment are recovered) will tend to select projects where the benefits are obtained rapidly, and will tend to reject projects where a substantial part of the benefits lies in the distant future. If the net present value is taken as the correct decision rule—as it normally should be—then consumers who use other rules will assess cost effectiveness incorrectly, and may thus fail to make optimal decisions.

A more general problem of non-optimization is that consumers may simply behave in ways that do not conform to the 'utility-maximizing' model of behaviour underlying standard economic analysis. Of course, many of the reasons why consumers may behave like this can be interpreted in terms of costs omitted in the analysis of optimal decisions; a consumer who 'cannot be bothered' to appraise alternative investments correctly may be interpreted as a consumer who optimizes, subject to large fixed costs in investment evaluations. Nevertheless, whilst this may be so, the omitted costs are clearly of a different nature to those discussed under the heading of omitted costs in the previous section, and the notion of 'non-optimization' may in practice be a more useful way of identifying the problems involved, than an interpretation in terms of further omitted costs of investments.

*Non-appropriability of benefits.* Cost-effective investments may not be undertaken if the person who benefits from energy-efficiency improvements differs from the person paying for them. This includes problems in tenanted housing, where the tenant may bear responsibility for paying energy bills, but where the landlord may be responsible for making any capital investments and improvements which would reduce energy use. Thus, for example, 92 per cent of owner-occupiers with accessible lofts have loft insulation but the proportion amongst tenants of private landlords is only 62 per cent (Henderson and Shorrock, 1989). In principle, landlord and tenant could bargain to ensure that an optimal level of energy-saving measures was installed; tenants could make payments either specifically, or in the form of higher rents, to induce their landlord to invest in energy saving on their behalf. However there are obvious problems with this where the improvements would benefit a number of different tenants, as, for example, in multi-occupied tenanted houses, or where a succession of short-stay tenants are involved. In the case of multi-occupancy the difficulties are the 'free-rider' incentives relating to the financing of the public good (tenant-financed energy-saving); with short-stay tenants, some beneficiaries will be future tenants, who cannot conceivably participate in any bargain.[7]

Non-appropriability of the benefits from energy-saving investment may also be a problem where properties are owner-occupied.[8] Owner-occupiers who

[7] Except, where rent-control legislation permits this, by paying higher rents, once the energy-saving measures are installed. The scope for this is, again, likely to be limited by possible information asymmetries about the dwelling.

[8] See Laquatra (1986) and Horowitz and Haeri (1990) for a discussion of the capitalization of energy-efficiency measures in house prices.

invest in energy-saving measures may be unable to reap the full benefits from their investment if they choose in future to sell the property, and if the benefits are not fully capitalized into the price because the future purchasers of their property cannot accurately assess the worth of past fuel-efficiency measures. Again, the problem can ultimately be resolved to one of information asymmetry; sellers may be better informed about the value of double glazing or loft insulation than the potential purchasers of their property.

*Credit-market failure.* To what extent should poverty be regarded as a source of market failure in energy-efficiency investment? A number of studies have alluded to the lower level of such investments amongst poorer households,[9] but it is not clear whether poverty as such, or other characteristics of the household (such as low energy use or tenure) should be seen as the underlying reason for low take-up. From a theoretical point of view, indeed, the level of current household income should not be a factor affecting the value of energy-efficiency measures; these have the character of investments, and an investment with a positive net present value is in principle worth while undertaking, regardless of the level of current household income. If current household income is insufficient to cover the costs of the investment, it will be worth while to borrow to finance the investment, so long as the real interest rate on loan finance does not exceed the internal rate of return on the investment.

On the other hand, the 'investment' nature of the installation of energy-saving measures gives rise to scope for take-up of energy-saving measures to be affected by market failures in the market for credit. Either energy-saving investment requires current consumption to be forgone, in order to obtain future energy savings, or it requires loan finance to be undertaken. Certain groups of the population, especially those with limited collateral, may be severely restricted in their access to credit at the market rate of interest. These problems may manifest themselves as a requirement for a high—possibly infinite—discount rate, depending on whether the lack of credit has already affected the time profile of individual consumption.

Nevertheless, problems of credit-market failure can be overstated. In the case of energy-efficiency investments, the capital outlays required are, in many cases, small. Moreover, availability of credit would appear to be a problem for only a few groups of the population; if anything, current experience seems to suggest that banks have been prepared to extend credit at normal interest rates well beyond the point at which individual borrowing levels are prudent and sustainable.

[9] e.g. Boardman (1991).

## 10.5 Past Policy

The balance-of-payments impact of higher oil prices after the 1973 and 1979 OPEC oil-price rises encouraged many of the oil-importing industrialized countries to employ a range of innovative policy measures to encourage domestic energy conservation. These have included schemes to provide financial incentives for insulation and conservation investments through taxes and direct subsidies, policies to improve the information available to private decision-makers about the energy use of products and dwellings, and command-and-control policies which set standards or specify technologies that have to be used in new and/or existing houses. Since the late 1970s the UK government has taken action to encourage energy efficiency in each of these areas, offering grants for loft insulation, promoting information campaigns and energy ratings schemes in order to increase public awareness and encourage informed decision-making in these areas, and steadily tightening the mandatory insulation levels in the building regulations for newly built houses.

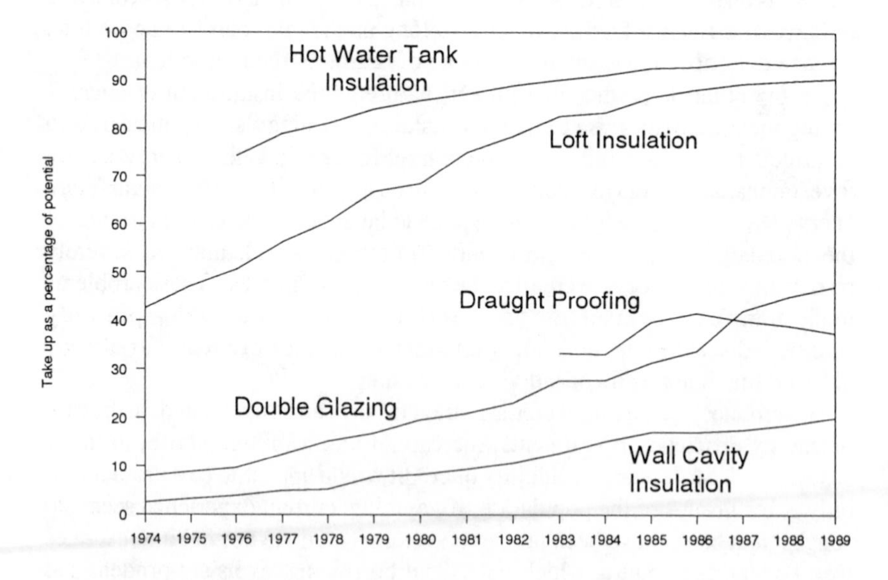


**Figure 10.1** *The Take-Up of Energy-Efficient Investments*

*Note*: Figures shown are percentages of all homes that are able to install the relevant measure. Thus, the overall potential varies between measures.
*Source*: Henderson and Shorrock (1989), Tables 2.i–2.v, and updated figures from BRE. All measurements are based on Audits of Great Britain data.

In the years after the OPEC price rises there were substantial increases in the take-up by households in the UK of certain energy-conservation measures, especially loft insulation (Figure 10.1). Whether this rapid increase in the take-up of domestic energy-conservation measures reflects the impact of the oil-price rises on individual behaviour, or the impact of the various government schemes introduced in response to the rise in oil prices, is almost impossible to assess with the information to hand, since both possible causes occurred at much the same time. Undoubtedly, at least some of the investments would have taken place without government intervention; the engineering-based studies we discussed in Section 10.3 show that the rates of return to certain types of domestic energy-conservation measures can be very large indeed, and these rates of return would have been increased sharply by the energy-price rises during the 1970s. Equally, the falls in real energy prices during the late 1980s were accompanied by a reduction in government schemes providing financial incentives for energy-efficiency investments, and again, disentangling the effects of policy change and prices is difficult.

### *Grants Schemes*

Grants schemes in the UK have concentrated almost entirely on loft insulation and can be divided into three categories: the Homes Insulation Act which provided grants to private householders; the Housing Investment Programme and other initiatives to encourage local authorities to insulate publicly owned housing; and single payments under social security benefit.[10]

*The Homes Insulation Act.* The first grants scheme was initiated by the central government in 1978 under the Homes Insulation Act. This programme allocated grants for loft insulation in all privately rented and owner-occupied dwellings. The grant covered £50 or 66 per cent of the cost of loft insulation—whichever was lower—for all households regardless of income. The public response to the grants was strong with approximately 400,000 homes insulating under the scheme in its first year.[11] Nevertheless, it is not clear what effect, if any, the scheme had on the take-up of loft insulation. Some or all of the grants paid out may have been deadweight, in the sense that those taking advantage of the grants would have paid for the insulation themselves had the grant not existed. Audits of Great Britain statistics report an increase of 610,000 homes with partial insulation from 1977 to 1978, suggesting that households were already eager to insulate before the scheme came into effect.

The Homes Insulation Act grant schemes were cut back sharply soon after they were introduced; the financial allocation was cut by about one-third in

[10] For a detailed discussion of these schemes see Boardman (1991).

[11] Pilkington plc and Oxford Economic Research Associates (1990).

1980. At the same time the Act was amended to favour old-age pensioners and disabled people on low incomes with a grant equal to 90 per cent of the cost of insulation. The programme continued throughout the 1980s, with various amendments including an insulation top-up grant made available in 1984 for up to an extra inch of insulation. This helped to bring those with existing levels of insulation up to the 100mm suggested level. The scheme of 66 per cent non-means-tested grants was terminated in 1988, by which time 3.4 million households had installed some level of insulation under the scheme, and the overall proportion of the housing stock with loft insulation had reached about 90 per cent.[12] The means-tested grant of 90 per cent to those on low incomes continued to operate, but take-up has decreased considerably as the diffusion of loft insulation has covered an increasingly large proportion of the housing stock.

*The Housing Investment Programme.* Along with the Homes Insulation Act, the government established a system of grants within the Housing Investment Programme (HIP) to local authorities in order to insulate all lofts in council properties. The programme was intended to last for ten years, along with the Homes Insulation Scheme, by which time it was expected that nearly all local-authority dwellings would have loft insulation. However, in 1980, while the government expanded eligibility for the Homes Insulation Act grants to include local-authority tenants, they withdrew all HIP funds specifically earmarked for the insulation schemes. The local authorities were still allowed to devote other housing investment funds towards energy-efficient investment.

Despite the limited central funding earmarked for energy-efficiency investments by local authorities, many local authorities have pursued energy-efficiency programmes, partly using general sources of housing investment finance, and partly establishing 'Neighbourhood Energy Action' schemes to build awareness among tenants of eligibility for single payments from DHSS to finance energy-efficiency measures. Over the 1980s there was steady progress towards loft insulation in local-authority housing, and by 1989 local-authority tenants were equally likely to have at least some level of loft insulation and draught-proofing in their homes compared with the country as a whole (Table 10.1). However, local authorities have invested less in high-cost measures such as double glazing, cavity-wall insulation, and central heating, and, in addition, figures for full insulation in local authority dwellings are significantly lower than in the country as a whole. These shortcomings in local-authority measures may be related partly to the high cost and the stringent capital constraint which has faced the local authorities,[13] and the fact that local

[12] Pilkington plc and Oxford Economic Research Associates (1990).
[13] Owen (1990).

authorities themselves are unlikely to benefit from the future energy savings resulting from better insulation of their housing stock. The scope for tenants, on the other hand, to take action on their own is limited, both by rules laid down by many local authorities which prohibit local tenants from making any alteration to the fabric of the building, and by the fact that if they move they cannot recover the cost of any investment they have made in their home.

*Single payments.* Until April 1988 single-payment grants for the purchase of simple draught-proofing measures were available to anyone on supplementary benefit with under £500 in savings. This grant covered 100 per cent of materials with no provisions for installation costs. Other funding available for energy-efficient investments was for hot-water tank insulation only if the household on supplementary benefit had recently moved house and was eligible for a furniture grant and the reimbursement of interest payments for investments made in insulation measures. Since April 1988, there has been a variety of policy initiatives designed to replace the single payments, though much of the responsibility has been fragmented between different departments and the local authorities. This fragmentation is bound to have caused a certain amount of confusion regarding eligibility and availability of grants for insulation measures.

In 1988, the single payments were replaced by the Energy Grant, which covers 90 per cent of the cost of draught-proofing materials. The grants are given conditional on the employment of a Neighbourhood Energy Action project to install the measures free of charge. This is a combined attempt by the Departments of the Environment and Employment and the Energy Efficiency Office (EEO) to encourage energy efficiency as well as providing work for the long-term unemployed with the ultimate goal of establishing these NEA projects as private businesses. Although the idea is innovative, in practice there are many pitfalls. If there is no NEA project in the local authority, then the grant is not available even to those who want to install the draught-proofing themselves. Hence, the link made between employment and the installation of energy-efficient measures has caused the issue of energy inefficiency of low-income dwellings to become secondary to employment concerns.[14]

More recent developments have addressed both the capital-constraint issue for low-income households in private accommodation and the information problem. The Minor Works Grant, as of April 1990, offers full grants to any household on means-tested benefit living in owner-occupied or private rented accommodation. Technically these households are eligible for up to three grants of £1,000 each for thermal-insulation measures. The grants are admin-

[14] Boardman (1991).

istered by the local authorities, though, who decide how much to allocate to this programme and may offer nothing at all.

The latest proposal from the EEO is the Home Energy-Efficiency Scheme (HEES) which is an attempt to combine grants for insulation with advisory services and labour costs. This is an extension of the Energy Grant, which will attempt to establish independent businesses out of the NEA groups. The same criticism of the Energy Grant applies to the HEES. The emphasis appears to be on the establishment of private energy-management consultants, rather than on aiding low-income families with their energy costs in an efficient way. This becomes evident with the discovery that these low-income families must pay a £15 contribution in order to receive the grant and the services. The suggested funding allocation for the HEES is also very limited.

### *Building Regulations*

Domestic building regulations were introduced in 1965 in order to combat the levels of condensation and mould growth in domestic housing, which are health hazards, rather than to save energy. It was not until 1976, after the 1973 oil crisis, that the regulations were extended to include energy-efficiency standards in domestic buildings. The 1976 Regulations state an aggregate requirement for the rate of heat loss through outer walls, windows, and the roof of all new homes built. In order to comply with these requirements, approximately 60mm of loft insulation would be needed, but no wall-cavity insulation would be required.[15]

The insulation standards required by the building regulations were tightened in a series of revisions in 1982, 1985, and 1990, and opportunities to 'trade-off' between different sources of heat loss have been introduced, including provisions for the use of solar energy. The current standards require approximately 150 mm of loft insulation and 50–75mm of outer wall cavity insulation.[16] The levels of energy efficiency now required are stringent, and are in fact rather higher than the optimal levels calculated by Pezzey (1984).

### *Information Schemes*

Government policy has focused on two methods of increasing information regarding conservation; the development of an Energy Ratings Index for houses, and the use of campaigns to increase general awareness of the importance of energy conservation.

[15] Pilkington plc and Oxford Economic Research Associates (1990).
[16] Pilkington plc and Oxford Economic Research Associates (1990).

*Energy Ratings.* Energy-ratings schemes, which provide an explicit measurement of the energy-efficiency levels of individual houses, can be used to provide home-buyers with greater information about the thermal efficiency and the likely running costs of different properties, and can also help home-owners identify worthwhile energy-efficiency investments. The idea is similar to the miles-per-gallon measurement of the fuel efficiency of automobiles, except that houses are far more heterogeneous than automobiles, and the practical assessment is therefore rather more difficult.

At present, there is no legal requirement for the use of energy ratings in housing transactions, as there is in Denmark and Norway on the resale of buildings. The government's involvement in this area has been confined to technical development, and to initiating one of the schemes currently in operation.

Energy rating has been under development for over twenty years. The government-supported Building Research Establishment has developed a sophisticated computer package for the calculation of the level of energy used in varying circumstances, and this BREDEM model has been widely used in practical applications. The early attempts made by Open University in their Energy Matters scheme as well as the HEAT (Homes Energy Audit and Advice and Treatment) scheme paved the way for more successful schemes such as the Milton Keynes Index (used by the Milton Keynes Development Corporation to impose minimum energy-ratings limits on all of the newly built houses in an area of the town) and the currently accepted National Home Energy Rating (NHER) and Starpoint Ratings.

The NHER was developed by the National Energy Foundation to increase consumer awareness of insulation levels in newly built houses. A privately run company, Starpoint, then developed a similar ratings system for energy rating of existing houses. Both schemes rate the energy efficiency of houses with the BREDEM model, although there are some differences in the approaches taken by the two schemes, firstly with regard to the scale used in the rating (both ratings move from zero upwards, designating an increase in the level of energy savings, but Starpoint's scale is 1 to 5 and NHER's scale is 1 to 10), and secondly in the purposes for which they are primarily designed.

The NHER was developed as a target level for new homes to achieve in energy use. The actual programme that calculates the rating can be used by anyone, but certification must be issued by a registered assessor. The rating is more elaborate than Starpoint, as it is aimed at newly built homes, and the materials and construction methods are therefore more uniform and up to date, and so easier to rate. The other major difference is that the NHER is location-specific, whilst Starpoint does not take locational factors into account in its rating of homes. Starpoint, on the other hand, sells energy rating as a service to individual customers; an auditor runs the programme and makes an assessment of the house for the client. The Starpoint rating can be seen as more than simply a ratings scheme, but also as an energy-conservation consultation where the auditor gives advice on the uptake of energy-efficient investments.

*Information campaigns.* The final area of policy consists of government-directed information campaigns designed to increase public awareness of energy conservation. There have been two major campaigns by the British government; one in response to the oil crisis of the early 1970s and the other as a result of the increased environmental awareness of the 1980s. Both campaigns consisted of promotions directed towards both the domestic and the industrial sectors. The effects of these campaigns are hard to measure. The increased awareness can be surveyed,[17] but the effect of this awareness on the actions of consumers is more complicated to assess.

The Save-It campaign was an emergency reaction to the 1973–4 oil crisis which consisted mainly of media advertising and promotional stickers and posters. The idea behind the campaign was to inform the public as well as actively to encourage private industry to use the Save-It message in their promotion of energy conservation. The Save-It logo became commonplace and the government, no doubt, succeeded in increasing awareness about the general issue of energy conservation.

The second of these campaigns was a more direct attempt at increasing people's awareness of the cost effectiveness of insulation. The Monergy campaign began by naming 1986 'Energy Efficiency Year'. The promotion was similar to the Save-It campaign in that it also advocated private-industry uptake of the Monergy logo, but the message was different. Rather than emphasizing a short-run solution to a price increase in energy products, the Monergy campaign concentrated on the long-term level of energy savings available to those who invested in insulation measures. Guides were published for home-owners listing the costs and savings of loft insulation and draught-proofing etc., and estimating the payback periods on these investments.

This campaign lasted for one year, at the end of which it is estimated by the Energy Efficiency Office that 80 per cent of the population became better informed on the importance of energy efficiency. The impact of this greater awareness on individual investments and energy consumption is harder to assess, and cannot be inferred from aggregate data on energy use. The rate of growth of energy consumption in 1986 was less that half that of 1985 (*Digest of UK Energy Statistics* reports UK domestic energy consumption growth of 11 per cent in 1985 and 4.5 per cent in 1986), but this decrease can with equal plausibility be attributed to other factors, such as the severity of the winter in

[17] See Hedges (1991).

those years and the relatively low level of energy consumed in 1984 (due to a mild winter), as to the awareness campaign.

### *Domestic Energy-Conservation Policies in Other Countries*

Direct subsidies, soft loans, and tax incentives were introduced by many OECD countries during the late 1970s and early 1980s.[18] These programmes lasted approximately five to ten years before it was concluded that all those who could gain from the financial incentives had done so, and many of the programmes have now come to an end. The current trend, in many countries, as in the UK, is away from subsidy policies (partly because of public-spending constraints), and, instead, to place greater emphasis on the information problem. For those who did not take advantage of the financial incentives offered in the past decade, there must be some obstacle to their realization of the high returns to be gained from the investments. The current direction of policy-makers is to enhance the information available to households, rather than to finance their investments.

As a result, nearly all OECD countries are currently engaged in some form of information and/or publicity campaign regarding energy efficiency. These are generally directed primarily towards industry in countries with milder climates, but include households in countries with more severe weather. Those countries that have taken the information problem one step further have experimented with energy audits and mandatory labelling. The US, for example, has required by law that utility companies offer an energy-auditing service under the Residential Conservation Service (RCS). This consists of a visit to the dwelling by a trained energy auditor who calculates the level of energy savings attainable from various insulation measures for the specific dwelling. Canada is also experimenting with this type of regulation and Denmark and Norway have required inspections by energy consultants upon the sale of a building. Many countries are also encouraging the development of a private market for energy-management services through training, grants, and tax incentives. Labelling of appliances has received a good deal of attention in North America and the EC is prepared to introduce an appliance-labelling system, but the labelling of buildings has yet to become mandatory in any OECD country other than Denmark and Norway.

Command-and-control policies are also tightening as a result of public concern for the environment. Almost every country in the OECD has mandatory insulation standards for newly built dwellings, though the enforcement is not always effective. The EC is currently preparing a model 'reference' code for building standards and emphasizes the importance of high standards in newly

[18] See IEA (1987).

built dwellings as it estimates that 20 per cent of the buildings standing in ten years will be built in the 1990s.[19] The Netherlands has taken building regulations one step further by enforcing insulation standards on government-subsidized renovations in order to improve the standards of the already existing housing stock. There is a close link between the effectiveness of building regulations and training measures for those employed in the building industry; training can reduce the costs of compliance, and in some cases can be an effective substitute for tighter regulation. A Swedish evaluation of building regulations concluded that many of the current regulations were applied to dwellings years before their enforcement because of the extensive training and information schemes directed towards builders in Sweden.

## 10.6 Policy Assessment and Conclusions

Policies towards domestic energy efficiency clearly have to be formulated and implemented against a background of considerable uncertainty. This uncertainty is of two types, uncertainty about the impact of policy measures on the take-up of energy-efficiency measures, and uncertainty about the environmental consequences of energy use.

As far as policy uncertainty is concerned, the existing evidence on the effectiveness of domestic energy-efficiency policies is seriously incomplete, in at least three important respects. First, as we have observed above, policy measures have tended to be introduced as a response to the balance-of-payments implications of high energy prices, which makes it difficult to disentangle the separate contributions of high energy prices and policy measures on the level of take-up. Second, the existing estimates of the desirable extent of energy-efficiency investment, which we discussed in section 10.3, whilst suggestive of the technical scope for improvement, may omit important elements of cost, and are, of course, very sensitive to assumptions about the future path of energy prices. Third, moreover, there is virtually no evidence on the practical significance of the various possible sources of market failure which we have identified in section 10.4 as possible explanations for the gap between the actual level of energy-efficiency investments and available estimates of the cost-effective level.

Uncertainty about the environmental consequences of energy use, and, hence, about the overall objectives of policy intervention, is equally great. Both the scientific predictions about the long-term impact of global warming and the economic estimates of the values (or costs) to be attributed to particular outcomes exhibit enormous margins of error. This uncertainty about the future

[19] See Commission of the European Communities Report (1984).

costs of global warming leads to consequent uncertainty about the scale of the necessary policy intervention; will supply-side policies such as fuel substitution in electricity generation yield enough reduction in carbon-dioxide emissions, for example, or are more extensive measures affecting the demand side also necessary?

The uncertainty both about the need for intervention and the impact of policy measures has implications for the design of policy about global warming, and, more specifically, towards domestic energy conservation. A pragmatic ordering of policy priorities is required, that recognizes the uncertainty regarding both the objectives and instruments of policy, and that places the greatest weight on policy measures that are less critically dependent on particular environmental outcomes or the precise scale of responses.

One method of encouraging the use of energy-efficient measures is through the price mechanism; charge a higher price for energy, to reflect the social as well as private costs of energy use, and the returns to energy-efficient investments will rise. Governments have been reluctant to raise energy prices in this way for several reasons; the impact of higher energy prices on industrial competitiveness, the inelasticity of energy demand, and the regressive nature of energy taxes. Sweden, Denmark, and Norway are the only countries in the OECD which have continued to increase energy taxation through the 1980s with the specific aim of encouraging conservation. According to the International Energy Agency (IEA), 'there is no country [in the OECD] where taxation and energy objectives are brought together in a systematic and well-balanced fashion'.[20] The IEA claims that this is generally because energy taxation is seen more as a method of raising revenue than as an instrument of environmental policy in its own right. The inconsistency of taxation and energy policy is strikingly evident in the current tax policy in the UK which actually discourages energy efficiency by charging VAT on home-insulation products yet not on energy consumption.

When, or if, pricing policy is ever used to encourage energy conservation, the existence of the market failures outlined in this paper will impede the efficient adjustment of energy demand. Hence, any price-based energy policy must be accompanied by an emphasis on the removal of market failures. As we have seen, there are three approaches that policy-makers can follow in order to remove these market failures. These are: first, schemes which aim to provide financial incentives through taxes and direct subsidies; second, policies to improve the information available to private decision-makers, for example, through information campaigns and energy-ratings schemes; and, third, command-and-control policies which set standards or specify technologies that have to be used in new and/or existing houses.

[20] IEA (1987) p. 112.

The uncertainty about the goals and impact of policy suggests that the full scope for 'no regrets' policy measures should be exploited. If some policy interventions are desirable, regardless of the future costs and benefits of global warming, then they should be implemented first. In addition, both costs and policy uncertainty will usually be minimized if policy seeks to build on existing measures first. In particular, the incremental modification of existing schemes can benefit from what is known about the scale of individual responses to the existing policy. We suggest the following three-step approach to policy towards domestic energy efficiency.

First, the scope for information policies should be fully exploited. These include both advertising and awareness schemes, and official support for the certification of the energy efficiency of products and dwellings. Both are directed towards improving the functioning of the market system, and will thus tend to encourage improvements in energy efficiency where they are most efficiently undertaken. The provision of information has important public-good aspects, and as we have seen may be affected by various market failures. These give rise to a need for public provision of a considerable amount of general information and advice. Where energy-efficiency information is provided by the private sector (e.g. by suppliers of equipment or services), there may also be an important role for the public sector in certification or guaranteeing the accuracy of the information, for example through public support for a system of energy rating.

Second, the building regulations provide a basis for policy which can draw on existing practice and experience. Although the building regulations, like other command-and-control policies, have the drawback of inflexibility, in that they apply uniformly to all, they sidestep the information problems and market failures that inhibit the effective application of market incentives to energy efficiency. Existing building regulations for new buildings are stringent, but only affect a proportion of the housing stock. One possible policy recommendation that would increase the insulation standards of the already existing housing stock would be to expand these regulations to include renovation of homes, as is currently being experimented with in the Netherlands, especially in the rental sector. The EEO is already currently targeting households that are in the process of making household improvements as a group likely to be influenced by increased information on energy efficiency. Their estimates suggest that the marginal cost of installing cavity-wall insulation while improvements are already being made is substantially lower than the cost of installation at other times. The cost of inconvenience to households already doing structural work is also probably close to zero. The standards to be applied to renovation may however have to be less stringent than in the existing building regulations, as there are more difficulties entailed in insulating already existing homes.

Third, although there may be a case for subsidizing energy-efficiency investment to reflect differences between the discount rates appropriate for public-sector and private-sector decisions, or as a second-best alternative to the absence of pollution charging for energy sources at the appropriate level, we would argue that the uncertainty about the environmental costs and benefits in this area means that government should only resort to subsidies when it has exhausted the potential for 'no regret' policies—those that would be worth while, even if the environmental damage from energy use turned out to be low or non-existent. As for the form that should be taken by any subsidy policies, we see no strong reason for limiting them to lower income households; although there may be some greater difficulty for poorer households in taking up beneficial energy-efficiency investments, the market failures in energy efficiency are wide-ranging, and by no means entirely confined to the poor.

## Bibliography


Barnett, R. (1986), 'An Economic Appraisal of Local Energy Conservation Schemes', *Energy Policy*, October, 425–36.

Boardman, B. (1991), *Fuel Poverty: From Cold Homes to Affordable Warmth*, London, Belhaven Press.

Commission of the European Communities (1984), 'Towards a European Policy for the Rational Use of Energy in the Building Sector', COM(84)614 final, Brussels.

Hausman, J. A. (1979), 'Individual Discount Rates and the Purchase and Utilization of Energy-Using Durables', *The Bell Journal of Economics*, 10, 33–54.

Hedges, A. (1991), *Attitudes to Energy Conservation in the Home*, London, HMSO.

Henderson, G. and Shorrock, L. (1989), *Domestic Energy Fact File*, Watford, BRE.

—— (1990), *Energy Use in Buildings and Carbon Dioxide Emissions*, Watford, BRE.

Horowitz, M. J. and Haeri, H. (1990), 'Economic Efficiency vs. Energy Efficiency: Do Model Conservation Standards Make Good Sense?', *Energy Economics*, April, 122–31.

House of Commons Energy Committee (1989), 'Energy Policy Implications of the Greenhouse Effect', Sixth Report, 1989–90, HMSO, 192–1.

Hunt, L. and Manning, N. (1989), 'Energy Demand Elasticities: Some Estimates for the UK Using the Cointegration Procedure', *Scottish Journal of Political Economy*, 36(2), 183–93.

Hutton, S. *et al.* (1985), 'Energy Efficiency in Low Income Households: An Evaluation of Local Insulation Projects', Energy Efficiency Series 4, London, HMSO.

International Energy Agency (1987), *Energy Conservation in IEA Countries*, Paris, OECD.

Jochem, E. and Gruber, E. (1990), 'Obstacles to Rational Electricity Use and Measures to Alleviate Them', *Energy Policy*, May, 340–50.

Johnson, P., McKay, S., and Smith, S. (1990), 'The Distributional Consequences of Environmental Taxes', IFS Commentary No. 23, London, Institute for Fiscal Studies.

Laquatra, J. (1986), 'Housing Market Capitalization of Thermal Integrity', *Energy Economics*, July, 134–8.

Owen, G. (1990), 'Energy Efficiency in Social Housing', NEA Policy Discussion Paper No. 3, January.

Pezzey, J. (1984), *An Economic Assessment of Some Energy Conservation Measures in Housing and Other Buildings*, Watford, BRE.

Pilkington plc and Oxford Economic Research Associates (1990), *Environmental Policy and Energy Demand: A Strategy for the UK*, September.

# 11 Environmental Policy in the United States

*Dallas Burtraw*
*Paul R. Portney*

## 11.1 Introduction

The United States has had environmental policies since it emerged as an independent nation more than 200 years ago. Until 1970, however, these policies were little more than a hodge-podge of mostly state and local governmental rules and regulations with an occasional federal law thrown in. Some of these state and local ordinances dealt explicitly with open burning of leaves, garbage, and other wastes—these laws were the precursors of modern-day air-pollution statutes. Other laws, again mostly local but with some exceptions, restricted the discharge of certain liquid and solid wastes into navigable waterways—these became the basis for eventually much more ambitious federal water-pollution legislation and regulation.

The year 1970 marked the dawning of what might be called the 'modern environmental era' in the United States. It was that year that both the Council on Environmental Quality (CEQ) and the Environmental Protection Agency (EPA) were created. The former is an advisory body within the Executive Office of the President; while the Chairman of the CEQ and its thirty or so staff members are not the only environmental advisers on the White House staff, they are perhaps foremost amongst them. The EPA, on the other hand, employs more than 16,000 people; its primary functions are to interpret, implement, and enforce for the executive branch of government the environmental laws passed

Dallas Burtraw is a Fellow and Paul Portney is Vice President and Senior Fellow of Resources for the Future, Washington, D.C. For very helpful comments on an earlier draft, they thank Chris Mendes, Katherine Probst, and Margaret Walls, while acknowledging their own responsibility for remaining errors.

by Congress. In other words, EPA's regulations add specificity and bring to life those laws. It is by far the largest and, arguably, the most important of the regulatory agencies in the US.

Finally, 1970 marked the passage of sweeping amendments to the federal Clean Air Act, in many ways the most far-reaching of all the US environmental laws. Important in their own right, the 1970 amendments to the Clean Air Act were equally significant because they signalled an impatience in Washington with the more decentralized approach to environmental policy in the US that characterized the pre-1970 period. For many reasons, then, environmental policy took a dramatic turn beginning in 1970; the focus in this paper is, accordingly, on this most recent twenty-year period.

'Environmental policy' often connotes not only those laws and regulations dealing with air and water pollution, toxic substances, and hazardous wastes, but also those dealing with forests, land use, agricultural policy, fisheries, etc. In the US, though, the latter issues have a separate history, are the responsibility of different agencies, and are referred to as natural-resource rather than environmental issues. The intent here is to observe this distinction and concentrate attention on matters related to environmental pollution.[1] In some cases, this distinction is a blurred one—global climate change being perhaps the best example—but it is necessary if this overview is to be kept manageable.

In the next section, the basic approach to environmental regulation in the US is laid out. Distinctions are drawn between: (1) laws that call for the establishment of ambient environmental goals (that is, specific environmental objectives that must be met); (2) laws that require the adoption of specific types of control technologies or, at the very least, establish limitations on the amount(s) of pollution that particular kinds of sources can emit; (3) laws that are aimed at specific products in commerce (such as chemicals or pesticides); and (4) laws designed to clean up pollution that has already taken place. It goes without saying that matters are more complicated than this; typically, major environmental laws combine one or more elements of these approaches.

Following that, information is presented on the costs and benefits associated with US environmental laws. While something is known of these impacts, it should be emphasized at the very outset that it is often distressingly little. A final section addresses a particularly interesting question that arises in any federal system: which environmental responsibilities are properly the function of the federal government, and which might best be left to lower levels of government?

[1] For a discussion of natural-resource policy, see Portney (1982*a*). Frederick and Sedjo (forthcoming, 1991) discuss trends in natural-resource use.

## 11.2 Basic Statutory Framework

There are seven major environmental laws in the US, the combined length of which runs, quite literally, to several thousand pages. Thus, it is not easy to summarize their major features in any article of this length.[2] Nevertheless, there are some unifying characteristics which run throughout all the laws that make comparisons possible. These laws are discussed in chronological order.

*The Clean Air Act*

As indicated above, the 1970 amendments to the Clean Air Act substantially enlarged the federal role in US air-pollution policy.[3] Prior to that time, air pollution had largely been left to the fifty states to control, the federal role having been largely confined to passing money to the states so that they could hire skilled professionals for the task. In 1970, however, the Congress proclaimed that henceforth it would be the responsibility of the new EPA to: (1) establish nationally uniform ambient (or outdoor) air quality standards for a number of the most common air pollutants; (2) promulgate what were called 'new source performance standards'—that is, limitations on the maximum amount of these same pollutants that could be emitted by any new or substantially modified industrial facility; (3) require each of the fifty states to establish very detailed programmes (called State Implementation Plans) that would, over time, impose controls on existing sources of pollution in those areas where the air quality standards were being violated; and (4) establish emission limitations on all sources of what have come to be known as 'hazardous' or 'toxic' air pollutants, as distinct from the more common, garden-variety pollutants found everywhere.[4] Finally, in the 1970 amendments Congress took upon itself the responsibility for determining the maximum emissions that new motor vehicles would be allowed to discharge; it established a schedule according to which new cars, trucks, buses, and motorcycles would gradually have to become less and less polluting over time.

Thus, with the EPA having established the goals of air-pollution control—e.g. the national ambient standards—the emissions standards pertaining to both

[2] For a detailed legal description of these seven (and other) environmental laws, see Novick, Stever, and Mellon (1987). For a detailed analysis of the economic and policy issues inherent in US environmental law, see Portney (1990*a*).

[3] For a fuller description, see Stern (1982) and Portney (1990*a*).

[4] This latter distinction is somewhat artificial, it must be admitted. The very reason for concern about the more common air pollutants for which ambient standards were to be established was that they, too, could be hazardous at high enough levels. Nevertheless, US air-pollution policy has been sharply bifurcated since 1970, with virtually all of the attention until recently having been devoted to establishing, and then trying to ensure compliance with, the nationally uniform ambient air quality standards.

stationary and mobile sources, combined with the controls the states were to impose on the existing plants, were supposed to ensure that all parts of the country then in violation would gradually come into compliance with the standards. In 1977, Congress amended the Act again to ensure that those parts of the country which at that time enjoyed air quality substantially better than the standards would be required to maintain those levels. This requirement, which effectively established a two-tiered system of air quality, was referred to as 'prevention of significant deterioration'.

While matters are somewhat more complicated than this description would imply, this is the approach that has basically been followed in the US for the last twenty years. Towards the end of 1990, however, Congress again substantially modified the major parts of the Clean Air Act. Two changes are particularly noteworthy. First, impatient with the slow pace at which EPA had been regulating hazardous air pollutants, Congress required EPA to write technology-based emissions standards (requiring the 'Maximally Achievable Control Technology') for sources of nearly 200 specific pollutants according to a very strict and precise time schedule.

Second, out of a concern about 'acid rain', Congress wrote into law a requirement that annual emissions of sulphur dioxide from coal-fired electric power plants be reduced by about 10 million tons per year (or about 50 per cent) over a ten-year period. This marked the first time that Congress had directly regulated the total quantity of emissions from any source category (emission *rates* had been established for cars and for factories but these did not cap aggregate emissions). Equally important, Congress provided for a novel approach to these emissions reductions. That is, it explicitly allowed each affected utility plant to reduce its emissions by less than initially required so long as it secured a greater-than-required emissions reduction from other regulated (or unregulated) sources. So long as the total emissions reduction is that stipulated in the law, such 'trading' between sources is permitted. In effect, this will create a market for emissions reductions which, it is hoped, will minimize the total cost associated with the overall 10 million ton reduction.[5]

### *The Clean Water Act*

A very different tack was taken in water-pollution control.[6] Prior to 1972, the individual states were responsible for establishing water quality standards (that is, *ambient* standards like those established by the federal EPA under the Clean

[5] Possible restrictions on the trading that utilities would like to do by the federal EPA, by its state offices, or by individual state public utility regulators could greatly reduce the possible cost savings (see Bohi and Burtraw, 1991). It remains to be seen how the market for emissions allowances takes shape.

[6] For a detailed discussion, see Freeman (1990).

Air Act), and then formulating detailed plans for controlling individual sources of water pollution so that these ambient standards would be met. For a variety of reasons, the Congress lost faith in the state efforts in the early 1970s and radically restructured water-pollution control in the US. Virtually scrapping the water-quality-based approach, in 1972 Congress mandated that it would be the responsibility of the EPA to issue technology-based discharge standards for all major sources of water pollution in the US—steel and chemical plants, leather tanneries, electroplaters, food-processing plants, etc.[7] Municipal sewage-treatment facilities were also given deadlines by which they had to install basic, then more advanced, and finally—in some cases—quite sophisticated water-pollution-control equipment. To ease the financial burden on the municipalities (but not the privately owned firms regulated under the law), the Clean Water Act also introduced substantial federal subsidies to help build these sewage treatment plants.

While the Clean Water Act has been amended several times since 1972, its basic structure remains the same today. True, the size of the subsidies to local governments for building sewage-treatment plants has been reduced, and several other relatively minor changes have been made, but the effluent (or source-discharge) standards that EPA began to promulgate in 1972 still account for the lion's share of water-pollution control in the US today. Although the Act is due to be re-examined in 1991, no major changes to its basic approach are being seriously contemplated.

*The Federal Insecticide, Fungicide, and Rodenticide Act*

The year 1972 also marked the passage of the Federal Insecticide, Fungicide, and Rodenticide Act (for ease, generally referred to as FIFRA), the nation's basic law for the regulation of pesticides and herbicides used on crops. FIFRA differs from the Clean Air and Clean Water Acts, and several other environmental laws as well, in that it establishes restrictions on the manufacture and use of agricultural *products*. This is to be contrasted with limitations in the former laws on the *residuals* that are emitted during the course of production. This distinction goes a long way towards explaining the somewhat unique nature of pesticide regulation discussed later.

The most important provision in FIFRA is the requirement that no new herbicide or pesticide can be sold in the US unless the EPA has approved it. Similarly, any proposed new use of such a product—for instance, applying to maize a pesticide that theretofore had only been used on wheat—must also receive EPA approval. Before EPA will grant such approval, the manufacturer

[7] States may establish ambient water quality standards if the technology-based discharge standards set by EPA are not sufficient to protect water quality.

must generally conduct and submit the results of extensive tests designed to identify possible acute and also long-term hazards to human health and the environment that could result from use of the product in question. The burden of demonstrating that the new product is safe rests with the manufacturer. Based on these tests, the EPA can impose certain restrictions on the use of the product as preconditions of approval. For example, the concentration of specific active ingredients in the pesticide or herbicide can be limited; labelling requirements may be imposed; limitations can be imposed on the number of applications per hectare per period of time; and limitations can also be imposed on the length of time the product must sit on the crops before field hands are allowed to harvest the crops.

Finally, FIFRA also gives the EPA the power to review those products that were already on the market in 1972 when EPA was given expanded regulatory power. EPA can restrict or even cancel the use of existing pesticides or herbicides posing 'unreasonable' risks to health and/or the environment; the key difference between EPA's powers for these products already in commerce, *vis-à-vis* a proposed new product, is that the burden of proof falls on EPA to prove the harmfulness of these existing products while the burden is on the manufacturer to prove the safety of any proposed new product.

### *The Safe Drinking Water Act*

In 1974 Congress passed the Safe Drinking Water Act to protect the quality of the water provided by public water systems. Generally speaking, this law requires the EPA to establish planning 'goals' for the reduction of each drinking-water contaminant—these are referred to as recommended maximum contaminant levels (or RMCLs) which are to provide a margin of safety against adverse health effects. In addition, the Agency is required to issue binding national drinking-water regulations for the same contaminants. These latter regulations—also referred to as maximum contaminant levels (or MCLs)—are to be set as close to the RMCLs as is feasible.

Frustrated with the slow pace of regulation, in 1986 the Safe Drinking Water Act was amended to require the EPA to accelerate its rule-making: Congress directed that eighty-three new drinking water standards be prepared within the next three years, that the EPA issue regulations requiring public water systems to monitor for certain unregulated pollutants, that EPA take a series of measures to protect underground aquifers and also surface water supplies, and that the EPA take a variety of other measures as well. However, the basic thrust of the Act—the establishment of RMCLs and subsequent MCLs—remained the same.

### *The Toxic Substances Control Act*

Motivated by a concern about the effects of chemicals on health, Congress passed the Toxic Substances Control Act in 1976.[8] Quite similar in spirit to the pesticide law described above, the Act gives EPA the authority to deny manufacturers the right to introduce new chemicals into commerce if it feels these substances will pose unreasonable risks to human health or the environment. Also as in the case of pesticides, the EPA can limit or even ban proposed new uses of such chemicals. However, there is an important distinction that must also be understood. While the burden of proof of safety for new pesticides rests with the manufacturer, the burden of proof lies with EPA in the case of new chemicals to show that they will be harmful if used as intended. In addition, no testing data are routinely required for the proposed chemical, although the EPA can require such testing in those circumstances where it believes the chemical poses an 'imminent hazard.'

Existing chemicals pose the same problem to the EPA under the toxic substance law as existing pesticides did (and still do) under FIFRA. That is, with more than 60,000 existing chemicals in commerce at the time TSCA was passed, EPA has been under great pressure to test the pre-existing chemicals for toxicity and to regulate those about which there are reasons to be concerned. Finally, it should be added that when adequate test data are available and suggest a potentially serious problem, the EPA has the right under TSCA to control virtually every aspect under which the chemical is produced, transported, distributed, used, and disposed of—including outright bans.

### *The Resource Conservation and Recovery Act*

Also in 1976, Congress passed the Resource Conservation and Recovery Act (or RCRA) which was designed to establish comprehensive regulations governing the generation, transportation, storage, and disposal of hazardous and also solid wastes. In a sense, RCRA was intended to address wastes disposed of on land, in the same way the Clean Air and Clean Water Acts were intended to take care of their respective environmental media.[9]

Among other features, RCRA requires the EPA to: (1) establish definitions for what constitutes hazardous waste and what does not; (2) design and implement a tracking system through which hazardous wastes could be followed from the time they were generated to the time they were disposed of at a (permitted) facility through incineration, land disposal, or other means; (3) promulgate regulations spelling out the measures that had to be taken at

[8] See Shapiro (1990) for a more detailed description.

[9] For a fuller description and analysis, see Dower (1990).

every permitted hazardous-waste handling facility, including the imposition of design standards—for instance, engineering requirements that had to be met at each site (such as double clay liners of a specified thickness for landfills); and (4) write regulations for the first time for municipal solid-waste disposal sites (ordinary garbage dumps). States were given a great deal of authority to implement these regulations, particularly those dealing with solid waste.

In 1984, in reaction to the slow pace of activity during the first eight years under the statute (and partially in reaction to its belief that the Reagan administration was less than zealous about environmental matters), Congress made significant changes to RCRA. In particular, it instructed the EPA to write new regulations (and do so quickly) that would have the effect of restricting the land disposal of virtually all hazardous wastes unless the Administrator of the EPA could demonstrate that such a ban would not be necessary to protect public safety. In effect, then, these changes had the effect of shifting the burden of proof from those concerned with harm to those convinced of the safety of land disposal. Finally, amongst other changes, Congress brought under the RCRA regulatory system thousands of smaller generators of hazardous wastes that had been exempted by the 1976 law, as well as a vast number of possibly *l*eaking *u*nderground *s*torage *t*anks (one of the few bits of humour in US environmental policy is that this latter programme has come to be known acronymically as the LUST programme!).

*The Superfund*

When Congress passed RCRA in 1976, it assumed that it had solved the problems associated with hazardous-waste disposal. It had not. When in 1978 wastes from an abandoned disposal site—closed long ago—began to leak into basements and yards in a suburb of Buffalo, New York called Love Canal, it became clear that regulating *existing* generators, transporters, and disposers of such wastes would not make the products of past disposal activities disappear. Fearing that such problems would be ubiquitous, in 1980 Congress passed the Comprehensive Emergency Response, Compensation, and Liability Act; it has come to be known as the Superfund law (after the trust fund it established to pay for clean-ups).

In addition to appropriating some federal monies to be used for the clean-up of abandoned sites, the Superfund included a number of other provisions, many of which have become quite controversial. In order to minimize the federal share of clean-ups, Superfund contains a broad definition of the liability of private parties. For instance, it retroactively imposes what is known as strict liability. In other words, if in the past—even the very distant past—a company had been disposing of its wastes in accordance with the very best practices of the time, the company was still liable under Superfund for today's clean-up costs. Moreover, Superfund provided for what is known as joint and several liability as well. This means that even if EPA knows that a particular firm was responsible for only a small fraction of the wastes disposed of at a site, it has the power to require that firm to pay the entire cost of the clean-up; it is then up to the firm to try to recover from the other contributors—at least those that are still financially viable. Finally, to augment further the federal contribution to the cleanup fund, Congress instituted an excise-like tax on petroleum feedstocks in manufacturing, and further broadened this tax in 1986 to include a number of other industries as well.

### *The Role of Economics*

These brief descriptions illustrate the major environmental laws of the US, but they beg a basic question: what role do economic considerations play in the regulations written under these laws? The answer is a resounding 'It depends'! For instance, depending upon the law in question, EPA officials may: (1) be *required* to balance health and/or ecosystem protection against regulatory costs in setting standards; (2) be *allowed* to take costs into account in establishing technology-based source discharge standards; (3) be explicitly *prohibited* from taking costs into account in setting standards; or (4) be required to use some combination of the above (although this might seem to be contradictory). A brief explanation is in order.

Many economists would prefer to see environmental standards—whether pertaining to ambient conditions or to emissions from individual sources—set on the basis of a judicious balancing of benefits and costs at the margin. This is far from the prevailing approach in the US. However, two of the seven major statutes discussed above—the Federal Insecticide, Fungicide, and Rodenticide Act and also the Toxic Substances Control Act—not only allow but actually require such balancing. Specifically, both statutes direct EPA officials to take action against 'unreasonable' risks to human health or the environment; moreover, both laws make it clear that, in determining which risks are or are not unreasonable, the economic benefits associated with the use of the pesticide or chemical substance in question should be factored into the equation. Thus, under both laws, if two substances posed identical risks, one might have been banned or its use sharply restricted while no action was taken against the other. This could happen if the latter substance provided significant economic benefits (it greatly increased yields, say) and could not easily be replaced, while many possible substitutes existed for the former.

As suggested above, this benefit–cost balancing approach is not the rule in US environmental policy. Consider the Clean Air Act, for example. Rather than permitting EPA officials to take costs into account when establishing the national ambient air quality standards, Congress instead appears to have forbidden such an approach. The ambient standards are to be set so as to 'provide an adequate margin of safety . . . requisite to protect the public health'. While the balancing of health benefits against compliance costs is not explicitly prohibited in the law, a series of court decisions has established that such a balancing was not what Congress had in mind in writing the Clean Air Act.[10]

Does it not make sense, one might ask, to require air-quality standards to be set at levels that will ensure public health? Do we really want to trade off dollars against health? To most economists, it would seem, the answer to this latter question is yes. This is so for two reasons. First, it appears to be impossible to find a level of pollution other than zero at which health risks are non-existent. There will always be some individual so sensitive that even trace amounts of pollutants in the air will pose risks to him or her. Since zero concentrations are a practical impossibility, however, we must then face the question of just how much risk we are willing to accept. This would appear to be the kind of question for which economics would be useful, even essential.

Second, what if a 'safe' level of pollution did exist? Would we then automatically set the air quality standard(s) at that level? Not necessarily. Since resources are scarce, it is at least possible that the marginal cost associated with going to the safe level from a somewhat less strict standard would not be justified by the additional health protection the safe level would afford. Nor is this trade-off merely one of health versus dollars. The real costs of additional air-pollution control are the opportunities forgone in other areas—these might very well take the form of increased expenditures for vaccinations, pre-natal care for expectant mothers, etc. In other words, the real trade-offs might be health versus health, in which case the balancing approach to standard-setting looks less crass and mercenary.

The reluctance to permit cost–benefit analysis is not confined to ambient standard setting. As discussed above, for instance, the EPA is also required under the Clean Air Act to develop emissions standards for all new or substantially modified sources of the major air pollutants. In writing these standards, the EPA is allowed to consider whether the emissions limitations are 'economically achievable', but not whether these standards can be justified by the benefits they will provide. For instance, suppose the EPA was trying to determine whether or not to require all newly constructed petroleum refineries, say, to install certain equipment to reduce emissions of volatile organic compounds (or VOCs). Under the Clean Air Act, EPA may take into account the financial impact of the proposed regulations on the companies choosing to build new refineries—in principle, the standards should be affordable. But if the contemplated requirement was affordable, EPA could not decline to impose it

[10] See *Lead Industries Association, Inc. v. EPA* (1980).

on the grounds that the air-quality improvements it would effect would not be worth the additional costs borne by the companies.

Generally speaking, and with the exceptions noted above, this pattern runs throughout the rest of US environmental laws. That is, when setting standards for drinking water, river or lake quality, conditions at hazardous-waste clean-up sites, or other environmental media, the EPA is generally forbidden from balancing costs against health benefits in setting ambient standards. This kind of cost–benefit balancing is generally also frowned upon when the Agency sets new source-performance standards under the Clean Water Act, the Resource Conservation and Recovery Act, and so on. As under the Clean Air Act, however, the new source standards are required to be economically affordable.

What about this requirement that the emissions standards required of all new sources be affordable? Is this not enough economics to inject into environmental policy? The answer, we believe, is no. First, in many industries in the US the likelihood of new facilities being built is slim. No new petroleum refineries have been constructed in the US for nearly twenty years, and new plant construction is virtually nil in the steel, chemical, aluminium, and other basic industries as well.[11] Thus, environmental regulation falls predominantly upon existing facilities under many of the environmental laws. One justification that is offered for tough new source-performance standards is the need to avoid the construction of new 'dirty' industrial infrastructures that will be long-lived and perpetuate existing environmental problems. However, there is a perverse kind of incentive created by the affordability criterion for new sources. Specifically, it says that profitable and successful companies that are making lots of money are capable of installing very expensive kinds of pollution-control equipment, and therefore should be forced to do so; at the same time, this logic suggests marginally profitable, often poorly run companies should not be required to do very much. Yet a ton of sulphur dioxide from the smokestack of a nearly bankrupt firm does no less damage than one from the stack of a real moneymaker. Why, then, control them differentially? Would this not reward inefficiency and penalize its opposite? Seemingly so, and this is reason to be concerned about its application in setting source emissions standards.[12]

There is one final respect in which economics is sometimes used in environmental regulation that bears mention here. Under some of the environmental laws, the EPA is encouraged to select the most cost-effective of the options available to accomplish an environmental goal. For instance, in

[11] Some have argued, in fact, that this is due to the very strict standards the EPA has established for new plants. See Crandall (1983), for example.

[12] One might also be concerned about the distribution of costs when standards precipitate the closure of a facility and the unemployment that would result. Sensitivity to the ability to pay may be a component of common notions of equity that local governments are better able to appreciate. We revisit this issue in the last section of this paper.

selecting possible clean-up remedies at abandoned hazardous-waste disposal sites under Superfund, the Agency is directed to choose a remedy that is 'permanent' but also cost-effective. That is, the EPA is allowed to choose the least expensive from among a number of possible clean-up strategies. Cost-effectiveness is also encouraged under that section of the Clean Water Act directing the EPA to establish discharge standards for industrial polluters.[13]

More important than the fact that cost-effectiveness is permitted or encouraged in some US environmental statutes is the way EPA has sometimes gone about pursuing it. In several cases, the Agency has facilitated the creation of markets for pollution 'rights'. For example, under the Clean Air Act, petrol refiners were directed to reduce and eventually almost completely eliminate the lead content of their fuel. Beginning in 1983 the EPA implemented this programme by allowing some producers to cut back the lead content of their fuels by less than the original requirement so long as they could find another refiner willing to make a correspondingly larger-than-required reduction. In other words, a market emerged for lead reductions such that those who most reduced the lead content of their fuels were those who could do so most inexpensively; analogously, those making less than the originally required reductions were those who would have found it prohibitively expensive to do so. Trading was discontinued after the maximum amount of lead in petrol was set at 0.1 grams per gallon in 1987 (this much was allowed so as to avoid potential damage to some engines). In addition, 'banking' of lead rights was allowed between 1985 and 1987 to allow some refiners to reduce the lead content of their fuel to the standard of 0.1 grams ahead of schedule, and to sell credits to other refiners who delayed their compliance. In this way, a decentralized approach to environmental protection made it possible to accomplish the desired reductions for less than a more traditional, command-and-control approach would have cost. This is obviously similar to the market that will be created for sulphur-dioxide-emissions reductions under the recent amendments to the Clean Air Act.

Nor are these the only incentive-like mechanisms extant in air-pollution policy. For instance, since 1975 EPA has required firms wishing to locate polluting facilities in areas where the air quality standards are already being violated to more than offset any new emissions they would create with compensating reductions elsewhere in that area. In other words, prospective new entrants must purchase pollution reductions from existing sources that are greater than the emissions they would generate. This market for pollution reductions is so lively that 'brokerage firms' dealing in pollution reductions now exist in southern California and other areas.[14] There is much interest at the

[13] See Fraas and Munley (1989).

[14] See Tietenberg (1985) and Liroff (1986) for a discussion of these market-based approaches to air-pollution control.

EPA today in extending these incentive mechanisms to other environmental regulatory problems. For instance, the Agency is giving preliminary thought to making use of deposit-refund approaches to such things as car batteries, spent solvents, and other household products; at the same time, tradable discharge permits are said to be receiving serious consideration in water-pollution control. As of yet, however, these applications are no more than gleams in the eyes of policy analysts. Outside the air-pollution field, there are virtually no serious examples of decentralized, market-like approaches to pollution control that are in actual operation.

It would be misleading to conclude this discussion of cost- effectiveness without pointing out at least one unfortunate instance where the environmental laws of the US have impeded the search for least-cost approaches to environmental quality. Perhaps the most egregious example pertains to emissions limitations on any new coal-fired power plant a firm might wish to build. Not only was any new plant constrained in the past to emit no more than 1.2 pounds of sulphur dioxide per million BTUs of energy generated, but it had to do so in one particular way according to the Clean Air Act—by installing expensive flue-gas desulphurization equipment. Companies were not allowed to meet the emission standard by burning the low-sulphur coal that is plentiful in the US, even though this would have reduced the costs associated with meeting the emissions standard considerably.

Why not permit electric utilities the flexibility to meet the standard the best way they see fit? Because if they were granted this flexibility, many would have elected the low-sulphur coal approach, which in turn would have reduced the demand for high-sulphur coal in the central and eastern US. Because the United Mine Workers represents many more high- than low- sulphur coal miners, and because the union formed a powerful political coalition with environmentalists in 1977,[15] Congress wrote into the Clean Air Act itself certain provisions that forced utilities to install expensive pollution-control equipment rather than meet the standards in the more natural (e.g. low-sulphur coal) way. This attempt to serve both environmental and employment objectives in one piece of legislation resulted in consumers in the US paying a much higher price for electricity than was necessary.[16] The 1990 amendments made some important changes regarding emissions standards for new coal-fired plants. Power plants are no longer forced to install this removal equipment. However, under the allowance-trading programme for sulphur dioxide reductions, incentives still exist for such installation. It is too soon to see whether the road-block to cost-effectiveness that has existed since 1977 is still there.

[15] See Ackerman and Hassler (1981).
[16] See Portney (1982*b*).

## 11.3 Environmental Benefits and Costs: Empirical Evidence

It would be nice to be able to report careful and comprehensive estimates of the benefits and costs associated with the laws described above (actually, with the regulations written pursuant to these laws). This is not possible, however, since relatively little effort goes into the economic analysis of proposed or actual regulations—relative, that is, to their likely economic impacts, pro or con. However, there is some evidence worth mentioning.

### *Costs*

The regulatory edifice erected over the past twenty years contains myriad requirements for businesses, governmental agencies, and individuals. How much is spent in the US each year to comply with these regulatory requirements? Subject to a number of caveats to be discussed below, one estimate of annual compliance expenditures (as they are generally called) associated with federal environmental regulation[17] pegs such spending at about $100 billion annually (in current dollars).[18]

Two observations should be made about this estimate. First, the magnitude is eye-catching. $100 billion is about 2 per cent of US GNP; as best can be determined, this is a greater share devoted to environmental protection than that of any other Western democracy. Second, this estimate does not include the costs associated with the recent amendments to the Clean Air Act described above. Since these will cost the US at least $25 billion per year (in current dollars) once fully implemented in ten years—and perhaps as much as $35 billion annually[19]—this total will increase significantly as the 1990s wear on. Nor does this estimate reflect the likely increase in the cost of cleaning up abandoned waste-disposal sites owned by private parties and by the federal government. These costs are increasing faster than virtually any other component of environmental spending.

Several caveats are in order. First, making estimates of annual compliance expenditures is no easy matter. It depends in large part on the reports of the regulated businesses themselves, and they have at least some incentive to exaggerate the costs they are incurring as a result of federal environmental regulation. Also, future projections depend on assumptions about likely technological development over time. It might be the case that sulphur dioxide is commonly controlled via the installation of 'widgets' today, but there is no

[17] This does not include the cost of complying with state and/or local regulations imposed independently.

[18] See US Environmental Protection Agency (1991).

[19] See Portney (1990*b*).

reason to believe that widgets will be the control technology of the future. This inability to forecast future technological change may impart a consistent upward bias to estimates of compliance expenditures.

Finally, economists will wish to note that while estimates of annual compliance expenditures are necessary to determine the true social costs associated with environmental regulation, they are not the same thing. The former are measured by out-of-pocket expenses for new pollution-control equipment, cleaner fuels, etc. The latter, however, are properly measured by the aggregate amount of compensation required to make all those who suffer utility losses as a result of regulation no worse off than they were before; this would include compensation for higher final-product prices, lost earnings from unemployment, and so on.[20]

### *Benefits*

Before reviewing estimates of the benefits associated with US environmental laws and regulations, a word or two is in order about how economists make such estimates. Simply put, the benefits associated with a particular policy are measured by individuals' willingness to pay for the favourable effects the policy produces. To illustrate, the Clean Water Act improves water quality (compared to what it would have been in the absence of the law). This in turn means that more or better recreation is possible, in the form of fishing, swimming, boating, and so on; it means that less money must be spent to purify water drawn for drinking and bathing; industries using water in production processes spend less to treat it in advance of use; and other favourable effects may be noticed as well. Benefit estimation requires ascertaining, for each individual favourably affected by these developments, the maximum amount he or she would be willing to pay for these changes. Aggregate benefits to society are simply the sum of these individual willingnesses to pay.

Several brief observations about this approach. First, since your willingness to pay for cleaner water depends importantly on your income, benefits do too. If one is unhappy with the existing distribution of income, one may cast a jaundiced eye on cost–benefit analysis. Second, if no individual anywhere is willing to pay anything for a policy change, there are no benefits associated with it. In other words, cost–benefit analysis recognizes no inherent values that transcend individual valuations. Thus, neither trees nor birds nor microorganisms have value unless some persons value them.

However, these values need not be restricted to the crassly commercial. Thus, if (as seems likely) many people are willing to pay something to see certain

[20] For an excellent technical discussion and empirical estimate of the relationship between compliance expenditures and true social costs, see Kopp and Hazilla (1990).

species preserved, or air or water quality maintained, even though they never expect to derive any tangible commercial benefit as a result, that is nevertheless a very real economic benefit that should properly be counted in a cost–benefit analysis. Cost–benefit analysis is anthropocentric, then, since values derive from humans alone, but it is *not* confined to market transactions by any means. In fact, it was invented for policy evaluation in those very circumstances where markets alone could not be relied upon to provide a Pareto optimal allocation of resources.

Two principal approaches are used to determine aggregate willingness to pay for environmental improvements. While they are much too complex to be neatly summarized here,[21] they are: (1) the direct approach (sometimes referred to as the contingent valuation method), in which carefully constructed questionnaires are used to elicit individuals' valuations of proposed changes in environmental quality;[22] and (2) indirect methods, in which individuals' actions in a variety of market or other settings reveal information about their valuations of environmental 'goods'.[23]

No effort has been made in the US to estimate total annual benefits associated with all the environmental laws discussed above. That is, there is no analogue to EPA's estimate of total annual compliance expenditures. This is unfortunate because it leads to misleading and unfair comparisons between total costs but only partial benefits.

In 1982, Freeman came the closest to preparing a comprehensive estimate of aggregate annual environmental regulatory benefits when he reviewed and synthesized a variety of previous analyses of air- and water-pollution-control benefits.[24] He found that, as of 1978, the 'most likely value' of the annual benefits associated with the Clean Air Act was $38 billion (in 1989 dollars), with health benefits constituting more than three-quarters of the total. Since the US population grew about 11 per cent between 1978 and 1989, annual air-pollution-control benefits presumably would be even greater were Freeman to conduct a similar analysis today. Note that according to the EPA, the annual cost in 1989 of complying with the Clean Air Act was about $30.9 billion ($1989). Thus, it would appear that the air-pollution-control provisions in place in 1989 generated benefits in excess of costs, perhaps by as much as $8–10 billion annually.

[21] For a rigorous discussion of environmental benefit estimation, see Freeman (1979).

[22] See Mitchell and Carson (1989) for a recent and comprehensive discussion of the strengths and weaknesses of this approach.

[23] For example, differences in property values between polluted and clean neighbourhoods can be used to make inferences about willingness to pay for air-quality improvements. So, too, can compensating wage differentials between safe and risky jobs reveal something about the implicit value of risk reductions.

[24] See Freeman (1982).

What about the 1990 amendments to the Clean Air Act that Congress passed? Portney (1990) recently analysed these changes. Subject to very great uncertainties, he concluded that while the changes made are likely to cost $30–35 billion annually once fully implemented,[25] annual benefits would fall in the range of $6–25 billion, with a most likely estimate of $14 billion. In other words, the changes Congress made in 1990 appear to carry with them a much less favourable cost–benefit balance than the provisions that were in place until that time.

Freeman also carefully reviewed and synthesized estimates of water-pollution-control benefits. He found that, by 1985, annual water-pollution-control benefits would be about $16 billion ($1989). Recreation benefits (from swimming, boating, and fishing) comprised about half of this total, with the rest accounted for by gains to commercial fishing, improved aesthetics, and reduced costs to municipalities, households, and commercial concerns. According to the EPA, though, in 1985 the US incurred about $34 billion for water-pollution-control expenditures—more than twice Freeman's benefit estimate. Based on Freeman's review, then, it would appear that the Clean Water Act does much less well from a cost–benefit perspective than the Clean Air Act.

It would be nice to report that similarly comprehensive estimates exist for the Safe Drinking Water Act, the two hazardous-waste laws, or the statutes governing chemicals and also pesticides and herbicides. They do not. There are many studies that look at the effects of changes in this or that provision of a particular law, but none which take a crack at estimating programme-wide annual benefits.[26] While this leaves the way open for future researchers, it is frustrating not to be able to draw overall conclusions about the sum total of US environmental programmes.

Suffice it to say in summary that these programmes are quite expensive, that they generate significant benefits (which in some cases appear to exceed the costs and, in others, not), that these benefits could be had at less cost to society if more use were made of incentive-like mechanisms, and that controversy will rage always about each of these conclusions.

## 11.4 Environmental Federalism

To this point, we have focused our discussion of US environmental policy at the national (or federal) level. In principle, however, unless pre-empted by the federal government, authority in the US political system is reserved for the

[25] This is an estimate of compliance costs which, as noted previously, is only a proxy for social costs which may be higher or lower.

[26] Kneese (1984) reviews a great many individual benefit studies, and in a way accessible to non-economists.

states.[27] The traditional basis for national action on domestic policy matters is the perceived failure of the states to guarantee rights for individuals—such as the right to interstate commerce, due process of law, and equal protection.[28] Until the late 1960s, the involvement of the national government in environmental programmes was minimal. As we pointed out above, however, the environmental movement that has blossomed since then has invoked a major role for the federal government, especially since the creation of the Environmental Protection Agency (EPA) in 1970. The appropriate federal role in the determination and implementation of environmental policy is the subject we address in this section.

State and local governments remain very important in US environmental policy for at least three reasons. First, they retain almost exclusive authority in matters pertaining to land-use planning, an area of activity that has flourished ever since the 1920s. Without doubt, the most significant interactions between individuals and their environment result from local land-use decisions. However, this area of immense importance is well beyond the scope of this paper. A second reason for interest in sub-national governments is that they have important responsibilities under federal laws, which we have alluded to above and discuss briefly below. Third, increasingly states are passing their own environmental laws that are often stricter than their federal counterparts.

The term 'federalism' describes the complicated relationship in US politics between federal, state, and local governments. It usually refers to the rights and prerogatives reserved for state-level government for the determination and implementation of policy, or the delegation of authority to states, under the federal system.[29] Frequently, the term 'federalism' is used as a metaphor for state sovereignty or restrictions on the federal government's powers.[30] With respect to environmental policy, the central political debate generally boils down to issues such as whether national legislation should 'pre-empt' state

[27] The tenth amendment to the US Constitution grants that powers 'not delegated to the United States by the Constitution, nor prohibited by it to the states, are reserved to the States respectively, or to the people'.

[28] The authority of the US government to pre-empt state and local laws is based on the 'supremacy clause' in Article VI, paragraph 2 of the US Constitution which grants the US government the authority to exercise limited powers without interference from the states.

[29] The term federalism is a historical anachronism that may seem misleading. In the formative years of the US political system around 1800 the Federalist party included those who subscribed to a strong role for a central government. Thomas Jefferson's Republican Party favoured states' rights. The term 'federalism' evolved from the great compromise that set forth a division of power, and today the term suggests the inverse of federal authority.

[30] The 'new federalism' of recent usage refers to political initiatives to decentralize authority and funding in many areas of public policy. This initiative was begun by President Nixon in 1972 with passage of the State and Local Fiscal Assistance Act, and expanded by President Reagan's efforts to defund many federal activities beginning in 1981. See Lester (1990) for a survey.

legislation entirely; whether national legislation should serve as a floor ('meet or exceed') or a ceiling for state regulatory efforts; and, frequently, where lies responsibility for funding.[31]

This portrait of controversy is potentially misleading, however. Federalism should be recognized to be much broader than a contest for authority; it is a system of political interdependence in which outcomes are negotiated and responsibilities are shared.[32] Even where Congressional involvement has been the greatest, state governments retain a great deal of discretion in environmental policy-making.[33]

As with the consideration of benefits and costs in the environmental laws, there are diverse allocations of responsibility between the levels of government. The major programmes for air, water, and hazardous-waste management usually reserve the role for setting standards to the federal government and delegate all or part of daily implementation to the states. For example, as we discussed previously, under the Clean Air Act the federal government sets ambient air quality standards but largely delegates implementation and enforcement efforts to the states. States may adopt stricter ambient standards, but the national standards serve as a floor for all locations. This approach to federalism has been labelled 'partial pre-emption' or 'meet or exceed.'

When states default on enforcement under the Clean Air Act, the EPA can develop its own plan for the state. However, experience indicates that such an outcome has been less than satisfactory for both parties.[34] An alternative enforcement tool of the federal government is the 'cross-over sanction' that enables the government to encumber funding in indirectly related programmes. For example, if states fail to meet air-pollution standards they may be penalized by the federal government through the withholding of highway funds.[35]

[31] Indeed, there is reason for the debate to boil. Congress has enacted about 354 statutes in US history that pre-empt state and local authority, about 190 of which have been enacted between 1969 and 1989 (Hawkins, 1990).

[32] O'Brien (1989).

[33] See Derthick (1987) and The Conservation Foundation (1984), ch. 8.

[34] For instance, in 1981 the state of Idaho voted not to fund the state's air-quality programme forcing the EPA to administer it at an eventual cost five times as great, causing 'more problems than it solved' from the perspective of both state and federal officials. Also, in 1982 the state of Iowa returned responsibilities for its municipal water-monitoring programme to the EPA. But the EPA managed only 15 per cent of the inspections conducted previously by the state. See The Conservation Foundation (1984), p. 458.

[35] A similar approach may be used by a state to secure co-operation from local jurisdictions to attain air-quality goals. For example, in 1977 the California State Water Resources Board imposed a moratorium on new sewer hook-ups in Orange County by denying approval for a $10 million federal sewer grant. The action had the support of other state agencies including the California Air Resources Board and was intended to coerce Orange County to develop housing policies that would reduce commuting needs.

However, there exist limits on federal action. For instance, in the 1970s the courts ruled against the EPA's efforts to use the threat of fines, sanctions, and contempt citations for state officials to force states to implement transportation measures—such as parking bans and bus lanes—to improve air quality. Essentially the courts determined that if the states choose not to co-operate with a federal programme, they can be fully pre-empted but they cannot be forced to implement federal regulations. The federal government must exercise its own authority to implement regulations directly, a task which it is not well suited to doing at the local level. The threat of the EPA taking over state responsibilities for implementation is frequently likened to a 'gorilla in the closet'; as we indicated previously, a better analogy may be that of the bull in a china shop. Consequently, both sides have significant negotiating power under environmental federalism.

The Clean Water Act and Safe Drinking Water Act are similar to the Clean Air Act: the design and implementation of programmes under these acts are delegated in large measure to the states. More than two-thirds of the states have assumed responsibility for implementing these regulations. A third area where significant enforcement authority has been delegated to the states is regulation of the transportation and storage of hazardous waste under the Resource Conservation and Recovery Act (RCRA); however, design of programmes is restricted to the federal level.

In contrast, under the Toxic Substances Control Act and also the Federal Insecticide, Fungicide, and Rodenticide Act, the federal government has exclusive responsibility in the design of programmes and their enforcement. The Comprehensive Environmental Response, Compensation, and Liability Act (CERCLA) is also managed almost entirely at the federal level. States can exercise considerable control under CERCLA, however, either by withholding their contribution toward site clean-up to stall activities, or by imposing standards that exceed those of the federal government and providing the additional funds necessary for the clean-up. States may also enter into co-operative agreements that allow them to initiate remedial action, although the EPA retains oversight responsibility. But in response to federal delays, many states also have initiated their own clean-up laws.

The trend in federal funding for the development and enforcement of environmental laws was downward in the early part of the 1980s and has now stabilized and even increased slightly under President Bush. State contributions to environmental efforts have increased consistently, however, especially with regard to hazardous-waste management. As a consequence, grants from EPA to the states cover less than half of total state expenditures for air, water, and hazardous- and solid-waste management costs.

Naturally state influence in the implementation of environmental policy has increased as state contributions to funding have increased. In addition, on a number of environmental fronts, states are seizing the initiative from Washington on policy, including recycling and solid-waste management, hazardous-waste management, groundwater protection, indoor air pollution, and even the use of chlorofluorocarbons.[36] A leading example is the siting of hazardous-waste land-fills, which has fallen off sharply due to new tough state laws and is now far below the rate at which new wastes are being created. Many industry representatives have responded with calls for federal pre-emption and uniform national standards.

These examples illustrate a mosaic of policies that no doubt contains patterns of special interest and historical circumstance, but hopefully if one looks carefully one also may find some guiding principles.[37] We turn attention now to examining the rationale for state control in some detail, following which we consider the rationale for federal involvement.[38]

The fundamental theoretical motivation for a federalist system of decentralized decision-making stems from the widely held Jeffersonian ideal of direct democracy. This ideal is in accord with prevalent ideas about environment protection which hold that people need to be in closer contact with their environment and more aware and responsive to the effect that their actions have upon it. These sentiments also resemble the prevalent economic prescriptions for environmental protection—namely policies that attempt to internalize the environmental consequences of individual actions into individual decision-making.

At first appearance, it seems reasonable that those levels of government that are closest to environmental problems are also those best situated to seek a remedy. Transferring authority for environmental protection to higher levels of government makes the potential remedy for a problem more abstract to local residents and indeed, their attempts to seek a solution will have less of an effect. Consequently people are likely to feel less empowered.

[36] See for examples Kriz (1989) and the annual reports by the Fund for Renewable Energy and the Environment, 'The State of the States', beginning in 1987.

[37] Natural-resource policy provides many additional illustrations of the divisions of responsibility under federalism. At one extreme, the development of water resources has historically been left to the states. For example, even where federal law applies to the siting of hydroelectric facilities, states retain control of water in the reservoir. This decentralization has led to tremendous experimentation and differentiation among the states, even in the 20th century. The traditional doctrine of riparian rights gives control over a waterway to owners of land along its banks. A contradictory doctrine of appropriative rights gives priority according to chronological use. Many states experimented with some combination of the two systems (see Pisani, 1987). It is interesting to note that the historical variation in state laws for the allocation of water greatly complicated federal efforts to set uniform quality standards and partially explains the adoption of technology-based standards for water pollution.

[38] See also Schwab (1988).

A related concern, labelled the 'Leviathan hypothesis' from public choice theory, suggests that as citizens turn over control of public spending and regulation to higher levels of government, the amount of spending and the nature of decision-making will reflect the preferences of politicians, bureaucrats, and special-interest lobbyists rather than those of individuals.[39] This concern, manifest in the belief that governments have the tendency to grow beyond the size that would efficiently provide services, supplied the intellectual fodder for President Reagan's efforts in the early 1980s to seek 'regulatory relief' through his 'new federalism'.

The proximity of local government to its constituency is likely to lend it greater sensitivity to equity in the distribution of costs. When the costs of a national environmental regulation fall disproportionately on one firm, or especially on the residents of one jurisdiction, the outcome may offend our common notion of equity. Local government is more likely to be responsive to this concern.

It also seems reasonable that local governments will employ more creative policies in seeking a solution to an environmental problem, due to the flexibility that attends their size and proximity to the problem.[40] The serendipitous benefit of local experimentation to the rest of the nation is best stated by US Supreme Court Justice Louis Brandeis: 'It is one of the happy incidents of the federal system that a single courageous State may, if its citizens choose, serve as a laboratory; and try novel social and economic experiments without risk to the rest of the country.'[41]

Many economists find further appeal in the theoretical efficiency that results from competition between local jurisdictions when policy-making occurs at the local level. One familiar hypothesis suggests that people vote with their feet—that is, they decide where to locate their homes and businesses on the basis of the array of private and public goods, services, and amenities including the quality of the environment that alternative areas offer.[42] To the extent that there exists mobility in the population, this should promote competition between jurisdictions for residents and for economic growth, which in turn provides citizens with choices and improves the quality and variety of alternatives people face generally. And to the extent that people have differing preferences or different incomes, there are potential economic gains to be realized by allowing communities to specialize in accommodating individual desires.

[39] Brennan and Buchanan (1980).

[40] For example, local government may be more sensitive to issues such as the age of the capital stock. If a facility that faces regulatory evaluation for pollution is new, a requirement to retrofit with pollution-control equipment may make sense. If the facility is old with a relatively short remaining life, other instruments such as fines in order to instil the incentive to reduce pollution, rather than retrofit requirements that may be economically unfeasible, may be a better solution.

[41] *New State Ice Company v. Liebmann*, 285 US 262, 311 (1932).

[42] Tiebout (1956).

Most importantly perhaps, from an environmental perspective, there are technical reasons why local government may be the most appropriate locus for environmental policy-making. National standards are likely to be insensitive to variations in local geography. For instance, differences in geologic structure of a streambed may mean that the same effluent discharge may have very different effects in different areas. Simply the speed of the streamflow will make a difference in terms of the impact of oxygen-demanding organic material or plant nutrients such as phosphorus and nitrogen on water quality. And at one particular stream, seasonal variations in temperature and streamflow will matter as well. Yet none of these important characteristics is factored into federal policy-making.

In principle, of course, states could adopt quality-based standards to supplement the technology standards of the Clean Water Act. In practice, however, there is inadequate technical or financial support for doing so, and enforcement and monitoring efforts are already over-extended. Furthermore, even if a state were to adopt comprehensive quality-based standards and make a commitment to funding necessary enforcement activities, it would not have the flexibility to relax federal technology standards on dischargers in cases where the impact on water quality is minimal.

Furthermore, the benefits and costs of pollution control may vary with geography, so that uniform (minimum) air-quality standards such as would be enforced under the Clean Air Act may not be appropriate from a cost–benefit perspective. For instance, our research has found that the economically efficient standard for total suspended particulates for Baltimore—the concentration at which marginal benefits are equalized with marginal costs—is nearly 50 per cent greater than the optimal standard for St Louis.

But this system of federalism is like Durga, the multiple-armed goddess from Hindu religion. It seems that for each point we have mentioned in favour of local government responsibility for environmental regulation, there is an 'on the other hand'.

Lower levels of government may be closest to environmental problems but many—in fact, most—environmental problems do not respect political borders. The water pollution from an upstream manufacturer may cause problems in a downstream city or state. Fish and animals that migrate across many jurisdictions may be harmed seriously by sources of pollution in one location. Acid deposition in Canada and Scandinavia emanates in part from the US and the UK, respectively. So while the cost of pollution controls in one jurisdiction typically are borne entirely in that jurisdiction, frequently the benefits of an improved environment are spread widely across many jurisdictions, providing an inadequate incentive for local governments to protect the environment. These are classic examples of the problem of externalities in economic theory, which serves as a prominent explanation for the perceived inability of states and local governments to deal individually with many pollution problems. In fact, as the acid rain example above suggests, in some cases even national governments are not large enough neatly to surround some environmental problems.

Even where environmental damages do not spill over in purely physical terms to other jurisdictions, there is another respect in which externalities may occur. As mentioned above, the benefits of environmental quality include the value that a person places on the enjoyment of a resource outside of the marketplace, such as a scenic panorama, that may be located in a jurisdiction distant to his or her own. Individuals may be willing to pay for maintaining the quality of the panorama even if they do not plan on visiting it, perhaps because they do not want to rule out the possibility they may visit it one day in the future. Even if the chance they or their progeny will ever visit a scenic place such as the Arctic National Wildlife Refuge in Alaska is nil, they may experience psychic or vicarious rewards (perhaps by looking at photographs) just from its existence. Economists label these 'use', 'option', and 'existence' values, and are increasingly able to measure them in a consistent fashion.[43] The implication of this theory for the question of federalism is that even in the absence of transboundary pollution problems, an individual jurisdiction may fail adequately to consider all the benefits of environmental protection in policy-making, because of the non-market values that accrue to persons outside the jurisdiction. In brief, economic theory suggests that the fate of the Arctic National Wildlife Refuge should not be left to the Alaskans alone.

A related issue involves the consideration of the welfare of future generations. Residents of a jurisdiction may be able to 'take the money and run' if exploitation of the local environment leads to short-term economic gain, without concern for the long-term environmental effects that may 'spill over' on to future residents. To date, national governments have considered inadequately the question of intergenerational equity, but it seems clear that local governments are even less well positioned to do so. Elected representatives at all levels have fairly short-run incentives to perform. Ironically, it may be the longevity of bureaucracy that best lends itself to consideration of the long-run future and our environmental heritage.

Even in the absence of spillovers, there remain several justifications for national standards of environmental quality. First, national standards can serve a co-ordinating role to achieve co-operation among states when the socially efficient level of environmental quality may not be achievable by states acting individually. For example, if the state of Connecticut was to require much more complete labelling and safer packaging of garden herbicides than other states in the north-east region of the country, manufacturers would incur special costs. Ostensibly these costs would be passed on to Connecticut consumers, or the

[43] See Mitchell and Carson (1989).

products withdrawn from the market there altogether, and it may be that the benefits of this policy would not justify the cost for state residents. However, if the policy were adopted on a broader scale, the cost for Connecticut residents would be less because needless redundancy in the marketing practices of herbicide manufacturers would be eliminated and the benefits might exceed the costs. This example illustrates economies of scale that may occur in many areas including manufacturing, marketing, administration, and enforcement. Furthermore, there may be complementarity between the policies of the states, for example, in the reduction of urban smog along the north-east corridor either through emission standards or transportation planning, that invites a co-ordinated approach to policy.

There may also exist economies of scale on the benefits side of the issue; for example, uniform minimum standards reduce the risk stemming from imperfect information. There is no doubt a tremendous benefit from assurances that the water is (reasonably) safe to drink in every airport in the US, that chemical trucks on the highway in every state are (reasonably) safe, and so on.

Uniform standards also may promote economic development. Firms that operate in different states frequently complain about the costs of learning about and complying with multiple sets of regulations. Historically these differences constituted an implicit, and often intentional, barrier to entry. The hypothesis of 'the visible hand' in American economic history suggests that it was the demise of these local impediments to trade due to enforcement of the interstate commerce clause of the US Constitution that led to economies of scale in the organization of firms and economic growth in the twentieth century.[44] Evidence is inconclusive on this point, however. Local control in the allocation of water is recognized to have been a boon to economic development of the western states, due to the particular characteristics of different regions, though it has also led to a wasteful allocation of the resource.[45]

Meanwhile, variations in laws can constitute an unfair disadvantage for businesses. For example, in early 1984 some Oklahoma coal companies successfully appealed for federal enforcement of strip-mining laws in the state, arguing that lax enforcement constituted an unfair advantage for their competitors who were in non-compliance.[46]

Such concerns might be thought to suggest that national standards should entirely pre-empt state laws, serving as a ceiling as well as a floor on environmental regulation, but this conclusion does not necessarily follow. A distinction must be made between quality (or performance) standards, and

[44] Chandler (1977).

[45] Local differentiation in water law also helps explain the reason the Clean Water Act focused on technology rather than quality-based standards. Variations in state laws greatly complicate efforts to attain uniform national standards (Pisani, 1987, p. 137). See also Frederick (forthcoming 1991).

[46] The Conservation Foundation (1984), p. 422.

technology standards. When states enact, say, ambient environmental quality standards that exceed the national norm, the effects they create such as cost disadvantages for businesses (and consumers) are largely internalized into their own state.[47] One cannot make a general case for federal pre-emption in this circumstance. Variations in technology-based standards, on the other hand, are more amenable to use as a barrier to entry without any perceptible environmental benefits.[48] Uniform technology standards as well as enforcement efforts among the states do stabilize the climate for business and facilitate interstate commerce.

Competition between jurisdictions, suggested previously as a mechanism to promote the responsiveness of government, can also work against the public interest. In order to divert economic activity away from other areas, jurisdictions may compete by relaxing environmental regulations to a level that is below that which maximizes social welfare from the national perspective. Furthermore, communities may 'easy ride' on the provision of 'non-excludable public goods' like parks or a healthy environment in neighbouring jurisdictions.[49] Empirical studies have not been able definitively to identify these effects, nor have they been able to disprove them either. To the extent these forms of destructive competition are important effects, national minimum standards for environmental quality can help to remedy them.

A final counterpoint to the idea that local government best represents Jeffersonian ideals is the observation that in practice, even at the local level, governmental institutions are sometimes undemocratic. The mayor or the governor are not likely to live next to a local waste dump, while the less enfranchised are. Furthermore, even in the absence of informational problems, a national minimum level of quality may satisfy paternalistic or humanistic goals for much the same reason we mandate flush toilets in building codes.

Even in the town of Strawberry Fields where everyone is nice, however, direct democracy may fail to deliver the economically efficient policy. If all of the benefits for an environmental improvement accrue to a relatively few individuals while the costs are borne equally across the population, even

[47] Differing standards among the states imposes a cost burden on industries that must accommodate many different regulations. If there are many differences among the states, the economic loss that results from higher costs for industry may justify a co-ordinating role for the federal government. However, in the presence of a uniform minimum standard nationally, it is unlikely that many states will exceed that standard without also clamouring for raising it. When just a few states exceed the federal standard it is not obvious why higher costs cannot be passed on to the consumers in those states.

[48] This point is explicitly recognized in the product-standard limitation clause of the legislation enabling the Occupational Safety and Health Administration, which discourages differences in product-design standards among the states that might serve to restrict interstate commerce (Foote, 1987, p. 47).

[49] Burtraw and Harrington (1991).

if the benefits greatly outweigh the costs, direct democracy may fail to deliver a policy because for most individuals the costs outweigh the benefits.[50] Greater homogeneity of the population and more evenly dispersed benefits and costs are both conducive to efficient decision-making at the local level. Greater heterogeneity is better suited to a higher level of government, however, which is further removed from short-run political constraints.[51] Thus, interfering policies from the national government may be more than paternalistic—they may in some cases provide a genuine safety net for all members of society.[52]

So, there exist at least two points of view on all the issues we have raised. What criteria can one use to evaluate the proper level of government to determine environmental policy?[53] This discussion brings forth two perspectives. The economic perspective is a functional one. That is, it asks what level of government is technically best situated to be able to gather and process information about benefits and costs, calculate an appropriate policy response, and implement the result so as to maximize social welfare.[54]

A second perspective is less functional and more political.[55] It considers the variations in interest-group power at different levels of government, and was articulated well in the 1971 Report of the President's Council of Economic Advisers:

> [Policy] rules require that the gains and losses entailed by different levels of environmental quality be weighed, the Government agency making the rules must be responsive to those who bear the gains and losses . . . As a practical matter, much of the damage from pollution will be 'measured' by political pressures from those damaged.[56]

These two views are not incompatible, but their integration requires a broad-minded analysis.

The justifications for lower levels of government to take the lead in environmental policy can be summarized in four categories. One is that local

[50] See Olson (1969), as well as the literature on median voter models beginning with Bowen (1943).

[51] Oates and Schwab (1988).

[52] To the extent this safety net also includes national health insurance for at least some segments of the population, there is an additional reason for the federal government to be concerned about local standards for environmental health.

[53] Some useful guidelines can be found in US Congressional Budget Office (1988).

[54] Clearly, the theory allows that these tasks may be divided between levels of government. Seminal literature in this area includes Olson (1969) and Oates (1972).

[55] See Elliot *et al.* (1985).

[56] US Council of Economic Advisers (1971), p. 121; cited in S. Peltzman and T. N. Tideman, 'Local Versus National Pollution Control: Note', *American Economic Review*, **62**(5), December 1972. For an example of this view see Noam (1982).

government is, by definition, closest to the people, with all the benefits that follow. Second is its facility to innovate. Third is the opportunity for local governments to fashion policies tailored to the variations in tastes, incomes, and prices between different areas. Fourth are the technical characteristics that make the impact of each environmental problem distinct.

We observe that the justifications for higher levels of governments also collapse into four categories. One is the spillover of costs and/or benefits. Second is the ability to facilitate desirable co-ordination among local governments. Third is the ability to inhibit destructive competition between local governments. Fourth is the appeal of enlightened paternalism.

We are led to conclude that it is wrong-headed to attempt, or even to desire, to resolve definitively the hierarchy of authority in environmental policy. The justifications we have outlined inherently conflict; yet the variety of approaches to federalism offer a rich tool-box of policy instruments and strategies. Clearly, there will be times where what we really need is a left-handed monkey wrench. If US history is any indication, indeed it may be small-minded to look for consistency in the application of federalism.

## 11.5 Conclusions

In conclusion, we offer a few brief comments about the role for economics in the future of US environmental policy, addressing first the research agenda for environmental economics, and secondly environmental federalism. Economists themselves may only weakly appreciate (and non-economists may not appreciate at all) the important distinction between estimates of costs that come from industry's cost of compliance with environmental laws, and true social costs.[57] The former is only a proxy for the latter. Similarly, observable economic benefits are only a proxy for total social benefits of environmental policy. New techniques in modern welfare economics portend significant advances in the measurement of these costs and benefits.

As environmental policy has become more comprehensive over the last two decades, there are fewer and fewer cases where the benefits of possible new regulations greatly exceed the costs—in essence, the obvious problems have been addressed. Also, other social problems are making competing demands on the public treasury, and at the same time there is increasing concern for domestic economic productivity in an era of global competitiveness. Neither the public nor private sectors have resources that can painlessly be diverted to environmental protection. In short, those who maintain hope for continuing

[57] The former may be characterized as static, partial equilibrium estimates while the latter invites dynamic, general equilibrium analysis.

improvements in the quality of our environment must look harder for the 'good deals'. One important opportunity for reducing the costs of environmental policy is through incentive regulation, such as the example of tradable emission allowances that we mentioned. US environmental policy illustrates that these two areas—the measurement of social costs and benefits, and the development of incentive-based regulation—represent two important areas for further economic research.

At the outset of our discussion on environmental federalism we mentioned that one of the central debates concerns the issue of pre-emption. In closing we offer our perspective. First, there is little justification for total pre-emption by the federal government of local environmental initiatives. Some problems really are local ones and ought to be addressed there. On the other hand, we identified a number of reasons why federal partial pre-emption, at least to establish minimum standards, would be attractive if not essential for sound policy-making.

Second, in light of this survey, there are areas where current US environmental policy might deserve re-evaluation. Standards concerning drinking-water protection, the extent of clean-up at abandoned hazardous-waste disposal sites, and the technological configuration of solid-waste land-disposal sites—where currently the federal government has much authority—may lend themselves to increased local determination. In each of these cases, there are some reasons to consider federal pre-eminence. Often a concern about intergenerational effects is one such reason. But it would appear that these are problems whose extent is confined geographically and, thus, well suited to more carefully tailored individual approaches.

By the same token, in several areas there appears to be a *greater* need for federal leadership. One such area is the encouragement of recycling, where one role for the federal government could be to develop procurement policies that would stimulate the demand for recycled materials. In addition, as we rest on the verge of the 'global millennium', there are many emerging international problems that require federal attention, including the continued use of chlorofluorocarbons, global warming, and the loss of species habitat and diversity. Many states in the US have begun to adopt policies in these areas, but this is clearly the wrong forum for regulatory action. One can only hope that state efforts eventually provoke federal action.

## Bibliography

Ackerman, B. and Hassler, W. (1981), *Clean Coal/Dirty Air*, New Haven, Yale University Press.

Bohi, D. R. and Burtraw, D. (forthcoming 1991), 'Utility Investment Behavior and the Emission Trading Market', *Energy and Natural Resources*.

Bowen, H. (1943), 'The Interpretation of Voting in the Allocation of Resources', *Quarterly Journal of Economics*, 58, 27–48.

Brennan, G. and Buchanan, J. (1980), *The Power to Tax: Analytical Foundations of a Fiscal Constitution*, New York, Cambridge University Press.

Burtraw, D. and Harrington, W. (1991), '"Easy Riding" in Community Provision of Non-Excludable Public Goods', Washington, D.C., Resources for the Future, Working Paper.

Chandler, A. (1977), *The Visible Hand*, Belknap Press.

The Conservation Foundation (1984), *State of the Environment: An Assessment at Mid-Decade*, Washington, D.C..

Crandall, R. (1983), *Controlling Industrial Pollution*, Washington, D.C., Brookings Institution.

Derthick, M. (1987), 'American Federalism: Madison's Middle Ground in the 1980s', *Public Administration Review*, 47(1), 66–74.

Dower, R. (1990), 'Hazardous Wastes', in P. Portney (ed.), *Public Policies for Environmental Protection*, Washington, D.C., Resources for the Future, 151–94.

Elliott, E. D., Ackerman, B. A., and Millian, J. C. (1985), 'Toward a Theory of Statutory Evolution: The Federalization of Environmental Law', *Journal of Law, Economics and Organization*, 1(2), 313–40.

Foote, S. B. (1987), 'New Federalism or Old Federalization: Deregulation and the States', in H. N. Scheiber (ed.), *Perspectives on Federalism: Papers from the First Berkeley Seminar on Federalism*, University of California, Berkeley, Institute of Governmental Studies.

Fraas, A. and Munley, V. (1989), 'Economic Objectives within a Bureaucratic Decision Process: Setting Pollution Control Requirements under the Clean Water Act', *Journal of Environmental Economics and Management*, 17, 23–35.

Frederick, K. D. (forthcoming 1991), 'Water Resources', in K. D. Frederick and R. A. Sedjo (eds.) (forthcoming 1991), *America's Renewable Resources: A Historical Perspective on Their Use and Management*, Washington, D.C., Resources for the Future.

— and Sedjo, R. A. (eds.) (forthcoming 1991), *America's Renewable Resources: A Historical Perspective on Their Use and Management*, Washington, D.C., Resources for the Future.

Freeman, A. M. (1979), *The Benefits of Environmental Improvement: Theory and Practice*, Washington, D.C., Resources for the Future.

— (1982), *Air and Water Pollution Control: A Benefit–Cost Assessment*, New York, John Wiley and Sons.

— (1990), 'Water Pollution Policy', in P. Portney (ed.), *Public Policies for Environmental Protection*, Washington, D.C., Resources for the Future.

Fund for Renewable Energy and the Environment (1987), 'The State of the States', Washington, D.C.

Hawkins, R. B. Jr. (1990), 'Pre-emption: The Dramatic Rise of Federal Supremacy', *Journal of State Government*, 63(1), 10–14.

Kneese, A. (1984), *Measuring the Benefits of Clean Air and Water*, Washington, D.C., Resources for the Future.

Kopp, R. and Hazilla, M. (1990), 'Social Cost of Environmental Quality Regulations: A General Equilibrium Analysis', *Journal of Political Economy*, 98, 853–73.

Kriz, M. E. (1989), 'Ahead of the Feds', *National Journal*, 9 December, 2989–93.

*Lead Industries Association, Inc. v. EPA*, 647 F. 2d 1130, 10 ELR 20643, DC. Cir. 1980.

Lester, J. P. (1990), 'A New Federalism? Environmental Policy In The States', in N. J. Vig and M. E. Kraft (eds.), *Environmental Policy in the 1990s: Toward A New Agenda*, Washington, D.C., Congressional Quarterly Press.

Liroff, R. (1986), *Reforming Air Pollution Regulation: The Toil and Trouble of EPA's Bubble*, Washington, D.C., The Conservation Foundation.

Mitchell, R. C., and Carson, R. T. (1989), *Using Surveys to Value Public Goods: The Contingent Valuation Method*, Washington, D.C., Resources for the Future.

*New State Ice Company v. Liebmann*, 285 USC 262, 311 (1932).

Noam, E. (1982), 'The Choice of Governmental Level in Regulation', *KYKLOS*, 35, 278–91.

Novick, S., Stever, D., and Mellon, M. (1987), *Law of Environmental Protection*, New York, Clark Boardman Co.

Oates, W. E (1972), *Fiscal Federalism*, New York, Harcourt Brace Jovanovich, Inc.

— and Schwab, R. M. (1988), 'Economic Competition among Jurisdictions: Efficiency Enhancing or Distortion Inducing?', *Journal of Public Economics*, 35, 333–54.

O'Brien, D. M. (1989), 'Federalism as a Metaphor in the Constitutional Politics of Public Administration', *Public Administration Review*, 49(5), 411–19.

Olson, M. (1969), 'The Principle of "Fiscal Equivalence": The Division of Responsibilities among Different Levels of Government', *American Economic Review*, 65(2), 479–87.

Pisani, D. J. (1987), 'Federalism, Water Law, and the American West, 1886–1928', in H. N. Scheiber (ed.), *Perspectives on Federalism: Papers from the First Berkeley Seminar on Federalism*, University of California, Berkeley, Institute of Governmental Studies.

Portney, P. (1982*a*), *Current Issues in Natural Resource Policy*, Washington, D.C., Resources for the Future.

— (1982*b*), 'How *Not* to Create a Job', *Regulation*, 35–8.

— (1990*a*), *Public Policies for Environmental Protection*, Washington, D.C., Resources for the Future.

— (1990*b*), 'Economics and the Clean Air Act', *Journal of Economic Perspectives*, 4(4), 173–81.

Schwab, R. M. (1988), 'Environmental Federalism', *Resources*, 92, Washington, D.C., Resources for the Future.

Shapiro, M. (1990), 'Toxic Substances Policy', in P. Portney (ed.), *Public Policies for Environmental Protection*, Washington, D.C., Resources for the Future, 195–242.

Stern, A. (1982), 'History of Air Pollution Legislation in the United States', *Journal of Air Pollution Control Assocation*, 32, 44–61.

Tiebout, C. M. (1956), 'A Pure Theory of Local Expenditures', *Journal of Political Economy*, 64, 416–24.

Tietenberg, T. (1985), *Emissions Trading*, Washington, D.C., Resources for the Future.

US Congressional Budget Office (1988), 'Environmental Federalism: Allocating Responsibilities For Environmental Protection', September, Washington, D.C..

US Council of Economic Advisors, (1971), 'Economic Report of the President', Washington, D.C.

US Environmental Protection Agency (1991), 'Environmental Investments: The Cost of a Clean Environment', report.

# Index